FREE DVD   FREE   FREE DVD

Essential Test Tips DVD from Trivium Test Prep

Dear Customer,

Thank you for purchasing from Cirrus Test Prep! Whether you're looking to join the military, get into college, or advance your career, we're honored to be a part of your journey.

To show our appreciation (and to help you relieve a little of that test-prep stress), we're offering a **FREE *Praxis Essential Test Tips DVD**** by Cirrus Test Prep. Our DVD includes 35 test preparation strategies that will help keep you calm and collected before and during your big exam. All we ask is that you email us your feedback and describe your experience with our product. Amazing, awful, or just so-so: we want to hear what you have to say!

To receive your **FREE *Praxis Essential Test Tips DVD***, please email us at 5star@cirrustestprep.com. Include "Free 5 Star" in the subject line and the following information in your email:

1. The title of the product you purchased.
2. Your rating of 1 – 5 (with 5 being the best).
3. Your feedback about the product, including how our materials helped you meet your goals and ways in which we can improve our products.
4. Your full name and shipping address so we can send your **FREE *Praxis Essential Test Tips DVD*.**

If you have any questions or concerns please feel free to contact us directly at 5star@cirrustestprep.com.

Thank you, and good luck with your studies!

* Please note that the free DVD is <u>not included</u> with this book. To receive the free DVD, please follow the instructions above.

Praxis II Social Studies Rapid Review Study Guide

CONTENT AND INTERPRETATION (5086) TEST PREP AND PRACTICE QUESTIONS

Copyright © 2017 by Cirrus Test Prep

ALL RIGHTS RESERVED. By purchase of this book, you have been licensed one copy for personal use only. No part of this work may be reproduced, redistributed, or used in any form or by any means without prior written permission of the publisher and copyright owner.

Cirrus Test Prep is not affiliated with or endorsed by any testing organization and does not own or claim ownership of any trademarks, specifically for the Praxis Social Studies: Content Knowledge and Interpretation (5086) exam. All test names (and their acronyms) are trademarks of their respective owners. This study guide is for general information only and does not claim endorsement by any third party.

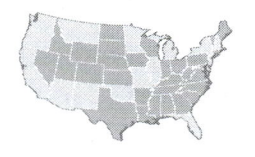

Table of Contents

Online Resources i
Introduction iii

US History 1
    NORTH AMERICA BEFORE EUROPEAN CONTACT 1
    COLONIAL NORTH AMERICA 5
    REVOLUTION AND THE EARLY UNITED STATES 13
    CIVIL WAR, EXPANSION, AND INDUSTRY... 22
    ✓ THE UNITED STATES BECOMES A GLOBAL POWER 32
    POSTWAR AND CONTEMPORARY UNITED STATES 40

World History.. 49
    EARLY CIVILIZATIONS AND THE GREAT EMPIRES 49
    FEUDALISM THROUGH THE ERA OF EXPANSION 58
    ARMED CONFLICTS 74
    GLOBAL CONFLICTS 83
    POST-COLD WAR WORLD.. 97

Government 101
    POLITICAL THEORY... 101
    CONSTITUTIONAL UNDERPINNINGS OF THE US GOVERNMENT........................... 107
    STRUCTURES AND POWERS OF THE FEDERAL GOVERNMENT 112
    AMERICAN POLITICAL SYSTEMS 134
    COMPARATIVE POLITICS AND INTERNATIONAL RELATIONS 139

Geography 149
What is Geography? 149
Human Characteristics of Place 162
Economic Patterns 171
Political Geography 180
Human-Environment Interaction 185
Movement 193

Economics 201
Fundamental Economic Concepts 201
Types of Economic Systems 208
Supply and Demand 210
Elasticity 215
Factors of Production 218
Behavior of Firms 221
Types of Markets 227
Government Intervention 229
Macroeconomics 231

Psychology 243
Lifespan Development 243
Learning, Memory, and Cognition 255
Personality 264
Social Psychology 267
Motivation and Stress 271

Sociology 275
Social Perspective and Methods of Inquiry 276
Culture, Socialization, and Social Organization 279
Social Hierarchy 290
Social Change, Movement, and Demography 297

Practice Test 299
Answer Key 327

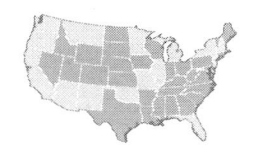

Online Resources

To help you fully prepare for your Praxis Social Studies (5086) exam, Cirrus includes online resources with the purchase of this study guide.

Practice Test

In addition to the practice test included in this book, we also offer an online exam. Since many exams today are computer-based, getting to practice your test-taking skills on the computer is a great way to prepare.

Flash Cards

A convenient supplement to this study guide, Cirrus's flash cards enable you to review important terms easily on your computer or smartphone.

Cheat Sheets

Review the core skills you need to master the exam with easy-to-read Cheat Sheets.

From Stress to Success

Watch *From Stress to Success*, a brief but insightful YouTube video that offers the tips, tricks, and secrets experts use to score higher on the exam.

Reviews

Leave a review, send us helpful feedback, or sign up for Cirrus promotions—including free books!

Access these materials at:

www.cirrustestprep.com/praxis-5086-online-resources

Introduction

Congratulations on choosing to take the Praxis Social Studies: Content Knowledge and Interpretation (5086) exam! By purchasing this book, you've taken the first step toward becoming a social studies teacher.

This guide will provide you with a detailed overview of the Praxis, so you know exactly what to expect on test day. We'll take you through all the concepts covered on the test and give you the opportunity to test your knowledge with practice questions. Even if it's been a while since you last took a major test, don't worry; we'll make sure you're more than ready!

What is the Praxis?

Praxis Series tests are a part of teaching licensure in approximately forty states. Each state uses the tests and scores in different ways, so be sure to check the certification requirements in your state by going to www.ets.org/praxis/states. There, you will find information detailing the role of the Praxis tests in determining teaching certification in your state, what scores are required, and how to transfer Praxis scores from one state to another.

The social studies tests are interdisciplinary; they test your ability to understand relationships among fields in social studies. These include U.S. and world history, U.S. government/civics, economics, geography, and behavioral sciences. You'll integrate your knowledge of all of these subjects in order to answer the questions correctly.

What's on the Praxis?

The content in this guide will prepare you for the Praxis Social Studies: Content Knowledge and Interpretation (5086) exam. This test assesses whether you possess the knowledge and skills necessary to become a secondary school social studies teacher using both a multiple-choice section and a written section that includes three constructed-response essay questions. These three essay questions are interdisciplinary and designed to exercise your critical thinking skills and gauge your ability to interpret social studies resources like maps and charts.

You have a maximum of two hours to complete the entire test. It is recommended that you spend approximately ten minutes on each short essay and an hour and a half on the multiple-choice questions, but you may use the two hours allotted as you see fit.

Praxis Social Studies: Content and Interpretation (5086) Content			
Section	**Concepts**	**Number of Questions**	**Percentage**
Multiple-choice (Part A)	US History	18	15%
	World History	18	15%
	Government/Civics	18	15%
	Economics	13	11%
	Geography	13	11%
	Behavioral Sciences	10	8%
Short Content Essays (Part B)		3	25%
Total		93 questions	2 hours

You will answer approximately eighteen multiple-choice questions (fifteen percent of the test) on U.S. history. The test will require knowledge of North American geography, pre-colonial civilizations, the purposes of European colonization of the continent, and how pre-colonial peoples interacted with European colonizers. Be prepared for questions about the American Revolution and the foundations of the United States government and Constitution. The test will cover developments in the nineteenth century, including westward expansion, political division, the Civil War, Reconstruction, industrialization, urbanization, and immigration. The Progressive Era and the New Deal are covered as well. Be aware not only of United States involvement in the First and Second World Wars, but also of their impact on both foreign and domestic policy. Prepare for thematic questions that will test your knowledge of the impact of labor and technology on the economy, changing political trends from the New Deal and Great Society to conservatism, the impact of religion on society, and civil rights and changing perceptions of race, ethnicity, and gender roles throughout the twentieth century. Questions are also likely to explore the United States' role as a world power during the Cold War and into the twenty-first century.

You will answer approximately eighteen multiple-choice questions (fifteen percent of the test) on world history. In general, you will be expected to understand how world societies and civilizations have been shaped by conflict, technology, and religion; ideologies like nationalism, totalitarianism and other political philosophies; economic movements like industrialization and the market economy; and major demographic trends. The test will also presume an understanding of transglobal similarities in gender and family expectations, and the impact of trade within and among cultures. Specific questions may ask about the classical civilizations in Europe and Asia and their transformation from 300 – 1400 C.E.; European developments from the Renaissance through the Enlightenment; colonization, trade, and other global interactions from 1200 – 1750 C.E.; the consequences of nationalism and European imperialism from 1750 – 1914 C.E.; the causes and consequences of the First and Second World Wars (like decolonization and the rise of the Soviet Union); and the important developments of the post-Cold War world (such as globalization and fundamentalism).

You will answer approximately eighteen multiple-choice questions (fifteen percent of the test) on government/civics. Generally, you will need to have a solid understanding of major political concepts, orientations, and theorists. United States government, its constitutional foundation, national political institutions, and the three branches of government will be covered on the test. You will also be assessed on your knowledge of how national political institutions' processes, structures, and powers function. Expect questions about the effects of civil rights, political ideology, political parties, special interest groups, and the media on politics. In addition to domestic U.S. government, you'll be asked questions about comparative politics and international relations. The test will presume knowledge of the types of government, such as parliamentary and federal; in addition, prepare to be asked about types of regimes, such as democracies, autocracies, and oligarchies. International relations will be tested on a theoretical and practical level: for example, how theory relates to cooperation among nations and diplomacy in practice. You'll also be tested on the powers and problems of international laws and organizations, such as NATO and the United Nations.

You will answer approximately thirteen multiple-choice questions (eleven percent of the test) on economics. The test will assess the two major content areas of economics: micro and macro. Questions about the former cover concepts such as economic systems, distribution of income, behavior of firms, product markets, market efficiency, governmental controls, factors of production, and choice and opportunity costs. Macroeconomics questions ask about measures of economic performance, fiscal and monetary policies, money and banking, inflation and economic growth, exchange rates and international trade, business cycles, and unemployment.

You will answer approximately thirteen multiple-choice questions (eleven percent of the test) on geography. Questions will not only ask you to glean information from maps, projections, and geographical data, but also to analyze and organize this information in conjunction with your own spatial understanding and mental maps. You will be asked to identify patterns and interpret data from a variety of sources and to display your understanding of concepts like political geography, state formation, and contemporary areas of conflict. An understanding of human geography is also essential to this section. Prepare to answer questions about demographic patterns and change. The test will also cover interrelationships of humans and their environments and how culture, economics, migration and settlement, development, industrialization, and globalization affect those relationships.

You will answer approximately ten multiple-choice questions (eight percent of the test) on behavioral sciences. Behavioral sciences focus on human behavior and its influencing factors: these include learning, identity, and development as well as society, social groups, and institutions. The test will also cover how culture, diversity, and adaptation affect human behavior.

How is the Praxis Scored?

The multiple-choice questions are equally weighted. The ninety multiple-choice questions comprise 75 percent of your overall score, while the three constructed-response essays comprise the other 25 percent. The preceding tables offer a breakdown of the concepts covered in the multiple-choice sections of the test. Keep in mind that some multiple-choice questions are experimental questions for the purpose of the Praxis test writers and will not count toward your overall score. However, since those questions are not indicated on the test, you must respond to every question. There is no penalty for guessing on Praxis tests, so be sure to eliminate answer choices and answer every question. If you still do not know the answer, guess; you may get it right!

On the constructed-response section, the graders of the responses assign a score of 0 – 3 to each response. A score of a 3 is earned by a response that shows thorough understanding of the prompt by being accurate and complete. An adequate understanding of the prompt with a mostly complete and accurate answer will earn a score of 2, while a score of a 1 will be given to an answer that shows little understanding of the prompt with mostly inaccurate or incomplete information. A response that does not answer the questions or is wholly incorrect will receive a score of 0. The scores of the three constructed-response essays are equally weighted to comprise twenty-five percent of your overall score.

Your score report will be available two to three weeks after the test date and will stay on your Praxis account for one year, but you can also opt for a paper report. The score report includes your score and the passing score for the states you identified as score recipients.

How is the Praxis Administered?

This test is administered as a paper-and-pencil test or as a computerized test. You are encouraged to take the version of the test that is most comfortable for you. There is no difference between the two versions; both have the same time-limit and cover the same content. The Praxis website allows you to take a practice test to acclimate yourself to the computerized format if you choose to take this version.

The Praxis Series tests are available at testing centers across the nation. To find a testing center near you, go to http://www.ets.org/praxis/register. At this site, you can create a Praxis account, check testing dates, register for a test, or find instructions for registering via mail or phone.

On the day of your test, be sure to bring your admission ticket (which is provided when you register) and photo ID. The testing facility will provide pencils and erasers and an area outside of the testing room to store your personal belongings. You are allowed no personal effects in the testing area. Cell phones and other electronic, photographic, recording, or listening devices are not permitted in the testing center at all, and bringing those items may be cause for dismissal, forfeiture of your testing fees, and cancellation of your scores. For details on what is and is not permitted at your testing center, refer to http://www.ets.org/praxis/test_day/bring.

About Cirrus Test Prep

Cirrus Test Prep study guides are designed by current and former educators and are tailored to meet your needs as an incoming educator. Our guides offer all of the resources necessary to help you pass teacher certification tests across the nation.

Cirrus clouds are graceful, wispy clouds characterized by their high altitude. Just like cirrus clouds, Cirrus Test Prep's goal is to help educators "aim high" when it comes to obtaining their teacher certification and entering the classroom.

About This Guide

This guide will help you master the most important test topics and also develop critical test-taking skills. We have built features into our books to prepare you for your tests and increase your score. Along with a detailed summary of the test's format, content, and scoring, we offer an in-depth overview of the content knowledge required to pass the test. Our sidebars provide interesting information, highlight key concepts, and review content so that you can solidify your understanding of the exam's concepts. Test your knowledge with sample questions and detailed answer explanations in the text that help you think through the problems on the exam and two full-length practice tests that reflect the content and format of the Praxis. We're pleased you've chosen Cirrus to be a part of your professional journey!

US History

NORTH AMERICA BEFORE EUROPEAN CONTACT

NORTHEASTERN SOCIETIES

Prior to European colonization, diverse Native American societies controlled the continent; they would later come into economic and diplomatic contact, and military conflict, with European colonizers and United States forces and settlers.

Major civilizations that would play an important and ongoing role in North American history included the **Iroquois** and **Algonquin** in the Northeast. Both of those tribes would also be important allies of the English and French, respectively, in future conflicts, in that part of the continent.

The Iroquois actually consisted of five tribes, the **Mohawk**, **Seneca**, **Cayuga**, **Oneida**, and **Onondaga**—which organized into the regionally powerful **Iroquois Confederacy**, bringing stability to the eastern Great Lakes region.

While many Native American, or First Nations, people speak variants of the Algonquin language, the **Algonquin** people themselves have historically been a majority in what is today Quebec and the Great Lakes region. Active in the fur trade, the Algonquin developed important relationships with French colonizers and a rivalry with the Iroquois.

THE MIDWEST

Later, the young United States would come into conflict with the Shawnee, Lenape, Kickapoo, Miami, and other tribes in the Midwestern region of Ohio, Illinois, Indiana, and Michigan in early western expansion. These tribes later formed the **Northwest Confederacy** to fight the United States.

The **Shawnee** were an Algonquin-speaking people based in the Ohio Valley; however their presence extended as far east and south as the present-day Carolinas and Georgia. While socially organized under a matrilineal system, the Shawnee had male kings. Also Algonquin-speaking, the Delaware-based **Lenape** were considered by the Shawnee to be their "grandfathers" and thus accorded respect. Another Algonquin-speaking tribe, the **Kickapoo** were originally from the Great Lakes region but would move throughout present-day Indiana and Wisconsin. The **Miami** moved from Wisconsin to settle and farm in the Ohio Valley. They also took part in the fur trade.

The Southeast

In the South, major tribes included the Chickasaw and Choctaw, the descendants of the **Mississippi Mound Builders** or Mississippian cultures, societies that built mounds from around 2,100 to 1,800 years ago as burial tombs or the bases for temples. Both tribes were organized in matrilineal clans, and both spoke Muskogean languages. The **Chickasaw** were based in northern Mississippi and Alabama and western Kentucky and Tennessee; they shared agricultural practices with the Iroquois. The **Choctaw**, whose origins trace to the Deep South and Florida, spoke a similar language to the Chickasaw. These two tribes would later form alliances with the British and French, fighting proxy wars on their behalf.

Figure 1.1. Mississippi Mounds

The **Creek**, also descended from the Mississippian peoples, originated in Alabama, Georgia, South Carolina, and Florida. The Muskogean-speaking Creek would later participate in an alliance with the Chickasaw and Choctaw—the Muscogee Confederacy—to engage the United States, which threatened tribal sovereignty.

Unlike the Chickasaw, Choctaw, and Creek, the **Cherokee** spoke (and speak) a language of the Iroquoian family. It is thought that they migrated south to their homeland in present-day Georgia sometime long before European contact, where they remained until they were forcibly removed in 1832. Organized into seven clans, the Cherokee were also hunters and farmers like other tribes in the region, and would later come into contact—and conflict—with European colonizers and the United States of America.

GREAT PLAINS, SOUTHWEST, PACIFIC NORTHWEST

Farther west, tribes of the Great Plains like the **Sioux**, **Cheyenne**, **Apache**, **Comanche**, and **Arapaho** would later come into conflict with American settlers during westward expansion. Traditionally nomadic or semi-nomadic, these tribes depended on the **buffalo** for food and materials; therefore they followed the herds.

In the Southwest, the **Navajo** controlled territory in present-day Arizona, New Mexico, and Utah. The Navajo were descendants of the cliff-dwelling **Ancestral Pueblo** or **Anasazi**, who had settled in the Four Corners area. The Navajo practiced pastoralism and lived in semi-permanent wooden homes called *hogans*. The Navajo had a less hierarchical structure than other Native American societies, and engaged in fewer raids than the Apache to the north.

Figure 1.2. Ancestral Pueblo Cliff Palace at Mesa Verde

In the Pacific Northwest, fishing was a major source of sustenance, and Native American peoples created and used canoes to engage in the practice. Totem poles depicted histories. The **Coast Salish**, whose language was widely spoken throughout the region, dominated the Puget Sound and Olympic Peninsula area. Farther south, the **Chinook** controlled the coast at the Columbia River.

Ultimately, through both violent conflict and political means, Native American civilizations lost control of most of their territories and were forced onto reservations by the United States. Negotiations continue today over rights to land and opportunities and reparations for past injustices.

SAMPLE QUESTIONS

1) **Which of the following best describes the political landscape of the Northeast before European contact?**

    A. Many small, autonomous tribes scattered throughout the region fought over land and resources.

    B. Several organized tribes controlled the region, including a major confederation.

    C. A disorganized political landscape would facilitate European colonial domination.

    D. The land was largely uninhabited, allowing easy exploitation of resources.

    Answer:

    B. **Correct.** Powerful tribes controlled trade and territory; among these were the powerful Iroquois Confederacy.

2) **How do the movements of the tribes of the Northwest (throughout present-day Indiana, Illinois, Ohio, Michigan, and Wisconsin) illustrate tribal interactions before European contact and during colonial times?**

    A. Having been pushed westward by the Iroquois, the Lenape are just one example of forced migration in early North American history.

    B. The migration of the Miami from Ontario to the Ohio Valley illustrates the diffusion of the Algonquin language throughout the continent.

    C. Despite the wide geographic range of the Shawnee, Kickapoo, Miami, and Lenape, all these peoples spoke variants of the Algonquin language; this shows the importance of this language for many Native American tribes whether or not they were Algonquin people.

    D. Ongoing conflict between the Northwest Algonquin Confederacy, based in Ontario and the Upper Midwest, and the Iroquois Confederacy, based in the eastern Great Lakes region and present-day upstate New York, resulted in instability that forced tribes to move throughout the region.

    Answer:

    C. **Correct.** While the Algonquin people were primarily located in what is today Quebec and southern Ontario, the Algonquin language was spoken widely throughout North America among both settled and semi-settled non-Algonquin peoples.

3) At the time of European contact, the Southeastern United States was mainly populated by
   A. the Mississippi Mound Builders.
   B. settled tribes who spoke Muskogean and Iroquoian languages.
   C. nomadic tribes who spoke Muskogean and Iroquoian languages.
   D. the Ancestral Pueblo cliff dwellers.

   Answer:
   B. **Correct.** The Choctaw, Creek, Chickasaw, and others were Muskogean-speaking peoples; the Cherokee spoke an Iroquoian language. Both tribes were settled.

4) Tribes living in the Great Plains region were dependent on which of the following for survival?
   A. buffalo for nutrition and materials for daily necessities
   B. domesticated horses for hunting and warfare
   C. access to rivers to engage in the fur trade
   D. three sisters agriculture

   Answer:
   A. **Correct.** The Great Plains tribes depended on buffalo, which were plentiful before European contact and settlement, for food; they also used buffalo parts for clothing and to make necessary items.

5) How were the Navajo influenced by the Ancestral Pueblo, or Anasazi?
   A. The Navajo continued the practice of pastoralism, herding horses throughout the Southwest.
   B. The Navajo expanded control over land originally settled by the Ancestral Pueblo.
   C. The Navajo began building cliff dwellings, improving on the Anasazi practice of living in rounded homes built from wood.
   D. The Navajo developed a strictly hierarchical society, abandoning the looser organization of the Ancestral Pueblo.

   Answer:
   B. **Correct.** The Ancestral Pueblo had settled in what is today the Four Corners region; the Navajo came to control land extending through present-day Arizona, New Mexico, and Utah.

COLONIAL NORTH AMERICA

The Americas were quickly colonized by Europeans after Christopher Columbus first laid claim to them for the Spanish, and the British, French, and Spanish all held territories in North America throughout the sixteenth, seventeenth, eighteenth, and nineteenth centuries.

SPAIN IN THE WEST AND SOUTHWEST

Spanish **conquistadors** like **Hernando de Soto** and **Francisco Vasquez de Coronado** explored and conquered what is today the southwestern United States. Spanish colonization also meant spreading Christianity, so colonizers established **missions** throughout the region. The Spanish Crown granted **encomiendas**, land grants to individuals to establish settlements, allowing the holder to ranch or mine the land. Colonists demanded tribute and forced labor from local Native peoples, essentially enslaving them, to profit from the land. Spain's holdings ultimately extended through the Southwest, parts of the Rocky Mountains, and California. Spain also controlled the Gulf Coast, including New Orleans and Florida.

Throughout this region, Spanish colonizers encountered resistance from Native Americans. Spain temporarily lost land for two years after the 1680 **Pueblo Revolt**. Sometimes referred to as part of the ongoing **Navajo Wars**, this revolt included several Native American tribes. Spain eventually reconquered the territory, subjugating the peoples living in the region to colonial rule.

The conflict led to friction among Spanish thinkers over the means, and even the notion, of colonization. The priest **Bartolomé de las Casas**, who lived in the Americas, was appalled at the oppression of colonization and argued for the rights and humanity of Native Americans. On the other hand, **Juan de Sepulveda**, who never left Spain, argued that the Native Americans needed the rule and "civilization" brought by Spain, justifying their treatment at the hands of colonizers.

Despite ongoing conflict between Native Americans and Spanish colonizers, there was social mixing among the people. Intermarriage and fraternization resulted in a stratified society based on race in Spanish and Portuguese colonies throughout the Western Hemisphere. According to the **casta** system, race determined an individual's place in the societal hierarchy, with white people most privileged. The term **mestizo** referred to people of mixed white European and Native American, who were more privileged than the Native American peoples.

The Spanish also introduced African people to the Americas. Forced labor and diseases like **smallpox** had decimated Native American populations in Mexico and the Southwest. Consequently, in order to exploit these resource-rich lands, Spanish colonizers took part in the European-driven **trans-Atlantic slave trade**, kidnapping African people or purchasing them on the West African coast, bringing them to the Americas and forcing them into slavery in mines and plantations.

FRENCH HEGEMONY IN THE MIDWEST AND NORTHEAST

Unlike Spain, which sought not only profit but also to settle the land and convert Native Americans to Christianity, France was mainly focused on trade. **Jacques**

Cartier claimed New France (Quebec) for France in the sixteenth century. French explorers like **Samuel de Champlain** reached land in Vermont, northern New York, and the eastern Great Lakes region, consolidating control of France's North American colonies in 1608.

European demand was high for **fur** and beaver pelts from the Northeast. French colonists were also more likely to establish agreements and intermarry with local Native Americans than other European powers; they did not establish settlements based on forced labor or arrive with families. The term *métis* described mixed-race persons. Eventually France would control the valuable trade routes throughout the Great Lakes and the Mississippi region through Louisiana and New Orleans.

ENGLAND AND THE THIRTEEN COLONIES

Unlike the Spanish and French, the English brought their families to North America, with the goal of establishing agricultural settlements. In the sixteenth century, Sir Walter Raleigh established the Roanoke colony in present-day Virginia; while this settlement mysteriously disappeared by 1590, interest in colonization reemerged as **joint-stock companies** sought royal charters to privately develop colonies on the North American Atlantic coast. The first established colony, **Jamestown**, was also located in Virginia, and became so profitable that the Crown took it over in 1624.

Tobacco was the primary cash crop in Virginia. Since tobacco grew on plantations, Virginia required **indentured servants** to farm it. These workers were freed from servitude after a period of work. Some did come from Africa. However in 1660, the **House of Burgesses**, which governed Virginia, declared that all blacks would be lifelong slaves even if they had been indentured servants. The South became increasingly socially stratified, with enslaved persons, indentured servants, landowners, and other classes. The Carolinas and Georgia would also become important sources of tobacco (and rice); South Carolina institutionalized slavery in North America for the next two centuries by adopting the slave codes from Barbados.

While Jamestown and Virginia were populated by diverse groups of settlers, businessmen, indentured servants, and slaves, the demographics were different farther north. In New England, **Separatists**, members of the Church of England who believed it had strayed too far from its theological roots, had come to North America seeking more religious freedom. The first group of Separatists, the Pilgrims, arrived on the *Mayflower* in 1620 and had drawn up the **Mayflower Compact**, guaranteeing government by the consent of the governed. They were later joined by the **Puritans**, who had been persecuted in England. The colonial Puritan leader **John Winthrop** envisioned the Massachusetts

> **DID YOU KNOW?**
>
> Slavery was not as widespread in the northern colonies as it was in the South, as the climate in the North did not support plantation agriculture. Demand for slaves was therefore higher in the South, where unskilled labor was needed to harvest tobacco and later, cotton.

Bay Colony in the model of the biblical *City upon a Hill*, rooted in unity, peace, and what would be a free, democratic spirit. These philosophies would later inform the American Revolution.

A form of social stratification existed in New England as well: according to Puritan belief, wealth and success showed that one was a member of the **elect**, or privileged by God. Poorer farmers were generally tenant farmers; they did not own land and rarely made a profit.

The concepts of religious tolerance were not isolated to New England. The mid-Atlantic region was well suited for agriculture and trade, with fertile lands and natural harbors. The commercial settlement of New Amsterdam came under English control in 1664 and was renamed New York; in 1682, the Quaker **William Penn** founded the city of Philadelphia. Pennsylvania, New Jersey, and Delaware were founded in the Quaker spirit as part of Penn's **Holy Experiment** to develop settlements based on tolerance.

> **DID YOU KNOW?**
>
> Quakerism promotes equality, community, non-violence, conflict resolution, and tolerance. These ideas are at the root of the name of Philadelphia, the "City of Brotherly Love."

Earlier in the region, in 1649 the **Maryland Toleration Act** had ensured the political rights of all Christians there, the first law of its kind in the colonies. This was due, in part, to the influence of **Lord Baltimore**, who had been charged by Charles I to found a part of Virginia (to be called Maryland) as a Catholic haven—helping him maintain power in an England divided between Catholics and Protestants.

The North American colonial economy was part of the **Atlantic World**, taking part in the **Triangular Trade** among the Americas, Africa, and Europe, where slaves were exchanged in the Americas for raw materials and goods, raw materials were shipped to Europe to be processed into goods for the benefit of the colonial powers, and these goods were sometimes exchanged for slaves in Africa. In this way, North America was part of the **Columbian Exchange**, the intersection of goods and people throughout the Atlantic World.

Exploitation of colonial resources and the dynamics of the Columbian Exchange supported **mercantilism**, the prevailing economic system: European powers controlled their economies in order to increase global power. Ensuring a beneficial **balance of trade** is essential; the country must export more than it imports. An unlimited supply of desirable goods obtainable at a low cost made this possible, and the colonies offered just that. In this way, European powers would be able to maintain their reserves of gold and silver rather than spending them on imports. Furthermore, those countries that obtained access to more gold and silver—notably, Spain, which gained control of mines in Central America and Mexico—exponentially increased their wealth, dramatically changing the balance of economic power in Europe. Long-term consequences included the decline of feudalism and the rise of capitalism.

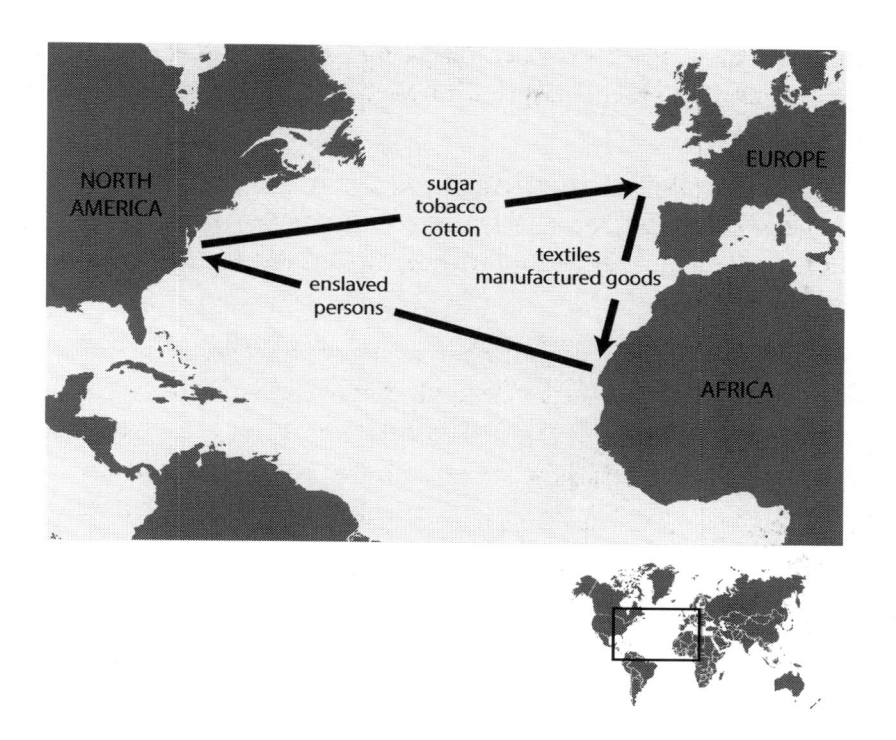

Figure 1.3. Triangular Trade

COLONIAL CONFLICT

Throughout the chaos in England during the **English Civil War**, policy toward the colonies had been one of **salutary neglect**, allowing them great autonomy. However, stability in England and an emerging culture of independence in the Thirteen Colonies caught the attention of the British Crown. To protect the British mercantilist system, the **Navigation Acts** were enacted in 1651, forbidding colonial trade with any other countries. **Bacon's Rebellion** against the colonial governor of Virginia in 1676 embodied the growing resentment of landowners, who wanted to profit rather than redirect revenue to Britain. Following the 1688 Glorious Revolution in England, many colonists expected more autonomy; however, new leadership continued to limit self-rule.

American colonists were also increasingly influenced by Enlightenment thought. John Locke's ***Second Treatise*** was published in 1689; critical of absolute monarchy, it became popular in the colonies. Locke's concepts of government by consent of the governed and the natural rights of persons became the bedrock of the United States government. Locke argued for **republicanism**: that the people must come together to create a government for the protection of themselves and their property, thereby giving up some of their natural rights. However, should the government overstep its bounds, the people have the right to overthrow it and replace it.

In the mid-eighteenth century, a sense of religious fervor called the **Great Awakening** spread throughout the colonies; people became devoted to God beyond the confines of traditional Christianity. Many universities were founded during this time to train ministers; the Great Awakening helped develop a more singularly North American religious culture.

Meanwhile, North America served also as a battleground for France and England, already in conflict in Europe and elsewhere. In the mid-seventeenth century, the Algonquin and Iroquois, allied with the French and English, respectively, fought the **Beaver Wars** for control over the fur trade in the northeastern part of the continent. The Iroquois would ultimately push the Shawnee and other tribes associated with the Algonquin from the Northeast and Great Lakes area farther west to present-day Wisconsin.

France had come to control the vast **Louisiana Territory**, from the Ohio Valley area through the Mississippi Valley, the area down the Mississippi River to its capital of New Orleans, and as far as the reaches of the Missouri River and the Arkansas/Red River stretching west. Not only did France clash with Britain in the northern part of the continent, but the two colonial powers came into conflict in the South as well. In 1736, French forces, allied with the Choctaw, attacked the English-allied Chickasaw as part of France's attempts to strengthen its hold on the southeastern part of North America in the **Chickasaw Wars**.

Figure 1.4. *Join, or Die.*

Following another period of salutary neglect in the colonies, in 1754, French and English conflict exploded once again in North America as fighting broke out in the Ohio Valley. The British government organized with North American colonial leaders to meet at Albany; **Benjamin Franklin** helped organize the defensive Albany Plan of Union and argued for this plan in his newspaper, the *Pennsylvania Gazette*, using the famous illustration *Join, or Die*. However, the Crown worried that this plan allowed for too much colonial independence, adding to tensions between the Thirteen Colonies and England.

The Seven Years' War broke out in Europe in 1756; this conflict between the British and French in North America was known as the **French and Indian War**. War efforts in North America accelerated; ultimately, Britain emerged as the dominant power on the continent. France had allied with the Algonquin, traditional rivals of the British-allied Iroquois. However, following defeats by strong colonial military leaders like **George Washington** and despite its strong alliances and long-term presence on the continent, France eventually surrendered. Britain gained control of French territories in North America—as well as Spanish Florida—in the 1763 **Treaty of Paris** which ended the Seven Years' War.

SAMPLE QUESTIONS

6) How did Spanish and French colonization in North America differ?

   A. Both intermarried with Native Americans; however the Spanish took a more aggressive approach in spreading Christianity.

   B. Spain sought accord and agreement with Native Americans, while France forced marriages as part of settling the land.

   C. France colonized the Southwest; Spain colonized the Northeast and Midwest.

   D. France imported enslaved Africans as part of the Triangular Trade in order to support New France, while Spain mainly exploited the labor of local Native American tribes.

   Answer:

   A. **Correct.** Spain established missions to spread Christianity, in addition to settling and exploiting the land; France worked to establish networks of trade and did not concentrate on religious conversion (although the Church was present and at work in its colonies). Both intermarried locally.

7) On the Atlantic coast of North America, which of the following contributed to demographic differences between North and South?

   A. a climate that supported plantation agriculture in the southern colonies, which resulted in high demand for African slaves

   B. geography favorable to ports in the Northeast, resulting in diverse and tolerant centers of commerce and trade in Boston, New York, and Philadelphia

   C. a climate that supported small-scale agriculture and family farms in the northern colonies, which resulted in a very low demand for African slaves

   D. all of the above

Answer:

D. Correct. All of the above answer choices are true.

8) The mid-Atlantic colonies of Pennsylvania, Delaware, and New Jersey were founded on what premise?

   A. to be a beacon of unity and humanity, reminiscent of John Winthrop's *City upon a Hill*
   B. to reflect tolerance, as part of William Penn's *Holy Experiment*
   C. to turn a profit, in accordance with their roots in joint-stock companies seeking royal charters
   D. to conquer land and convert Native American tribes to Christianity

Answer:

B. Correct. William Penn founded these colonies in the spirit of his tolerant Quaker faith.

9) How did the British and French rivalry spill over into North America?

   A. While Britain and France were often on opposite sides in European conflict, they found common ground against Native Americans in North America.
   B. European conflicts between Catholics and Protestants affected Catholic French and Protestant English settlers; related violence from the Hundred Years' War broke out between them as a result.
   C. These European powers engaged in proxy wars, supporting powerful tribes jockeying for control of land in the Great Lakes and southeastern regions of North America.
   D. France and Britain formed an alliance to prevent Spain from moving eastward on the continent.

Answer:

C. Correct. The Beaver Wars, the Chickasaw Wars, and later the French and Indian War, which was part of the Seven Years' War, are all examples of British-French conflict playing out in North America.

10) Which of the following were factors in stirring up colonial discontent?

   A. Locke's *Second Treatise*
   B. trade restrictions like the Navigation Acts
   C. the Great Awakening
   D. all of the above

Answer:

D. Correct. All of the above are true.

Revolution and the Early United States

The American Revolution

Despite British victory in the French and Indian War, Britain had gone into debt. Furthermore, there were concerns that the colonies required a stronger military presence following **Pontiac's Rebellion** in 1763. The leader of the **Ottawa** people, Pontiac, led a revolt that extended from the Great Lakes region through the Ohio Valley to Virginia. As this land had been ceded to England from France (lacking any consultation with the native inhabitants) the Ottawa people and other Native Americans resisted further British settlement and fought back against colonial oppression. **King George III** signed the **Proclamation of 1763**, an agreement not to settle land west of the Appalachians, in an effort to make peace; however much settlement continued in practice.

As a result of the war and subsequent unrest, Britain once again discarded its colonial policy of salutary neglect; furthermore, in desperate need of cash, the Crown sought ways to increase its revenue from the colonies.

King George III enforced heavy taxes and restrictive acts in the colonies to generate income for the Crown and punish disobedience. England expanded the **Molasses Act** of 1733, passing the **Sugar Act** in 1764 to raise revenue by taxing sugar and molasses. Sugar was produced in the British West Indies and widely consumed in the Thirteen Colonies. In 1765, Britain enforced the **Quartering Act**, requiring colonists to provide shelter to British troops stationed in the region.

The 1765 **Stamp Act**, the first direct tax on the colonists, triggered more tensions. Any document required a costly stamp, the revenue reverting to the British government. **Patrick Henry** protested the Stamp Act in the Virginia House of Burgesses; the tax was seen as a violation of colonists' rights, given that they did not have direct representation in British Parliament. In Britain, it was argued that the colonists had **virtual representation** and so the Act—and others to follow—were justified.

As a result, colonists began boycotting British goods and engaging in violent protest. **Samuel Adams** led the **Sons and Daughters of Liberty** in violent acts against tax collectors. In response, the Chancellor of the Exchequer Charles Townshend enforced the punitive **Townshend Acts** which imposed more taxes and restrictions on the colonies; customs officers were empowered to search colonists' homes for forbidden goods with **writs of assistance**. **John Dickinson's** *Letters from a Farmer in Pennsylvania* and Samuel Adams' **Massachusetts Circular Letter** argued for the repeal of the Townshend Acts (which were, indeed, repealed in 1770) and demanded *no taxation without representation*. Samuel Adams continued to stir up rebellion with his **Committees of Correspondence**, which distributed anti-British propaganda.

Protests against the Quartering Act in Boston led to the **Boston Massacre** in 1770, when British troops fired on a crowd of protesters. By 1773, in a climate of continued unrest driven by the Committees of Correspondence, colonists protested the latest taxes on tea levied by the **Tea Act** in the famous **Boston Tea**

Party by dressing as Native Americans and tossing tea off a ship in Boston Harbor. In response, the government passed the **Intolerable Acts**, closing Boston Harbor and bringing Massachusetts back under direct royal control.

In response to the Intolerable Acts, colonial leaders met in Philadelphia at the **First Continental Congress** in 1774 and issued the *Declaration of Rights and Grievances*, presenting colonial concerns to the King, who ignored it. However, violent conflict began in 1775 at **Lexington and Concord**, when American militiamen (**minutemen**) had gathered to resist British efforts to seize weapons and arrest rebels in Concord. On June 17, 1775, the Americans fought the British at the **Battle of Bunker Hill**; despite American losses, the number of casualties the rebels inflicted caused the king to declare that the colonies were in rebellion. Troops were deployed to the colonies; the Siege of Boston began.

> **DID YOU KNOW?**
>
> King George III also hired Hessian mercenaries from Germany to supplement British troops; adding foreign fighters only increased resentment in the colonies and created a stronger sense of independence from Britain.

In May 1775, the **Second Continental Congress** met at Philadelphia to debate the way forward. Debate between the wisdom of continued efforts at compromise and negotiations and declaring independence continued. The king ignored the Congress's *Declaration of the Causes and Necessities of Taking Up Arms*, which asked him to consider again the colonies' objections; he also ignored the **Olive Branch Petition** which sought compromise and an end to hostilities. **Thomas Paine** published his pamphlet **Common Sense**; taking Locke's concepts of natural rights and the obligation of a people to rebel against an oppressive government, it popularized the notion of rebellion against Britain.

By summer of 1776, the Continental Congress agreed on the need to break from Britain; on July 4, 1776, it declared the independence of the United States of America and issued the **Declaration of Independence**, drafted mainly by **Thomas Jefferson** and heavily influenced by Locke.

Americans were still divided over independence; **Patriots** favored independence while those still loyal to Britain were known as **Tories. George Washington** had been appointed head of the Continental Army and led a largely unpaid and unprofessional army; despite early losses, Washington gained ground due to strong leadership, superior knowledge of the land, and support from France (and to a lesser extent, Spain and the Netherlands). The tide turned in 1777 at **Valley Forge**, when Washington and his army lived through the bitterly cold winter and managed to overcome British military forces. The British people did not favor the war and voted the Tories out of Parliament; the incoming Whig party sought to end the war. In the 1783 **Treaty of Paris**, the United States was recognized as a country, agreeing to repay debts to British merchants and provide safety to those British loyalists who wished to remain in North America. The American Revolution would go on to inspire revolution around the world.

FEDERALISTS AND DEMOCRATIC-REPUBLICANS

Joy in victory was short-lived. Fearful of tyranny, the Second Continental Congress had authorized only a weak central government, adopting the **Articles of Confederation** to organize the Thirteen Colonies—now states—into a loosely united country. A unicameral central government had the power to wage war, negotiate treaties, and borrow money. It could not tax citizens, but it could tax states. It also set parameters for westward expansion and establishing new states: the **Northwest Ordinances** of 1787 forbade slavery north of the Ohio River. Areas with 60,000 people could apply for statehood. However, it soon became clear that the Articles of Confederation were not strong enough to keep the nation united.

The new country was heavily in debt. Currency was weak, taxes were high, and instability loomed. Daniel Shays led **Shays' Rebellion**, a revolt of indebted farmers who sought to prevent courts from seizing property in Massachusetts and to protest debtor's prisons. Furthermore, debt and disorganization made the country appear weak and vulnerable to Great Britain and Spain. If the United States was to remain one country, it needed a stronger federal government.

> **DID YOU KNOW?**
>
> The Northwest Ordinances also effectively nullified King George III's Proclamation of 1763, which promised Native Americans that white settlement would not continue in the Ohio Valley region. The United States did not recognize the Proclamation, and tensions would build.

Alexander Hamilton and **James Madison** called for a **Constitutional Convention** to frame a stronger federal government in a written constitution. Madison and other **Federalists** like **John Adams** believed in **separation of powers**, republicanism, and a strong federal government.

To determine the exact structure of the government, delegates at the convention settled on what became known as the **Great Compromise**, a **bicameral legislature**. Two plans had been presented: the **New Jersey Plan**, which proposed a legislature composed of an equal number of representatives from each state (which would benefit smaller states), and the **Virginia Plan**, which proposed a legislature composed of representatives proportional to the population of each state. States with large populations of enslaved African Americans accounted for those persons with the **Three-Fifths Compromise**, which counted a slave as three-fifths of a person. While represented in a state's population to determine that state's representation in Congress, enslaved persons had no place in the political process. The states adopted both plans, creating the **House of Representatives** and the **Senate**, to represent the large and small states at the federal level.

Despite the separation of powers provided for in the Constitution, **Anti-Federalists** like **Thomas Jefferson** called for even more limitations on the power of the federal government. The first ten amendments to the Constitution, or the **Bill of Rights**, a list of guarantees of American freedoms, was a concession to the

Anti-Federalists, who would later become the **Democratic-Republican Party** (eventually, the Democratic Party).

To convince the states of the benefits of federalism and to ratify the Constitution, Hamilton, Madison, and John Jay wrote the *Federalist Papers*. Likewise, the Bill of Rights helped sway the hesitant. In 1791, the Constitution was ratified. **George Washington** was elected president, with John Adams serving as vice president; Washington appointed Hamilton as Secretary of the Treasury and Jefferson as Secretary of State.

Hamilton prioritized currency stabilization and repayment of debts; he also believed in establishing a national bank—the **Bank of the United States (BUS)**. He also favored tariffs and excise (sales) taxes, which Anti-Federalists—who became known as **Democratic-Republicans**—vehemently opposed. in 1795, rebellion against the excise tax on whiskey broke out; the **Whiskey Rebellion** indicated unrest in the young country and was put down by militia.

President Washington issued the **Neutrality Proclamation** in 1793, keeping the US out of the French Revolution. However, British and French ships accosted American ships in the Atlantic and forced American sailors into naval service (**impressment**). **Jay's Treaty**, an attempt at reinstating neutrality, was unsuccessful and unpopular; it only negotiated the removal of British forts in the western frontier. Furthermore, Spain became concerned about changes in the continental balance of power. President Washington had Thomas Pickney negotiate a new treaty with Spain; giving the US rights on the Mississippi River and in the Port of New Orleans, **Pickney's Treaty** was a diplomatic success and ratified by all thirteen states. The **Northwest Indian Wars** continued in the Ohio region; ultimately the Americans gained territory in Ohio and Indiana following the defeat of allied tribes at the **Battle of Fallen Timbers** in 1794.

> **DID YOU KNOW?**
>
> Federalists were generally from the North and were usually merchants or businessmen; Anti-Federalists were usually from the South or the rural west, and farmed the land.

In President Washington's **Farewell Address**, he recommended the United States adhere to neutrality in international affairs, setting a precedent for early American history. Vice President John Adams, a Federalist, became the second president. France continued to seize American ships, so Adams sent representatives to negotiate; however, in what became known as the **XYZ Affair**, the Americans were asked for bribes in order to even meet with French officials. The insulted Americans began an undeclared conflict in the Caribbean until the **Convention of 1800** negotiated a cessation of hostilities.

During the Adams administration, the Federalists passed the harsh **Alien and Sedition Acts**. The Alien Act allowed the president to deport "enemy aliens"; it also increased the residency requirements for citizenship. The Sedition Act forbade criticism of the president or of Congress. Divisions between the Federalists and the Democratic-Republicans were deeper than ever and the presidential elections of 1800 were tense and controversial. Nevertheless, Thomas Jefferson was elected to the presidency in 1801 in a non-violent transfer of power.

Jefferson repealed the Alien and Sedition Acts and shrank the federal government. Economic policies favored small farmers and landowners, in contrast to Federalist policies, which supported big business and cities. However, Jefferson also oversaw the **Louisiana Purchase**, which nearly doubled the size of the United States. This troubled some Democratic-Republicans, who saw this as federal overreach, but the Louisiana Purchase would be a major step in westward expansion.

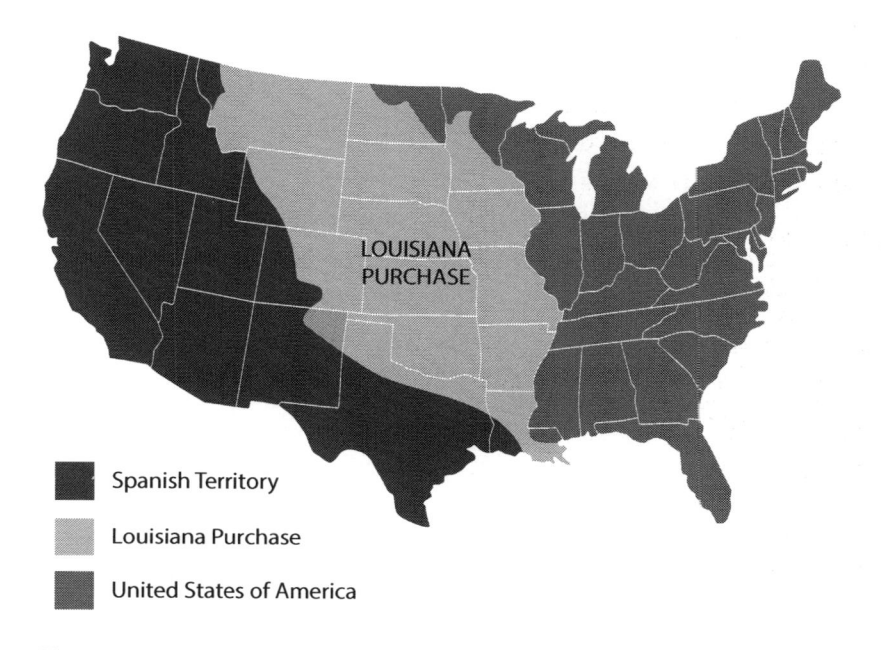

Figure 1.5. Louisiana Purchase

Jefferson was also forced to manage chaotic international affairs. Britain and France, at war in Europe, were attempting to blockade each other's international trade, threatening US ships and commerce. In an attempt to avoid the conflict, Congress passed the **Embargo Act** in 1807, restricting international trade. However this law only damaged the US economy further. At the end of Jefferson's presidency, Congress passed the **Non-Intercourse Act**, which allowed trade with foreign countries besides Britain and France; under President **James Madison**, tensions would remain high.

Monroe Doctrine and Manifest Destiny

British provocation at sea and in the northwest led to the **War of 1812**. Growing nationalism in the United States pressured Madison into pushing for war after the **Battle of Tippecanoe** in Indiana, when **General William Henry Harrison** fought the **Northwest Confederacy**, a group of tribes led by the Shawnee leader **Tecumseh**. The Shawnee, Lenape, Miami, Kickapoo, and others had come together not only out of common interest—to maintain control over their lands—but also because they followed Tecumseh's brother **Tenskwatawa**, who was considered a prophet.

Despite the Confederacy's alliance with Britain, the United States prevailed. Congress declared war with the intent to defend the United States, end commercial disruption and impressment of Americans at sea, and destabilize British Canada. The war resulted in no real gains or losses for either the Americans or the British. Yet at the war's end, the United States had successfully reaffirmed its independence. The Federalists, who had opposed the war, eventually collapsed. Patriotism ran high.

The **Era of Good Feelings** began with the presidency of **James Monroe** as a strong sense of public identity and nationalism pervaded in the country. In a religious revival called the **Second Great Awakening**, people turned from Puritanism to Baptist and Methodist faiths, following revolutionary preachers and movements. In art and culture, romanticism and reform movements elevated the "common man," a trend that would continue into the presidency of Andrew Jackson.

From a financial perspective, the country would again struggle. Disagreement over the **Tariff of 1816** divided industrialists, who believed in nurturing American industry, from Southern landowners, who depended on exporting cotton and tobacco for profit. Later, following the establishment of the **Second Bank of the United States**, the **Panic of 1819** erupted when the government cut credit following overspeculation on western lands; the BUS wanted payment from state banks in hard currency, or **specie**. Western banks foreclosed on western farmers.

With the Louisiana Purchase, the country had almost doubled in size. In the nineteenth century, the idea of **manifest destiny**, or the sense that it was the fate of the United States to expand westward and settle the continent, prevailed. Also in 1819, the United States purchased Florida from Spain in the **Adams-Onis Treaty**. The **Monroe Doctrine**, James Monroe's policy that the Western Hemisphere was "closed" to any further European colonization or exploration, asserted US hegemony in the region.

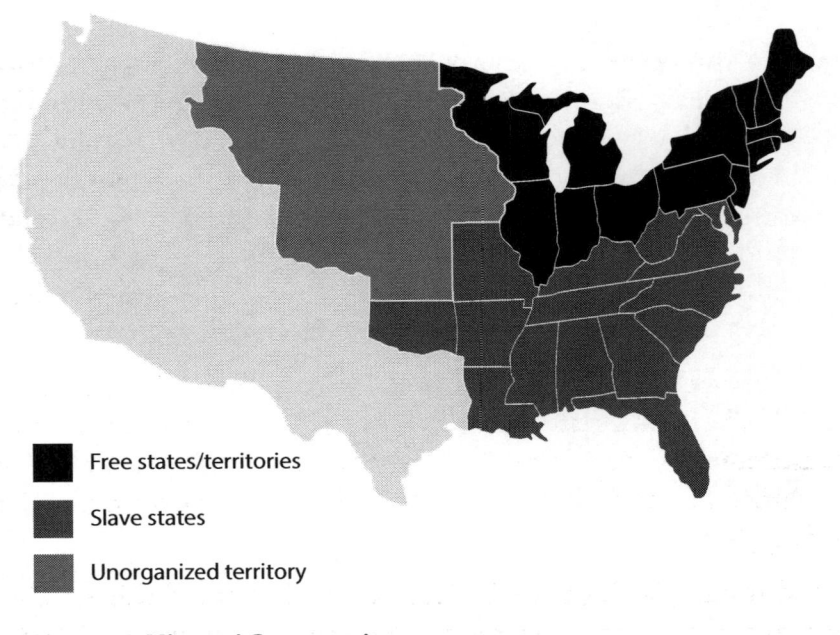

Figure 1.6. Missouri Compromise

Westward expansion triggered questions about the expansion of slavery, a divisive issue. Slavery was profitable for the southern states which depended on the plantation economy, but increasingly condemned in the North. Furthermore, the Second Great Awakening had fueled the **abolitionist** movement. In debating the nature of westward expansion, the Kentucky senator **Henry Clay** worked out a compromise. The **Missouri Compromise**, also known as the **Compromise of 1820**, allowed Missouri to join the union as a slave state, but provided that any other states north of the **thirty-sixth parallel (36°30')** would be free. Maine would also join the nation as a free state. However, more tension and compromises over the nature of slavery in the West were to come.

Jacksonian Democracy

Demographics were changing throughout the early nineteenth century. Technological advances had increased cotton yield; therefore, more persons were enslaved than ever before, bringing more urgency to the issue of slavery. In addition, **immigration** from Europe to the United States was increasing. Reactionary **nativist** movements like the **Know-Nothing Party** feared the influx of non-Anglo Europeans, particularly Catholics, and discrimination was widespread, especially against the Irish. Other technological advances like the **railroads** and **steamships** were speeding up westward expansion and improving trade throughout the continent; a large-scale **market economy** was emerging. With early industrialization and changing concepts following the Second Great Awakening, women were playing a larger role in society, even though they could not vote.

Most states had extended voting rights to white men who did not own land or substantial property: **universal manhood suffrage**. Elected officials would increasingly come to better reflect the electorate, and the brash war hero Jackson was popular among the "common man."

During the election of 1824, Andrew Jackson ran against **John Quincy Adams**, Henry Clay, and William Crawford, all Republicans (from the Democratic-Republican party); John Quincy Adams won. By 1828, divisions within the party had Jackson and his supporters known as Democrats, in favor of small farmers and inhabitants of rural areas, and states' rights. Clay and his supporters became known as **National Republicans** and, later, **Whigs**, a splinter group of the Democratic-Republicans which supported business and urbanization; they also had federalist leanings. Thus the **two-party system** emerged.

Andrew Jackson's popularity with the "common man," white, male farmers and workers who felt he identified with them, and the fact that owning property was no longer a requirement to vote, gave him the advantage and a two-term presidency. Jackson rewarded his supporters, appointing them to important positions as part of the **spoils system**.

Opposed to the Bank of the United States, he issued the **Specie Circular**, devaluing paper money and instigating the financial **Panic of 1837**. Despite his opposition to such deep federal economic control, Jackson was forced to contend with controversial tariffs. The **Tariff of 1828**, or **Tariff of Abominations**, benefitted northern industry, but heavily affected southern exports. Senator **John C. Calhoun** of South Carolina argued for **nullification**, the right of a state to declare a law null and void if it was harmful.

Tensions increased with the **Tariff of 1832**; Calhoun and South Carolina threatened to secede if their economic interests were not protected. Jackson managed the **Nullification Crisis** without resorting to violence, working out a compromise in 1833 that was more favorable to the South.

Socially and politically, white men of varying levels of economic success and education had stronger political voices and more opportunities in civil society. However, women, African Americans, and Native Americans did not. With continental expansion came conflict with Native Americans. Despite efforts by the Cherokee, who unsuccessfully argued for the right to their land in the Supreme Court case *Cherokee Nation v. Georgia* (1831), President Jackson enforced the 1830 **Indian Removal Act**, forcing tribes from their lands in the Southeast. Thousands of people were forced to travel mainly on foot, with all of their belongings, to Indian Territory (today, Oklahoma) on the infamous **Trail of Tears**, to make way for white settlers. Violent conflicts would continue on the Frontier farther west between the US and the Apache, Comanche, Sioux, Arapaho, Cheyenne, and other tribes throughout the nineteenth century.

SAMPLE QUESTIONS

11) How did the Quartering Act impact the colonists?

    A. Colonists were forced to take British soldiers into their homes; protests against the Act led to the Boston Tea Party.

    B. Colonists were forced to build quarters for British soldiers who were stationed locally.

    C. Colonists had to provide one-quarter of their earnings to support British soldiers stationed locally.

    D. Colonists were forced to take British soldiers into their homes; protests against the Act led to the Boston Massacre.

Answer:

    D. **Correct.** Anger at being forced to provide shelter for British soldiers led to protests; in 1770, British soldiers fired on protests against the Quartering Act in what came to be called the Boston Massacre.

12) **What was the impact of Shays' Rebellion?**
    A. It showed resistance to imposing excise taxes on whiskey and other consumer goods.
    B. It illustrated the need for a stronger federal government in the young United States.
    C. Taxes engineered by Hamilton during the Washington administration were cut.
    D. The radical Democratic-Republicans emerged to protest the Bank of the United States.

    Answer:
    B. Correct. Shays' Rebellion, in which Daniel Shays led a rebellion of indebted farmers shortly after the end of the Revolution, showed the need for a stronger federal government to ensure national stability and was a major factor in planning the Constitutional Convention.

13) **What was the impact of United States' rejection of the Proclamation of 1763?**
    A. A series of conflicts between the Americans and the Northwest tribes (later, the Northwest Confederacy) culminated in the War of 1812. Ultimately, the US would control the land.
    B. The French and British formed the Northwest Confederacy, allying against the United States to control more land in North America.
    C. A series of conflicts between the Americans and the Northwest tribes culminated in the War of 1812. Ultimately, the Northwest Confederacy would control the land for another century before ceding it to Canada.
    D. The Northwest Confederacy of British and American soldiers united to drive Native American tribes from what is today the Midwest region of the United States, allowing whites to establish settlements there.

    Answer:
    A. Correct. Despite efforts by the tribes to retain control over their land, they would eventually lose a series of conflicts and the United States would establish states in the Midwest and Ohio Valley region.

14) **How did the Missouri Compromise reflect divisions over slavery?**
    A. It showed disagreement over the nature of westward expansion.
    B. It showed the impact of the abolitionist movement on politics.
    C. It showed how the Second Great Awakening had influenced society.
    D. all of the above

    Answer:
    D. Correct. All of the answer choices are true.

15) How did demographics play a part in democratic change during the early and mid-nineteenth century, particularly in the context of Jacksonian Democracy?

- A. The rising strength of industry in the Northeast, coupled with the beginnings of railroads, strengthened support for pro-business politicians and the business class.
- B. Wealthy European immigrants shifted the balance of power away from the "common man" to business owners and the elites, leading to the rise of the powerful Whig party.
- C. Universal manhood suffrage shifted the balance of political power away from the elites; immigration accelerated westward expansion and began to power early industry and urban development.
- D. Jackson's focus on strengthening the federal government dissatisfied the South, leading to the Nullification Crisis.

Answer:

C. Correct. Universal manhood suffrage allowed all white males, whether or not they owned property, to vote; the "common man" had a voice in government, and Jackson enjoyed their support. Likewise, an influx of poor European immigrants changed the country's demographics, providing more workers for early industry, more settlers to populate the west, and a stronger voice in government against the wealthy.

Civil War, Expansion, and Industry

The Road to Conflict

The Civil War was rooted in ongoing conflict over slavery, states' rights, and the reach of the federal government. Reform movements of the mid-nineteenth century fueled the abolitionist movement. The Missouri Compromise and the Nullification Crisis foreshadowed worsening division to come.

In 1836, Texas, where there were a great number of white settlers, declared independence from Mexico. In 1845, Texas joined the Union; this event, in addition to US hunger for land, triggered the **Mexican-American War**. As a result of the **Treaty of Guadalupe Hidalgo**, which ended the war following Mexico's surrender, the United States obtained territory in the Southwest and gold-rich California. The population of California would grow rapidly with the **gold rush** as prospectors headed west to try their fortunes. However, Hispanics who had lived in the region under Mexico lost their land and were denied many of the rights that whites enjoyed—even though they had been promised US citizenship and equal rights under the treaty. They also suffered from racial discrimination.

Meanwhile, social change in the Northeast and growing Midwest continued. As the market economy and early industry developed, so did the **middle class**. The role of **women** changed; extra income allowed many to stay at home. The

Cult of Domesticity, a popular cultural movement, encouraged women to become homemakers and focus on domestic skills. However, women were also freed up to engage in social activism. Activists like **Susan B. Anthony** and **Elizabeth Cady Stanton** worked for women's rights, including women's suffrage, culminating in the 1848 **Seneca Falls Convention** led by the **American Woman Suffrage Association**. Women were also active in the temperance movement. Organizations like the Woman's Christian Temperance Union advocated for the prohibition of alcohol, which was finally achieved with the Eighteenth Amendment, although it was later repealed with the Twenty-First.

Reform movements continued to include abolitionism, which ranged from moderate to radical. The American Colonization Society wanted to end slavery and send former slaves to Africa. The activist, writer, and former slave **Frederick Douglass** advocated for **abolition**. Douglass publicized the movement along with the American Anti-Slavery Society and publications like Harriet Beecher Stowe's *Uncle Tom's Cabin*. The radical abolitionist **John Brown** led violent protests against slavery. Abolitionism became a key social and political issue.

The industrial change in the North did not extend to the South, which continued to rely on plantations and cotton exports. Nor were the majority of demographic changes occurring in the South. Differences among the regions grew, and disputes over extending slavery into new southwestern territories obtained from Mexico continued. Another compromise was needed.

Anti-slavery factions in Congress had attempted to halt the extension of slavery to the new territories obtained from Mexico in the 1846 **Wilmot Proviso**, but these efforts were unsuccessful. The later **Compromise of 1850** admitted the populous California as a free state and Utah and New Mexico to the Union with slavery to be decided by **popular sovereignty**, or by the residents. It also reaffirmed the **Fugitive Slave Act**, which allowed slave owners to pursue escaped slaves to free states and recapture them. It would now be a federal crime to assist escaped slaves, an unacceptable provision to many abolitionists.

Shortly thereafter, Congress passed the **Kansas-Nebraska Act of 1854** which allowed those two territories to decide slavery by popular sovereignty as well, effectively repealing the Missouri Compromise. A new party, the **Republican Party**, was formed by angered Democrats, Whigs, and others as a result; later, one of its members, Abraham Lincoln, would be elected to the presidency. Violence broke out in Kansas between pro- and anti-slavery factions in what became known as **Bleeding Kansas**.

In 1856, an escaped slave, **Dred Scott**, took his case to the Supreme Court to sue for freedom. Scott had escaped to the free state of Illinois and sought to stay there; his former "owner" had argued that he could get him back regardless of the state he was in. The Court heard the case, *Scott v. Sandford*, and ruled in favor of Sandford, upholding the Fugitive Slave Act, the Kansas-Nebraska Act, and nullifying the Missouri Compromise. The Court essentially decreed that African Americans were not entitled to rights under US citizenship.

In 1858, a series of debates between Illinois Senate candidates, Republican **Abraham Lincoln** and Democrat **Stephen Douglas**, showed the deep divides in the nation over slavery and states' rights. During the **Lincoln-Douglas Debates**, Lincoln spoke out against slavery, while Douglas supported the right of states to decide its legality on their own. In 1860, Lincoln was elected to the presidency. Given his outspoken stance against slavery, South Carolina seceded immediately, followed by Mississippi, Alabama, Florida, Louisiana, Georgia, and Texas. They formed the Confederate States of America, or the **Confederacy**, on February 1, 1861, under the leadership of **Jefferson Davis**, a senator from Mississippi.

Shortly after the South's secession, Confederate forces attacked Union troops in Charleston Harbor, South Carolina; the **Battle of Fort Sumter** sparked the Civil War. As a result, Virginia, Tennessee, North Carolina, and Arkansas seceded and joined the Confederacy. West Virginia was formed when the western part of Virginia refused to join the Confederacy.

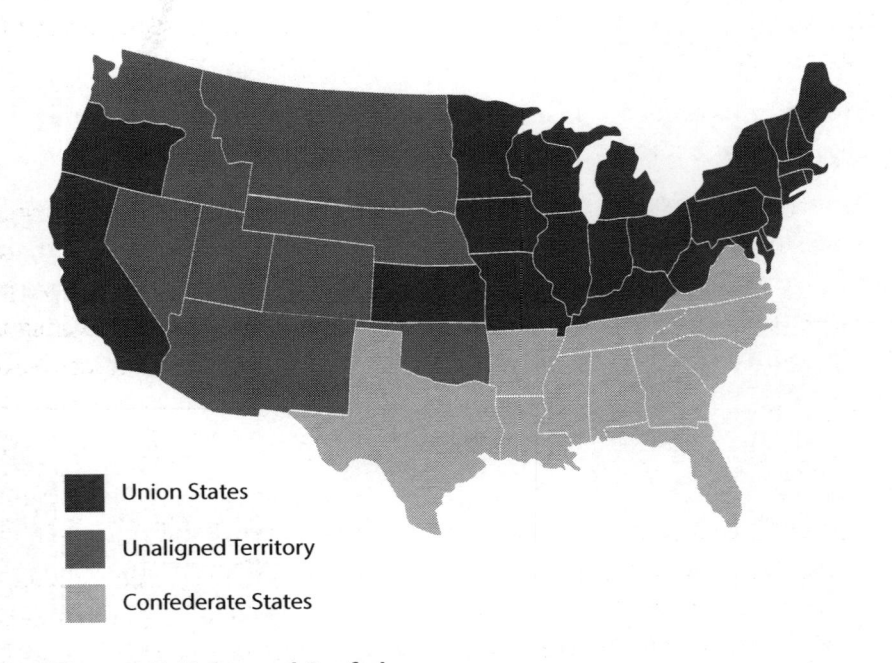

Figure 1.7. Union and Confederacy

Both sides believed the conflict would be short-lived; however, after the First Battle of Bull Run when the Union failed to rout the Confederacy, it became clear that the war would not end quickly. The Union developed the **Anaconda Plan**, which "squeezed" the Confederacy through a naval blockade and Union control of the Mississippi River. Since the South depended on international trade for much of its income, a naval blockade would have serious economic ramifications.

However, the Second Battle of Bull Run was a tactical Confederate victory, led by **General Robert E. Lee** and Stonewall Jackson. The Union army remained intact, but the loss was a heavy blow to Union morale. The Battle of Antietam was the first battle to be fought on Union soil. Union General George B. McClellan halted General Lee's invasion of Maryland, but failed to defeat Confederate forces. Undaunted, on January 1, 1863, President Lincoln decreed the end of slavery in the rebel states with the **Emancipation Proclamation**. The **Battle of Gettysburg** was a major Union victory. It was the bloodiest battle in American history up to this point; the Confederate army would not recover.

> **DID YOU KNOW?**
>
> President Lincoln later delivered the Gettysburg Address onsite, in which he framed the Civil War as a battle for human rights and equality.

Meanwhile, Union forces led by **General Ulysses S. Grant** gained control over the Mississippi River, completing the Anaconda Plan. The **Battle of Atlanta** was the final major battle of the Civil War, and the Confederacy fell. One of the final conflicts of the war, the Battle of Appomattox Court House, finally resulted in Confederate surrender at Appomattox, Virginia, on April 9, 1865, where General Lee surrendered to General Grant. The war ended shortly after.

AFTERMATH AND RECONSTRUCTION

Despite the strong leadership and vast territory of the Confederacy, a larger population, stronger industrial capacity (including weapons-making capacity), the naval blockade of Southern trade, and superior leadership resulted in Union victory. Yet bitterness over Northern victory persisted, and President Lincoln was assassinated on April 15, 1865. Post-war **Reconstruction** would continue without his leadership.

Before his death, Lincoln had crafted the **Ten Percent Plan**: if ten percent of a Southern state's population swore allegiance to the Union, that state would be readmitted. However Lincoln's vice president, Andrew Johnson, enforced Reconstruction weakly and the white supremacist **Ku Klux Klan** emerged to intimidate and kill black people in the South; likewise, states enacted the oppressive **Black Codes** to limit the rights of African Americans.

> **DID YOU KNOW?**
>
> Despite ratifying the amendments, Southern states instituted the Black Codes to continue oppression of freedmen, or freed African Americans, who faced ongoing violence.

As a result, Congress passed the **Civil Rights Act** in 1866, granting citizenship to African Americans and guaranteeing African American men the same rights as white men (later reaffirmed by the Fourteenth Amendment). Eventually former Confederate states also had to ratify the 1865 **Thirteenth Amendment**, which abolished slavery; the **Fourteenth Amendment**, which upheld the provisions of the

Civil Rights Act; and the **Fifteenth Amendment**, which in 1870 granted African American men the right to vote.

Conflict over how harshly to treat the South persisted in Congress and in 1867, a Republican-led Congress passed the **Reconstruction Acts**, placing former Confederate states under the control of the US Army, effectively declaring martial law. Tension and bitterness existed between many Northern authorities and Southern leaders. At the same time, Reconstruction modernized Southern education systems, tax collection, and infrastructure. The **Freedmen's Bureau** was tasked with assisting freed slaves (and poor whites) in the South.

While technically enslaved African Americans had been freed, many slaves were not aware of this; others still remained voluntarily or involuntarily on plantations. All slaves were eventually freed; however, few had education or skills. Despite the Fourteenth Amendment, the rights of African Americans were regularly violated. The **Jim Crow laws** enforced **segregation** in the South.

In 1896, the Supreme Court upheld segregation in *Plessy v. Ferguson* when a mixed-race man, Homer Plessy, was forced off a whites-only train car. When Plessy challenged the law, the Court found that segregation was indeed constitutional, holding that *separate but equal* did still ensure equality under the law. This would remain the law until *Brown v. Board of Education* in 1954.

Black leaders like **Booker T. Washington** and **W.E.B. DuBois** sought solutions. Washington believed in gradual desegregation and vocational education for African Americans, providing it at his **Tuskegee Institute**. DuBois, on the other hand, favored immediate desegregation and believed African Americans should aim for higher education and leadership positions in society. His stance was supported by the advocacy group, the **National Association for the Advancement of Colored People (NAACP)**. These differing views reflected diverse positions within and beyond the African American community over its future. Furthermore, many blacks fled the South for opportunities in the North and West, as part of a greater demographic movement known as the **Great Migration**.

Resentment over the Reconstruction Acts never truly subsided, and military control of the South finally ended with the **Compromise of 1877**, which resolved the disputed presidential election of 1876, granting Rutherford B. Hayes the presidency, and removed troops from the South.

While the Civil War raged and during the chaotic post-war Reconstruction period, settlement of the West continued. California had already grown in population due to the gold rush. In the mid-nineteenth century, **Chinese immigrants** came in large numbers to California, in search of gold but arriving to racial discrimination instead. At the same time, however, the US was opening up trade with East Asia, thanks to **clipper ships** that made journeys across the Pacific Ocean faster and easier. Earlier in 1853, **Commodore Matthew Perry** had used "gunboat diplomacy" to force trade agreements with Japan; even earlier, the United States had signed the **Treaty of Wangxia**, a trade agreement, with Qing Dynasty China.

Unlike Chinese immigrants, Americans of European descent were encouraged to settle the Frontier. The **Homestead Act of 1862** granted 160 acres of land in the West to any settler who promised to settle and work it for a number of years. Frontier life was hard, however, as the land of the Great Plains was difficult to farm. Meanwhile, ranching and herding cattle became popular and profitable. White settlers also hunted the buffalo; mass buffalo killings threatened Native American survival.

Conflict between Native American tribes and white settlers was ongoing. The United States came to an agreement with the Sioux in South Dakota, offering them land as part of the burgeoning **reservation** system. However, by the late nineteenth century, gold was discovered in the Black Hills of South Dakota on the **Great Sioux Reservation**, and the US reneged on its promise. The resulting **Sioux Wars** culminated in the 1876 **Battle of Little Big Horn** and General George Custer's famous "last stand." While the US was defeated in that battle, reinforcements would later defeat the Sioux and the reservation system continued. The spiritual **Ghost Dance Movement** united Plains tribes in the belief that whites would eventually be driven from the land. In 1890, the military forced the Sioux to cease this ritual; the outcome was a massacre at **Wounded Knee** and the death of the Sioux chief, **Sitting Bull**.

In 1887, the **Dawes Act** ended federal recognition of tribes, withdrew tribal land rights, and forced the sale of reservations—tribal land. It also dissolved Native American families. Children were sent to boarding schools, where they were forced to abandon their languages and cultures.

THE GILDED AGE AND THE SECOND INDUSTRIAL REVOLUTION

Back in the Northeast, the market economy and industry were flourishing. Following the war, the **Industrial Revolution** accelerated in the United States. The Industrial Revolution had begun with textile production in Great Britain, fueled in great part by Southern cotton. It evolved in the United States with the development of heavy industry into what would be called the **Second Industrial Revolution**.

The **Gilded Age** saw an era of rapidly growing income inequality, justified by theories like **Social Darwinism** and the **Gospel of Wealth**. These argued that the wealthy had been made rich by God and were more deserving of wealth than others. Much of this wealth was generated by heavy industry in the Second Industrial Revolution (the first being textile driven in Europe). Westward expansion required railroads; railroads required steel, and industrial production required oil: all these commodities spurred the rise of powerful companies like John D. Rockefeller's Standard Oil and Andrew Carnegie's US Steel.

The creation of **monopolies** and **trusts** helped industrial leaders consolidate their control over the entire economy; a small elite grew to hold a huge percentage of income. Monopolies let the same business leaders control the market for their own products. Business leaders in varying industries (monopolies) organized into trusts, ensuring their control over each other's industries, buying and selling from each other, and resulting in the control of the economy by a select few. These processes were made possible thanks to **vertical** and **horizontal integration** of industries. One company would dominate each step in manufacturing a good, from obtaining raw materials to shipping finished product, through vertical integration. Horizontal integration describes the process of companies acquiring their competition, monopolizing their markets. With limited governmental controls or interference in the economy, American **capitalism**—the free market system—was becoming dominated by the elite.

However, the elite were also powering industrial growth. Government corruption led only to weak restrictive legislation like the **Interstate Commerce Act** of 1887, which was to regulate the railroad industry, and the **Sherman Antitrust Act** (1890), which was intended to break up monopolies and trusts, in order to allow for a fairer marketplace; however, these measures would remain largely toothless until President Theodore Roosevelt's "trust-busting" administration in 1901.

Not only were products from the US market economy available in the United States; in order to continue to fuel economic growth, the United States needed more markets abroad. **New Imperialism** described the US approach to nineteenth and early twentieth century imperialism as practiced by the European powers. Rather than controlling territory, the US sought economic connections with countries around the world.

While the free markets and trade of the **capitalist** economy spurred national economic and industrial growth, the **working class**, comprised largely of poor European and Chinese immigrants working in factories and building infrastructure, suffered from dangerous working conditions and other abuses. As the railroads expanded westward, white farmers suffered: they lost their land to corporate interests. In addition, Mexican Americans and Native Americans were harmed and lost land as westward expansion continued with little to no regulations on land use. African Americans in the South, though freed from slavery, were also struggling under **sharecropping**, in which many worked for the same people who had enslaved them, leasing land and equipment at unreasonable rates, essentially trapped in the same conditions they had lived in before.

These harmful consequences led to the development of reform movements, social ideals, and change.

Populism and the Progressive Era

The **People's (Populist) Party** formed in response to corruption and industrialization injurious to farmers (later, it would also support reform in favor of the working class, women, and children). Westward expansion destroyed farmland, pushing small farmers off their land and into debt. Small farmers were also unable to keep up with mechanized farming. Groups like the **National Grange** advocated for farmers. More extreme groups like **Las Gorras Blancas** disrupted the construction of railroads altogether in efforts to protect land from corporate interests.

Farmers were also concerned about fiscal policy. In order to reduce their debt, they believed that a **silver standard** would inflate crop prices by putting more money into national circulation, and formed the **Greenback-Labor Party**. The 1890 **Sherman Silver Purchase Act** allowed Treasury notes to be backed in both gold and silver. However, continuing economic troubles led to the **Panic of 1893**, and the act was repealed.

Meanwhile, the **Colored Farmers' Alliance** formed to support sharecroppers and other African American farmers in the South. Jim Crow laws remained in place in much of the South, reaffirmed by the Supreme Court case *Plessy v. Ferguson*. The NAACP was formed to advocate for African Americans nationwide and still functions today.

At the same time, the **labor movement** emerged to support mistreated industrial workers in urban areas. **Samuel Gompers** led the **American Federation of Labor (AFL)**, using **strikes** and **collective bargaining** to gain protections for industrial workers. The **Knights of Labor** further empowered workers by integrating unskilled workers into actions. The activist **Mother Jones** revolutionized labor by including women, children, and African Americans into labor actions.

Poor conditions led to philosophies of reform. Many workers were inspired by **socialism**, the philosophy developed in Europe that the workers should own the means of production and that wealth should be distributed equally, taking into account strong economic planning. Other radical movements included **utopianism**, whose adherents conceptualized establishing utopian settlements with egalitarian societies. More modern philosophies included the **Social Gospel**, the notion that it was society's obligation to ensure better treatment for workers and immigrants. With the continual rise of the **middle class**, women took a more active role in advocating for the poor and for themselves. Women activists also aligned with labor and the emerging **Progressive Movement**.

With the Progressive **Theodore Roosevelt**'s ascension to the presidency in 1901 following President William McKinley's assassination, the Progressive Era reached its apex. The *trust-buster* Roosevelt enforced the Sherman Antitrust Act and prosecuted the powerful **Northern Securities** railroad monopoly under the Interstate Commerce Act, breaking up trusts and creating a fairer market. He led government involvement in negotiations between unions and industrial powers, culminating in what was known as a *square deal* for fairer treatment of workers. The Progressive Era also saw a series of acts to protect workers, health, farmers, and children under Presidents Roosevelt and Taft.

Roosevelt also continued overseas expansion following McKinley's **Spanish-American War** (1898–1901), in which the US gained control over Spanish territory in the Caribbean, Asia, and the South Pacific.

The Spanish-American War had been the first time the United States had engaged in overseas military occupation and conquest beyond North America, contrary to George Washington's recommendations in his Farewell Address.

During this period, the US annexed Hawaii, Guam, Puerto Rico, and took over the Panama Canal Zone; Cuba became a US protectorate; and the US annexed the Philippines, which would fight an ongoing guerrilla war for independence.

Spanish abuses in Cuba had concerned Americans; however, many events were exaggerated in the media. This sensational **yellow journalism** aroused popular interest in intervention in Cuba. The discovery of a diplomatically embarrassing letter from the Spanish minister de Lôme, along with the mysterious explosion of the battleship USS *Maine* in Havana, spurred the US into action.

Many Americans did not support intervention, however. According to the **Teller Amendment**, Cuba would revert to independence following the war. The US signed a peace treaty with Spain in 1898. As a result, it controlled Puerto Rico and Guam. Despite having promised independence to the Philippines, McKinley elected to keep it; furthermore, under the **Platt Amendment**, the United States effectively took over Cuba despite previous promises.

The **Roosevelt Corollary** to the Monroe Doctrine, which promised US intervention in Latin America in case of European intervention there, essentially gave the US total dominance over Latin America. Under the **Hay-Pauncefote Treaty**, Great Britain relinquished its claims to the Panama Canal Zone to the US. This **new imperialism** expanded US markets and increased US presence and prestige on the global stage.

SAMPLE QUESTIONS

16) Which of the following is true about the roots of the Civil War?

    A. Disagreement over the institution of slavery precipitated the Nullification Crisis, an early example of Southern discontent with the federal government.

    B. High numbers of immigrants moving to the North in the early nineteenth century represented a threat to the smaller South, which wanted to maintain control over the slaves.

    C. Lincoln and Douglas provoked anti-slavery sentiment in their debates around the country, bringing attention to a previously uncontested issue.

    D. The Missouri Compromise, the Compromise of 1850, and the Kansas-Nebraska Act reflected dissent over the future of the country—whether slavery should be extended as the United States grew.

    Answer:

    D. **Correct.** These pieces of legislation represent ongoing efforts to bridge the gap between differences in views over slavery in determining the future of the country.

17) **How did the Dawes Act impact Native Americans in the West?**

   A. It forced them to move from their ancestral lands to what is today Oklahoma.

   B. It revoked tribal rights to land and federal recognition of tribes, forcing assimilation.

   C. It granted them land on reservations: for example, the Sioux received deeds to the Great Sioux Reservation in the Black Hills of South Dakota.

   D. It provided 160 acres of land to any settler willing to farm land on the Great Plains for at least five years, threatening Native American rights to land.

   Answer:

   B. Correct. The punitive Dawes Act forced assimilation by revoking federal recognition of tribes, taking lands allotted to tribes and dissolving reservations, and forcing children into assimilationist schools (thereby dividing families).

18) **How was a small elite of wealthy businesspersons able to dominate the economy during the Gilded Age?**

   A. The Sherman Antitrust Act put a few expert business leaders in charge of economic policy.

   B. Monopolies and trusts, developed through horizontal and vertical integration, ensured that the same business leaders controlled the same markets.

   C. Industrialization was encouraging the United States to shift to a planned economy in keeping with philosophical changes in Europe.

   D. The silver standard allowed specific businesspeople holding large silver reserves to dominate the market.

   Answer:

   B. Correct. Horizontal and vertical integration of industries allowed the same companies—and people—to control industries, or create monopolies. Those elites who monopolized specific markets organized trusts so that one group controlled entire sectors of the economy.

19) **How did the Spanish-American War change perceptions of the United States?**

   A. It was clear to Europe and Latin America that the United States had military and territorial, in addition to economic, aspirations as an imperial power.

   B. The United States had begun to prove itself as a military power on the global stage, with strong naval capabilities.

   C. It was clear that nationalism was strong among the American people.

   D. all of the above

Answer:

D. Correct. All of the above answer choices satisfy the question.

20) How did the Progressive Movement change the United States during the Second Industrial Revolution?

   A. Trade unions fought for workers' rights and safety; the Social Gospel, an early philosophy of charity and philanthropy, developed to support the poor and urban disadvantaged.
   B. The Seneca Falls Convention drew attention to the question of women's suffrage.
   C. Progressives argued to extend rights and protections to Native Americans, particularly those displaced by settlement on the Great Plains.
   D. The Supreme Court ruled segregation unconstitutional in *Plessy v. Ferguson*.

Answer:

A. Correct. Unions improved conditions for industrial workers; the Social Gospel imparted a sense of social responsibility that manifested in laws and regulations protecting the rights and safety of workers, farmers, the poor, and others.

The United States Becomes a Global Power

Socioeconomic Change and World War I

Social change led by the Progressives in the early twentieth century resulted in better conditions for workers, increased attention toward child labor, and calls for more livable cities.

The Roosevelt administration focused its attention on economic change at the corporate level. The **Sherman Antitrust Act**, despite its intended purpose—to prosecute and dissolve large trusts and create a fairer market place—had actually been used against unions and farmers' alliances. Under Roosevelt, the Act was used to prosecute enormous trusts like the **Northern Securities Company**, which controlled much of the railroad industry, and **Standard Oil**. Actions like this earned Roosevelt his reputation as a trust-buster.

Continuing economic instability also triggered top-down reform. Banks restricting credit and overspeculating on the value of land and interests, coupled with a conservative gold standard, led to the **Panic of 1907**. To stabilize the economy and protect the banking system, Congress passed the **Federal Reserve Act** in 1913. Federal Reserve banks were established to cover twelve regions of the country; commercial banks had to take part in the system, allowing "the Fed" to control interest rates and avoid a similar crisis.

During the Progressive Era, while the United States became increasingly prosperous and stable, Europe was becoming increasingly unstable. Americans were divided over how to respond. Following the Spanish-American War, debate had arisen within the US between **interventionism** and **isolationism**—whether the US should intervene in international matters or not. Interventionists believed in spreading US-style democracy, while isolationists believed in focusing on development at home. This debate became more pronounced with the outbreak of World War I in Europe.

> **DID YOU KNOW?**
>
> Jacob Riis's groundbreaking book and photo essay *How the Other Half Lives* revealed the squalor and poverty the poor urban classes—often impoverished immigrants—endured, leading to more public calls for reform.

Inflammatory events like German **submarine warfare** (U-boats) in the Atlantic Ocean, the sinking of the *Lusitania*, which resulted in many American civilian deaths, the embarrassing **Zimmerman Telegram** (in which Germany promised to help Mexico in an attack on the US), and growing American **nationalism**, or pride in and identification with one's country, triggered US intervention. The US declared war in 1917. With victory in 1918, the US had proven itself a superior military and industrial power. Interventionist **President Woodrow Wilson** played an important role in negotiating the peace; his **Fourteen Points** laid out an idealistic international vision, including an international security organization. However, European powers negotiated and won the harsh **Treaty of Versailles**, which placed the blame for the war entirely on Germany and demanded crippling **reparations** from it, one contributing factor to **World War II** later in the twentieth century. The **League of Nations**, a collective security organization, was formed, but a divided US Congress refused to ratify the Treaty, so the US did not join it. Consequently, the League was weak and largely ineffective.

Divisions between interventionists and isolationists continued. Following the Japanese invasion of Manchuria in 1932, the **Stimson Doctrine** determined US neutrality in Asia. Congress also passed the **Neutrality Acts** of the 1930s in face of conflict in Asia and ongoing tensions in Europe.

Fear of homegrown radicals—particularly communists and anarchists—and xenophobia against immigrants led to the **Red Scare** in 1919 and a series of anti-immigration laws. Congress limited immigration specifically from Asia, Eastern Europe, and Southern Europe with the racist **Emergency Quota Act** of 1921 and **National Origins Act** of 1924.

The ongoing Great Migration of African Americans to the North led to differing views on black empowerment. Leaders like **Marcus Garvey** believed in self-sufficiency for blacks, who were settling in urban areas and facing racial discrimination and isolation. Garvey's **United Negro Improvement Association** would go on to inspire movements like the Black Panthers and the Nation of Islam; however, those radical philosophies of separation were at odds with the NAACP, which believed in integration. Tensions increased with 1919 race riots. In the South, the Ku Klux

Klan was growing in power, and blacks faced intimidation, violence, and death; **lynchings**, in which African Americans were kidnapped and killed, sometimes publicly, occurred frequently.

Despite race riots and discrimination in northern cities, African American culture did flourish and become an integral part of growing American popular culture. The **Harlem Renaissance**, the development and popularity of African American-dominated music (especially **jazz**), literature, and art, was extremely popular nationwide and contributed to the development of American pop culture.

Early technology like radio, motion pictures, and automobiles—products available to the middle class through credit—emerged in the 1920s, changing the US middle class and encouraging a culture of consumption. Furthermore, the women's rights movement was empowered by the heightened visibility of women in the public sphere; the **Nineteenth Amendment**, giving all women the right to vote, was ratified in 1920. However, the **Roaring Twenties**, a seemingly trouble-free period of isolation from chaotic world events, would come to an end.

Great Depression

Following WWI, the United States had experienced an era of consumerism and corruption. The government sponsored **laissez-faire** policies and supported **manufacturing**, flooding markets with cheap consumer goods. Union membership suffered; so did farmers, due to falling crop prices. While mass production helped the emerging middle class afford more consumer goods and improve their living standards, many families resorted to **credit** to fuel consumer spending. These risky consumer loans, **overspeculation** on crops and the value of farmland, and weak banking protections helped bring about the **Great Depression**, commonly dated from October 29, 1929, or *Black Tuesday*, when the stock market collapsed. During the same time period, a major drought occurred in the Great Plains, affecting farmers throughout the region. Millions of Americans faced unemployment and poverty.

Speculation, or margin buying, meant that speculators borrowed money to buy stock, selling it as soon as its price rose. However, since the price of stocks fluctuated, when buyers lost confidence in the market and began selling their shares, the value of stocks fell. Borrowers could not repay their loans; as a result, banks failed.

Following weak responses by the Hoover administration, **Franklin Delano Roosevelt** was elected to the presidency in 1932. FDR offered Americans a *New Deal*: a plan to bring the country out of the Depression. During the *First Hundred Days* of FDR's administration, a series of emergency acts (known as an *alphabet soup* of acts due to their many acronyms) was passed for the immediate repair of the banking system. The **Glass-Steagal Act** established the **Federal Deposit Insurance Corporation (FDIC)** to insure customer deposits in the wake of bank failures. The **Securities and Exchange Commission (SEC)** was established later to monitor stock trading and punish violators of the law. The **Agricultural Adjustment Act (AAA)** subsidized farmers to reduce production, benefitting them by raising the prices of commodities. The **Home Owners Loan Corporation (HOLC)** refinanced mortgages to protect homeowners from losing their homes, and the **Federal Housing Administration (FHA)** was created for the long term to insure low-cost mortgages.

Figure 1.8. Soup Kitchen During the Great Depression

The **Tennessee Valley Authority (TVA)**, was the first large-scale attempt at regional public planning; despite being part of the First Hundred Days, it was a long-term project. While intended to create jobs and bring electricity to the impoverished, rural inhabitants of the Tennessee Valley area, one of its true objectives was to accurately measure the cost of electric power, which had been supplied by private companies. The TVA was the first public power company and still operates today.

FDR did not only address economic issues; a number of acts provided relief to the poor and unemployed. The federal government allotted aid to states to be distributed directly to the poor through the **Federal Emergency Relief Act**. The federal government distributed funding to states through the **Public Works Administration (PWA)** for the purpose of developing infrastructure and to provide construction jobs for the unemployed. Likewise, the **Civilian Conservation Corps (CCC)** offered employment in environmental conservation and management projects. Later, during the **Second New Deal**, the **Works Progress Administration (WPA)** was established. The WPA was a long-term project that generated construction jobs on national infrastructure projects. It also employed writers and artists through the **Federal Writers' Project** and the **Federal Art Project**.

The New Deal addressed labor issues as well. The **Wagner Act** ensured the right to unionize and established the **National Labor Relations Board (NLRB)**. Strengthening unions guaranteed collective bargaining rights and protected workers.

FDR was a Democrat in the Progressive tradition; the Progressive legacy of social improvement was apparent throughout the New Deal and his administration. The New Deal and its positive impact on the poor, the working class, unions, and immigrants led these groups to support the Democratic Party.

INTERNATIONAL AFFAIRS AND WORLD WAR II

The entire world suffered from the Great Depression, and Europe became increasingly unstable. With the rise of the extremist Nazi Party in Germany, the Nazi leader Adolf Hitler led German takeovers of several European countries and threatened US allies, bombing Britain. However, the United States, weakened by the Great Depression and bound by the Neutrality Acts, remained militarily uncommitted in the war. However, the Neutrality Act of 1939 allowed cash-and-carry arms sales to combat participants; in this way, the United States could support its allies (namely, Great Britain).

FDR was increasingly concerned about the rise of fascism in Europe, seeing it as a global threat. To ally with and support Great Britain without technically declaring war on Germany, FDR convinced Congress to enact the **Lend-Lease Act**, directly supplying Britain with military aid, in place of cash-and-carry. In response to the nonaggression pact signed by Hitler and Stalin, FDR and the British Prime Minister **Winston Churchill** signed the **Atlantic Charter**, which laid out the anti-fascist agenda of free trade and self-determination. To garner domestic support, FDR spoke publicly about the **Four Freedoms**: freedom of speech, freedom of religion, freedom from want, and freedom from fear.

However, after the Japanese attack on **Pearl Harbor** on December 7, 1941, the US entered the war. Despite being attacked by Japan (a German ally), the United States focused first on the European theater. The Allied powers—the US, Great Britain, and the Soviet Union—agreed that Hitler was the primary global threat. The United States focused on eliminating the Nazi threat in the air and at sea, destroying Nazi U-boats (submarines) in the Atlantic. The US also engaged Germany in North Africa, defeating its troops to approach fascist Italy from the Mediterranean. On June 6, 1944, or **D-Day**, the US led the invasion of German-controlled Europe at Normandy. After months of fighting, following the exhausting **Battle of the Bulge** when the Allies faced fierce German resistance, the Allies entered Germany and ended the war in Europe.

The United States was then able to focus more effectively on the war in the Pacific. The United States had broken Japanese code, yet the **Navajo Code Talkers**, using the Navajo language, made it impossible for Japan to crack US code. The US strategy of **island hopping** allowed it to take control of Japanese-held Pacific islands, proceeding closer to Japan itself despite **kamikaze** attacks on US ships, in which Japanese fighter pilots intentionally crashed their planes into US ships. President **Harry Truman** had taken power following FDR's death in 1945. Rather than force a US invasion of Japan, which would have resulted in massive casualties, he authorized the bombing of **Hiroshima** and **Nagasaki** in Japan, the only times that **nuclear weapons** have been used in conflict. The war ended with Japanese surrender on September 2, 1945.

The **United Nations** was formed in the wake of the Second World War, modeled after the failed League of Nations. Unlike the League, however, it included a **Security Council** of major world powers, which could intervene militarily in unstable global situations. With most of Europe destroyed, the US and the Soviet Union emerged as the two global **superpowers**.

In 1945, Stalin, Churchill, and Roosevelt had met at the **Yalta Conference** to determine the future of Europe. The Allies had agreed on free elections in European countries. However, following the war the USSR occupied Eastern Europe, preventing free elections. The United States saw this as a betrayal of the agreement at Yalta. Furthermore, while the US-led **Marshall Plan** began rebuilding Europe, the USSR consolidated its presence and power in Eastern European countries, forcing them to reject Marshall aid. This division would destroy the alliance between the Soviets and the West, leading to the **Cold War** between the two superpowers and the emergence of a **bipolar world**.

> **DID YOU KNOW?**
>
> Japanese-Americans faced discrimination at home due to their ethnicity. Forced into internment camps, Japanese-Americans challenged this violation of their rights in *Korematsu v. US*; however, the Supreme Court ruled in favor of the government.

COLD WAR AT HOME AND ABROAD

With the collapse of the relationship between the USSR and the US, fear of **communism** grew. Accusations of communist sympathies against public figures ran rampant during the **McCarthy era** in the 1950s, reflecting domestic anxieties.

The **Truman Doctrine** stated that the US would support any country threatened by authoritarianism (communism). This policy lead to the **Korean War** (1950 – 1953), a conflict between the US and Soviet- and Chinese-backed North Korean forces, which ended in a stalemate. The policy of **containment**, to contain Soviet (communist) expansion, defined US foreign policy. According to **domino theory**, once one country fell to communism, others would quickly follow. Other incidents included the **Bay of Pigs** invasion in Cuba (1961), a failed effort to topple the communist government of Fidel Castro, and the **Cuban Missile Crisis** (1962), when Soviet missiles were discovered in Cuba and military crisis was narrowly averted, both under the administration of the popular President **John F. Kennedy**.

Meanwhile, in Southeast Asia, communist forces in North Vietnam were gaining power. Congress never formally declared war in Vietnam but gave the president authority to intervene militarily there through the **Gulf of Tonkin Resolution** (1964). However, this protracted conflict—the **Vietnam War**—also led to widespread domestic social unrest, which only increased with US deaths there, especially after the Vietnamese **Tet Offensive** (1968). The US ultimately withdrew from Vietnam. North Vietnamese forces, led by **Ho Chi Minh**, took over the entire country.

SAMPLE QUESTIONS

21) Which of the following precipitated US entry into the First World War?
    A. the sinking of the *Lusitania*
    B. nationalism stirred up by the Zimmerman telegram
    C. the threat of German U-boats in the Atlantic
    D. all of the above

    Answer:
    D. Correct. All of the above events together precipitated US entry into the First World War.

22) How did the United States change in the 1920s?
    A. The Great Migration ceased.
    B. African American culture became increasingly influential.
    C. The Great Depression caused high unemployment.
    D. Thanks to the New Deal, millions of Americans found jobs.

    Answer:
    B. Correct. The Harlem Renaissance is one example of the emergence of African American culture in the public sphere; as US popular culture developed, African American contributions influenced it.

23) What was the purpose of the United Nations Security Council?
    A. to provide a means for international military intervention in case of conflict that could threaten global safety, in order to avoid another world war
    B. to provide a forum for the superpowers to maintain a dialogue
    C. to provide a means for countries to counter the power of the US and USSR in an effort to limit the reach of the superpowers
    D. to develop a plan to rebuild Europe and Japan

Answer:

A. Correct. The Security Council was (and is) able to militarily intervene in cases of armed conflict that could pose a global threat.

24) **How did the New Deal repair the damage of the Great Depression and help the United States rebuild?**

   A. Immediate economic reforms stabilized the economy during the First Hundred Days; later, longer-term public works programs provided jobs to relieve unemployment and develop infrastructure.

   B. Social programs initiated during the First Hundred Days provided jobs for Americans; measures to protect homeowners, landholders, and bank deposits followed to guarantee financial security.

   C. Programs like the Tennessee Valley Authority helped the government determine proper pricing and institute price controls for important public goods.

   D. FDR proposed supporting banks and big business with federal money in order to reinvigorate the market by limiting government intervention.

Answer:

A. Correct. FDR focused on immediate economic stabilization upon taking office, then attacked poverty and unemployment on a sustainable basis.

25) **Why did the former allies, the United States and the Soviet Union, turn against each other following the end of the Second World War?**

   A. Stalin felt that the Marshall Plan should have been extended to the Soviet Union.

   B. Because of the fear of communism in the United States, the US had considered invading the USSR following the occupation of Nazi Germany.

   C. Despite assurances to the contrary, the USSR occupied Eastern European countries, preventing free elections in those countries.

   D. The Soviet Union was concerned that the United States would use the nuclear bomb again.

Answer:

C. Correct. Stalin's refusal to permit free elections in the countries of Eastern Europe was considered a betrayal of the agreement reached at Yalta, and a major reason for the collapse of the US-Soviet relationship.

Postwar and Contemporary United States

Civil Rights and Social Change

During the 1960s, the US experienced social and political change, starting with the election of the young and charismatic John F. Kennedy to the presidency. Later, President **Lyndon B. Johnson**'s administration saw the passage of liberal legislation in support of the poor and of civil rights. The **Civil Rights Movement**, led by activists like the **Rev. Dr. Martin Luther King, Jr.** and **Malcolm X**, fought for African American rights in the South, including the abolition of segregation, and also for better living standards for Blacks in northern cities.

Civil rights came to the forefront with the 1954 Supreme Court case ***Brown v. Board of Education***, when the Warren Court (so-called after Chief Justice Earl Warren) found segregation unconstitutional, overturning its decision in *Plessy v. Ferguson*. *Brown* took place shortly after the desegregation of the armed forces, and public support for civil rights and racial equality was growing.

The **Southern Christian Leadership Conference (SCLC)** and Dr. King believed in civil disobedience, non-violent protest. In Montgomery, Alabama, **Rosa Parks**, an African American woman, was arrested for refusing to give up her seat to a white man on a bus. Buses were segregated at the time, and leaders including Dr. King organized the successful **Montgomery Bus Boycott** to challenge segregation. Building on their success, civil rights activists, now including the **Student Nonviolent Coordinating Committee (SNCC)**, led peaceful protests, sit-ins, and boycotts against segregation at lunch counters, in stores, at public pools, and other public places.

The movement grew to include voter registration campaigns that included students and other activists (both black and white) from around the country—the **Freedom Riders**, so-called because they rode buses from around the country to join the movement in the South. The movement gained visibility as non-violent protesters at government and public facilities and on university campuses faced violence from the police and state authorities, including attacks by water cannons and police dogs.

The Civil Rights Movement became a major national issue. Civil rights workers organized the **March on Washington** in 1963, when Dr. King delivered his famous *I Have a Dream* speech. Widespread public support for civil rights legislation was impossible for the government to ignore. In 1964, Congress passed the **Civil Rights Act**, which outlawed segregation.

However, African Americans' voting rights were still not sufficiently protected. According to the Fifteenth and Nineteenth Amendments, all African Americans—men and women—had the right to vote, but many Southern states restricted voting with literacy tests and poll taxes, which disproportionately affected African Americans. Dr. King and civil rights workers organized a march from Selma to Montgomery, Alabama, to draw attention to this issue; however it ended in violence as marchers were attacked by police. In 1965, led by President Lyndon B. Johnson, Congress passed the **Voting Rights Act**, which forbade restrictions impeding the ability of African Americans to vote, including literacy tests. Separately, the **Twenty-Fourth Amendment** made poll taxes unconstitutional.

Figure 1.9. March on Washington

Meanwhile, **Malcolm X** was an outspoken proponent of **black empowerment**, particularly for African Americans in urban areas. Unlike Martin Luther King, Jr., who believed in integration, Malcolm X and other activists, including groups like the **Black Panthers**, believed that African Americans should focus on strengthening their own communities rather than advocating for integration and legislative change.

The Civil Rights Movement extended beyond the Deep South. **Cesar Chavez** founded the **United Farm Workers (UFW)**, which organized Hispanic and migrant farm workers in California and the Southwest to advocate for unionizing and collective bargaining. Farm workers were underpaid and faced racial discrimination. The UFW used boycotts and non-violent tactics similar to those used by civil rights activists in the South; Cesar Chavez also used hunger strikes to raise awareness of the problems faced by farm workers.

> **DID YOU KNOW?**
>
> Today, some states have instituted voter identification laws similar to literacy tests and poll taxes, which disproportionately affect minorities.

The Civil Rights Movement also included **feminist** activists who fought for fairer treatment of women in the workplace and for women's reproductive rights. The **National Organization for Women** and feminist leaders like **Gloria Steinem** led the movement for equal pay for women in the workplace. The landmark case of *Roe v. Wade* struck down federal restrictions on abortion.

The **American Indian Movement (AIM)** brought attention to injustices and discrimination suffered by Native Americans nationwide. Ultimately it was able to achieve more tribal autonomy and address problems facing Native American communities throughout the United States.

In New York City in 1969, the **Stonewall riots** occurred in response to police repression of the gay community. These riots and subsequent organized activism are considered the beginning of the LGBT rights movement.

Johnson launched a **War on Poverty**, passing reform legislation to support the poor. The **Medicare Act** provided medical care to elderly Americans; the creation of the **Department of Housing and Urban Development** increased the federal role in housing and urban issues. Johnson's **Head Start** program provisded early intervention for disadvantaged children before elementary school (and still does today); the **Elementary and Secondary Education Act** increased funding for primary and secondary education. Additionally, the **Immigration Act of 1965** overturned the provisions of the Emergency Quota Act, ending the racist limitations on immigrants to the US.

At the same time, LBJ's overseas agenda was increasingly unpopular. Adhering to containment and domino theory, Johnson drew the United States deeper into conflict in Southeast Asia. The **Vietnam War** was extremely unpopular in the US due to high casualties, the draft (mandatory military service for young men) and what seemed to many to be the purposelessness of the war. Student activists engaged in widespread protest. The emergence of a youth **counterculture** added to a sense of rebellion among Americans, usurping government authority and challenging traditional values.

THE RISE OF CONSERVATISM

Radical social change in the 1960s, coupled with the toll of the Vietnam War on the American public, led to backlash against liberalism. Social and political **conservatism** arose as a response to the increased role of government in public life, high rates of government spending, and challenges to traditional social norms. The conservative **Richard Nixon** became president in 1970.

During Nixon's administration, the conflict in Vietnam ended and a diplomatic relationship with China began. Nixon also oversaw economic reforms—he lifted the gold standard in an effort to stop **stagflation**, a phenomenon when both unemployment and inflation are high at the same time. Ending the gold standard reduced the value of the dollar in relation to other global currencies, and foreign investment in the United States increased. However, the Nixon administration also suffered from corruption. A burglary at the Democratic National Headquarters, based at the Watergate Hotel, was connected to the Oval Office. The **Watergate scandal** eventually forced Nixon to resign, further destroying many Americans' faith in their government.

During the 1970s, the economy suffered due to US involvement in the Middle East. US support for Israel in the Six Day War and 1973 Yom Kippur War caused the Arab-dominated **OPEC** (the Organization of Petroleum Exporting Countries) to boycott the US. As a result, oil prices skyrocketed. In the 1979 Iranian Revolution and **hostage crisis**, when staff at the US embassy in Tehran were taken hostage by anti-American activists, the economy suffered from another oil shock. While President Jimmy Carter had been able to negotiate peace between Israel and Egypt in the **Camp David Accords**, he was widely perceived as ineffective. Carter lost the presidency in 1980 to the conservative Republican **Ronald Reagan**.

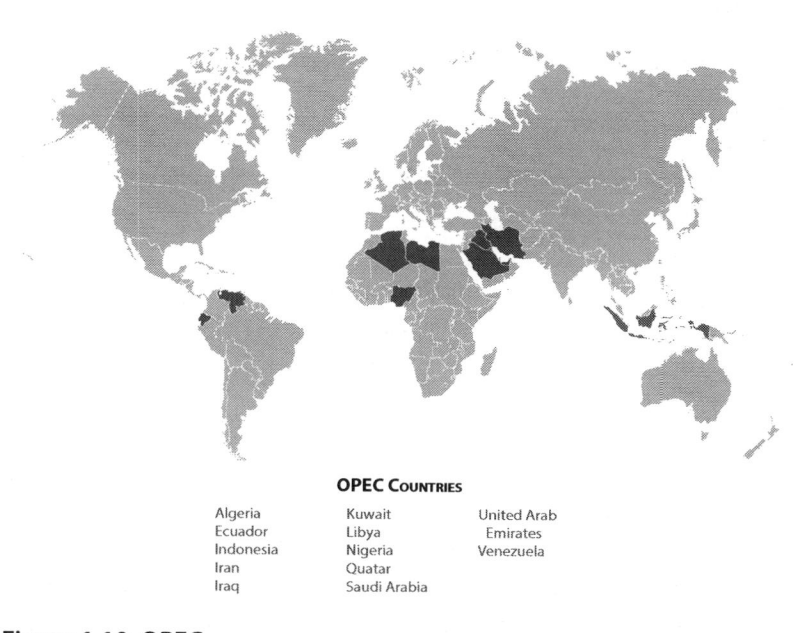

OPEC COUNTRIES

Algeria	Kuwait	United Arab
Ecuador	Libya	Emirates
Indonesia	Nigeria	Venezuela
Iran	Quatar	
Iraq	Saudi Arabia	

Figure 1.10. OPEC

Reagan championed domestic tax cuts and an aggressive foreign policy against the Soviet Union. The Reagan Revolution revamped the economic system, cutting taxes and government spending. According to supply-side economics (popularly known as *Reaganomics* or *trickle-down economics*), cutting taxes on the wealthy and providing investment incentives would cause wealth to "trickle down" to the middle and working classes and the poor. However, tax cuts forced Congress to cut or eliminate social programs that benefitted millions of those same Americans. Later, the **Tax Reform Act** of 1986 ended progressive income taxation.

Despite promises to lower government spending, the Reagan administration invested heavily in the military in an **arms race** with the Soviet Union. The Reagan administration also funded advanced military technology to intimidate the Soviets, despite having signed the **Strategic Arms Limitation Treaties (SALT I and II)** limiting nuclear weapons and other strategic armaments in the 1970s. Ultimately, the US would outspend the USSR militarily, a precipitating factor in the fall of the USSR.

Conservative values became publicly popular. Since the Civil Rights Movement, many Southern Democrats switched loyalties to the Republican Party. At the same time, the Democrats gained the support of African Americans and other minority groups who benefitted from civil rights and liberal legislation. During the Reagan era, conservative Republicans espoused a return to "traditional" values. **Christian fundamentalism** became popular, particularly among white conservatives. Groups like **Focus on the Family** lobbied against civil rights reform for women and advocated for traditional, two-parent, heterosexual families.

THE END OF THE COLD WAR AND GLOBALIZATION

The administration of **George H. W. Bush** signed the Strategic Arms Reduction Treaty (**START**) with the Soviet Union in 1991, shortly before the dissolution of the USSR. It would enter into force in 1994 between the US and the Russian Federation to limit the large arsenals of strategic weapons possessed by both countries.

With the collapse of the Soviet Union in 1991, the balance of international power changed. The bipolar world became a unipolar world, and the United States was the sole superpower. The first major crisis occurred in the Middle East when Iraq, led by **Saddam Hussein**, invaded oil-rich Kuwait. The US intervened, with international support. The resulting **Gulf War**, or **Operation Desert Storm** (1991)— cemented the status of the US as the world's sole superpower; Saddam's forces were driven from Kuwait, and Iraq was restrained by sanctions and no-fly zones.

With the election of President **Bill Clinton** in 1992, the US took an active international role, helping broker peace deals in the former Yugoslavia, Northern Ireland, and the Middle East. Clinton's election also indicated a more liberal era in American society: while conservative elements remained, changing attitudes toward minorities in the public sphere and increased global communication (especially with the advent of the internet) were a hallmark of the 1990s.

As part of **globalization**, the facilitation of global commerce and communication, the Clinton administration prioritized free trade. The United States signed the **North American Free Trade Agreement (NAFTA)** with Mexico and Canada, removing trade restrictions throughout North America. The Clinton administration also eased financial restrictions in the United States. These changes were controversial: many American jobs went overseas, especially manufacturing jobs, where labor was cheaper. Furthermore, globalization facilitated the movement of people. **Immigration reform** would be a major issue into the twenty-first century.

Clinton faced dissent in the mid-1990s with a conservative resurgence. A movement of young conservatives elected to Congress in 1994 promised a **Contract with America**, a conservative platform promising a return to lower taxes and traditional values. Clinton also came under fire for personal scandals. Despite these controversies and political division, society became increasingly liberal. Technology like the **internet** facilitated national and global communication, media, and business; minority groups like the LGBT community engaged in more advocacy; and environmental issues became more important to the public.

The Twenty-First Century

By the end of the twentieth century, the United States had established itself as the dominant global economic, military, and political power. The US dominated global trade: American corporations established themselves globally, taking advantage of free trade to exploit cheap labor pools and less restrictive manufacturing environments (at the expense of American workers). American culture was widely popular: since the early twentieth century, American pop culture like music, movies, television shows, and fashion was enjoyed worldwide.

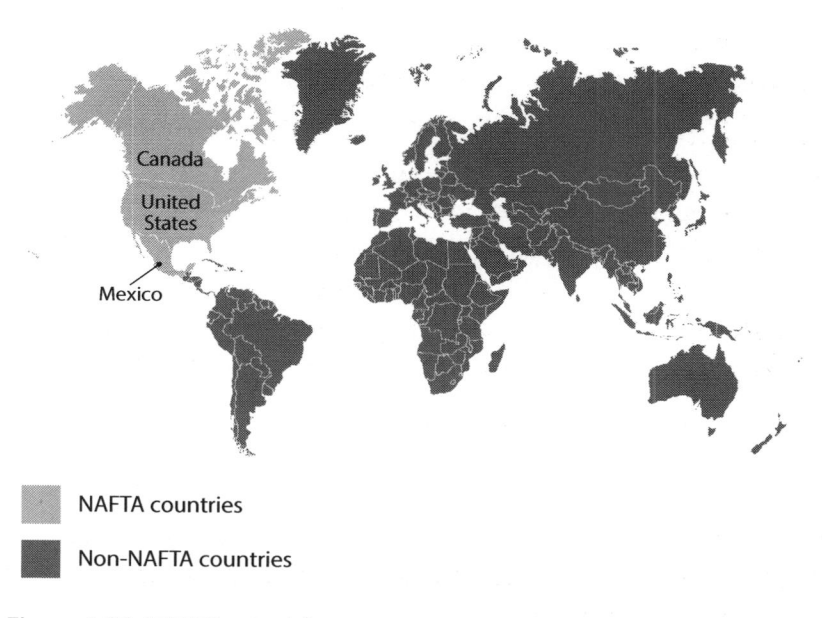

Figure 1.11. NAFTA countries

However, globalization also facilitated global conflict. The United States had been relatively untouched by large-scale terrorist attacks. That changed on **September 11, 2001**, when the terrorist group **al Qaeda** hijacked airplanes, attacking New York and Washington, DC, in the largest attack on US soil since the Japanese bombing of Pearl Harbor. The 9/11 attacks triggered an aggressive military and foreign policy under the administration of President **George W. Bush**, who declared a *War on Terror*, an open-ended global conflict against terror organizations and their supporters.

Following the attacks, the US struck suspected al Qaeda bases in Afghanistan, beginning the **Afghanistan War**, during which time the US occupied the country. Suspected terrorist fighters captured there and elsewhere during the War on Terror were held in a prison in **Guantanamo Bay**, Cuba, which was controversial because it did not initially offer any protections afforded to prisoners of war under the Geneva Conventions.

President Bush believed in the doctrine of **preemption**, that if the US was aware of a threat, it should preemptively attack the source of that threat. In 2003, the US attacked Iraq, believing that Iraq held **weapons of mass destruction** that could threaten the United States. This assumption was later revealed to be false; however, the **Iraq War** deposed Saddam Hussein and led to a long-term occupation of the country as well as destabilization and violence in Iraq.

At home, Congress passed the **USA Patriot Act** to respond to fears of more terrorist attacks on US soil; this legislation gave the federal government unprecedented—and, some argued, unconstitutional—powers of surveillance over the American public.

Despite the tense climate, social liberalization continued in the US. Following the Bush administration, during which tax cuts and heavy reliance on credit helped push the country into the **Great Recession**, the first African American president, **Barack Obama**, was elected in 2008. Under his presidency, the US emerged from the recession, ended its occupations of Iraq and Afghanistan, passed the Affordable Care Act, which reformed the healthcare system, and legalized same-sex marriage. The Obama administration also oversaw the passage of consumer protection acts, increased support for students, and safety nets for homeowners.

In 2016, the celebrity real estate developer **Donald Trump** won the presidency in an intensely contested election against **Hillary Clinton**, former senator, Obama's secretary of state, and the first female Democratic nominee for president. Economic malaise, racial tensions, urbanization, and other issues are thought to be contributing to national division. Some strongly support Trump, whose isolationist policies include withdrawing from the international Paris Agreement to combat climate change, banning citizens of some Muslim-majority countries from the US, and cutting involvement in NATO. Others vehemently disagree with his positions, accuse him of corruption, and are suspicious of the authenticity of his election, fearing it was unfairly influenced by the Russian Federation.

SAMPLE QUESTIONS

26) Why did the Civil Rights Movement continue to push for legislative change even after the passage of the 1964 Civil Rights Act?

   A. While the Civil Rights Act provided legal protections to African Americans and other groups, many believed it did not go far enough as it did not outlaw segregation.
   B. Leaders like Malcolm X believed further legislative reform would ensure better living conditions for blacks in cities.
   C. Civil rights leaders wanted legislation to punish white authorities in the South that had oppressed African Americans.
   D. Legal restrictions like literacy tests, poll taxes, and voter registration issues inhibited African Americans from exercising their right to vote, especially in the South.

   Answer:
   D. **Correct.** Despite the end to legal segregation, discrimination was deeply entrenched, and laws still existed to prevent African Americans from voting. Civil rights activists worked to ensure the passage of the Voting Rights Act in 1965.

27) Which of the following best describes liberalism under LBJ?

   A. Liberalism was the philosophy that the government should be deeply involved in improving society at home, and work on fighting communism abroad.
   B. According to liberalism, the US should devote its resources to improving life at home for the disadvantaged, but refrain from direct intervention in international conflict.
   C. Liberals believed in moderate social programs, but that spending should be limited.
   D. Liberalism frowns upon conflict intervention, as shown by the mass demonstrations against the Vietnam War in the 1960s.

   Answer:
   A. **Correct.** LBJ believed in forming a Great Society and launched government programs to support the disadvantaged; he also waged an unsuccessful war against communism in Southeast Asia.

28) Which of the following best describes globalization?

   A. the free movement of goods and services across borders
   B. easier communication worldwide thanks to technology like the internet
   C. facilitated movement of persons from one country to another
   D. all of the above

Answer:

D. Correct. Globalization is a multifaceted phenomenon that takes into account all the factors listed above.

29) How did Reagan's economic policies affect working class and poor Americans?

    A. They had little effect on these classes because the United States has a free market economy.
    B. They increased taxes by eliminating the progressive income tax and cut social programs needed by many disadvantaged people.
    C. They benefitted the working and middle classes by cutting taxes and increasing investment opportunities.
    D. Despite Reagan's tax cuts, the government was able to fund all social programs, so lower income Americans who used them were unaffected by changes in revenue.

Answer:

B. Correct. Low taxes on the wealthy were thought to encourage investment in the economy; as a result, wealth would "trickle down" to other Americans. In practice, lower taxes meant less government revenue, and many social programs were cut.

30) Which best describes the Bush doctrine of preemption?

    A. The US believed that in order to contain terrorism, it had to occupy countries that might harbor terrorists.
    B. Fearing that the entire Middle East would succumb to terrorists, the Bush administration established a presence in the centrally located country of Iraq to avoid a "domino effect" of regime collapse.
    C. The Bush administration justified international intervention and foreign invasion without previous provocation in order to preempt possible terrorist attacks.
    D. The US held prisoners captured during the War on Terror at Guantanamo Bay, where they were not treated as prisoners of war under the Geneva Conventions.

Answer:

C. Correct. Preemption was used to justify the 2003 invasion of Iraq, on the assumption that Iraq had weapons of mass destruction it intended to use or to provide for terrorist attacks against the United States.

World History

EARLY CIVILIZATIONS AND THE GREAT EMPIRES

PALEOLITHIC AND NEOLITHIC ERAS

The earliest humans were hunter-gatherers until the development of agriculture in about 11,000 BCE. 60,000–70,000 years ago, early humans began migrating from Africa, gradually spreading out across the continents.

Early human history begins with the **Paleolithic** era. During this period, early **hominids** like our ancestors *Homo sapiens sapiens* and *Homo neanderthalensis* exhibited the use of rudimentary tools based on stone, before metalworking. Hence, the term ***Stone Age*** describes this period.

From approximately 11,000–10,500 BCE, humans started settled communities, developed agricultural practices, and began domesticating animals. They also started using metal to make tools, weapons, and other objects. This was the beginning of the **Neolithic** period, characterized by behavioral and technological change like the invention of the wheel. During the **Bronze Age**, humans began working with copper and tin, creating stronger tools and weapons.

MIDDLE EAST AND EGYPT

Settled societies organized into larger centralized communities characterized by early social stratification and rule of law. The earliest known examples of these were in the **Fertile Crescent**, the area in North Africa and Southwest Asia stretching from Egypt through the Levant and into Mesopotamia.

Around 2500 BCE the **Sumerians** emerged in the Near East. Developing irrigation and advanced agriculture, they were able to develop city-states. They also invented **cuneiform**, the first alphabet, which allowed advanced governance and administration. Sumer featured city-states, the potter's wheel, early astronomy and mathematics, literature, and religious thought.

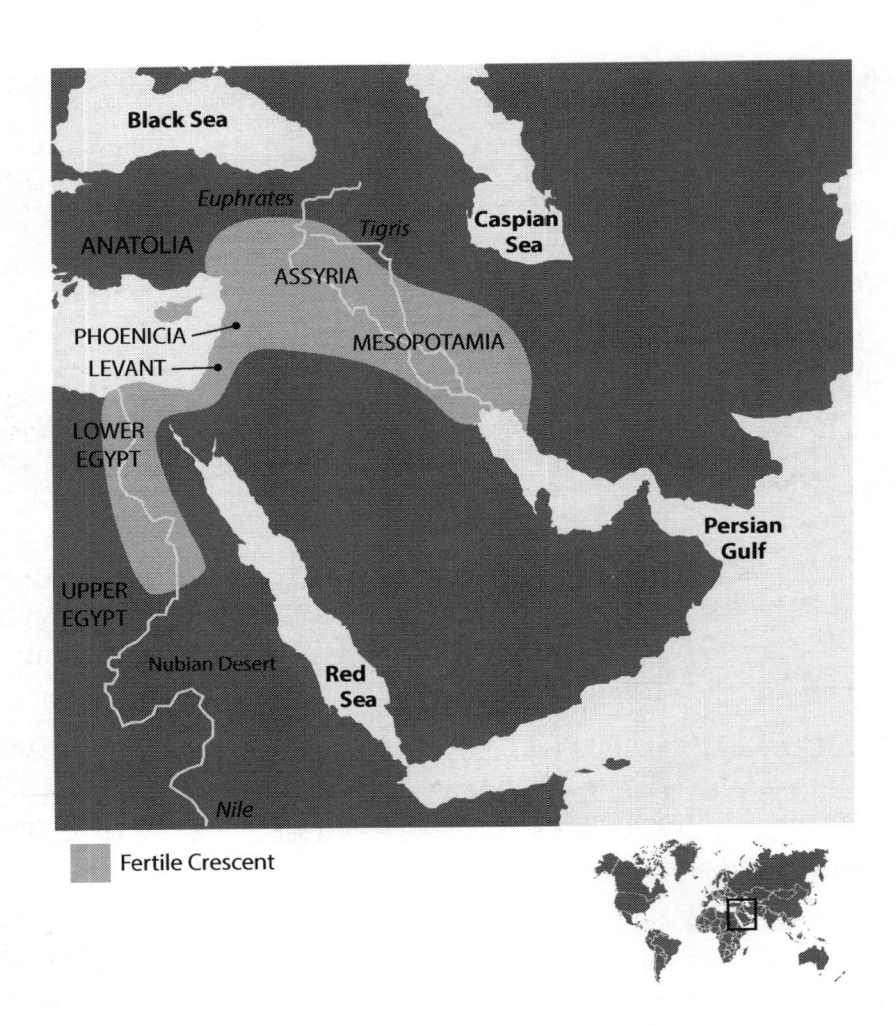

Figure 2.1. Fertile Crescent

Eventually the Sumerians were overcome by Semitic-speaking, nomadic peoples in the Fertile Crescent: the result was the **Akkadian Empire**. Around the eighteenth century BCE, the Akkadians had given way to **Babylonia** in Southern Mesopotamia and **Assyria** in the north. These two civilizations would develop roughly concurrently.

Assyria had developed as a powerful city-state in northern Mesopotamia. Influenced by the Sumerians and Akkadians, the Assyrians developed unique sculpture and jewelry, established regional military dominance, and played an important role in regional trade. At odds with Babylonia over the centuries, the Assyrian Empire had grown to encompass most of the Fertile Crescent.

Like Assyria, Babylonia inherited elements of Akkadian and Sumerian civilization. By the eighteenth century BCE, King Hammurabi in Babylonia had developed courts and an early codified rule of law—**the Code of Hammurabi**—which meted out justice on an equal basis: "an eye for an eye, a tooth for a tooth."

Babylonia continued urban development supported by organized agriculture, warfare, administration, and justice; Babylon became a major ancient city. Babylonia developed more advanced astronomy, medicine, mathematics, philosophy, art, and literature like the *Epic of Gilgamesh*.

Around 1200 BCE Mesopotamia became vulnerable to the **Hittites** from Anatolia. The Hittites had developed in the Bronze Age but flourished in the **Iron Age**, developing expertise in metallurgy to create strong weapons; they also mastered horsemanship and invented chariots. Thus the Hittites became a strong military power and a threat to regional empires and their commercial interests.

> **DID YOU KNOW?**
>
> Settled communities needed the reliable sources of food and fresh water a temperate climate could provide. Surpluses of food allowed for cultural and civilizational development, not just survival.

Meanwhile, development had been under way in the **Nile Valley** in ancient **Egypt**. Known for their pyramids, art, and pictorial writing (**hieroglyphs**), the ancient Egyptians emerged as early as 5000 BCE; evidence of Egyptian unity under one monarch, or **pharaoh**, dates to the First Dynasty, around 3000 BCE.

Despite the surrounding Sahara Desert, the land along the Nile River was arable. Irrigation enabled the Egyptians to develop settled communities. Civilizations emerged on the Upper and Lower Nile, unifying under the early dynasties led by pharaohs, with the Egyptian capital at **Memphis**.

By the fourth dynasty, Egypt's civilizational institutions, written language, art, and architecture were well developed. It was during this period that the famous **pyramids** were erected at Giza as burial tombs. In addition, the complex religious mythology of ancient Egypt had become established. Egypt grew in power from 1550 to 1290 BCE. Led by the powerful Pharaoh **Thutmose III**, Egypt expanded into the Levant.

Later, **King Akhenaten (Amenhotep IV)** abolished the Egyptian religion, establishing a cult of the sun linked to himself. During this period Egypt saw a surge of iconoclastic art and sculpture. However, his successors returned to traditional values. Under **Ramesses II**, Egypt battled the Hittites in the Levant, reaching a stalemate. Egypt fell into decline, losing control of the Levant and eventually falling to Assyria.

> **QUICK REVIEW**
>
> What were the contributions of the early Middle Eastern civilizations? List several.

INDIA

Meanwhile, early civilizations also developed farther east. The **Indus Valley Civilizations** flourished in the Indian Subcontinent and the Indus and Ganges river basins. The **Harappan** civilization was based in Punjab from around 3000 BCE. The major cities of **Harappa** and **Mohenjo-daro** featured grid systems indicative of detailed urban planning; they may be the earliest planned cities in the world. In addition, Harappan objects found in Mesopotamia reveal trade links between these civilizations.

Later, concurrent with the Roman Empire, the **Gupta Empire** emerged in India. During this period, the Golden Age of India, the region was economically strong. Oceanic trade flourished with China, East Africa, and the Middle East in spices, ivory, silk, cotton, and iron, which was highly profitable as an export.

The Guptas encouraged music, art, architecture, and Sanskrit literature and philosophy. While practitioners of Hinduism, the empire was tolerant of Buddhists and Jains. Organized administration and rule of law made it possible for **Chandragupta II** to govern a large territory throughout the Subcontinent. However, by 550 BCE, invasions from the north by the Huns and internal conflicts within the Subcontinent led to imperial decline.

CHINA

In China, the **Shang dynasty**, the first known dynasty, ruled the **Huang He** or **Yellow River** area around the second millennium BCE and developed the earliest known Chinese writing. Like the early civilizations in the Middle East, the Shang dynasty featured the use of bronze technology, horses, wheeled technology, walled cities, and other developments.

Around 1056 BCE the **Zhou** dynasty emerged and China expanded to the **Chiang Jiang** (Yangtze River) region. Family aristocracies controlled the country in a hierarchy similar to later European feudalism, setting the foundation for hierarchical rule and social stratification.

The concept of the **Mandate of Heaven**, in which the emperor had a divine mandate to rule, emerged. The unstable period toward the end of the Zhou dynasty was known as the **Spring and Autumn Period**; during this time **Confucius** lived (c. 551 – 479 BCE). His teachings would be the basis for Confucianism, the foundational Chinese philosophy emphasizing harmony and respect for hierarchy.

Following the chaotic **Warring States Period** (c. 475 – 221 BCE) the short-lived but influential **Qin dynasty** emerged, unifying disparate Chinese civilizations and regions under the first emperor, **Qin Shihuangdi**. This dynasty (221 – 206 BCE) was characterized by expanded infrastructure, standardization in weights and measures, writing, and currency. The administrative **bureaucracy** established by the emperor was the foundation of Chinese administration until the twentieth century.

> **DID YOU KNOW?**
>
> Shared customs like the use of silkworms, jade, chopsticks, and the practice of Confucianism also indicated early Chinese unity.

Figure 2.2. Great Wall of China

In addition, the emperor constructed the **Great Wall of China**, and his tomb is guarded by the famous **terracotta figurines**. During the Qin dynasty, China expanded as far south as Vietnam.

The **Han dynasty** took over in 206 for the next 300 years (206 BCE–220 CE), retaining Qin administrative organization and adding Confucian ideals of hierarchy and harmony.

The Americas

Prehistoric peoples migrated to the Americas from Asia during the Paleolithic period, and evidence of their presence dates to at least 13,000 years ago.

From around 1200 BCE, the **Olmec** civilization developed on the Mexican Gulf Coast. Its massive sculptures reflect complex religious and spiritual beliefs. Later civilizations in Mexico included the **Zapotecs**, **Mixtecs**, **Toltecs**, and **Mayas** in the Yucatán peninsula, developing irrigation to expand agriculture.

Meanwhile, in South America, artistic evidence remains of the **Chavin**, **Moche**, and **Nazca** peoples, who preceded the later Inca civilization and empire. The Chavin style influenced later Andean art. The construction of the Nazca lines, enormous sketches engraved in the ground, remains a mystery.

In North America, the ancient mounds in the Mississippi region may be ancient spiritual structures. Precolonial North American peoples are discussed in the US history chapter.

PERSIA AND GREECE

The **Persian** emperor **Cyrus** conquered the Babylonians in the sixth century BCE. His son **Darius** extended Persian rule from the Indus Valley to Egypt, and north to Anatolia by about 400 BCE, where the Persians encountered the ancient Greeks. **Greek** (or Hellenic) culture impacted the development of European civilization.

Greece was comprised of city-states like **Athens**, the first known **democracy**, and the military state **Sparta**. Historically these city-states had been rivals; however, they temporarily united against Persia. It was during this period, the **Golden Age** of Greek civilization, that much of the Hellenic art, architecture, and philosophy known today emerged.

> **QUICK REVIEW**
>
> How is Greek philosophy relevant today?

The term *democracy* comes from the Greek word **demokratia**—"people power." It was participatory rather than representative; officials were chosen by groups rather than elected.

In this period and into the fourth century BCE, the **Parthenon** was built, as were other characteristic examples of ancient Greek sculpture and architecture. **Socrates** began teaching, influencing later philosophers like **Plato** and **Aristotle** who established the basis for modern western philosophical and political thought.

Despite its status as a democracy, Athens was not fully democratic: women did not have a place in politics, and Athenians practiced slavery. Furthermore, those men eligible to participate in political life had to prove that both of their parents were Athenian (the criterion of double descent).

Toward the end of the fifth century BCE, Athens and Sparta were at odds during the **Peloponnesian War** (431–404 BCE), which ultimately crippled the Athenian democracy permanently. Later in the fourth century BCE, Philip II of Macedonia was able to take over most of Greece. His son **Alexander** (later known as Alexander the Great) proceded to conquer Persia, spreading Greek civilization throughout Western and Central Asia.

ROME

Meanwhile, in Italy, the ancient Romans were consolidating their power. The city of **Rome** was founded by the eighth century BCE; it became strong thanks to its importance as a trade route for the Greeks and other Mediterranean peoples. Early Roman culture drew from the **Etruscans**, inhabitants of the Italian peninsula, and the Greeks, from whom it borrowed elements of architecture, art, language, and even religion.

Rome became a republic in 509 BCE and elected lawmakers (senators) to the **Senate**. The Romans developed highly advanced infrastructure and began conquering areas around the Mediterranean, expanding to North Africa.

With conquest of territory and expansion of trade came increased slavery, and working class Romans (**Plebeians**) were displaced; at the same time, the wealthy ruling class (**Patricians**) became more powerful and corrupt. Resulting protest movements led to legislative reform and republican stabilization, strengthening the republic by the first century BCE.

While militarily and economically strong, the republic was increasingly divided between the wealthy ruling class (the **Optimates**) and the discontented working, poor, and military class (the **Populare**). The Senate weakened due to its own corruption, and the leaders **Julius Caesar**, **Pompey**, and **Crassus** took control in a short-lived triumvirate.

Caesar took over and began to transition Rome from a republic to an empire. Caesar was assassinated by a group of senators in 44 BCE; however, in that short time he had been able to consolidate and centralize imperial control. His nephew **Octavian** eventually took control of Rome in 31 BCE. He took the name **Augustus Caesar**, becoming the first Roman emperor.

At this time, Rome reached the height of its power, and the empire enjoyed a period of stability known as the *Pax Romana.* Rome controlled the entire Mediterranean region and lands stretching as far north as Germany and Britain, territory into the Balkans, far into the Middle East, Egypt, North Africa, and Iberia.

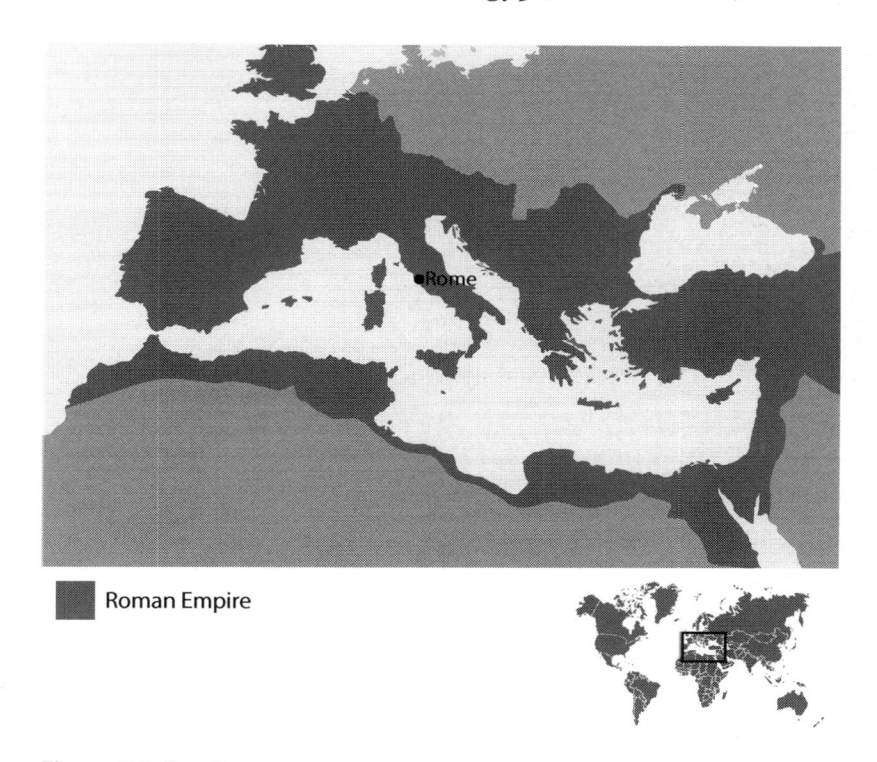

Figure 2.3. Pax Romana

In this time of relative peace and prosperity, Latin literature flourished, as did art, architecture, philosophy, mathematics, science, and international trade throughout Rome and beyond into Asia and Africa. A series of emperors would follow and Rome remained a major world power, but it would never again reach the height of prosperity and stability that it did under Augustus.

It was during the time of Augustus that a Jewish carpenter named Jesus in Palestine began teaching that he was the son of the Jewish God, and that his death would provide salvation for all of humanity. Jesus was eventually crucified; followers of **Jesus Christ**, called Christians, preached his teachings of redemption throughout Rome. Despite the persecution faced by early Christians, **Christianity**'s universal appeal and applicability to people of diverse backgrounds would allow it to spread quickly.

By 300 CE, Rome was in decline. The Christian emperor **Constantine** moved the capital to **Constantinople** and established Christianity as an official religion. The balance of power and stability shifted to the east.

This political shift enabled the western (later, Catholic) church to gain power in Rome. Over time, the Catholic Church would become one of the most powerful political entities in the world; today, there are around one billion Catholics worldwide.

DID YOU KNOW?

These clans and others from Central Asia were able to defeat the Romans in the north and settle in Europe, thanks to their equestrian skills, superior wheels, and iron technology.

The western part of the Roman Empire gradually fell into disarray and succumbed to invading European clans like the **Anglo-Saxons**, the **Franks**, the **Visigoths**, the **Ostrogoths**, and the **Slavs**. The last emperor was killed in Rome in **476 CE**, marking the end of the empire.

Meanwhile the eastern part of the Roman Empire, with its capital at Constantinople, evolved into the **Byzantine Empire**. The Byzantine emperor **Justinian** (527 – 565 CE) reconquered parts of North Africa, Egypt, and Greece, established rule of law, and reinvigorated trade with China.

He also nurtured Christianity, building the **Hagia Sophia**, the cathedral and center of orthodox Christianity. Over time, a clear schism would emerge between the church in Rome and Christians in Constantinople, creating the Roman Catholic Church and the Greek Orthodox Church.

During the early Middle Ages in Europe and the Byzantine Empire, the roots of another civilization were developing in the Arabian Peninsula. In the seventh century, the Prophet **Muhammad** began teaching **Islam**. Based on the teachings of Judaism and Christianity and following the same god, Islam presented as the final version of these two religions. Like Christianity, it held universal appeal.

SAMPLE QUESTIONS

1) What is required for a settled community?

    A. domesticated animals
    B. a source of fresh water
    C. technology
    D. weapons

    Answer:

    B. Correct. Fresh water permits a reliable food source, which allows for settlement; people need not travel in search of food.

2) The earliest known form of alphabetic writing (using characters to create words) is

    A. cuneiform, developed by the Egyptians.
    B. cuneiform, developed by the Sumerians.
    C. hieroglyphs, developed by the Egyptians.
    D. hieroglyphs, developed by the Sumerians.

    Answer:

    B. Correct. The Sumerians developed cuneiform. Hieroglyphs are pictographs.

3) The Shang and Zhou dynasties are particularly relevant in Chinese history for their contributions in

    A. developing Chinese administration.
    B. centralizing Chinese imperial power as symbolized through the terracotta figurines in the imperial tombs.
    C. forming a Chinese identity through the development of written language, the Emperor's Mandate of Heaven, and fostering Confucianism.
    D. ensuring China's safety by building the Great Wall of China.

    Answer:

    C. Correct. Written Chinese developed under the Shang dynasty, and the Mandate of Heaven emerged under the Zhou dynasty; furthermore, other cultural traditions emerged during these periods.

4) The Athenian concept of democracy embraced
   A. participatory democracy, in which local groups made decisions directly by vote.
   B. an anonymous electoral process similar to that of the United States in which officials were elected.
   C. people of all backgrounds, so that all residents of Athens had a stake in the political process.
   D. an educated electorate in order to ensure the best possible decision-making.

   Answer:
   A. **Correct.** The Athenian notion of *demokratia*, or people power, was participatory rather than representative.

5) How did Julius Caesar rise to and retain power?
   A. He invaded Rome with his armies from Gaul, and used his military resources to control the empire.
   B. He was elected president of the Senate by the people thanks to widespread political support.
   C. He took control of the Senate thanks to his charisma and popularity among the people.
   D. As part of the Triumvirate, he was guaranteed a leadership position.

   Answer:
   C. **Correct.** The Senate's corruption and weakness, and Caesar's popularity with the Populare, enabled him to take and retain control.

Feudalism Through the Era of Expansion

The Middle Ages in Europe

The Byzantine Empire remained a strong civilization. Constantinople was a commercial center, strategically located at the Dardanelles, connecting Asian trade routes with Europe. Later, missionaries traveled north to Slavic Russia, spreading Christianity and literacy. Russian Christianity was influenced by Byzantine doctrine, what would become Greek Orthodox Christianity.

Despite the chaos in Western Europe, the church in Rome remained strong, becoming a stabilizing influence. However, differences in doctrine between Rome and Constantinople became too wide to overcome. Beginning in 1054, a series of **schisms** developed between the two. Eventually two entirely separate churches emerged: the **Roman Catholic Church** and the **Greek Orthodox Church**.

In Europe, the early Middle Ages (or ***Dark Ages***) from the fall of Rome to about the tenth century, were a chaotic and unsafe time. What protection and stability existed were represented and maintained by the Catholic Church and the feudal system.

Society and economics were characterized by decentralized, local governance, or **feudalism**, a hierarchy where land and protection were offered in exchange for loyalty. Feudalism was the dominant social, economic, and political hierarchy of the European Middle Ages.

In exchange for protection, **vassals** would pledge **fealty**, or **pay homage** to **lords**. Lords were landowners who rewarded their vassals' loyalty with land, or **fiefs**, and protection. Economic and social organization revolved around **manors**, self-sustaining areas possessed by lords but worked by peasants. The peasants were **serfs**. Tied to the land, they worked for the lord in exchange for protection; however they were not obligated to fight. Usually they were also granted some land for their own use. While not true slaves, their lives were effectively controlled by the lord.

Warriors who fought for lords, called **knights**, were rewarded with land and could become lords in their own right. Lords themselves were vassals of other lords; that hierarchy extended upward to kings or the Catholic Church. The Catholic Church itself was a major landowner and political power. In a Europe not yet dominated by sovereign states, the **Pope** was not only a religious leader, but also a military and political one.

Small kingdoms were scattered throughout Europe, and stable trade was difficult to maintain. One exception to the chaos was the Scandinavian **Viking** civilization. From the end of the eighth century until around 1100, the Vikings expanded from Scandinavia thanks to their seafaring skills and technology. The Vikings traded with the Byzantine Empire and European powers. They traveled to and raided parts of Britain, Ireland, France, and Russia.

> **DID YOU KNOW?**
>
> There were limits on sovereign power. In 1215, English barons forced King John to sign the Magna Carta, which protected their property and rights and is the basis of Britain's current parliamentary system.

Meanwhile, by the eighth century the North African **Moors**, part of the expanding Islamic civilization, had entered Iberia and were a threat to Christian Europe. **Charles Martel**, leader of the **Franks** in what is today France, defeated the Moors in 732 CE, stopping further Islamic incursion into Europe. Instability followed Charles Martel's death, however, and **Charlemagne**, the son of a court official, eventually took over the Franks.

Charlemagne was able to maintain Frankish unity, extend Frankish control into Central Europe, and protect the **Papal States** in central Italy. Parts of Western and Central Europe became organized under Charlemagne, who was crowned emperor of the Roman Empire by Pope Leo III in 800 CE. While in retrospect this seems long after the end of Rome, at the time many Europeans still perceived themselves as still part of a Roman Empire. Today Charlemagne's rule is referred to as the **Carolingian Empire**.

Charlemagne brought stability to Western and Central Europe during a period when two powerful, non-Christian, organized civilizations—the Vikings in the north and the Islamic powers in the south—threatened what was left of western Christendom, and when insecurity was growing to the east with the decline of the Byzantines and the emergence of the Islamic Umayyad Caliphate in Damascus. His reign strengthened the Roman Catholic Church and enabled a resurgence of Roman and Christian scholarship.

It was also under Charlemagne that the feudal system became truly organized, bringing more stability to Western Europe. In 962 CE, **Otto I** became emperor of the **Holy Roman Empire** in Central Europe, a confederation of small states which remained an important European power until its dissolution in 1806.

In 1066, **William the Conqueror** left Normandy in northwest France. The **Normans** established feudalism, Christianity, and economic organization in England. Intermarriage and conquest resulted in English control of parts of France, too. Conflict between Britain and France would continue for several centuries, while rulers in Scandinavia and Northwest Europe consolidated power.

THE ISLAMIC WORLD AND CHINA

Meanwhile, in the wake of the decline of the Byzantine Empire, **Arab-Islamic empires**, characterized by brisk commerce, advancements in technology and learning, and urban development, arose in the Middle East.

Before the rise of Islam in the seventh century, the Arabian Peninsula was located at the intersection of the Byzantine Empire, and the **Sasanians** (Persians), who practiced **Zoroastrianism**. Both of these empires sought to control trade with Central and eastern Asia along the Silk Road as well as with Christian Axum (Ethiopia).

In Arabia itself, Judaism, Christianity, and animist religions were practiced by the Arab majority. The Prophet **Muhammad** was born in Mecca around 570; he began receiving messages from God (Allah), writing them as the **Qur'an**, the Islamic holy book. He preached the religion of **Islam** around 613 as the last, most correct version of the monotheistic religions. Driven from **Mecca** to Medina in 622, Muhammad and his followers recaptured the city and other major Arabian towns by the time of his death, establishing Islam and Arab rule in the region.

Islam appealed to many in the disorganized region. The religion's demands (the **Five Pillars of Islam**) asked followers to declare faith in one god (Allah), pray five times daily, donate 10 percent of their earnings to the community, make a pilgrimage at least once in their lifetimes to Mecca, and fast during the holy month of Ramadan. Anyone could easily convert to the religion, and it brought stability and social organization to a chaotic region and time.

> **DID YOU KNOW?**
>
> A caliph was considered both a political and a religious leader.

After Muhammad's death in **632 CE**, his followers went on to conquer land north into the weakening Byzantine Empire. The Muslim Arabs led incursions into Syria, the Levant, and Mesopotamia, taking over these territories. Thanks to military, bureaucratic, and organizational skill as well as their ability to win over dissatisfied minorities, the Arabs eventually isolated the Byzantines to parts of Anatolia and Constantinople and crushed the Persian Sasanians.

> **DID YOU KNOW?**
>
> Ali's followers called themselves the *party of Ali* or, in Arabic, the *shiat Ali*, which is the origin of the word *Shia* or *Shi'ite* Muslims.

However, disagreements over leadership led to conflict among Muslims and the Sunni-Shi'a Schism. The **Shi'ites**, who centered in Mesopotamia, believed that Muhammad's cousin Ali was the rightful heir to the early Islamic empire. The followers of the Meccan elites became known as **Sunnis**, "orthodox" Muslims with a focus on community rather than genealogy. Over the centuries, other differences would develop.

The **Umayyad Caliphate** (empire), based in Damascus, was named for the leading Meccan tribe that had supported Muhammad from the beginning. By 750, the Arabs would control land from North Africa to the Indus River Valley and Spain (al-Andalus).

- Expansion under the Prophet Muhammad, 612 – 632
- Expansion under the Rashidun, 632 – 655
- Expansion under the Umayyad Caliphate, 661 – 750

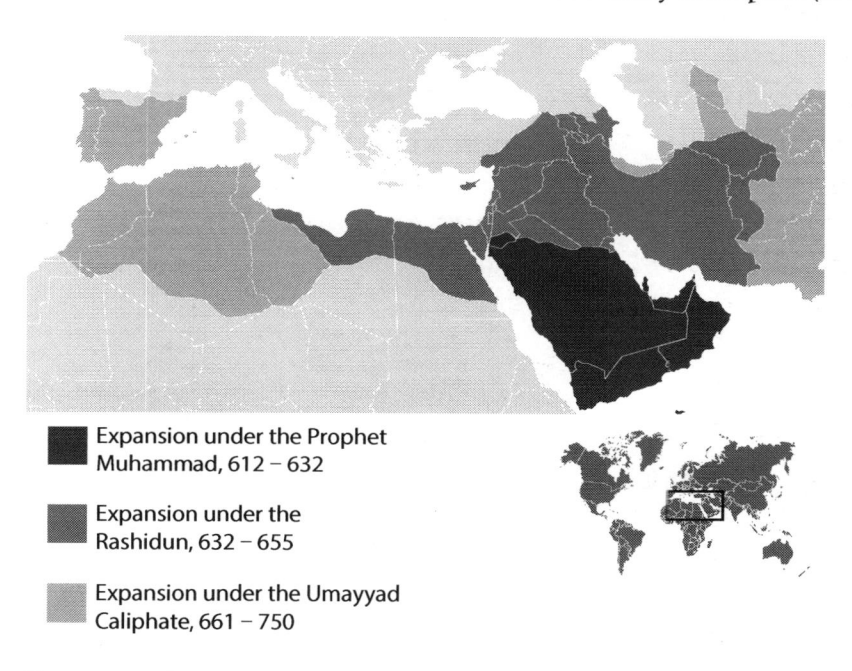

Figure 2.4. Islamic Expansion

Ongoing conflict among Arab elites resulted in the **Abbasid Caliphate** in 750 CE. The Umayyads were overthrown by the Arab-Muslim Abbasid family, which established a new capital in Baghdad. The Abbasids professionalized the military, helping consolidate imperial control and improving tax collection.

The administration and stability provided by the caliphates fostered an Arabic literary culture. Stability permitted open trade routes, economic development, and cultural interaction throughout Asia, the Middle East, North Africa, and parts of Europe.

Thanks to the universality of the Arabic language, scientific and medical texts from varying civilizations—Greek, Persian, Indian—could be translated into Arabic and shared throughout the Islamic world. Arab thinkers studied Greek and Persian astronomy and engaged in further research. Arabs studied mathematics from around the world and developed algebra, enabling engineering, technological, artistic, and architectural achievements.

Around this time, the **Song dynasty (960 – 1276)** controlled most of China. Under the Song, China experienced tremendous development and economic growth. Characterized by increasing urbanization, the Song featured complex administrative rule, including the difficult competitive written examinations required to obtain prestigious bureaucratic positions in government.

Most traditions recognized as Chinese emerged under the Song, including the consumption of tea and rice and common Chinese architecture. The Song engaged not only in overland trade along the Silk Road, exporting silk, tea, ceramics, jade, and other goods, but also sea trade with Korea, Japan, Southeast Asia, India, Arabia, and even East Africa.

CONFLICT AND CULTURAL EXCHANGE

Cultural exchange was not limited to interactions among Christian Europeans, Egyptians, and Levantine Muslims. International commerce was vigorous along the **Silk Road,** the term for trading routes which stretched from the Arab-controlled Eastern Mediterranean to Song dynasty China, where science and learning also blossomed.

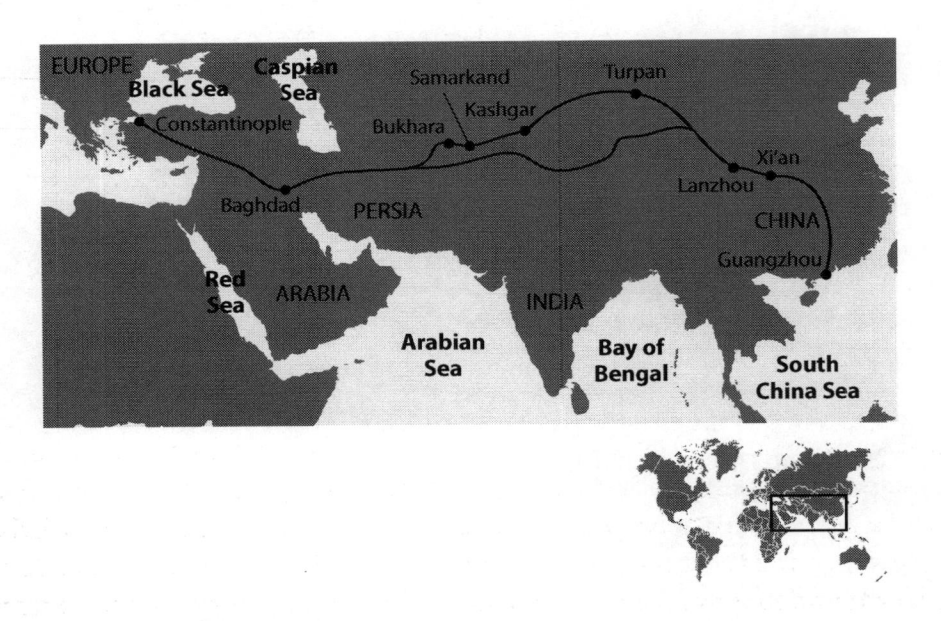

Figure 2.5. The Silk Road

The Silk Road reflected the transnational nature of Central Asia. The nomadic culture of Central Asia lent itself to trade among the major civilizations of China, Persia, the Near East, and Europe. Buddhism and Islam spread into China. Chinese, Islamic, and European art, pottery, and goods were interchanged among the three civilizations—early globalization. The Islamic hajj (the pilgrimage to Mecca) spurred cultural interaction, too.

> **QUICK REVIEW**
>
> How did the Silk Road and Islam *both* contribute to global cultural exchange?

Islam also spread along trans-Saharan trade routes into West Africa and the Sahel. Brisk trade between the gold-rich **Kingdom of Ghana** and Muslim traders based in Morocco brought Islam to the region around the eleventh century. The Islamic **Mali Empire** (1235–1500), based farther south in **Timbuktu**, eventually extended beyond the original Ghanaian boundaries to the West African coast and controlled the valuable gold and salt trades. It became a center of learning and commerce. However, by 1500, the **Songhai Empire** had overcome Mali and dominated the Niger River area.

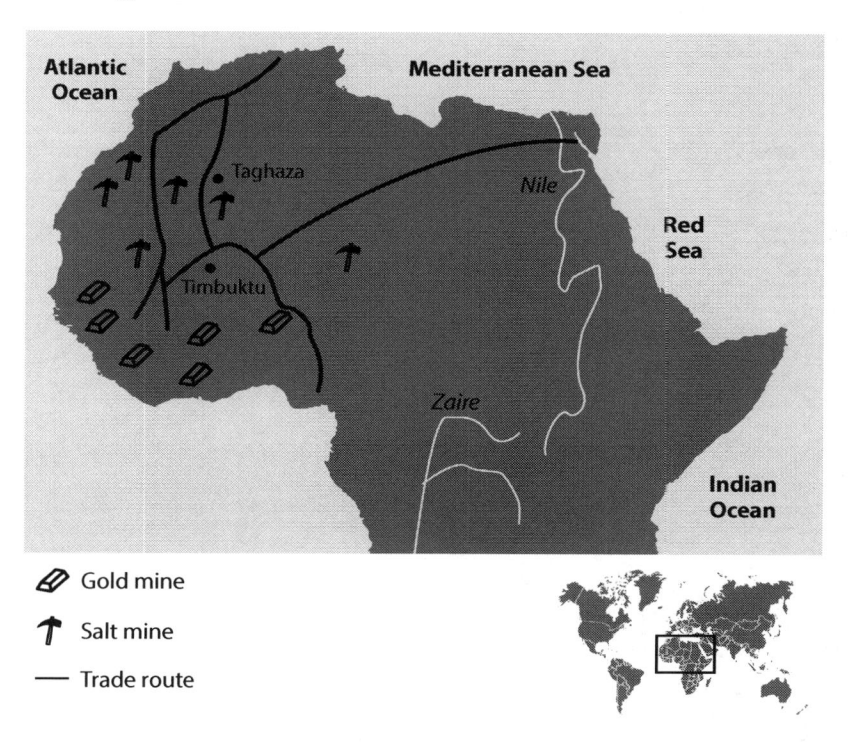

Figure 2.6. Trans-Saharan Trade Routes

Loss of Byzantine territory to the Islamic empires meant loss of Christian lands in the Levant to Muslims. In 1095, the Byzantine Emperor asked **Pope Urban II** for help to defend Jerusalem and protect Christians there. European Christians were easily inspired to fight in what became known as the **First Crusade**. The pope offered lords and knights the chance to keep lands and bounty they conquered. He also offered Crusaders **indulgences**—forgiveness for sins committed in war and guarantees they would enter heaven.

Meanwhile, towards the end of the tenth century, the Abbasid Caliphate was in decline. The Shi'ite **Fatimids** took control of Syria and Egypt, addressing the Shi'ite claim to the caliphate. Other groups took control of provinces in Mesopotamia, Arabia, Spain, and Central Asia.

Figure 2.7. Great Mosque Cordoba

Despite conflict in Europe, Christians found they had more in common with each other than with Muslims and united to fight in the Middle East. The decline of the Abbasids had left the Levant vulnerable, and Christian Crusaders established settlements and small kingdoms in Syria and on the eastern Mediterranean coast, conquering major cities and capturing Jerusalem by 1099.

The Crusades continued over several centuries. The Kurdish military leader **Salah al-Din** (Saladin) defeated the Fatimids in Egypt and reconquered Jerusalem in 1187, driving European Christians out for good. Following Salah al-Din's death, the **Mamluks (1250–1517)** controlled Egypt.

> **DID YOU KNOW?**
>
> During the Hundred Years' War, Joan of Arc led the French in the 1429 Battle of Orléans, inspiring French resistance to the English.

While the Crusades never resulted in permanent European control over the Holy Land, they did open up trade routes between Europe and the Middle East, stretching all the way along the Silk Road to China. This increasing interdependence led to the European Renaissance.

Ongoing interactions between Europeans and Muslims exposed Europeans, who could now afford them thanks to international trade, to improved education and goods. However, the **Bubonic (Black) Plague** also spread to Europe as a result of global exchange, killing off a third of its population from 1347–1351. The plague had a worldwide impact: empires fell in its wake.

Back in Europe, conflict reached its height throughout the thirteenth and fourteenth centuries: the **Hundred Years' War** (1337–1453). France was in political chaos, decentralized and at times without a king; suffering the effects of the Black Plague; vulnerable to English attack; and periodically under English rule. While conflict would continue, England lost its last territory in France, Bordeaux, in 1453.

> **DID YOU KNOW?**
>
> Ferdinand and Isabella launched the Inquisition, an extended persecution of Jews and Jewish converts to Christianity who continued to practice Judaism in secret. Muslims were also persecuted and forced to convert to Christianity or be exiled.

In Spain, despite some coexistence between Christians and Muslims under Muslim rule, raids and conflict were ongoing during the lengthy period of the Christian **Reconquista** of Iberia, which did not end until 1492 when Christian powers took Grenada, uniting Spain.

EMPIRES IN TRANSITION

Beyond Egypt and the Levant, the collapse of the Abbasid Caliphate led to instability and decentralization of power in Mesopotamia, Persia, and Central Asia; smaller sultanates (territories ruled by sultans, regional leaders) emerged, and production and economic development declined. **Tang dynasty** China closed its borders and trade on the Silk Road declined. In the eleventh century, the nomadic Seljuks dominated the region from Central Asia through parts of the Levant. However, the Seljuks lacked effective administration or central authority.

Islam remained a unifying force throughout the region, and political instability and decentralization paradoxically allowed local culture to develop, particularly Persian art and literature. Furthermore, Islam was able to thrive during this period: local religious leaders (*ulama*) had taken up community leadership positions, and Islam became a guiding force in law, justice, and social organization. Yet political decentralization ultimately left the region vulnerable to the Mongol invasions of the twelfth and thirteenth centuries.

> **DID YOU KNOW?**
>
> During this period, Persian-influenced Sufi (mystical) Islam and poetry developed; Shi'ite theology and jurisprudence also developed as part of a strengthening independent Shi'ite identity.

In the Near East, the **Mongol invasions** destroyed agriculture, city life and planning, economic patterns and trade routes, and social stability. After some time, new patterns of trade emerged, new cities rose to prominence, and stability allowed prosperity, but the Mongol invasions dealt a blow to confidence in Islam.

Likewise, in China, the Mongols destroyed local infrastructure, including the foundation of Chinese society and administration—the civil service examinations. However, in order to govern the vast territory effectively, the Mongols in China took a different approach. Genghis Khan's grandson **Kublai Khan** conquered China and founded the Mongol **Yuan dynasty** in 1271, maintaining administrative infrastructure and education in the Confucian tradition.

Mongol attempts at imperial expansion in China into Japan and Southeast Asia, coupled with threats from the Black Plague, financial problems, and flooding, led to the decline of the Yuan dynasty and the rise of the Han Chinese **Ming dynasty** in 1368. The Ming reasserted Han Chinese control and continued traditional methods of administration; however the construction of the **Forbidden City**, the home of the Emperor in Beijing, helped consolidate imperial rule. The Ming also encouraged international trade.

Mongol decline was not only isolated to China; in Russia, **Ivan the Great** brought Moscow from Mongol to Slavic Russian control. In the late fifteenth century, Ivan had consolidated Russian power over neighboring Slavic regions. A century later, **Ivan the Terrible** set out to expand Russia further. Named the first **tsar**, or emperor, Ivan reformed government, recognized orthodox Christianity, and reorganized the military. However, overextension of resources and his oppressive entourage, the *oprichnina*, depopulated the state and gave him the reputation as a despotic ruler.

Farther south in Central Asia, the Mongol descendants, **Babur** found the **Mughal Empire** of India. Despite his Mongol roots, Babur identified as Turkic due to his tribal origins, and enjoyed support from the powerful Ottoman Empire in Turkey. In 1525, Babur set out for India. By 1529, he had secured land from Kandahar in the west to Bengal in the east; his grandson, **Akbar**, would consolidate the empire, which at the time consisted of small kingdoms. The Mughals would rule India until the eighteenth century and nominally control parts of the country until British takeover in the nineteenth century.

During Mughal rule in India, the Ming dynasty fell in China and the Qing took over. In 1644, the Ming fell to a peasant revolt; the **Manchu**, a non-Han group from the north, took the opportunity to seize Beijing and take the country. Despite their status as non–Han Chinese, the Manchu were accepted; thus began the **Qing dynasty**, under which China would become the dominant power in East Asia and a successful multiethnic state. They would also be China's last imperial rulers, losing power in 1911.

> **DID YOU KNOW?**
>
> The Mughal emperor Shah Jahan built the Taj Mahal in 1631.

Meanwhile, in Persia, the **Safavids** emerged in 1501. A major rival of the Ottoman Empire, the Safavids were a stabilizing force in Asia. Following Sufism, the Safavids supported art, literature, architecture, and other learning. Their organized administration brought order and stability to Persia throughout their rule, which lasted until 1736, when the **Qajar dynasty** took over.

Despite the instability inland, Indian Ocean trade routes had continued to function since at least the seventh century. These oceanic routes connected the Horn of Africa, the East African Coast, the Arabian Peninsula, Southern Persia, India, Southeast Asia, and China. The ocean acted as a unifying force throughout the region, and the **monsoon winds** permitted Arab, Persian, Indian, and Chinese merchants to travel to East Africa in search of goods such as ivory and gold—and slaves.

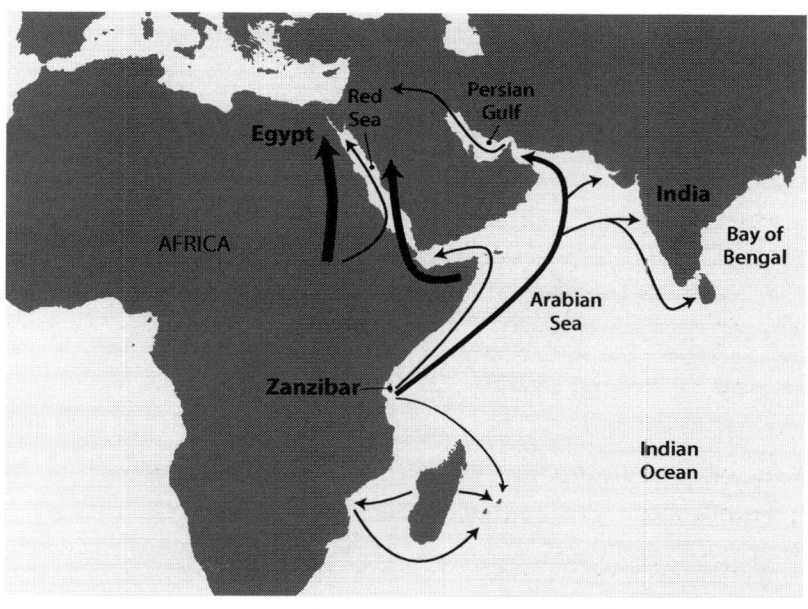

Figure 2.8. Indian Ocean Slave Trade

Despite the civilizational achievements of the Islamic empires, Tang and later Ming dynasty China, and the Central Asian and Indian empires that would emerge from the Mongols, the **East African slave trade** remained vigorous until the nineteenth century. Arabs, Asians, and other Africans kidnapped African people and sent them to lives of slavery throughout the Arab world and South Asia. Later, Europeans would take part in the trade, forcing Africans into slavery in colonies throughout South and Southeast Asia, and on plantations in Indian Ocean islands such as Madagascar.

Further north, the Ottoman Turks represented a threat to Central Europe. Controlling most of Anatolia from the late thirteenth century, the Ottomans spread west into the Balkans, consolidating their rule in 1389 at the **Battle of Kosovo**. In 1453 they captured Istanbul, from which the **Ottoman Empire** would come to rule much of the Mediterranean world.

Under the leadership of **Mehmed the Conqueror** in the fifteenth century and his successors, the Ottomans would conquer Pannonia (Hungary), North Africa, the Caucasus, the Levant and Mesopotamian regions, western Arabia, and Egypt. Under **Suleiman the Magnificent** (1520 – 1566), the **Ottoman Empire** consolidated control over the Balkans, the Middle East, and North Africa and would hold that land until the nineteenth century.

The capture of Istanbul (Constantinople) had represented the true end of the Byzantine Empire; the remaining Christian Byzantines, mainly isolated to coastal Anatolia, Constantinople, and parts of Greece, fled to Italy, bringing Greek, Middle Eastern, and Asian learning with them and enriching the emerging European Renaissance.

THE EUROPEAN RENAISSANCE

The **Renaissance**, or *rebirth*, included the revival of ancient Greek and Roman learning, art, and architecture. Not only did the Renaissance inspire new learning and prosperity in Europe, enabling exploration, colonization, profit, and later imperialism, but it also led to scientific and religious questioning and rebellion against the Catholic Church and, later, monarchical governments.

Reinvigoration of classical knowledge was triggered in part by Byzantine refugees from the Ottoman conquest of Constantinople, including scholars who brought Greek and Roman texts to Italy and Western Europe. The fall of Constantinople precipitated the development of **humanism** in Europe, a mode of thought emphasizing human nature, creativity, and an overarching concept of truth in all philosophical systems (the concept of **syncretism**). Emerging in Italy, the seat of the Catholic Church, humanism was supported by some popes, including Leo X. However in the long term it represented a threat to religious, especially Catholic, orthodoxy, however, as it allowed for the questioning of religious teaching. Ultimately humanism would be at the root of the **Reformation** of the sixteenth century.

Art, considered not just a form of expression but also a science in itself, flourished in fifteenth century Italy, particularly in **Florence**. While artists worked throughout Italy and found patrons in the Vatican among other places, the Florentine **Medici family** funded extensive civic projects, construction, décor, and public sculpture throughout Florence, supporting Renaissance art in that city.

Meanwhile, scholars like Galileo, Isaac Newton, and Copernicus made discoveries in what became known as the **Scientific Revolution**, rooted in the scientific knowledge of the Islamic empires, which had been imported through economic and social contact initiated centuries prior in the Crusades. Scientific study and discovery threatened the power of the Church, whose theological teachings were often at odds with scientific findings and logical reasoning.

> **QUICK REVIEW**
>
> The Scientific Revolution changed European thinking. What was the impact of using reason and scientific methodology rather than religion to understand the world?

Also in the mid-fifteenth century, in Northern Europe, **Johann Gutenberg** invented the **printing press**; the first book to be published would be the Bible. With the advent of printing, texts could be more widely and rapidly distributed, and people had more access to information beyond what their leaders told them. Combined with humanism and increased emphasis on secular thought, the power of the Church and of monarchs who ruled by divine right was under threat. Here lay the roots of the **Enlightenment**, the basis for reinvigorated European culture and political thought that would drive its development for the next several centuries—and inspire revolution.

Transnational cultural exchange had also resulted in the transmission of technology to Europe. During the sixteenth century, European seafaring knowledge, navigation, and technology benefitted from Islamic and Asian expertise; European explorers and traders could now venture beyond the Mediterranean. Portuguese and Dutch sailors eventually reached India and China, where they established ties with the Ming Dynasty. Trade was no longer dependent on the Silk Road. Improved technology also empowered Europeans to explore overseas, eventually landing in the Western Hemisphere, heretofore unknown to the peoples of Eurasia and Africa.

MESOAMERICAN AND ANDEAN CIVILIZATIONS

In the Americas, the **Maya**, who preceded the Aztecs in Mesoamerica, came to dominate the Yucatán peninsula around 300. They developed a complex spiritual belief system accompanied by relief art, and built pyramidal temples that still stand today. In addition, they developed a detailed calendar and a written language using pictographs similar to Egyptian hieroglyphs; they studied astronomy and mathematics. Maya political administration was organized under monarchical city-states from around 300 until around 900, when the civilization began to decline.

As smaller Mesoamerican civilizations had weakened and collapsed, the **Aztecs** had come to dominate Mexico and much of Mesoamerica. Their military power and militaristic culture allowed the Aztecs to dominate the region and regional trade. The main city of the Aztec empire, **Tenochtitlan**, was founded in 1325 and, at its height, was a major world city home to several million people.

Aztec civilization was militaristic in nature and divided on a class basis: it included slaves, indentured servants, serfs, an independent priestly class, military, and ruling classes. The Aztecs shared many beliefs with the Mayans; throughout Mesoamerica the same calendar was used. Central in the Aztec religion was worship of the god **Quetzalcoatl**, a feathered snake.

Figure 2.9. Quetzalcoatl

Meanwhile, in the Andes, the **Incas** had emerged. Based in **Cuzco**, the Incas had consolidated their power and strengthened in the area, likely due to a surplus of their staple crop maize, around 1300. They were able to conquer local lords and, later, peoples further south, thanks in part to domesticated llamas and alpacas which allowed the military to transport supplies through the mountains.

Inca engineers built the citadel of **Machu Picchu** and imperial infrastructure, including roads throughout the Andes. Thanks to highly developed mountain agriculture, they were able to grow crops at high altitudes and maintain waystations on the highways stocked with supplies.

COLONIZATION OF THE WESTERN HEMISPHERE

Interest in exploration grew in Europe during the Renaissance period. Technological advancements made complex navigation and long-term sea voyages possible, and economic growth resulting from international trade drove interest in market expansion. Global interdependence got a big push from Spain when King Ferdinand and Queen Isabella agreed to sponsor **Christopher Columbus**'s exploratory voyage in 1492 to find a sea route to Asia, in order to speed up commercial trade there. Instead, he stumbled upon the Western Hemisphere, which was unknown to Europeans, Asians, and Africans to this point.

Columbus landed in the Caribbean; he and later explorers would claim the Caribbean islands and eventually Central and South America for Spain and Portugal. However, those areas were already populated by the major American civilizations. Following bloody conflict with the Aztec and Inca Empires, Spain took over the silver- and gold-rich Mesoamerican and Andean territories, and the Caribbean islands where sugar became an important cash crop.

The economic system that resulted was **mercantilism**, whereby the colonizing or *mother country* took raw materials from the territories for the colonizers' own benefit. Governments amassed wealth through protectionism and increasing exports at the expense of other rising colonial powers. This eventually involved developing goods and then selling them back to those colonized lands at an inflated price.

The *encomienda* system granted European landowners the "right" to hold lands in the Americas and demand labor and tribute from the local inhabitants. Spreading Christianity was another important reason for European expansion. Local civilizations and resources were exploited and destroyed.

> **QUICK REVIEW**
>
> What was destructive about the *encomienda* system?

The **Columbian Exchange** enabled mercantilism to flourish. Conflict and illness brought by the Europeans—especially **smallpox**—decimated the Native Americans, and the Europeans were left without labor to mine the silver and gold or to work the land. **African slavery** was their solution.

Slavery was an ancient institution in many societies worldwide; however, with the Columbian Exchange slavery came to be practiced on a mass scale the likes of which the world had never seen. Throughout Africa and especially on the West African coast, Europeans traded for slaves with some African kingdoms and also raided the land, kidnapping people. European slavers took captured Africans in horrific conditions to the Americas; those who survived were enslaved and forced to work in mining or agriculture for the benefit of expanding European imperial powers.

The Columbian Exchange described the **triangular trade** across the Atlantic: European slavers took kidnapped African people from Africa to the Americas, sold them at auction and exchanged them for sugar and raw materials; these materials were traded in Europe for consumer goods, which were then exchanged in Africa for slaves, and so on.

Enslaved Africans suffered greatly, forced to endure ocean voyages crammed on unsafe, unhygienic ships, sometimes among the dead bodies of other kidnapped people, only to arrive in the Americas to a life of slavery in mines or on plantations. Throughout this period, Africans did resist both on ships and later, in the Americas; **maroon communities** of escaped slaves formed throughout the Western Hemisphere, the **Underground Railroad** in the nineteenth-century United States helped enslaved persons escape the South, and **Toussaint L'Ouverture** led a successful slave rebellion in Haiti, winning independence from the French for that country in 1791.

> **QUICK REVIEW**
>
> Explain the Columbian Exchange.

However, the slave trade continued for centuries. The colonies and later independent countries of the Western Hemisphere continued to practice slavery until the nineteenth century; oppressive legal and social restrictions based on race continue to affect the descendants of slaves to this day throughout the hemisphere.

During the eighteenth century, Spain and Portugal were preeminent powers in global trade thanks to colonization and **imperialism**, the possession and exploitation of land overseas. However, Great Britain became an important presence on the seas; it would later dominate the oceans throughout the nineteenth century.

Though Britain would lose its territories in North America after the American Revolution, it maintained control of the resource-rich West Indies. The kingdom went on to dominate strategic areas in South Africa, New South Wales in Australia, Mauritius in the Indian Ocean, and Madras and Bengal in the Indian Subcontinent, among other places. Later, in the nineteenth century, Britain would expand its empire further. Likewise, France gained territory in North America and in the West Indies; despite losses to Britain in the eighteenth century, that country would also expand its own global empire in the nineteenth century.

> **SAMPLE QUESTIONS**
>
> 6) Which of the following explains why the Eastern Roman Empire remained stable and transitioned to the Byzantine Empire while Rome in Western Europe collapsed?
>
>   A. Feudalism contributed to instability in Western Europe, and so that part of the continent disintegrated into a series of small states.
>
>   B. The schism between the Catholic and Greek Orthodox Churches tore the empire apart.
>
>   C. Muslims entered Constantinople and took it from Christian Roman control.
>
>   D. Imprudent alliances in the West led to Roman collapse, while strong leadership and centralization in the East developed a new empire.

Answer:

D. Correct. Security alliances with Germanic and Gothic tribes left Western Rome vulnerable to their attack; meanwhile in the east, centralized power in Constantinople and strong leadership, particularly under Justinian, led to the rise of the powerful Byzantine Empire.

7) Following the death of Muhammad, Muslim leadership became so divided that the religious movement eventually split into Sunnis and Shi'ites. This was due to

   A. disagreement over succession to his place as leader.
   B. disagreement about the importance of conquest.
   C. disagreement over the theological nature of Islam.
   D. disagreement over whether to accept Christians and Jews as *People of the Book*.

Answer:

A. Correct. The Meccan elites believed that they should take over leadership of Islam and continue the movement beyond the Arabian Peninsula; however Ali and Fatima, Muhammad's cousin and daughter, believed Ali was Muhammad's rightful successor as his closest living male relative.

8) Despite the violence of the Crusades, they were also beneficial for Europe in that they

   A. resulted in substantial, long-term land gains for European leaders in the Middle East.
   B. introduced European powers to the concept of nation-states, the dominant form of political organization in the Middle East.
   C. exposed Europe to Islamic and Asian science, technology, and medicine.
   D. enhanced tolerance of Islam throughout Europe.

Answer:

C. Correct. Europeans who traveled to the Levant to fight returned home with beneficial knowledge and technology.

9) Which of the following was a result of the rise of the Ottoman Turks?

   A. Christian Byzantines left Constantinople for Western Europe, bringing classical learning with them.
   B. The Ottomans were able to conquer the Balkans, the Levant, and eventually North Africa and the Middle East, establishing a large Islamic empire.
   C. The Ottomans represented an Islamic threat to European Christendom, given their grip on the Balkan Peninsula.
   D. all of the above

Answer:

D. **Correct.** All of the answer choices apply.

10) Which of the following best explains the Atlantic Triangular Trade?

   A. American raw materials were transported to Africa, where they were exchanged for enslaved persons; enslaved persons were taken to the Americas, where they turned raw materials to consumer goods for sale in Europe.
   B. European consumer goods were sold in the Americas at a profit; these goods were also sold in Africa in exchange for raw materials and for enslaved persons, who were taken to the Americas.
   C. European raw materials were sent to the Americas to be transformed into consumer goods by people who had been kidnapped from Africa and enslaved. These consumer goods were then traded in Africa for more slaves.
   D. Enslaved African people were traded in the Americas for raw materials; raw materials harvested by slaves went to Europe where they were utilized and turned to consumer goods; European consumer goods were exchanged in Africa for enslaved people.

Answer:

D. **Correct.** American raw materials (like sugar and tobacco) were used in Europe and also turned into consumer goods there. European goods (as well as gold extracted from the Americas) were exchanged in Africa for enslaved persons, who were forced to harvest the raw materials in the Americas.

Armed Conflicts

Reformation and New Europe

While Spain and Portugal consolidated their hold over territories in the Americas, conflict ensued in Europe. With the cultural changes of the Renaissance, the power of the Catholic Church was threatened; new scientific discoveries and secular Renaissance thought were at odds with many teachings of the Church. The Catholic monk **Martin Luther** wrote a letter of protest to the Pope in 1517 known as the **Ninety-Five Theses**, outlining ways he believed the Church should reform; his ideas gained support, especially among rulers who wanted more power from the Church. Triggering the **Reformation**, or movement for reform of the Church, Luther's ideas led to offshoots of new versions of Christianity in Western Europe, separate from the Orthodox Churches in Russia and Greece. Protestant thinkers like Luther and **John Calvin** addressed particular grievances, condemning the **infallibility** of the Pope (its teaching that the Pope was without fault) and the selling of **indulgences**, or guarantees of entry into heaven.

In Britain, religious and ethnic diversity between Protestant England and Scotland, and Catholic Ireland, made the kingdom unstable. Conflict between Protestants and Catholics was fierce on the Continent as well. The **Thirty Years' War** (1618–1648) began in Central Europe between Protestant nobles in the Holy Roman Empire who disagreed with the strict Catholic **Ferdinand II**, king of Bohemia and eventually archduke of Austria and king of Hungary (what was not under Ottoman domination). Elected Holy Roman Emperor in 1619, Ferdinand II was a leader of the **Counter-Reformation**, attempts at reinforcing Catholic dominance throughout Europe during and after the Reformation in the wake of the Renaissance and related social change. Ferdinand was also closely allied with the Catholic **Hapsburg** Dynasty, which ruled Austria and Spain. Other Protestant-Catholic conflict occurred between Denmark, Sweden, Poland, the Netherlands, and the Papacy.

The tangled alliances between European powers resulted in war between not only France and Spain, but also Sweden and Austria, with the small states of the weakening Holy Roman Empire caught in the middle. The war had been centered on alliances and concerns about the nature of Christianity within different European countries. However, upon signing the 1648 **Treaty of Westphalia**, the European powers agreed to recognize **state sovereignty** and practice **non-interference** in each other's matters—at the expense of family and religious allegiance. 1648 marked a transition into modern international relations when politics and religion would no longer be inexorably intertwined.

The end of the Thirty Years' War represented the end of the notion of the domination of the Catholic Church over Europe and the concept of religious regional dominance, rather than ethnic state divisions. Over the next several centuries, the Church—and religious empires like the Ottomans—would eventually lose control over ethnic groups and their lands, later giving way to smaller **nation-states**.

As state sovereignty became entrenched in European notions of politics, so too did conflict between states. Upon the death of the Hapsburg Holy Roman Emperor **Charles VI** in 1740, the **War of the Austrian Succession** began, a series of Continental wars over who would take over control of the Hapsburg territories. These conflicts would lead to the Seven Years' War.

In 1756 Frederick the Great of Prussia attacked Austria, launching the **Seven Years' War**. In Europe, this war further cemented concepts of state sovereignty and delineated rivalries between European powers engaged in colonial adventure and overseas imperialism—especially Britain and France. It would kick-start British dominance in Asia and also lead to Britain's loss of its North American colonies, nearly bankrupting the Crown.

This time of change in Europe would affect Asia. European concepts of social and political organization became constructed around national sovereignty and nation-states. European economies had become dependent upon colonies and were starting to industrialize, enriching Europe at the expense of its imperial possessions in the Americas, in Africa, and increasingly in Asia.

Industrialization and political organization allowed improved militaries, which put Asian governments at a disadvantage. The major Asian powers—Mughal India, Qing China, the Ottoman Empire, and Safavid (and later, Qajar) Persia—would eventually succumb to European influence or come under direct European control.

THE AGE OF REVOLUTIONS

Monarchies in Europe had been weakened by the conflicts between Catholicism and Protestant faiths; despite European presence and increasing power overseas, as well as its dominance in the Americas, instability made the old order vulnerable. Enlightenment ideals would trigger revolution against **absolute monarchy**. Revolutionary actors drew on the philosophies of enlightenment thinkers like **John Locke**, **Jean-Jacques Rousseau**, and **Montesquieu**, whose beliefs, such as **republicanism**, the **social contract**, the **separation of powers**, and the **rights of man** would drive the Age of Revolutions.

William and Mary defeated James and consolidated Protestant control over England, Scotland, and Ireland under a Protestant constitutional monarchy in the **Glorious Revolution**. The 1689 **English Bill of Rights** established constitutional monarchy, in the spirit of the **Magna Carta**.

The **American Revolution** heavily influenced by Locke, broke out a century later. Please refer to Chapter One, "US History," for details.

The **French Revolution** was the precursor to the end of the feudal order in most of Europe. **King Louis XIV**, the *Sun King* (1643–1715), had consolidated the monarchy in France, taking true political and military power from the nobility. Meanwhile, French Enlightenment thinkers like Jean-Jacques Rousseau, Montesquieu, and **Voltaire** criticized absolute monarchy and the repression of freedom of speech and thought; in 1789, the French Revolution broke out.

The power of the Catholic Church had weakened and the Scientific Revolution and the Enlightenment had fostered social and intellectual change. Colonialism and mercantilism were fueling the growth of an early middle class: people who were not traditionally nobility or landowners under the feudal system were becoming wealthier and more powerful thanks to early capitalism. This class, the **bourgeoisie**, chafed under the rule of the nobility, which had generally inherited land and wealth (while the bourgeoisie earned their wealth in business).

> **DID YOU KNOW?**
>
> Louis XIV built the palace of Versailles to centralize the monarchy—and also to contain and monitor the nobility.

At the same time, panic over dwindling food supplies triggered the **Great Fear** among the enormous population of peasants in July 1789. Suspicion turned to action when the king sent troops to Paris, and on July 14 the people stormed the **Bastille** prison in an event still celebrated in France symbolic of the overthrow of tyranny. Following a period of violence, the monarchy was overthrown.

The French Revolution inspired revolutionary movements throughout Europe and beyond; indeed, the revolutionary principle of self-determination drove revolutionary France to support its ideals abroad.

Ongoing war in Europe and instability in France between republicans and royalists continued to weaken the revolution, but France had military successes in Europe. France had continued its effort to spread the revolution throughout the continent, led by **Napoleon Bonaparte**.

In 1804 Napoleon emerged as emperor of France and proceeded to conquer much of Europe throughout the **Napoleonic Wars**, changing the face of Europe.

By 1815, other European powers had managed to halt France's expansion; at the **Congress of Vienna** in 1815, European powers including Prussia, the Austro-Hungarian Empire, Russia, and Britain agreed on a **balance of power** in Europe. The Congress of Vienna was the first real international peace conference and set the precedent for European political organization.

> **DID YOU KNOW?**
>
> An important tenet of the revolutionary ethos in France was the concept of self-determination, or the right of a people to rule themselves, which threatened rulers fearing revolution in their own countries.

Latin American countries joined Haiti and the United States in revolution against colonial European powers. Inspired by the American and French Revolutions, **Simón Bolivar** led or influenced independence movements in **Venezuela**, **Colombia** (including what is today **Panama**), **Ecuador**, **Peru**, and **Bolivia** in the early part of the nineteenth century.

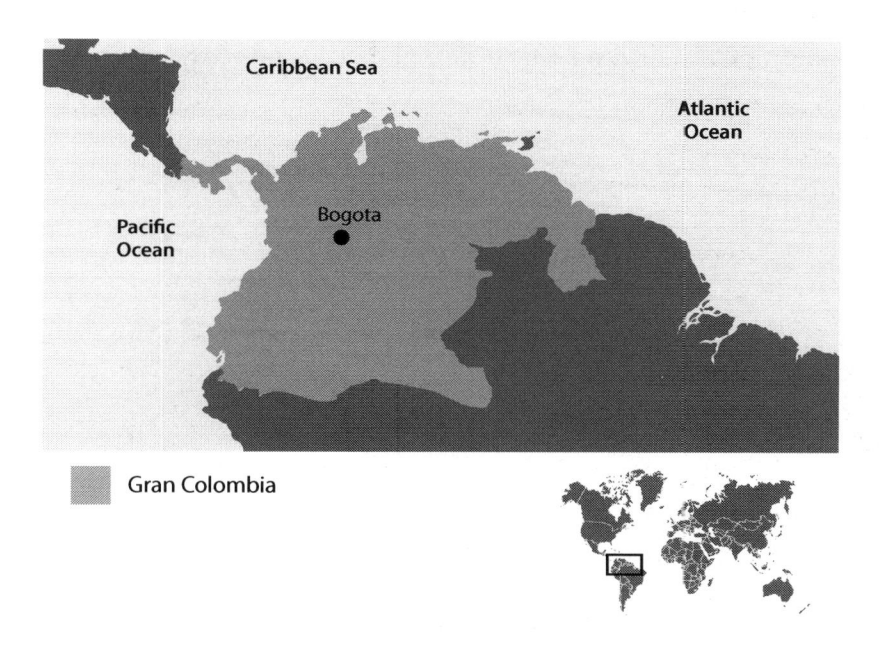

Figure 2.10. Gran Colombia

European Division

The nineteenth century was a period of change and conflict, and the roots of the major twentieth century conflicts—world war and decolonization—are found in it. Modern European social and political structures and norms, including **nationalism** and the **nation-state**, would begin to emerge. Economic theories based in the Industrial Revolution like **socialism** and eventually **communism** gained traction with the stark class divisions brought on by **urbanization** and industry.

Following the Napoleonic Wars, **Prussia** had come to dominate the German-speaking states that once comprised the Holy Roman Empire. By the nineteenth century and due in part to emphasis on military prowess, Prussia became an important military power and a key ally in the efforts against Napoleon.

Prussia had a particular rivalry with France, having lost several key territories during the Napoleonic Wars. In 1870, the militarily powerful kingdom went to war against France in the **Franco-Prussian War**, during which Prussia took control of **Alsace-Lorraine**, mineral-rich and later essential for industrial development.

Following the Franco-Prussian War, **Otto von Bismarck** unified those linguistically and culturally German states of Central Europe. Prussian power had been growing, fueled by **nationalism** and the **nation-state**, or the idea that individuals with shared experience (including ethnicity, language, religion, and cultural practices) should be unified under one government. In 1871, the **German Empire** became a united state. Bismarck encouraged economic cooperation, instituted army reforms and, perhaps most importantly, created an image of Prussia as a defender of German culture and nationhood, portraying other European states in opposition to that.

The concept of the nation-state spread throughout Central and Eastern Europe, which at the time was controlled by imperial powers like Austria-Hungary and the Ottoman Empire. Nationalism threatened imperial reach. It also led to **Italian Unification**.

Imperialism

As colonialism in the fifteenth and sixteenth centuries had been driven by mercantilism, conquest, and Christian conversion, so was seventeenth, eighteenth and nineteenth century imperialism driven by capitalism, European competition, and conceptions of racial superiority.

Britain and France, historic rivals on the European continent, were also at odds colonizing North America and in overseas trade. During the **Seven Years' War** (1756 – 1763), considered by many historians to be the first truly global conflict, these two powers fought in Europe and in overseas colonies and interests in North America and Asia.

The **French and Indian War**, as the Seven Years' War is called in North America, resulted in net gains for Britain, which won French colonies in Canada. However, the financial and military strain suffered by Britain in the Seven Years' War made it particularly vulnerable to later rebellion in the Thirteen Colonies, helping the Americans win the Revolutionary War there.

Britain went to war with France in Asia as well. In India, with the decline of the **Mughal Empire** and the rising power of colonial companies specializing in exporting valuable resources like spices and tea, smaller Indian kingdoms were forming alliances with those increasingly influential corporations. By 1803, British interests effectively took control of the Subcontinent and the Mughals were pushed to the north.

Britain would become the strongest naval power in the world and continue to expand its empire, especially in the search for new markets for its manufactured goods to support its industrial economy. During the reign of **Queen Victoria** (1837–1901) the British Empire would expand in Australia, India, and Africa.

Imperial expansion was driven by demand for raw materials for economic growth. The concept of the *white man's burden*, wherein white Europeans were "obligated" to bring their "superior" culture to other civilizations around the globe, also drove imperialist adventure, popularizing it at home in Britain and elsewhere in Europe. Still, other European powers like France, Germany, and even tiny Belgium controlled substantial colonial territory, exploiting natural resources and oppressing the people. Racism was a driving factor in their colonial expansion, too.

> **DID YOU KNOW?**
>
> Major European companies that dominated colonial trade and controlled territory in Asia included the British East India Company, the French East India Company, and the Dutch East India Company.

The European powers were immersed in what became known as the *Scramble for Africa*; the industrial economies of Europe would profit from the natural resources abundant in that continent, and the white man's burden continued to fuel colonization. At the **1884 Berlin Conference**, control over Africa was divided among European powers. Africans were not consulted in this process.

To gain access to closed **Chinese** markets, Britain forced China to buy Indian opium; the **Opium Wars** ended with the **Treaty of Nanking (1842)**. As a consequence, China lost power to Britain and later, other European countries, which gained **spheres of influence**, or areas of China they effectively controlled, and **extraterritoriality**, or privileges in which their citizens were not subject to Chinese law.

> **QUICK REVIEW**
>
> List some of the European powers' justifications for imperialism.

Discontent with the Qing dynasty was growing as Chinese people perceived that their country was coming under control of European imperialists. In 1900, the **Boxer Rebellion**, an uprising led by a Chinese society against the Emperor, was only put down with Western help. Meanwhile, living conditions for Chinese people continued to deteriorate.

In Japan, during the **Meiji Restoration** in 1868, the Emperor Meiji promoted modernization of technology, especially the military. Japan proved itself a world power when it defeated Russia in the **Russo-Japanese War** in 1905, and would play a central role in twentieth century conflict.

Industrial Revolution

Throughout this entire period, raw goods fueled European economic growth and development, leading to the **Industrial Revolution** in the nineteenth century. This economic revolution began with textile production in Britain, fueled by cotton from its overseas territories in North America, and later India and Egypt. The first factories were in Manchester, where **urbanization** began as poor people from rural areas flocked to cities in search of higher-paying unskilled jobs in factories.

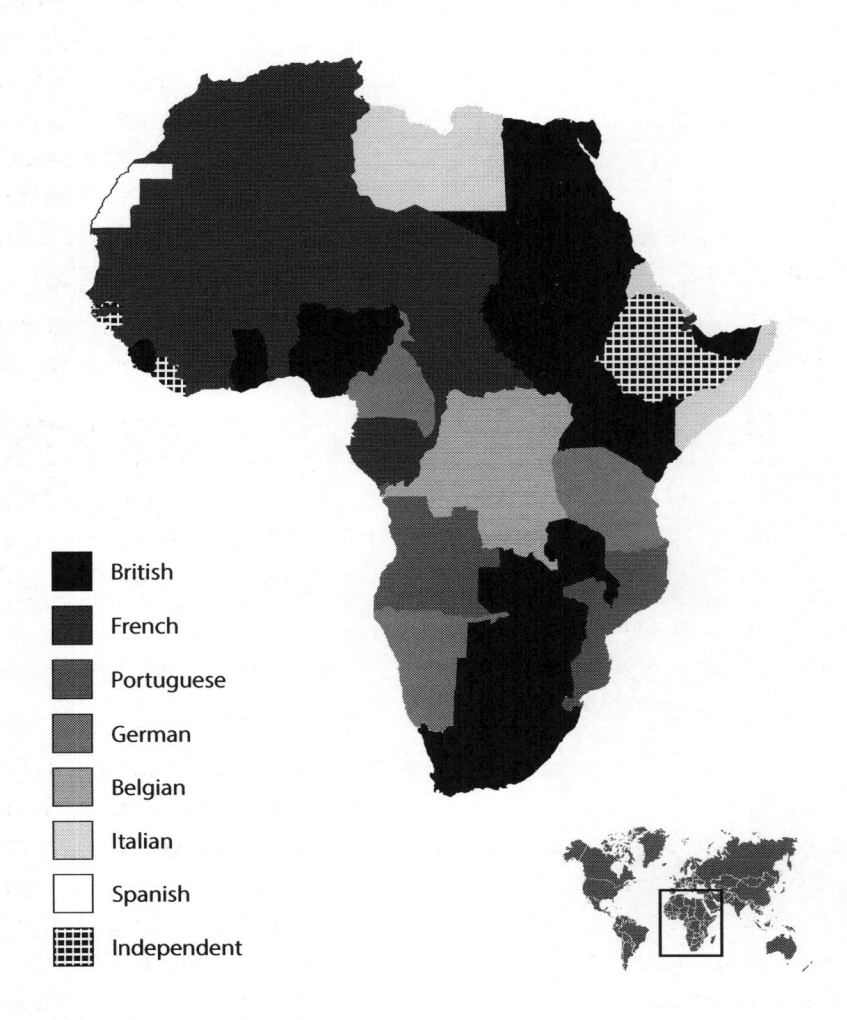

Figure 2.11. Imperial Africa

Early industrial technology sped up the harvesting and transport of crops and their conversion to textiles. This accelerated manufacturing was based on **capitalism**, the *laissez-faire* (or **free market**) theory developed by **Adam Smith**, who believed that an ***invisible hand*** should guide the marketplace—that government should stay out of the economy regardless of abuses of workers, the environment, or fairness in the marketplace, as the economy would eventually automatically correct for inequalities, price problems, and any other problematic issues.

Technology like the **spinning jenny** and **flying shuttle** exponentially increased the amount of cotton that workers could process into yarn and thread. Iron allowed for stronger machinery and would support the later **Second Industrial Revolution** in the late nineteenth and early twentieth century, which was based on **heavy industry**, railroads, and weapons.

To access the raw materials needed to produce manufactured goods, Britain and other industrializing countries in Western Europe needed resources—hence the drive for imperialism as discussed above. Cotton was harvested in India and Egypt for textile mills, minerals mined in South Africa and the Congo to power metallurgy. Furthermore, as industrialization and urbanization led to the development of early middle classes in Europe and North America, imports of luxury goods like tea, spices, silk, precious metals, and other items from Asia increased to meet consumer demand. Colonial powers also gained by selling manufactured goods back to the colonies from which they had harvested raw materials in the first place, for considerable profit.

Largely unbridled capitalism had led to the conditions of the early Industrial Revolution; workers suffered from abusive treatment, overly long hours, low wages or none at all, and unsafe conditions, including pollution. The German philosophers **Karl Marx** and **Friedrich Engels,** horrified by conditions suffered by industrial workers, developed **socialism**, the philosophy that workers, or the **proletariat,** should own the means of production and reap the profits, rather than the **bourgeoisie**, who had no interest in the rights of the workers at the expense of profit and who did not experience the same conditions.

> **DID YOU KNOW?**
>
> *The Communist Manifesto* contained the famous words *Workers of the world, unite!*

A different version of socialism would later help Russia become a major world power. The Russian intellectuals **Vladimir Lenin** and **Leon Trotsky** would take Marx and Engels's theories further, developing **Marxism-Leninism.** They embraced socialist ideals and believed in revolution; however they felt that **communism** could not be maintained under a democratic governing structure. Lenin supported dictatorship, more precisely the ***dictatorship of the proletariat***, paving the way for the political and economic organization of the Soviet Union. The Marxist Social Democrats, made up of the **Bolsheviks**, led by **Lenin**, and the **Mensheviks**, would gain power after the fall of the tsar in the early twentieth century. They would eventually take over the country in 1917.

SAMPLE QUESTIONS

11) **The Treaty of Westphalia**
    A. laid out the final borders of Europe, setting the stage for modern foreign policy.
    B. established the notion of state sovereignty, in which states recognized each other as independent and agreed not to interfere in each other's affairs.
    C. gave the Catholic Church more power in the affairs of Catholic-majority countries.
    D. established the notion of the nation-state, in which culturally and ethnically similar groups would control their own territory as sovereign countries.

    Answer:
    B. **Correct.** The Treaty of Westphalia was based on state sovereignty and non-interference, the core principles of modern international relations.

12) **An important factor leading to the French Revolution was**
    A. the corruption of Louis XIV.
    B. the strong organization of the Estates-General.
    C. support from the United States of America.
    D. the anti-monarchical philosophies of Enlightenment thinkers like Rousseau and Voltaire.

    Answer:
    D. **Correct.** Enlightenment thinking fueled the Age of Revolutions, and revolutionary French thinkers and writers like Rousseau, Voltaire, and others influenced revolutionary French leaders.

13) **Which of the following is NOT a way that the white man's burden influenced imperialism?**
    A. It inspired Europeans to settle overseas in order to improve what they believed to be "backward" places.
    B. Europeans believed in imperialism as in the best interest of native people, who would benefit from adopting European languages and cultural practices.
    C. Europeans believed it burdensome to be forced to tutor non-Europeans in their languages and customs.
    D. Many Europeans supported the construction of schools for colonial subjects and even the development of scholarships for them to study in Europe.

Answer:

- C. **Correct.** The idea of the white man's burden was not meant to suggest a literal burden; it was a paternalistic concept of responsibility used to justify imperial dominance.

14) **Marx and Engels believed**
  - A. that the proletariat must control the means of production to ensure a wageless, classless society to meet the needs of all equitably.
  - B. in the dictatorship of the proletariat, in which the workers would control the means of production in a non-democratic society.
  - C. that an organized revolution directed by a small group of leaders was necessary to bring about social change and a socialist society.
  - D. that the bourgeoisie would willingly give up control of the means of production to the proletariat.

Answer:

- A. **Correct.** Marx and Engels believed in abolishing wages and the class structure in exchange for a socialist society where the means of production were commonly held and in which income was equally distributed.

GLOBAL CONFLICTS

WORLD WAR I

Instability in the Balkans and increasing tensions in Europe culminated with the assassination of the Austro-Hungarian Archduke **Franz Ferdinand** by the Serbian nationalist **Gavrilo Princip** in Sarajevo on June 28, 1914. In protest of continuing Austro-Hungarian control over Serbia, Princip's action kicked off the **system of alliances** that had been in place among European powers.

Austria-Hungary declared war on Serbia, and Russia came to Serbia's aid. As an ally of Austria-Hungary, Germany declared war on Russia. Russia's ally France prepared for war; as Germany traversed Belgium to invade France, Belgium pleaded for aid from other European countries and so Britain declared war on Germany.

Germany had been emphasizing military growth since the consolidation and militarization of the empire under Bismarck in the mid-nineteenth century. Now, under **Kaiser Wilhelm II**, who sought expanded territories in Europe and overseas for Germany (including the potential capture of overseas British and French colonies), Germany was a militarized state and an important European power in its own right.

> **DID YOU KNOW?**
>
> The first international war to use industrialized weaponry, WWI was called "the Great War" because battle on such a scale had never before been seen.

In Europe, the 1914 **Battle of the Marne** between Germany and French and British forces defending France resulted in trench warfare that would continue for years, marking the Western Front. At **Gallipoli** in 1915, Australian and New Zealander troops fought the **Ottoman Empire**, allies of Germany, near Istanbul. Later that year, a German submarine, or **U-boat**, sank the *Lusitania*, a passenger ship in the Atlantic, killing many American civilians. In 1916, the **Battle of Verdun**, the longest battle of the war, ended in the failure of the Germans to defeat the French army. In 1916, the British navy pushed back the German navy in the **Battle of Jutland**; despite heavy losses, Britain was able to ensure that German naval power was diminished for the rest of the war. On July 1, 1916, the **Battle of the Somme** became part of an allied effort to repel Germany using artillery to end the stalemate on the Western Front; after four months, however, the front moved only five miles.

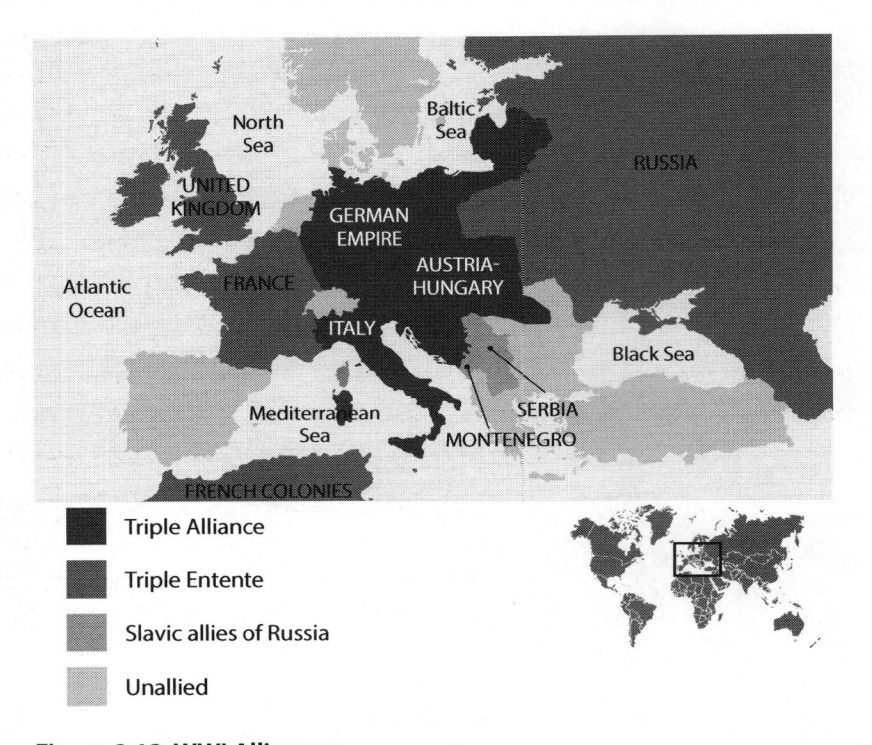

Figure 2.12. WWI Alliances

Finally, in 1917, the United States caught the **Zimmerman Telegram**, in which Germany secretly proposed an alliance with Mexico to attack the US. This finally spurred US intervention in the war; despite Russian withdrawal after the Bolshevik Revolution in October 1917, Germany was forced to surrender in the face of invasion by the US-supported allies.

According to the **Schlieffen Plan**, Germany had planned to fight a war on two fronts against both Russia and France. However, Russia's unexpectedly rapid mobilization stretched the German army too thin on the Eastern Front, while it became bogged down in **trench warfare** on the Western Front against the British, French, and later the Americans. Germany lost the war and was punished with the harsh **Treaty of Versailles,** which held it accountable for the entirety of the war. The Treaty brought economic hardship on the country by forcing it to pay **reparations**. Wilhelm was forced to abdicate and never again regained power in Germany. German military failure and consequent economic collapse due to the Treaty of Versailles and later worldwide economic depression set the stage for the rise of fascism and Adolf Hitler.

The Treaty also created the **League of Nations**, an international organization designed to prevent future outbreaks of international war; however, it was largely toothless, especially because the powerful United States did not join.

CHANGE IN THE MIDDLE EAST

The end of WWI also marked the end of the Ottoman Empire, which was officially dissolved in 1923. At the end of the war the Middle East was divided into **mandates**. The borders were decided by the **Sykes-Picot Agreement** between Britain and France, which divided the region into spheres of influence to be controlled by each power, and are essentially those national borders that divide the Middle East today.

In 1917, the secret **Balfour Declaration** promised the Jews an independent state in Palestine, but Western powers did not honor this agreement. In fact it conflicted directly with the Sykes-Picot Agreement, which held that Palestine would be governed internationally. The state of Israel was not established until 1948.

After the First World War, the secular nationalist **Mustafa Ataturk**, one of the Young Turks who pushed a secular, nationalist agenda, kept European powers out of Anatolia and abolished the Caliphate in 1924, establishing modern Turkey.

There was no more Caliph. Refugees and migrants had traveled throughout the Ottoman Empire over the course of the war, suddenly restricted by international borders from their places of origin. People lacked identification papers. Ethnic and religious groups were divided by what would become the borders of the modern Middle East.

The roots of two competing ideologies, **Pan-Arabism** and **Islamism**, developed in this context. According to Pan-Arabism, Arabs and Arabic speakers should be aligned regardless of international borders. Pan-Arabism eventually became an international movement espousing Arab unity in response to European and US influence and presence later in the twentieth century.

Islamism began as a social and political movement. The **Muslim Brotherhood** was established in Egypt in the 1920s, filling social roles that the state had abandoned or could not fill.

> **DID YOU KNOW?**
>
> In 1915, the Ottoman Empire launched a genocide against the Christian Armenian people, part of a campaign to control ethnic groups it believed threatened the Turkish nature of the empire. An estimated 1.5 million Armenians were forcibly removed from their homes and killed. To this day, the Turkish government denies the Armenian Genocide.

Eventually taking a political role, the Muslim Brotherhood's model later inspired groups like Hamas and Hezbollah.

Russian Revolution

By 1917, Russia was suffering from widespread food shortages and economic crisis; morale was low due to conscription and as the military suffered enormous losses and humiliating defeats under the command of Nicholas II. During WWI, this combination of failures at home and on the front only added to widespread dissatisfaction with the rule of the Tsar. The Tsar was forced to abdicate, and a period of violence and instability followed as different factions fought for power.

The communist Bolsheviks, led by Lenin and Trotsky, consolidated their power by nationalizing industry, developing and distributing propaganda portraying themselves as the defenders of Russia against imperialism, and forcefully eliminating dissent. Yet for many, it was more appealing to fight for a new Russia with hope for an improved standard of living than to return to the old times under the Tsar. In the **October Revolution** Lenin, Trotsky, and the Bolsheviks took control of Russia. By 1921, the Bolsheviks were victorious and formed the **Soviet Union** or **Union of Soviet Socialist Republics (USSR)**.

> **DID YOU KNOW?**
>
> In the 1920s, around twenty million Russians were sent to the *gulags*, or prison labor camps, usually in Siberia, thousands of miles from their homes. Millions died.

Following Lenin's death in 1924, the Secretary of the Communist Party, **Josef Stalin**, took power. Under Stalin's totalitarian dictatorship, the USSR became socially and politically repressive; the Communist Party and the military underwent **purges** where any persons who were a potential threat to Stalin's power were imprisoned or executed.

In 1931, Stalin enforced the **collectivization** of land and agriculture in an attempt to consolidate control over the countryside and improve food security. He had the *kulaks*, or landowning peasants, sent to the *gulags*, enabling the government to confiscate their land. By 1939, most farming and land was controlled by the government, and most peasants lived on collective land. However, systemic disorganization in the 1920s and 1930s resulted in famine and food shortages.

Stalin also focused on accelerating industrial development. Targeting heavy industry, these **Five Year Plans** increased production in industrial materials and staples like electricity, petroleum, coal, and iron; they also resulted in the construction of major infrastructure throughout the country from 1929 – 1938. However, conditions for the workers were dismal. The USSR quickly became an industrial power, but at the expense of millions who lost their lives in purges, forced labor camps, and famine.

CHANGE IN EAST ASIA

Following its victory in the Russo-Japanese War, Japan was recognized as a military power. It joined a world focused on industry and imperialism.

Having already embraced industrialization and modern militarization, Japan turned towards imperialism throughout Asia. In the **First Sino-Japanese War** (1894–1895), Japan gained influence and territory in mainland Asia. This conflict also revealed Chinese military and organizational limitations and showed Japanese military superiority.

Following the First World War, despite having provided assistance to the French and British in Asia, Japan began its own imperialist adventure in East and Southeast Asia not only to gain power and access to raw materials, but also to limit and eventually expel European rule in what Japan considered its *sphere of influence*. In 1931, Japan invaded **Manchuria**, creating the puppet state *Manchukuo*.

Meanwhile, China was undergoing political change. The **Xinhai Revolution** broke out in 1911, resulting in the overthrow of the Qing and the end of dynastic Chinese rule. However, despite Republican recognition by major international powers, the power vacuum left by the end of imperial China allowed the rise of warlords throughout the enormous country, and the government was unable to establish total control.

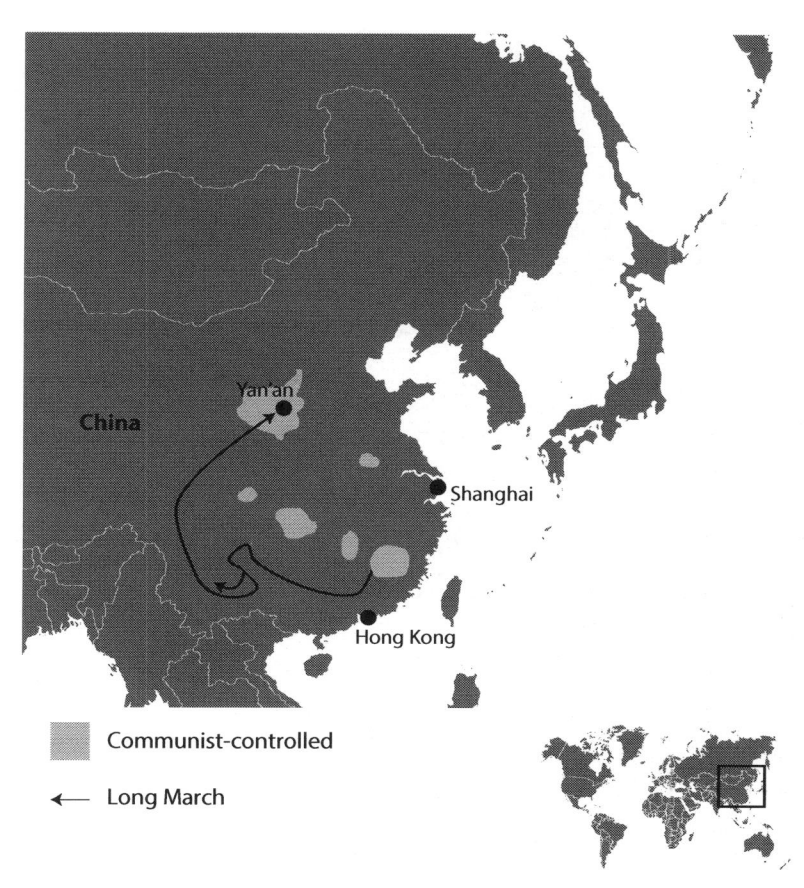

Figure 2.13. The Long March

The **Kuomintang (KMT)**, or Nationalist Party of the revolutionary government worked to consolidate government power; the KMT leader **Chiang Kai-shek** (or **Jiang Jieshi**) went on to take control of much of China back from the warlords.

At the same time, communism was emerging in China as a response to western imperialism. Temporarily working together, the KMT and **Chinese Communist Party** CCP were able to bring Chinese territory back under Republican control. However, Chiang turned against the CCP in 1927, driving it south.

The CCP focused its organizing activities in the countryside on the peasants, becoming powerful in southern China. Ongoing KMT attacks forced the CCP to retreat on the **Long March** north. During this time of hardship, **Mao Zedong** emerged as the leader of the movement.

World War II

Meanwhile, Germany suffered under the provisions of the Treaty of Versailles. In 1919, a democratic government was established at Weimar—the **Weimar Republic**. Germany was in chaos; the Kaiser had fled and the country was torn apart by war. However, the new government could not bring stability.

Blamed for WWI, Germany owed huge **reparations** according to the treaty to pay for the cost of the war, setting off **hyperinflation** and impoverishing the country and its people. The rise of communists and a workers' party that came to be known as the National Socialist Party, or **Nazi Party**, led to further political instability. Following the crash of the stock market in 1929, German unemployment reached six million; furthermore, the United States had called in its foreign loans. The Nazis, led by **Adolf Hitler**, gained support from business interests, which feared communist power in government.

Hitler maneuvered into the role of chancellor by 1933. His charisma and popular platform—to cancel the Treaty of Versailles—allowed him to rise. Nazi ideals appealed strongly to both industry and the workers in the face of global economic depression. Moreover, the Nazi Minister of Propaganda **Joseph Goebbels** executed an effective propaganda campaign, and would do so throughout Hitler's rule, known as the **Third Reich**.

Taking advantage of a series of crises, Hitler became the undemocratic *Führer*, or *leader*, of Germany, and the Nazis consolidated total control. They also set into motion their agenda of racism and genocide against "non-Aryan" (non-Germanic) or "racially impure" people.

Jewish people were particularly targeted. Germany had a considerable Jewish population; so did the other Central and Eastern European countries that Germany would come to control. Throughout the 1930s, the Nazis passed a series of laws limiting Jewish rights. **Kristallnacht** took place in 1938, an organized series of attacks on Jewish businesses, homes, and places of worship.

In 1939, Jews were forced from their homes into **ghettoes**, isolated and overcrowded urban neighborhoods. Millions of Jewish people were sent to **concentration camps**; the Nazis decided on the **Final Solution** to the "Jewish Question": to murder Jewish people by systematically gassing them at death camps. At least six million European Jews were murdered by the Nazis in the **Holocaust**.

Roma, Slavic people, homosexuals, disabled people, people of color, prisoners of war, communists, and others were also forced into slave labor in concentration camps and murdered there. Later, this concept of torturing and killing people based on their ethnicity in order to exterminate them would become defined as **genocide**.

Hitler was a **fascist**, believing in a mostly free market accompanied by a dictatorial government with a strong military. He sought to restore Germany's power and expand its reach through annexation and conquest. In 1939 Germany invaded **Poland** in what is commonly considered the beginning of the **Second World War**.

> **DID YOU KNOW?**
>
> The Atlantic Charter described values shared by the US and Britain, including restoring self-governance in occupied Europe and liberalizing international trade.

War exploded in Europe in 1939. Hitler gained control of more land than any European power since Napoleon, undefeated until the **Battle of Britain**. Despite staying out of combat, in 1941 the United States provided support and military aid to Britain through the **Lend-Lease Act**.

When Japan joined the **Axis** powers of Germany and Italy, the **Chinese Civil War** between communists and nationalists was interrupted by the Second Sino-Japanese War, when Japan tried to extend its imperial reach deeper into China.

At this time, Chiang was forced to form an alliance with Mao and the two forces worked together against Japan. By the end of the war, the CCP was stronger than ever, with widespread support from many sectors of Chinese society, while the KMT was demoralized and had little popular support.

In December of 1941, Japan, now part of the **Axis** along with Germany and Italy, attacked the United States at Pearl Harbor. Consequently, the US joined the war in Europe and in the Pacific, deploying thousands of troops in both theaters. Meanwhile, Japan continued its imperialist policies throughout Asia, threatening European interests and colonies there.

Back in Europe, having broken a promise to the Soviet Union, Hitler invaded Russia. But in 1942, the USSR defeated Germany at the **Battle of Stalingrad**, a turning point in the war during which the Nazis were forced to turn from the Eastern Front.

In 1944, the Allies invaded France on **D-Day**. While they liberated Paris in August, the costly **Battle of the Bulge** extended into 1945. Despite thousands of American casualties, Hitler's forces were pushed back. In the spring of 1945, when American and Soviet forces entered Germany, the Allies accepted Germany's surrender.

The war in the Pacific would continue, however. An American invasion of Japan would have likely resulted in hundreds of thousands of casualties. To avoid this, 1945, the US bombed the Japanese cities of **Hiroshima** and **Nagasaki** with nuclear weapons in 1945, the only time they have been used in combat. The tremendous civilian casualties did force the Emperor to surrender; at that point, the Second World War came to an end.

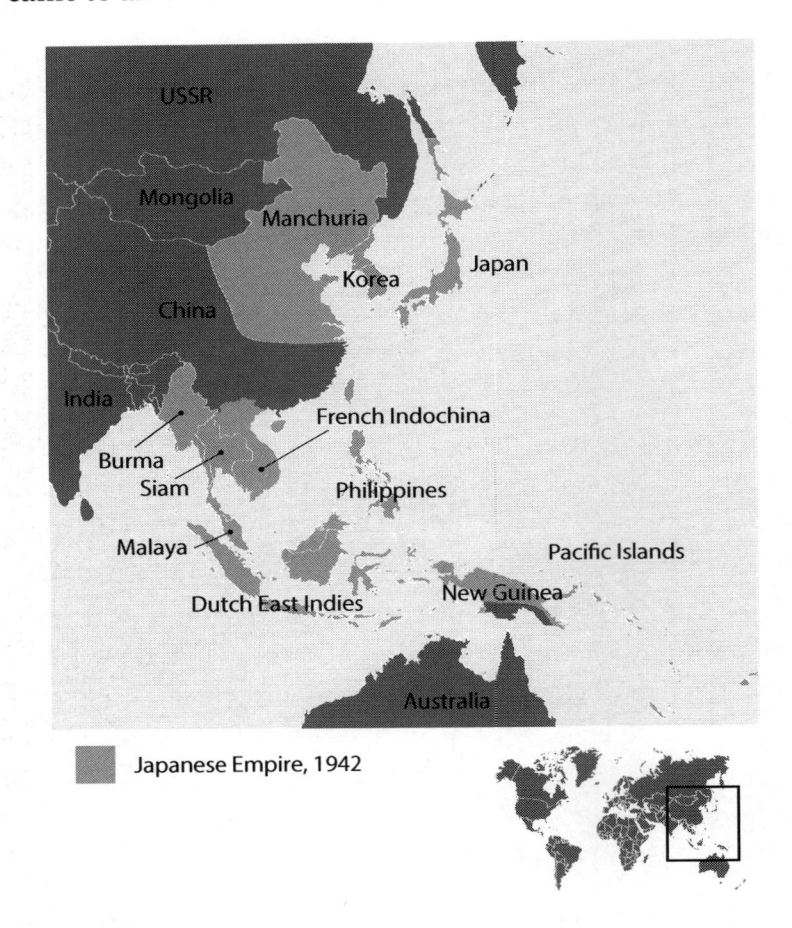

Figure 2.14. Japanese Expansion in Asia

That year in China, the Chinese Civil War recommenced; by 1949 the communists had emerged victorious. The KMT withdrew to Taiwan, while Mao and the CCP took over China, which became a communist country.

The extreme horrors of WWII helped develop the concept of **genocide**, or the effort to extinguish an entire group of people because of their ethnicity, and the idea of **human rights**. The **United Nations** was formed, based on the League of Nations, as a body to champion human rights and uphold international security. Its **Security Council** is made up of permanent member states which can intervene militarily in the interests of international stability.

Allied forces took the lead in rebuilding efforts: the US occupied areas in East Asia and Germany, while the Soviet Union remained in Eastern Europe. The Allies had planned to rebuild Europe according to the **Marshall Plan**; however, the USSR occupied eastern European countries, and they came under communist control. The **Cold War** had begun.

THE COLD WAR

At the Yalta Conference in February 1945, Stalin, Churchill, and Roosevelt had agreed upon the division of Germany, the free nature of government in Poland, and free elections in Eastern Europe. However, at the **Potsdam Conference** in July 1945, things had changed. Harry Truman had replaced Franklin D. Roosevelt, who had died in office, and Clement Atlee had replaced Winston Churchill. Stalin felt betrayed by the US use of the atomic bomb; likewise, the US and the British felt that Stalin had violated the agreement at Yalta regarding democracy in Eastern Europe.

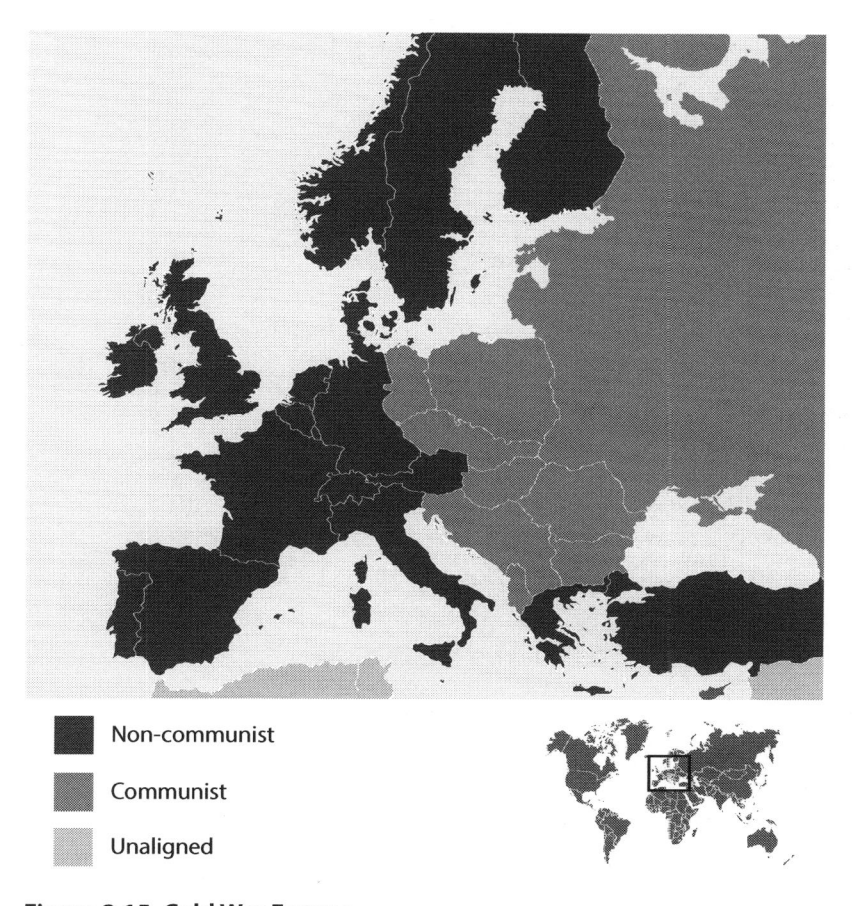

Figure 2.15. Cold War Europe

Stalin ensured that communists came to power in Eastern Europe, setting up satellite states at the Soviet perimeter in violation of the Yalta agreement. The Soviet rationale was to establish a buffer zone following its extraordinarily heavy casualties in WWII—around twenty million. In the words of the British Prime Minister

Winston Churchill, an *iron curtain* had come down across Europe, dividing east from west.

Consequently, western states organized the North Atlantic Treaty Organization or **NATO**, an agreement wherein an attack on one was an attack on all; this treaty provided for **collective security** in the face of the Soviet expansionist threat. The United States adopted a policy of **containment**, the idea that communism should be *contained*, as part of the **Truman Doctrine** of foreign policy.

In response, the Soviet Union created the **Warsaw Pact**, a similar organization consisting of Eastern European communist countries. **Nuclear weapons** raised the stakes of the conflict. The concept of **mutually-assured destruction**, or the understanding that a nuclear strike by one country would result in a response by the other, ultimately destroying the entire world, may have prevented the outbreak of active violence.

Germany itself had been divided into four zones, controlled by Britain, France, the US, and the USSR. Berlin had been divided the same way. Once Britain, France, and the US united their zones into West Germany in 1948 and introduced a new currency, the USSR cut off West Berlin in the **Berlin Blockade**. For nearly a year western powers provided supplies to West Berlin by air in the **Berlin Airlift**. Until 1961, refugees from the Eastern Bloc escaped to West Berlin. Furthermore, West Berlin was a center for Western espionage. In 1961, the USSR, now led by **Nikita Khrushchev**, closed the border and constructed the **Berlin Wall**.

> **QUICK REVIEW**
>
> How did the Cold War erupt between the Allies and the Soviet Union?

Korea had also been divided after the war, controlled by communists north of the **thirty-eighth parallel**. In 1950, the north invaded the south with Russian and Chinese support. According to the Truman Doctrine, communism needed to be contained. Furthermore, according to **domino theory**, if one country became communist, then more would, too, like a row of dominoes falling. Therefore, the United States became involved in the **Korean War** (1950 – 1953).

UN troops led by the US came to the aid of the South Koreans; China supported the North Koreans. War on the peninsula ended in a stalemate in 1953; tensions continue today.

Later, in **Cuba**, the revolutionary **Fidel Castro** took over in 1959. Allied with the Soviet Union, he allowed missile bases to be constructed in Cuba, which threatened the United States. During the **Cuban Missile Crisis** in 1962, the world came closer than ever to nuclear war when the USSR sent missiles to Cuba. President Kennedy and Premier Khrushchev were able to come to an agreement, and nuclear war was averted.

Despite this success, the United States engaged in a lengthy violent conflict in Southeast Asia. Supporting anti-communist fighters in Vietnam in keeping with containment and domino theory, the United States pursued the **Vietnam War** for almost a decade. The communist **Viet Cong** were waging a guerrilla war against France for independence, and the US became involved in the 1960s when France asked for aid.

Despite being outnumbered, Viet Cong familiarity with the difficult terrain, support from Russia and China, and determination eventually resulted in victory. Bloody guerrilla warfare demoralized the American military, but the 1968 **Tet Offensive** was a turning point. Despite enormous losses, the North Vietnamese won a strategic victory in this coordinated, surprise offensive. Extreme objection to the war within the United States, high casualties, and demoralization eventually resulted in US withdrawal in 1973.

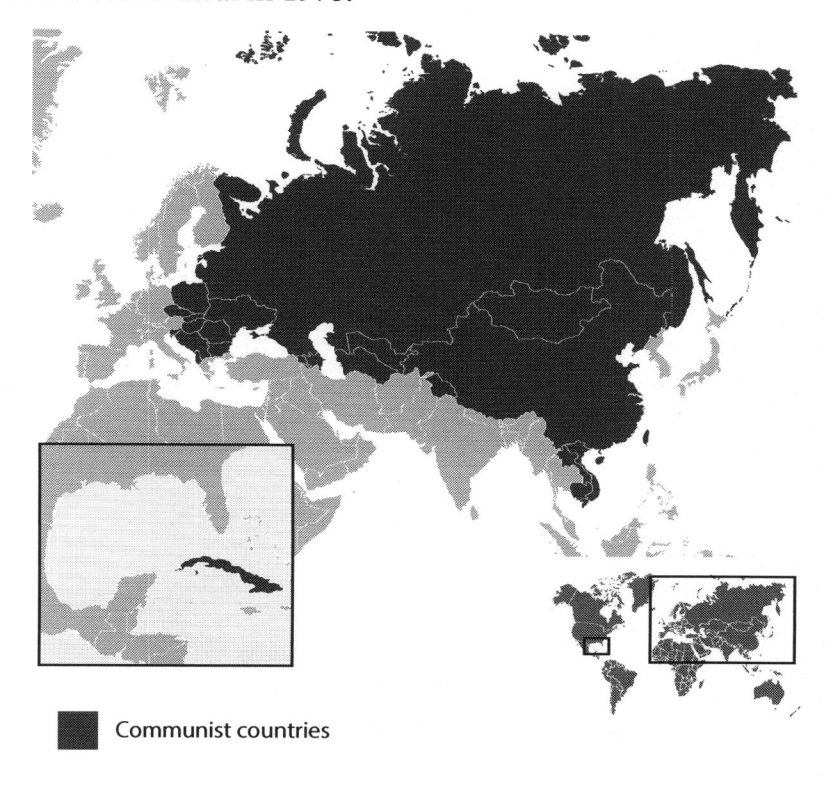

Figure 2.16. The Communist World

Toward the end of the 1960s and into the 1970s, the Cold War reached a period of **détente**, or a warming of relations. The US and USSR entered into arms treaties like the **Nuclear Non-Proliferation Treaty** and the **Strategic Arms Limitation Treaty** (**SALT I**). Some cultural exchanges and partnerships in outer space took place.

At the same time, the United States began making diplomatic overtures toward communist China. China and the USSR had difficult relations due to their differing views on the nature of

> **DID YOU KNOW?**
>
> Perhaps the most famous proposal in weapons technology of the Cold War was the Strategic Defense Initiative; popularly known as *Star Wars*, this outer-space based system would have intercepted Soviet intercontinental ballistic missiles.

communism. Following the **Sino-Soviet Split** of the 1960s, China had lost much Soviet support for its modernization programs. Despite advances in agriculture and some industrialization, Mao's programs like the **Great Leap Forward** had harmed the people. In 1972, US President Richard Nixon visited China, establishing relations between the communist government and the United States. Communist China joined the UN.

The climate would change again, however, in the 1970s and 1980s. The US and USSR engaged in proxy wars worldwide. In addition, the **arms race** was underway. President Ronald Reagan focused on weapons development in order to outspend the USSR on military technology.

DECOLONIZATION

Meanwhile, the former colonies of the fallen European colonial powers had won or were in the process of gaining their independence.

In 1949, the Indian leader **Mohandas Gandhi** had led a peaceful independence movement against the British, winning Indian independence. His assassination by Hindu radicals led to conflict between Hindus and Muslims in the **Subcontinent**, resulting in **Partition,** the bloody division of India into Pakistan and eventually Bangladesh.

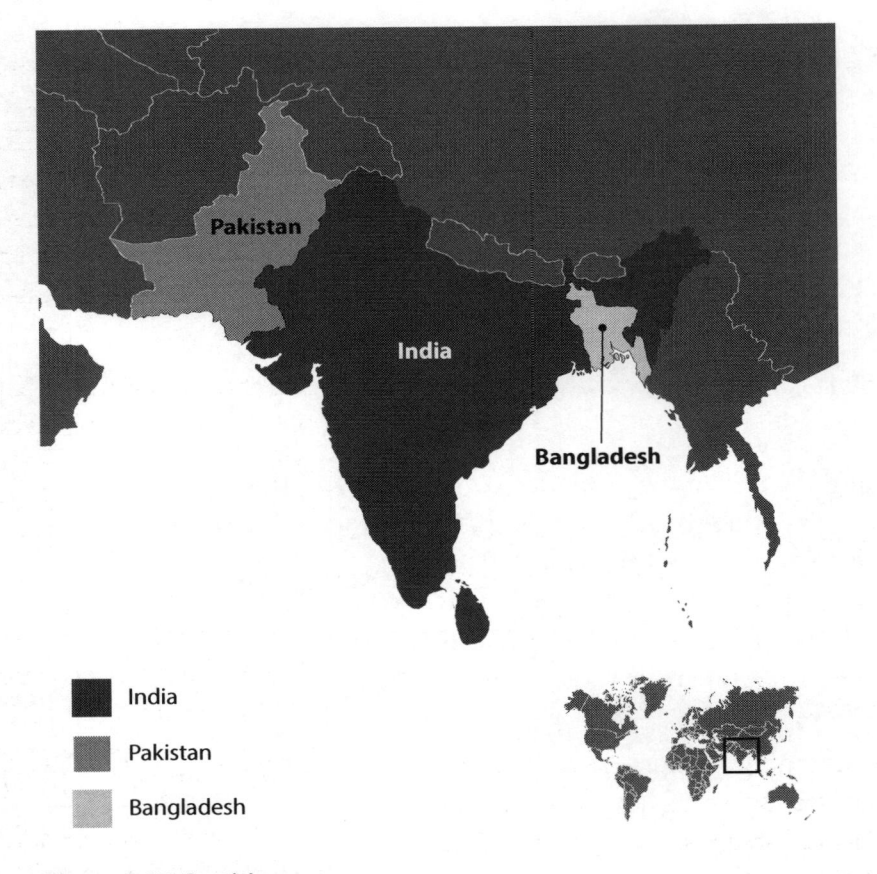

Figure 2.17. Partition

Bloody conflict in Africa like the **Algerian War** against France (1954–1962), the **Mau Mau Rebellion** against the British in Kenya in the 1950s, and violent movements against Belgium in the **Congo** resulted in African independence for many countries in the 1950s, 1960s, and 1970s; likewise, so did strong leadership by African nationalist leaders and thinkers like **Jomo Kenyatta, Julius Nyerere,** and **Kwame Nkrumah.** The apartheid regime in South Africa, where segregation between races was legal and people of color lived in oppressive conditions, was not lifted until the 1990s; **Nelson Mandela** led the country in a peaceful transition process.

In the Middle East, the European-controlled protectorates became independent states with arbitrary borders drawn and rulers installed by the Europeans. The creation of the state of **Israel** was especially contentious: in the 1917 **Balfour Declaration,** the British had promised the **Zionist** movement of European Jews a homeland; however, the US assured the Arabs in 1945 that a Jewish state would not be founded there. Israel emerged from confusion, chaos, and tragedy after the Holocaust in Europe, and violence on the ground in Palestine carried out by both Jews and Arabs. The conflict continues in the region today.

> **DID YOU KNOW?**
>
> The revolutionary Iranian government would go on to support Shi'a militants (the *Hezbollah*, or the *Party of God*) in the **Lebanese Civil War** throughout the 1980s; this group is also inspired by Islamism.

In Egypt, **Gamal Abdul Nasser** led the Pan-Arabist movement in the region. Egypt led the unsuccessful **Six Day War** in 1967 against Israel, a major setback for the Arab states. Israel took control of Arab territory. The Arab-Israeli conflict became a Cold War conflict during the 1973 **Yom Kippur War**: the US supported **Israel** and the USSR supported **Syria** and **Egypt**. Conflict continued until 1978, when the American president Jimmy Carter brokered peace between Israel and Egypt (and later, Jordan) in the **Camp David Accords**. By the 1970s, Pan-Arabism was no longer the popular, unifying movement it had once been.

The **Non-Aligned Movement** arose in response to the Cold War. Instead of the bipolar world of the Cold War (one democratic, led by the US, the other communist, led by the USSR), the Non-Aligned Movement sought an alternative: the **Third World**. Non-Aligned or Third World countries wanted to avoid succumbing to the influence of either of the superpowers, and many found a forum in the United Nations in which to strengthen their international profiles.

However, throughout the Cold War, **proxy wars** between the US and the USSR were fought around the world. In the 1980s, the United States began supporting anti-communists in Nicaragua, Afghanistan, Angola, Mozambique, and Ethiopia.

Iran had been under the oppressive regime of the western-supported **Shah Reza Pahlavi** for decades. By the 1970s, the Shah's corrupt, oppressive regime

> **QUICK REVIEW**
>
> Why were proxy wars important in the context of the Cold War?

was extremely unpopular in Iran, but it was propped up by the West. In the 1979 **Iranian Revolution**, diverse forces overthrew the Shah; shortly afterward, Islamist revolutionaries took over the country and established a conservative theocracy led by **Ayatollah Khomeini**.

Following the Iranian Revolution, the Iraqi leader **Saddam Hussein** declared war against Iran. While governed by Sunnis, Iraq was actually a Shi'ite-majority country, and Saddam feared Iran would trigger a similar revolution there. Iraq also sought control over strategic and oil-rich territories. The war raged from 1980 – 1990.

SAMPLE QUESTIONS

15) Which of the following was a weakness of the Schlieffen Plan?
    A. It overstretched the German army.
    B. It failed to anticipate a stronger resistance in France.
    C. It underestimated Russia's ability to mobilize its troops.
    D. all of the above

    Answer:
    D. **Correct.** All of the answer choices are true.

16) According to the Sykes-Picot Agreement,
    A. Israel would become an independent state.
    B. Husayn ibn Ali would become Caliph.
    C. Ataturk would lead an independent Turkey.
    D. Palestine would be under international supervision.

    Answer:
    D. **Correct.** Sykes-Picot put Palestine under the supervision of various international powers.

17) Which of the following led to the rise of the Nazis in early 1930s Germany?
    A. the impact of reparations and the support of German industrialists
    B. the impact of the Great Depression and the support of the workers
    C. support from the international communist movement and the impact of reparations on the German economy
    D. support from German industrialists and strong backing from other political factions in the Reichstag

    Answer:
    A. **Correct.** The Nazis planned to cease paying reparations, so their nationalist approach appealed to many Germans suffering from the hyperinflation that reparations had triggered. Furthermore, the

Nazis had the support of German industrialists, who feared the rise of communism among the working classes.

18) **The Cold War was rooted in**
    A. Stalin's unwillingness to cede control of East Berlin to the allies following the fall of the Nazis.
    B. the erection of the Berlin Wall.
    C. Stalin's failure to honor the agreement at Yalta, installing communist regimes in Eastern Europe rather than permitting free, democratic elections.
    D. the Cuban Missile Crisis.

    Answer:
    C. Correct. The Cold War was rooted in Stalin's creation of communist satellite states in Eastern and Central Europe.

19) **Which of the following precipitated the end of the Cold War?**
    A. the Iran Hostage Crisis
    B. the Soviet War in Afghanistan
    C. the Iran-Iraq War
    D. the Yom Kippur War

    Answer:
    B. Correct. The Soviet invasion of Afghanistan and the subsequent ten-year war sapped Soviet financial and military resources—and morale. This draining war, plus the high price of the arms race with the United States, contributed significantly to the fall of the Soviet Union.

POST-COLD WAR WORLD

In 1991, the Soviet Union fell when Soviet Premier **Mikhail Gorbachev**, who had implemented reforms like ***glasnost*** and ***perestroika*** (or *openness* and *transparency*), was nearly overthrown in a coup; a movement led by **Boris Yeltsin**, who had been elected president of Russia, stopped the coup. The USSR was dissolved later that year and Yeltsin became president of the Russian Federation. War in Afghanistan and military overspending in an effort to keep up with American military spending had weakened the USSR to the point of collapse, and the Cold War ended.

COLD WAR CONSEQUENCES

In 1990, Saddam Hussein, the leader of Iraq, invaded Kuwait, threatening the global oil supply. In response, the United States and other countries went to war—with a

UN mandate—to regain control of the world's petroleum reserves. The **Gulf War** cemented the US status as the sole superpower.

The changes following the fall of the Iron Curtain led to instability in the Balkans. In 1992, Bosnia declared its independence from the collapsing state of Yugoslavia. Violence broke out, and the **Bosnian War** raged from 1992 to 1995, resulting another European genocide—this time, of Bosnian Muslims.

Also following the Cold War, proxy wars throughout the world and instability in former colonies continued. In 1994, conflict in Central Africa resulted in the **Rwandan Genocide**. In **Zaire**, the country descended into instability following the fall of **Mobutu Sese Seko**, the US-supported dictator, in 1997.

In the 1980s, drought in the Horn of Africa led to widespread famine. The general public became more concerned about providing foreign aid to the suffering. In 1991 **Somalia** was broken up under the control of various warlords and clans; civilians suffered from starvation and violence even after a failed military intervention led by the United States. To this day there is no central government in much of Somalia.

COOPERATION AND CONFLICT

Following the end of the Cold War and post-decolonization, the balance of economic and political power began to change. The **G-20**, the world's twenty most important economic and political powers, includes many former colonies and non-European countries. The **BRICS**—Brazil, Russia, India, China, and South Africa—are recognized as world economic and political leaders.

Steps toward European unification had begun as early as the 1950s; the **European Union**, as it is known today, was formed in 1992. As the former Soviet satellite states moved from communism to more democratic societies and capitalistic economies, more countries partnered with the EU and eventually joined it, with twenty-eight members in 2015 and more in negotiations to join. However, European populism and rejection of globalism is rising: the United Kingdom voted to withdraw from the EU in 2016.

European Union countries remain independent, but they cooperate in international affairs, justice, security and foreign policy, environmental matters, and economic policy. Many also share a common currency, the **euro**.

Continental integration exists beyond Europe. In Africa, the **African Union** is a forum for African countries to organize and align political, military, economic, and other policies. It also organizes peacekeeping missions.

Globalization opened international markets through free-trade agreements like **NAFTA** (the North American Free Trade Agreement) and **Mercosur** (the South American free-trade zone). The **World Trade Organization** oversees international trade. Technological advances like improvements in transportation infrastructure and the **internet** made international communication faster, easier and cheaper.

However, more open borders, reliable international transportation, and faster, easier worldwide communication brought risks, too. The United States was attacked by terrorists on **September 11, 2001**, resulting in thousands of civilian casualties.

Following the attacks on 9/11, the United States attacked Afghanistan as part of the **War on Terror**. Afghanistan's radical Islamist **Taliban** government was providing shelter to the group that took responsibility for the attacks, **al Qaeda**. Led by **Osama bin Laden**, al Qaeda was inspired by Islamism and also by the radical Wahhabism of the Saudis. Bin Laden was killed by the United States in 2011 and control of Afghan security was turned over to the Afghan government in 2014, but the US still maintains a strong military presence in the country.

> **DID YOU KNOW?**
>
> While benefits of international trade include lower prices and more consumer choice, unemployment often increases in more developed countries, and labor and environmental violations are more likely in developing countries.

The Iraq War began in 2003 when the US invaded that country under the faulty premise that Saddam Hussein's regime was involved with al Qaeda and possessed weapons of mass destruction intended for terrorism. The war resulted in thousands of civilian and military casualties, destabilizing the region.

Elsewhere in the Middle East, reform movements began via the 2011 **Arab Spring**. Some dictatorial regimes have been replaced with democratic governments; other countries still experience limited freedoms or even civil unrest. In Syria, unrest erupted into an ongoing civil war. One consequence has been enormous movements of refugees into Europe, a factor in some Europeans' rejection of globalism.

Today, the Islamic State of Iraq and al Sham (**ISIS**) referring to Iraq and Syria (or Islamic State of Iraq and the Levant—ISIL) has arisen. ISIS has established a de facto state in Iraq and Syria with extremist Islamist policies and presents a global terror threat.

SAMPLE QUESTIONS

20) While immediately after the fall of the Soviet Union the US emerged as the sole superpower, in the twenty-first century, which phenomenon has so far characterized global governance?

    A. international terrorism
    B. international economic and political organizations
    C. international conflict
    D. the European Union

    Answer:

    B. Correct. While the United States remains a leading world power, the emergence of international organizations like the BRICS, the EU, the G-20, and the AU has empowered other countries; furthermore, international trade agreements are helping mold the international balance of power.

21) **What was one reason for the Bosnian War?**
    A. attacks by Bosniak Islamic extremists
    B. the dissolution of Yugoslavia
    C. the separation of Yugoslavia from the USSR
    D. attacks by Middle Eastern Islamic extremists

    Answer:
    B. **Correct.** One reason for the Bosnian War was the Yugoslav government's attempt to force the country to stay together; following the end of the Cold War and the collapse of communism, the formerly communist Yugoslavia had started to break up.

22) **What is one major role that the African Union plays?**
    A. The AU is a free trade area.
    B. The AU manages a single currency.
    C. The AU manages several peacekeeping forces.
    D. The AU represents individual African countries in international diplomacy.

    Answer:
    C. **Correct.** The AU organizes and manages peacekeeping forces in Africa; it also cooperates with the United Nations in peacekeeping.

23) **Which of the following is NOT a reason that the Soviet Union collapsed?**
    A. glasnost
    B. perestroika
    C. the war in Afghanistan
    D. the rise of the Taliban

    Answer:
    D. **Correct.** The Taliban did not emerge in Afghanistan until well after Soviet withdrawal from the country.

24) **Despite his alliance with the US-supported *mujahideen* in the war in Afghanistan against the Soviets, Osama bin Laden sponsored attacks against the United States because**
    A. he opposed a US military presence in Saudi Arabia.
    B. he opposed US support of Israel.
    C. he wanted to establish a global Islamist regime in accordance with the extremist, unorthodox beliefs rooted in Wahhabism.
    D. all of the above

    Answer:
    D. **Correct.** Bin Laden cited all of these reasons for his violent acts.

Government

POLITICAL THEORY

FUNDAMENTAL CONCEPTS IN POLITICAL THEORY

There are two basic reasons for government: to provide law and order, and to protect people from conflicts. To prevent and settle disputes between individuals, concrete rules of governance must be established. All formal governments require internal and external recognition of their authority.

Recognition from outside governments comes in the form of **sovereignty**, the right of a group to be free of outside interference. A group is sovereign when others outside of the group respect its right to govern its own affairs. Sovereignty can exist at different levels and to different degrees. For example, the United States has complete national sovereignty because other nations recognize the US government's right to rule its own people and manage its own affairs. Any attempt by another country to impose rules or regulate internal conflict would be viewed as a violation. Many wars have begun based on conflicts over sovereignty.

An organization like the National Rifle Association, on the other hand, has limited sovereignty. It is subject to state and federal laws and oversight. It has the right to make some rules regarding its own internal affairs. However, that level of sovereignty is limited; those rules may not interfere with those of the larger society. The sovereignty of groups—and more specifically of states—is an ongoing question within the United States.

Internal recognition of a government's authority is called its **legitimacy**, or the people's acceptance of their government's authority. If the people within the group do not believe in the government's right to power, it cannot function. Legitimacy has many sources, depending on the type of government: God, military might, or the people themselves. If a government loses its legitimacy, it cannot continue.

For example, during the Age of Reason rationality undermined popular belief in divine right (the idea that the king was chosen by God), destroying the legitimacy of the French monarchy. This allowed the unrest brewing in France to erupt in the French Revolution. Similarly, the Confederate states in the US South broke away from the Union at the beginning of the Civil War because they believed the federal government no longer represented them and was therefore illegitimate. A loss of legitimacy is at the center of every failed government and state.

SAMPLE QUESTIONS

1) Which of the following is NOT an example of the US protecting its national sovereignty?

   A. declaration of war after the bombing of Pearl Harbor
   B. signing of the Treaty of Paris at the end of the Revolutionary War
   C. President Eisenhower sending troops to Little Rock, Arkansas to integrate the schools
   D. patrolling the US-Mexico border

   Answer:

   C. **Correct.** In Little Rock, the governor of Arkansas refused to enforce the Supreme Court-ordered integration of public schools. President Eisenhower sent troops to Little Rock to enforce national authority over a noncompliant state. This was an internal matter, not a matter of state sovereignty.

2) Which of the following is an example of a legitimate government?

   A. the German Federal Republic in the 1990s
   B. the Dole government in Hawaii in the 1890s
   C. Mexican rule of Texas in the 1830s
   D. the rule of Maximilian I in Mexico in the 1860s

   Answer:

   A. **Correct.** Both former West and East German citizens recognized the newly unified German Federal Republic as the legal and political authority over both territories. Bringing the national capital back to Berlin legitimized the government in the eyes of the East, while maintaining the western currency and many western laws did so in the West.

Major Political Theorists

Our understanding of government today is based upon the ideas of key political theorists. Each questioned the purpose of government and came to different conclusions. While there are many significant theorists, the most important to note follow on the next page.

Niccolo Machiavelli (1469–1527) is best known for his work *The Prince*. He argues that public morality and private or personal morality are two very different ideas. According to Machiavelli, a good ruler understands that sometimes immoral acts are necessary for the public good. He also argued that legitimacy derives from power; therefore a leader's top priority is maintaining power at all costs. While some later readers have argued that *The Prince* was written as satire or hyperbole, its ideas guided Western politics for the next 400 years.

John Locke (1632–1704) was one of the most influential Enlightenment thinkers. His philosophical writings strongly influenced the American and French Revolutions, and he is responsible for many of the foundational ideas of American government. Locke argued that, by nature, all men (women were not widely considered as political actors) are free and equal and endowed with certain natural rights: life, liberty, and property. Thus he challenged the traditional view that men were bound by God to obey a monarchy, and instead argued that government was a natural outgrowth of the desire of individuals to protect their natural rights. Because of this desire, men relinquish some individual sovereignty to a neutral party (a government) which is responsible for maximizing the individual enjoyment of rights and serving the public good. As a result, a government's legitimacy derives from the consent of the people. Furthermore, when a government is no longer fulfilling its purpose and loses the people's consent, revolution is an appropriate and justified response. John Locke was not the first to consider this idea, also known as the **social contract**, but his conception of it strongly impacted later thinkers and is fundamental to the modern republic.

Baron de Montesquieu (1689–1755) is best known for his philosophical contributions to the political structure of the United States. Montesquieu wrote about the importance of balance of power in the success of a republic. He advocated for divided government: the **separation of powers**. Using Britain as his model, he argued that the most effective governments divided power among three different bodies or branches. He believed that powers should be equal, but differ in nature. Separation of powers, using a three-branch structure, is the central organizing principle of the American government.

Jean-Jacques Rousseau (1712–1778) extended the idea of the social contract in his work entitled *The Social Contract*. Like Locke, Rousseau believed that government was a natural extension of the individual's desire to protect and best enjoy their natural rights. However, Locke observed that such governments would inevitably be imbalanced and class based, as those with more resources protected their own rights at the expense of others. Eventually, a government would be overturned in revolution once the majority no longer recognized its legitimacy. Rousseau, instead, argued for government built on the **rule of law**. Rousseau argued that a common will exists, and it should be the basis of all laws. As a result, laws would apply to and benefit all equally, assuring stability. Rule of law was another Enlightenment idea which became a central tenet of the United States government.

Alexis de Tocqueville (1805–1859) is best known for his work *Democracy in America*. Published in 1835, it chronicled his travels throughout the United States and his political analysis of the young country. He celebrated the democratic underpinnings he saw in America—the emphasis on hard work and merit. However, he also believed that inequality drove economic growth and that "radical equality" led to mediocrity. De Tocqueville's writings are often referenced as an accurate and detailed analysis of the early stages of American democracy.

SAMPLE QUESTIONS

3) Which political theorist argued for the separation of powers?

   A. Jean-Jacques Rousseau
   B. Baron de Montesquieu
   C. John Locke
   D. Alexis de Tocqueville

   Answer:
   B. **Correct.** Montesquieu believed that the separation of powers into three branches of government was essential to the success of a republic.

4) The Declaration of Independence was most greatly influenced by which political theorist?

   A. John Locke
   B. Jean-Jacques Rousseau
   C. Niccolo Machiavelli
   D. Alexis de Tocqueville

   Answer:
   A. **Correct.** The inalienable rights described in the Declaration of Independence are a direct reference to the natural rights described by John Locke.

5) Which best describes social contract theory?

   A. Government is a necessary evil to provide order for the people.
   B. Government is an agreement between the ruler and subjects.
   C. Government exists as a promise to the people.
   D. Government exists at the will of the people.

   Answer:
   D. **Correct.** Social contract theory argues that government is the natural consequence of individuals' attempts to protect their natural rights. Individuals willingly relinquish some sovereignty to a governing body to maximize enjoyment of their rights. The people can remove the government if it does not serve its purpose.

6) **Which of the following is NOT true or consistent with Machiavelli's argument in *The Prince*?**

    A.   For a ruler to maintain power, the ends always justify the means.

    B.   Divine right is essential for a monarch to maintain legitimacy.

    C.   *The Prince* provides a blueprint for gaining and keeping power.

    D.   Rulers should not be judged by moral standards.

Answer:

    B.   **Correct.** Machiavelli was a pragmatist rather than a theorist. His writing focused on the best way for actual rulers to govern, rather than on determining the philosophical sources of their right to rule.

POLITICAL ORIENTATIONS

In modern government, political ideology can be sorted into two main categories: liberal and conservative. In the United States, liberals generally have a more expansive view of government, whereas conservatives have a more restrictive view.

Liberals (or *the left*) believe in the power and responsibility of government to effect positive change. They see the government as an effective protector of and provider for its citizens. As a result, liberals generally support a government that actively regulates the economy and implements extensive social programs. For example, liberals would advocate for a national healthcare system. Today, they support decreasing military spending and intervention, although they often make exceptions for humanitarian purposes. (Until the Vietnam War, liberals more typically favored overseas intervention to fight communism.) They believe the government should not curtail the rights of its citizens, and support the existence of implied rights like the right to privacy.

Conservatives (or *the right*) believe in the power and responsibility of the individual and private sector to effect positive change. They see the government as an ineffective agent of social change and believe its reach should be limited. They believe that government should only interfere in society to enable the individual or private entity to better operate. They support free-market solutions to economic problems and decreasing business regulations. They generally oppose government-run social programs, believing the free market is more efficient. For instance, most conservatives would believe a national healthcare system would lead to a decrease in the quality of care. They believe military power is necessary to maintain national sovereignty, so they advocate increased military spending and tend to be quicker to commit troops abroad.

While the liberal-conservative dichotomy generally covers opposing political ideologies in American politics, it is simplistic. Many American politicians are **moderates**. Moderates hold some views from each side of the spectrum. For example, a moderate might support increased military spending, but also support some social programs.

There are also extreme ideologies on the spectrum. On the far left, **socialists** advocate for a complete overhaul of the American economic and political system. They believe that the free market creates inequality, and that the market should be closely controlled by government to eliminate that inequality. They also advocate far-reaching government-run programs from healthcare to schools to utilities.

Libertarians, on the far right, support an extremely limited government. They do not support government programs of any kind and believe a completely unfettered market is most efficient and effective. They also believe the government should not intervene to curtail or protect individual rights. Their ideal government would undertake only the most basic tasks in order to ensure the functioning of the nation.

SAMPLE QUESTIONS

7) Which of the following would most likely be supported by liberals?

   A. an open trade agreement with China
   B. funding a new stealth bomber
   C. a law restricting the use of national forests
   D. vouchers for students to attend private schools

   Answer:

   C. **Correct.** Protection of the environment is a central liberal goal. Because liberals believe government should improve society, they believe the government must protect nature for its citizens.

8) Which of the following would a libertarian vote for, but not a liberal?

   A. regulation of business
   B. abortion rights
   C. criminal rights
   D. lower taxes

   Answer:

   D. **Correct.** A libertarian would certainly support lower taxes and would likely argue for their repeal. Taxes are collected to support government activity, most of which is opposed by libertarians. A liberal, however, would oppose lowering taxes, as liberals support a larger government role in society.

Constitutional Underpinnings of the US Government

Any study of the United States government must begin with its founding document: the Constitution. It was written as both an expression of ideals and as a practical framework for the functioning of the country. Designed to be a "living document," the Constitution and how it is interpreted has changed in the almost 230 years since it was written. However, its core principles have not. They continue to serve as the foundation and guiding light of American government and politics.

Still, it is important to understand that the Constitution was a product of the time in which it was written. The ideals that inform it grew directly out of the Enlightenment, and the governing structure it created was in direct response to both colonial discontent under Britain and problems faced by the new republic. In order to understand the government that emerged, it is necessary to understand this context.

Historical Context of the Constitution

In 1781, the Second Continental Congress convened to organize a government for the emerging nation. The colonies had broken away from Britain because of what they viewed as the oppressive rule of an overbearing central government. Therefore they intentionally designed a weak government under the framework of the Articles of Confederation. The Articles created a loose confederation of the future thirteen states, allowing them to retain considerable individual sovereignty.

The Articles established a **unicameral legislature** (only one house) with extremely limited authority. The Congress of the Confederation, as it was called, did not have the power to levy taxes or raise an army. Any laws had to be passed by a two-thirds vote, and any changes to the Articles had to be passed unanimously—essentially an impossible feat. The legislature was subordinate to the states. Representatives were selected and paid by state legislatures.

It quickly became clear that this government was too weak to be effective, and by 1787 the United States was in crisis. Unable to levy taxes, the federal government remained in debt from the war. In addition, without an organizing authority, states began issuing their own currencies and crafting competing trade agreements with foreign nations, halting trade and sending inflation through the roof. Without a national judicial system, there was no mechanism to solve economic disputes.

Discontent was particularly strong among farmers, who were losing their property. In 1786, Daniel Shays led a rebellion against Massachusetts tax collectors and banks. Unable to raise an army, the Congress of the Confederation was powerless to intervene. The rebellion was finally suppressed when citizens of Boston contributed funds to raise a state militia. **Shays' Rebellion** made it clear that the new government was unable to maintain order.

SAMPLE QUESTIONS

9) Why did the framers of the Articles of Confederation create a decentralized political system?

   A. to cancel the debts the states owed from the Revolution
   B. to prevent abuses of power like those that existed under British rule did not exist
   C. to delay the question of slavery
   D. to promote national sovereignty

   Answer:

   B. Correct. The perceived tyranny of Britain's rule was fresh on the minds of the framers. Their primary goal was to prevent it from re-emerging.

10) Which of the following ideas most influenced the framers of the Articles of Confederation?

    A. In order to have the consent of the people, all people must be allowed to vote.
    B. Three separate and balanced branches of government are essential for the protection of liberty.
    C. The central government's primary authority should be in monitoring trade.
    D. A strong central government threatens the liberty of the people.

    Answer:

    D. Correct. Fear of an overpowering central government was the primary factor considered in writing the Articles of Confederation.

11) Shays' Rebellion was considered a crisis of government because

    A. people were previously unaware of the amount of debt that remained from the Revolution.
    B. it illustrated the national government's inability to maintain order.
    C. it allowed foreign intervention in American affairs.
    D. civil liberties were once again threatened as they had been under British rule.

    Answer:

    B. Correct. The inability of the federal government to suppress the rebellion showed a major weakness in the new government.

12) Which of the following groups had the most to gain from a revision of the Articles of Confederation?

   A. small farmers
   B. members of state legislatures
   C. women
   D. merchants

   Answer:

   D. Correct. The Articles of Confederation lacked clear laws governing intrastate and international commerce, harming the merchants who relied on trade for income.

ENLIGHTENMENT IDEAS

Several key elements of the Enlightenment are reflected in the Constitution.

Rule of Law: In a nation ruled by law, governance is based on a body of written, or otherwise codified, law (such as the Constitution). No individual can make a governing decision in conflict with those laws.

Reason: The Constitution is a document based on reason. It lays out the structure of government and aims to limit government while still allowing it to fulfill its function. It also insists that governing decisions are made outside the scope of religion by actively separating the two.

Social Contract: The founders believed that government was a social contract, legitimized only by the consent of the people. This is also known as **popular sovereignty**. The Constitution protects individual liberty, life, and property.

Social Progress: Enlightenment thinkers believed in social progress. Therefore, the Constitution can be changed, allowing it to progress with the nation it governs.

SAMPLE QUESTIONS

13) Which of the following aspects of the Constitution reflects the social contract philosophy?

   A. the presidential cabinet
   B. checks and balances
   C. judicial review
   D. direct election of representatives

   Answer:

   D. Correct. The Constitution provides for the direct election of representatives to Congress. By selecting their leaders, the people grant them the authority to make governing decisions.

14) Which of the following best demonstrates the rule of law?
   A. The president and members of Congress can be charged with crimes.
   B. A government passes a law raising taxes, but later it does not require the wealthy to pay.
   C. Congress passes a law declaring the Constitution null and void.
   D. A king sentences his rival to death.

Answer:
   A. **Correct.** Those in authority are subject to punishment if they do not respect rule of law.

THE CONSTITUTION

A convention of the states was called to address problems in the young United States. At the **Constitutional Convention** in 1787, the old Articles were discarded in favor of a new governing document. There were five main goals for the new Constitution:

1. the protection of property
2. granting increased, but limited, power to the federal government
3. the protection of and limitations on majority rule
4. the protection of individual rights
5. the creation of a flexible framework for government

Each of these reflect the desire to balance authority and liberty. It is this balance that is at the core of the framework of the American government.

STRUCTURE OF THE FEDERAL GOVERNMENT

The crises of the 1780s made it clear that a stronger central government was needed. However, states did not want a central government that was strong enough to oppress the states or the people. The solution? Increase the power of the government, but prevent the concentration of power by dividing it.

The new Constitution reorganized the federal government into three branches—executive, judicial, and legislative—in keeping with Montesquieu's **separation of powers**. Each branch was given powers to limit the power of the other branches in a system called **checks and balances**. For example:

- The executive branch—via the role of president—has the power to veto (reject) laws passed by the legislature.
- The legislative branch can override the president's veto (with a two-thirds vote) and pass the law anyway.
- The judicial branch can determine the constitutionality of laws (**judicial review**).

The president has the power to appoint justices to the federal courts (including the Supreme Court), and the legislative branch—via the Senate—has the power to approve or reject presidential appointments.

The legislative branch also has the power to indict, try, and determine the guilt of a president for treason, bribery, and other "high crimes and misdemeanors." While not specifically defined in the Constitution, these are traditionally understood to be crimes such as perjury, abuse of power, misuse of funds, and dereliction of duty, specific to office holders.

The separation of powers did not address the relationship between the federal government and the states. Under the Articles, the federal government was completely beholden to the states for its very existence. However, it was clear that complete state sovereignty did not work. Instead, the Constitution created a **federal** relationship between the two levels of government. **Federalism** is a system in which both the state government and federal government retain sovereignty by dividing up the areas for which they are responsible.

Under the Constitution, the federal government handles matters that concern the population at large: for example, managing federal lands, coining money, and maintaining an army and navy. It also settles conflicts between the states via the federal judiciary and by regulating interstate trade. Matters of regional or local concern are handled by state or local governments. This relationship is best codified in the Tenth Amendment, which states that any powers not explicitly given to the federal government are reserved for the states. However, according to the **supremacy clause** (Article VI, Clause 2) the Constitution is the "supreme law of the land." Therefore, in cases of conflict between the states and the federal government, the federal government's authority generally supersedes that of the states.

The division of power has shifted over time. As the scope of the federal government has expanded, so too has its power. The federal government can also exert influence over state governments through **grant-in-aid**, money that is provided for a specific purpose, by attaching conditions to the funding. For example, grant-in-aid was given to the states in the late 1970s for highway improvement. However, states that accepted the money were required to set the drinking age at twenty-one years. In this way, the federal government influenced law that was technically beyond its purview.

SAMPLE QUESTIONS

15) **In the American federal system of government, the state governments' power derives from**

    A. the Constitution.
    B. the people of that state.
    C. the state legislatures.
    D. the people of the nation.

Answer:

B. Correct. Each state government is a democratic republic in which authority is derived from the consent of the governed.

16) Which of the following best illustrates the system of checks and balances?
    A. state and federal government power to levy taxes
    B. a governor's right to send the National Guard in a crisis
    C. the Senate's power to approve treaties signed by the president
    D. Congress's power to censure its members

Answer:

C. Correct. With the authority to approve treaties, the Senate can review and even restrain presidential foreign policy.

Structures and Powers of the Federal Government

In its original form, the federal government consisted of the three branches. Almost immediately upon the ratification of the Constitution, it began to grow and now includes a massive bureaucracy of departments and agencies.

Types of Powers

Governmental powers in the Constitution can be divided into six types:

Expressed Powers: Also known as **enumerated powers**, these are powers that are specifically granted to the federal government only. An example of an expressed power is the power to make treaties with foreign nations.

Implied Powers: These are powers the federal government has that are not in the Constitution. They derive from the elastic clause of the Constitution, Article I, Section 8. The **elastic clause** gives Congress the right to "make all laws necessary and proper" for carrying out other powers. For example, as new technologies like radio and television emerged, implied powers expanded the commerce clause to allow the federal government to regulate them.

The idea of implied powers was supported by the Supreme Court in *McCulloch v. Maryland* (1819). The state of Maryland tried to tax the Maryland branch of the Bank of the United States. When the bank refused to pay the tax, the case landed in the Maryland Court of Appeals; the court ruled that the Bank of the United States was unconstitutional, as the Constitution did not expressly give the federal government the power to operate a bank. Later, the Supreme Court overturned the ruling, citing the elastic clause.

Reserved Powers: These are powers that are held by the states through the Tenth Amendment, which states that all powers not expressly given to the federal government belong to the states. For example, the management of public education is a reserved power.

Inherent Powers: These are powers that derive specifically from US sovereignty and are inherent to its existence as a nation. For example, the powers to make treaties and to wage war are both inherent powers.

Concurrent Powers: These are powers that are shared equally by both the national and state government. The power to tax and the power to establish courts are both concurrent powers.

Prohibited Powers: These are powers that are denied to both the national government and the state governments. Passing bills of attainder (laws that declare someone guilty without a trial) is a prohibited power.

SAMPLE QUESTIONS

17) The power to coin money is an example of a(n)
    A. inherent power.
    B. prohibited power.
    C. concurrent power.
    D. expressed power.

    Answer:
    D. **Correct.** Article I of the Constitution states that Congress has the power to coin money.

18) The power to hold elections is an example of a(n)
    A. inherent power.
    B. prohibited power.
    C. concurrent power.
    D. expressed power.

    Answer:
    C. **Correct.** Federal, state, and local governments all have the authority to hold elections.

THE LEGISLATIVE BRANCH

At the writing of the Constitution, the branch of the federal government endowed with the most power was the legislative branch. Simply called **Congress**, this branch is composed of a bicameral legislature (two houses). Based on the British model, most colonies—and then states—had bicameral legislatures with an upper and lower house. While this structure was not originally adopted under the Articles of Confederation, the framers chose it when reorganizing the government. This was in large part due to a dispute at the convention over the structure of the legislative body—specifically the voting power of each state.

Small states advocated equal representation, with each state having the same number of representatives, each with one vote. Called the **New Jersey Plan**, this plan distributed decision-making power equally between the states, regardless of land mass or population. The more populous states found this system to be unfair. Instead, they argued for a plan called the **Virginia Plan**, based on **proportional representation**. Each state would be assigned a number of representatives based on its population (enslaved people deprived of their rights would even be counted, benefiting those states with large slave populations). In the end, the **Great Compromise** was reached. There would be two houses: the **House of Representatives** (the lower house) would have proportional representation, and the **Senate** (the upper house) would have equal representation.

This system had two other advantages. The House of Representatives would also be directly elected by the people, and the Senate by the state legislatures. This supported the federal structure of the government: one house would serve the needs of the people directly, and the other would serve the needs of the states. Also, it curbed federal power by fragmenting it and slowing down the legislative process.

POWERS OF CONGRESS

Article I of the Constitution outlines the structure and powers of Congress. As the most representative branch of government, the legislative branch was designed to be the most powerful. Hence, it has more expressed powers than the executive or judicial branches. In Section Eight of the Constitution, eighteen clauses list specific peacetime and war powers:

Table 3.1. Powers of Congress

Clause	Peacetime Powers	Clause	War Powers
1	To establish and collect taxes, duties, and excises	11	To declare war; to make laws regarding people captured on land and water
2	To borrow money	12	To raise and support armies
3	To regulate foreign and interstate commerce	13	To provide and maintain a navy
4	To create naturalization laws; to create bankruptcy laws	14	To make laws governing land and naval forces
5	To coin money and regulate its value; to regulate weights and measures	15	To provide for summoning the militia to execute federal laws, suppress uprisings, and repel invasions

Clause	Peacetime Powers	Clause	War Powers
6	To punish counterfeiters of federal money	16	To provide for organizing, arming, and disciplining the militia and governing it when in the service of the Union
7	To establish post offices and roads		
8	To grant patents and copyrights		
9	To create federal courts below the Supreme Court		
10	To define and punish crimes at sea; to define violations of international law		
17	To exercise exclusive jurisdiction over Washington, DC and other federal properties		
18	To make all laws necessary and proper to the execution of the other expressed powers (the elastic clause)		

SAMPLE QUESTIONS

19) **Congress was similar to the Congress of the Confederation in that**

   A. both were designed to be slow moving and deliberative.
   B. both represented the states only.
   C. both held very limited powers.
   D. both were unicameral.

   Answer:

   A. **Correct.** While Congress was designed to be more efficient and effective than the Congress of the Confederation, it was still divided into two houses with complicated structures to prevent consolidation of power through quick legislation.

20) **Which of the following congressional powers was a direct response to the failings of the Articles of Confederation?**

   A. the power to grant patents
   B. the power to make laws governing land forces
   C. the power to levy taxes
   D. the power to declare war

Answer:

C. Correct. An inability to levy taxes crippled the first federal government, making it unable to pay off its debt or function in any legitimate way.

HOUSE OF REPRESENTATIVES

The **House of Representatives** was designed to directly represent the people, and it was originally the only part of the federal government that was directly elected by the citizens. It is the larger of the houses; the number of representatives from each state is based on that state's population (**proportional representation**). Every state is guaranteed at least one representative. Apportionment of representatives is based on the census, so seats are reapportioned every ten years with the new census.

At the convention, the larger Southern states argued that their (non-voting) slave populations should count towards their overall population, therefore entitling them to more representatives. Northern states with few slaves disagreed. This issue was settled with the **Three-Fifths Compromise**. Each slave would be counted as three-fifths of a person for the purpose of the census. (Women, who could not vote until the ratification of the Nineteenth Amendment, were also counted in the census.)

The size of the House grew every ten years along with the population of the United States until 1929, when Congress set the number at 435 voting representatives. Today, each member of Congress represents approximately 700,000 people. Residents of Washington, DC and the US territories of Guam, American Samoa, and the US Virgin Islands are represented by non-voting observers; Puerto Rico is represented by a resident commissioner.

Each state legislature divides its state into congressional districts of approximately equal population. Political parties may battle in an attempt to draw the lines to ensure the maximum number of seats for their party. This is called **gerrymandering**. The Supreme Court has made several rulings to limit gerrymandering, including requiring each district to have equal population and contiguous or connected lines. It is also unconstitutional to draw lines based solely on race.

Members of the House of Representatives are elected for two-year terms to keep them beholden to the people. According to the Constitution, candidates must be at least twenty-five years old, have been a US citizen for at least seven years, and live in the state they are representing at the time of the election. The leader of the House is called the **Speaker of the House**. He or she is the leader of the majority party in the House.

Although it is technically considered the lower house, there are still **specific powers** that belong only to the House of Representatives:

- All revenue bills must start in the house. While the Senate may amend the bills, the framers wanted to keep budgetary power in the hands of the house most beholden to the people.

- The House may bring charges of **impeachment** against the president or a Supreme Court justice. Impeachment is the process by which a federal official can be officially charged with a crime. If found guilty, the official is removed from office. This followed the British model in which the House of Commons (the lower house) had the power to impeach, and the House of Lords (upper house) heard arguments and decided. In order to impeach a president or justice, a simple majority is required. Only Presidents Andrew Johnson and Bill Clinton have been impeached.
- The House must choose the president if there is no majority in the Electoral College. The House has only selected the president once: in 1824, Andrew Jackson, John Quincy Adams, and Henry Clay split the electoral vote. Jackson had the plurality (the greatest percentage), but did not win a majority. The vote went to the House, which elected John Quincy Adams.

THE SENATE

The **Senate** was designed to be the house of the states. To signify that no one state is more important than any other, representation in the Senate is apportioned equally, with two senators per state, making a total of 100 senators. Representatives were originally chosen by the state legislatures; there was no direct connection between the Senate and the people.

However, as the power of the federal government grew, the people increasingly came to think of it as representative of themselves rather than of the states. Corrupt state legislatures sold Senate seats to the highest bidder rather than electing the most qualified individual. Political machinations led to deadlocks in state legislatures over appointments, leaving Senate seats vacant for months at time. The Senate seemed a corrupt institution of the elite, disconnected from the democratic process. In 1913, the **Seventeenth Amendment** to the Constitution was ratified; it required the direct election of senators by the people of a state.

As the upper house, the Senate was designed to have greater autonomy than the House of Representatives. Thus, there are stricter requirements for candidacy. To be a senator, candidates must be at least thirty years old, have been a citizen of the United States for nine years, and—at the time of the election—live in the state they will represent.

Senators are elected for six-year terms, giving them time to make decisions that might be unpopular but in the best interest of the nation. Elections are staggered in three groups: one group of senators is up for election every two years. This ensures that all senators do not face re-election at the same time, allowing for more consistent governance.

The president of the Senate is the US vice president. However, he or she only has the power to vote in case of a tie. The vice president is often absent from the

Senate, in which case the **president pro tempore** presides. He or she is generally the longest-serving member of the Senate.

Much like the House, the Senate has certain unique powers:

- Whereas the House has the power to impeach, the Senate acts as the *jury* in the impeachment of a president, determining his or her guilt. To remove a president from office, the Senate must vote two-thirds in favor. This has never happened in American history.
- The Senate approves executive appointments and appointments to federal positions in the judicial system. These include members of the Supreme Court and other federal courts, the attorney general, cabinet members, and ambassadors.
- The Senate approves (ratifies) all treaties signed by the president.

SAMPLE QUESTIONS

21) Why did the framers give the House of Representatives the power to start revenue bills?

   A. Based on their qualifications, members of the House would have more economic knowledge.
   B. Members of the House would be less influenced by outside forces and political parties than members of the Senate.
   C. The House was more truly a national legislature; therefore, it should be in charge of the national budget.
   D. The frequency of elections for House of Representatives would make them more responsive to the will of the people in terms of spending.

   Answer:
   D. **Correct.** The framers thought it was important that those who spent the money be held most accountable to the people to avoid corruption and misuse.

22) Which of the following is NOT an example of how the Senate represents the states?

   A. the power to approve treaties
   B. equal representation of each state in the Senate
   C. vice president serves as president of the Senate
   D. selection of senators by state legislatures (before 1913)

   Answer:
   C. **Correct.** The vice president's role in the Senate has nothing to do with the influence of states on the national government. Instead, it is a way for the executive branch to check the legislative.

LAWMAKING

The primary function of the legislature is to write and pass laws. The process is intentionally cumbersome and complicated. The framers of the Constitution believed that the longer the process took, the more deliberation there would be, decreasing the risk of abuse of power.

Approximately 5,000 bills are introduced in Congress each year, only 2.5 percent of which become laws. There are no restrictions on who can write a bill. In fact, most are not written by Congress, but begin either in the executive branch or are written by special interest groups. A member of Congress is required, however, to introduce the bill. With the exception of revenue bills, bills can start in either house. Since the two houses have parallel processes, the same bill often starts in both houses at the same time.

Once it is placed in the "hopper," the bill is assigned a number and sent to the appropriate committee. Committees and their subcommittees are where most of the hard work of lawmaking is accomplished. Here bills are read, debated, and revised. It is also where most bills die, by either being **tabled** (put aside) in subcommittee or committee, or by being voted down. If a bill does get voted out of committee, it goes to the floor for debate. In the House of Representatives, the powerful **Rules Committee** not only determines which bills make it to the floor for debate, but also sets time limits for debate on each bill.

In the Senate, debate is unlimited. This allows for a unique tactic called the **filibuster**, in which a senator or group of senators continues debate indefinitely to delay the passage of a bill. Sixty votes are needed to end a filibuster, so to prevent one, senators often attempt to gather at least sixty votes for a bill before it comes to the floor.

After debate has ended, the members of each house vote on the bill. If it passes out of both houses, it moves to the **Conference Committee** which must transform the two draft bills into one. Then the unified bill returns to both houses for a final vote. If it passes, it proceeds to the president for signature or veto. If the president does veto the bill, it returns to Congress where both houses can vote again. If two-thirds of each house votes in favor of the bill, Congress overrides the veto and the bill will become law anyway. However, this rarely happens.

AMENDING THE CONSTITUTION

Congress is responsible for another significant legislative process: amending the Constitution. The framers understood that they could not foresee every threat to state sovereignty and personal liberty or every issue requiring government intervention. So they added Article V to the Constitution, which lays out a procedure for amending it, making the Constitution a *living document*.

Amendments to the Constitution can be introduced by Congress or the state legislatures. For Congress to propose an amendment to the Constitution, two-thirds of each house must vote in favor of the amendment. Alternatively, an amendment can be proposed if two-thirds of the states call for a national constitutional convention. All amendments to date, however, have been proposed by Congress. Either way, once the amendment has been officially proposed, it is not ratified until three-quarters of state legislatures (or special conventions convened by each state) approve it. There are twenty-seven amendments to the Constitution, the first ten of which were passed immediately in 1791. These first ten amendments, now called the **Bill of Rights**, were a condition for ratification imposed by **anti-federalists**. Concerned the federal government would be too powerful, they argued that individual liberties had to be explicitly protected. According to the amendments, the government may not:

> Amendment I: prohibit freedom of religion, speech, press, petition and assembly
>
> Amendment II: prohibit the right to bear arms
>
> Amendment III: quarter troops in citizens' homes
>
> Amendment IV: conduct unlawful search and seizures
>
> Amendment V: force anyone to testify against themselves or be tried for the same crime twice
>
> Amendment VI: prohibit the right to a fair and speedy trial
>
> Amendment VII: prohibit the right to a jury trial in civil cases (remember the original Constitution only guaranteed a jury in criminal cases)
>
> Amendment VIII: force citizens to undergo cruel and unusual punishment
>
> Amendment IX: violate rights that exist but are not explicitly mentioned in the Constitution
>
> Amendment X: usurp any powers from the states not given to them in the Constitution (so all other powers not listed in the Constitution belong to the states)

These will be discussed in more depth later in the chapter.

UNOFFICIAL CHANGES TO THE CONSTITUTION

While the only official way to change the Constitution is through the amendment process, other loopholes for change exist within its framework. These include:

- **Clarifying Legislation**: Using the **elastic clause**, legislation has been passed to clarify or expand the powers of the federal government. For example, the Judiciary Act of 1789 created the federal judiciary.
- **Executive Actions**: Although Congress holds most lawmaking power, the president can issue executive actions which have the force of law. The most famous of these is Abraham Lincoln's Emancipation Proclamation.

- **Judicial Decisions**: In *Marbury v. Madison* (1803) the Supreme Court established the precedent of **judicial review**, in which it determines the constitutionality of laws. In addition to strengthening the federal government, *Marbury v. Madison* specifically empowered the Supreme Court, laying the groundwork for its future transformative decisions.
- **Political Parties**: The rise of political parties changed the political landscape. Some aspects of American politics—like choosing the Speaker of the House and nominating presidential candidates—have come from political parties rather than through a formal legislative process.

PROHIBITED POWERS

Although Congress was made much more powerful by the Constitution, a real fear of tyranny existed among the framers. While Section 8 of the Constitution lists the powers of Congress, Section 9 lists what Congress cannot do. Most notable are:

1. No suspension of habeas corpus: A writ of habeas corpus is a legal demand a prisoner can make to profess their innocence in court. A means of preventing unreasonable imprisonment, this was viewed as an essential element of a just government. The Constitution forbids its suspension except in cases of rebellion or invasion.
2. No bills of attainder: A bill of attainder is a law that declares an individual or a group guilty of a crime without holding a trial. Much like with the writ of habeas corpus, this was seen as an essential protection in a fair society.
3. No ex post facto laws: An ex post facto law is a law which punishes an individual or group for breaking a law that was not a law when the act was committed. For example, slavery was abolished in 1865. If an ex post facto law was passed at that time, it would have punished anyone who had owned slaves before 1865.
4. No titles of nobility: It was important to the framers to provide safeguards against a return to monarchy. Therefore, they prohibited any American nobility.

SAMPLE QUESTIONS

23) Which of the following is an example of the "unwritten" Constitution?
    A. the Senate's confirmation of a Supreme Court justice
    B. the nomination of a presidential candidate at a nominating convention
    C. Congress writing a law regulating interstate commerce
    D. the House of Representatives voting to impeach the president

   Answer:

   B. Correct. This process for selecting a presidential nominee was created by the political parties and is not addressed in the Constitution.

24) **The clause of the Constitution that prohibits the suspension of writs of habeas corpus except in cases of rebellion or invasion demonstrates that the framers believed that**

 A. the people of the nation were likely to rebel.
 B. the president sometimes—like in cases of war—needs unlimited power.
 C. it is important to balance individual liberty with the security of the nation.
 D. the new laws would be resisted by most people.

Answer:

 C. **Correct.** Under the Articles of Confederation, it was clear that some limits on individual liberty were necessary. While it was still one of the highest priorities, the needs of the nation had to come first.

THE EXECUTIVE BRANCH

Defined by Article II of the Constitution, the executive branch enforces all federal law. Article II only provides for a president, vice president, and an unspecified number of executive departments. However, the executive branch has expanded considerably over the past 225 years along with the rest of the federal government. Today, the executive branch administers a federal bureaucracy that spends $3 trillion a year and employs 2.7 million people.

The president is the only executive role that is specifically outlined in the Constitution. The president serves a term of four years and may be re-elected once. While the term length was set in the original Constitution, the term limit was added in the Twenty-Second Amendment in 1951, in response to Franklin Delano Roosevelt's four elections to the presidency. Many felt that allowing unlimited terms opened the door for a de facto dictator and threatened liberty.

Qualifications: In order to qualify for the presidency, candidates must be natural-born American citizens, at least thirty-five years old, and have resided in the United States for at least fourteen years. While the Constitution does not specifically list requirements for the vice presidency, it does state that the vice president becomes the president in case of death, resignation, or impeachment. As a result, the vice president must meet the same qualifications as the president.

The **cabinet** consists of the heads of the executive departments and may advise the president. It is not directly referenced in the Constitution. Instead, it was derived from one line in Section 2: "he may require the opinion, in writing, of the principal officer in each of the executive departments, upon any subject relating to the duties of their respective offices."

George Washington instituted the first cabinet. He established four executive departments, so the first cabinet consisted of four positions: the Secretary of State, the Secretary of the Treasury, the Secretary of War (now, the Secretary of Defense) and the Attorney General. Over time, eleven executive departments were added, for a total of fifteen cabinet positions:

1. Department of Interior
2. Department of Agriculture
3. Department of Commerce
4. Department of Labor
5. Department of Energy
6. Department of Education
7. Department of Housing and Urban Development
8. Department of Transportation
9. Department of Veterans Affairs
10. Department of Health and Human Services
11. Department of Homeland Security

These fifteen departments employ more than two-thirds of all federal employees.

In addition to managing their departments, the members of the cabinet are also all in the line of presidential succession as established by the Presidential Succession Act (first passed in 1792 but most recently amended in 1947). The line of succession is as follows: following the vice president is the Speaker of the House, then the president pro tempore of the Senate, followed by each cabinet member in the order of the department's creation, beginning with the Secretary of State and ending with the Secretary of Homeland Security.

SAMPLE QUESTIONS

25) **The cabinet is made up of**

    A. the president's closest advisors.
    B. the heads of each executive department.
    C. the heads of each house of Congress and the chief justice of the Supreme Court.
    D. the secretaries of state, defense, the treasury, and the attorney general.

    Answer:

    B. Correct. Based on Section 2 of Article II of the Constitution, the cabinet is the embodiment of the president's right to seek advice from the heads of the executive departments.

26) Which of the following criteria must a vice president meet according to the Constitution?

  A. She or he must be a natural-born citizen of the United States.
  B. She or he must be of the same party as the president.
  C. She or he must have previously served in the legislature.
  D. There are no requirements specified.

Answer:

  D. **Correct.** The Constitution lists no specific requirements for the vice president. However, because they must be able to step in for the president, it is implied that they must meet the same criteria as the president.

POWERS OF THE EXECUTIVE BRANCH

Article II is considerably shorter than Article I because the framers intended the role and powers of the president to be more limited than those of Congress. However, the president does have a number of expressed powers.

Appointment Power: The president appoints federal officials. These include cabinet members, heads of independent agencies, ambassadors, and federal judges. Thus the president not only controls the executive branch and foreign policy, but also wields long-term influence over the judicial branch. However, the Senate must approve all presidential appointments according to the advice and consent clause of the Constitution. The president does have the power to remove appointees from office without Senate approval—with the exception of judges.

Commander in Chief: The first line of section 2 of Article II declares the president commander in chief of the army and navy—the supreme leader of US military forces. He or she can deploy troops and dictate military policy. However, Congress retains the power to declare war. Presidents have circumvented this check in the past by deploying troops without requesting a formal declaration of war. Because of this, in 1974 Congress passed the War Powers Resolution restricting the parameters of troop deployment.

Diplomat-in-Chief: The president is also considered the chief diplomat of the United States. He or she has the power to recognize other nations, receive ambassadors, and negotiate treaties. However, any treaties negotiated by the president must be approved by the Senate before taking effect. Today the US is a global power, and the president must manage international crises, negotiate international agreements, and monitor and maintain confidential information related to national and global security.

Judicial Powers: While the executive and judicial branches are quite separate, the president has powers intended to check the power of the judicial branch. Primarily, this is the power to appoint federal judges. The president may also grant pardons and reprieves for individuals convicted of federal crimes. as pardons are often seen to be politically motivated or a tool for those with political or personal connections. The number of pardons granted by presidents has fluctuated over time with Woodrow Wilson granting the most: 2,480. In recent years, presidents have issued fewer than one hundred pardons per president.

Legislative Powers: Like the judicial branch, the president is constitutionally accorded some legislative powers in order to limit the powers of the legislative branch. All laws that are passed end up on the president's desk. The president may sign the bill—in which case it becomes a law—or **veto** the bill. The president's veto prevents the bill from becoming law (unless Congress overrides the veto). The president is required to fully accept or reject a bill; he or she may not veto only sections of it. This is called a **line-item veto**, and the Supreme Court declared it unconstitutional in 1996. If the president does not wish to take such a clear stand on a bill, he or she can also simply ignore it. If the president does nothing for ten days, the bill automatically becomes law, even without a signature. If, however, there are less than ten days left in Congress's session, and the president does not sign the bill, it automatically dies. This is called a **pocket veto**.

The president also has the power to convene both houses of Congress to force them to consider matters requiring urgent attention.

While this is technically the extent of the president's legislative powers, in reality the position has a much greater legislative impact. The president sets the policy agenda both as the leader of their party and through the **State of the Union** address. Section 3 of Article II states that the president "shall from time to time give to the Congress information of the state of the union, and recommend to their consideration such measures as he [or she] shall judge necessary and expedient." This has evolved into an annual formalized address to Congress in which the president lays out executive legislative priorities.

ELECTION OF THE PRESIDENT

The framers wanted to ensure the president represented all of the states and was immune from the mob rule of democracy. As a result, they created the **Electoral College**. Over the years, the political parties have expanded the process into a nine-month series of elections.

Primaries/Caucuses: The first step in choosing a president is selecting the candidates. Originally, this was done in smoke-filled back rooms; it then became the provenance of party caucuses and then conventions, eventually evolving into the current system of primaries and caucuses. In a **primary** election, members of a political party in a state vote at a polling place for the candidate for their party. In ten states, a **caucus** system is used, in which members of a party in a state gather together at party meetings and vote for the candidate using raised hands or by gathering in groups.

National Nominating Convention: In July of the election year, the party holds a national nominating convention. Historically, this was where the candidate was chosen after days of heated debate and negotiation. However, because of the primary and caucus systems, delegates at the convention arrive already knowing whom their state supports. The delegates vote for the candidate who won their primary or caucus. The candidate with the most votes becomes the party's nominee.

Popular Vote: Presidential elections occur every four years on the first Tuesday in November. Today, all American citizens over the age of eighteen are allowed to vote. However, no voter qualifications are written into the Constitution; those were left to the states. In 1789, in every state, only propertied white men—one in fifteen white men—were allowed to vote. Starting with the removal of property qualifications during the Jacksonian era (1830s), the electorate expanded. Aside from property requirements, each expansion resulted from a new amendment to the Constitution.

Table 3.2. Constitutional Amendments Expanding Voting Rights

Amendment	Year	Provision
Fifteenth	1870	All male citizens, regardless of race, are allowed to vote.
Nineteenth	1920	All women are allowed to vote.
Twenty-Third	1961	Residents of the District of Columbia are allowed to vote in presidential elections.
Twenty-Fourth	1964	Poll taxes, an indirect restriction of black voting rights, are prohibited.
Twenty-Sixth	1971	All citizens over the age of eighteen are allowed to vote (in most states the voting age had previously been twenty-one years).

Electoral College: While the popular vote is tallied on Election Day, it does not determine the outcome of the presidential election; the Electoral College does. The Electoral College is composed of electors from each state who vote for the president. Electors are apportioned based on population; the number of a state's electors is the same as its number of representatives plus its number of senators (so each state has at least three electors). At first, most states allowed their state legislatures to choose their electors. By the end of the 1830s, almost every state allowed for the direct election of electors.

In the January following the election, electors gather in their states to cast their votes for president. Technically, electors are not bound to vote according to their state's popular vote. However, electors rarely take advantage of this right, and it has never affected the outcome of an election. Today, most states are winner-take-all, meaning the electors are expected to all vote in line with the outcome of the state's popular vote. The president must win a majority of the Electoral College: 270 votes.

The Electoral College was designed to elect a president for a scattered country with more regional than national focus. It favors small states and minority groups, giving them greater influence on the election than they would have in a direct election system. Today many people feel that the Electoral College is outdated. They argue it is undemocratic, for it gives undue importance to certain states. Instead, they support a direct election system.

SAMPLE QUESTIONS

27) Which of the following is an implied power of the president?
    A. granting pardons for federal crimes
    B. seeking ratification of a treaty from the Senate
    C. appointing a justice to the Supreme Court
    D. holding a regularly scheduled cabinet meeting

    Answer:
    D. Correct. While the Constitution does permit the president to seek the advice of executive department heads, it does not explicitly create a body like the cabinet which meets regularly with the president.

28) Which of the following earns the president the unofficial title of "Chief Legislator"?
    A. The president maintains US embassies abroad.
    B. The president votes in Congress in case of a tie.
    C. The president sets the agenda for much of what is debated in Congress.
    D. The president chooses the Speaker of the House.

    Answer:
    C. Correct. Using legislation promoted through various executive departments, the presidential role as leader of his or her party, and the State of the Union address, the president leads public policy.

29) Which action BEST exemplifies the president's role as Chief Executive?
    A. appointing a new Secretary of the Interior
    B. vetoing a bill
    C. negotiating a treaty with Russia
    D. receiving the ambassador from Finland

    Answer:
    A. Correct. As Chief Executive, the president is responsible for the management of the federal bureaucracy and all of the federal departments of the executive branch.

30) The Electoral College represents which of the beliefs of the framers of the Constitution?

A. Government derives its authority from the consent of the people.
B. Concentration of power can lead to tyranny.
C. The federal government derives its authority from the states.
D. The federal government needs greater power to provide stability to the nation.

Answer:

C. **Correct.** The Electoral College is designed to balance the power of the states and to best represent their interests without allowing a single state to dominate.

THE JUDICIAL BRANCH

The Constitution's framework for the judicial branch is the least detailed of the three branches. It is also a passive branch. Where the legislative branch creates laws, and the executive branch enforces those laws, the judicial branch can only act when an actual case is presented to it. It may not rule or make decisions based on hypotheticals. Yet this branch has grown to be at least as influential as the other two branches both in setting policy and molding the federal government.

The United States has a complex **dual court system**; each state has its own judicial system in addition to the federal one. Even though federal district courts handle over 300,000 cases a year, 97 percent of criminal cases are heard in state and local courts. While the federal courts hear more civil cases than criminal, the majority of these are still handled within the states.

State courts have **jurisdiction**—or the authority to hear a case—over most cases. Only cases that meet certain criteria are heard in federal courts. Most cases also can only be **appealed**—or reviewed by a higher court—up to the state supreme court. For the federal Supreme Court to review a state supreme court's decision, there must be an issue involving the interpretation of the federal Constitution.

Article III, the article of the Constitution which discusses the judicial branch, only details the Supreme Court. It then empowers Congress to create the rest of the judiciary, which it did beginning with the Judiciary Act of 1789.

The federal court system is composed of three levels of courts. First are the district courts. There are ninety-four district courts in the country, served by 700 judges. They handle eighty percent of all federal cases. The next level of courts consists of the twelve circuit courts of appeal. These courts review district court decisions and the decisions of federal regulatory agencies.

At the top is the **Supreme Court**. Sometimes called the "court of last resort," the Supreme Court reviews cases from the circuit court and from state supreme courts, and is the final arbiter of constitutionality. Decisions made by the Supreme

Court establish **precedents**, rulings that guide future court decisions at all levels of the judicial system.

While the Constitution delineates which kinds of cases the Supreme Court may hear, its real power was established by the precedent of an early case, *Marbury v. Madison* (1803). William Marbury—citing the Judiciary Act of 1789—sought relief from the court when James Madison, Secretary of State to the new president, did not deliver the federal appointment Marbury had been given by the previous president. The court ruled that while Madison was in the wrong, the section of the Judiciary Act cited by Marbury was unconstitutional. This established **judicial review**, the Supreme Court's power to determine the constitutionality of laws. This has become the most significant function of the court, allowing it to shape public policy.

Nine justices serve on the Supreme Court. Appointed by the president and approved by the Senate, Supreme Court justices serve for life. The Constitution does not provide any criteria for serving on the court. Traditionally, justices must demonstrate competence through high-level credentials or prior experience. Today, all of the justices on the Supreme Court hold law degrees from major universities and first served in federal district or appellate courts. They also generally share policy preferences with the president who appointed them, although judicial inclinations do not always align with political ones.

The court only has **original jurisdiction** (first court to hear the case) in three situations: 1) if a case involves two or more states; 2) if a case involves the US government and state government; or 3) if a case involves the US government and foreign diplomats. All other cases come to the Supreme Court through the federal appellate courts or the state supreme courts. Appellants must request a **writ of certiorari**, an order to the lower court to send up their decision for review. It receives approximately 9,000 requests for writs each year but typically only accepts eighty cases.

Once a case is accepted, each party must file a brief arguing its side, specifically referencing the constitutional issue in question. Other interested parties may also file **amicus briefs**, position papers supporting a particular side or argument. Then both parties present **oral arguments** in the Supreme Court. Each lawyer presents an oral summary of his or her party's argument and fields questions from the justices. Oral arguments are limited to thirty minutes per side. Next, the justices meet in private to discuss the case and to vote. The chief justice then assigns a justice to write the **majority opinion**, a detailed explanation of the majority's decision and reasoning. Other justices who did not vote with the majority may write **dissenting opinions**. While these have no force of law, they are a record of alternative reasoning which may be used in future cases. Sometimes justices also write **concurring opinions**, which agree with the majority's ruling, but provide different reasoning to support the decision.

Table 3.3. Supreme Court Cases

CASE NAME	RULING
Marbury v. Madison (1803)	This case established judicial review.
McCulloch v. Maryland (1819)	The court ruled that states could not tax the Bank of the United States; this ruling supported the implied powers of Congress.
Dred Scott v. Sandford (1857)	The Supreme Court ruled that enslaved persons were not citizens; it also found the Missouri Compromise unconstitutional, meaning Congress could not forbid expanding slavery to US territories.
Plessy v. Ferguson (1896)	This case established the precedent of separate but equal (segregation).
Korematsu v. US (1945)	This case determined that the internment of Japanese Americans during WWII was lawful.
Brown v. Board of Education (1954)	The Supreme Court overturned *Plessy v. Ferguson*; it ruled that separate but equal, or segregation, was unconstitutional.
Gideon v. Wainwright (1963)	The Supreme Court ruled that the court must provide legal counsel to poor defendants in felony cases.
Miranda v. Arizona (1966)	This ruling established that defendants must be read their due process rights before questioning.
Tinker v. Des Moines (1969)	This case established "symbolic speech" as a form of speech protected by the First Amendment.
Roe v. Wade (1973)	This case legalized abortion in the first trimester throughout the United States.
Bakke v. Regents of University of California (1978)	This case ruled that while affirmative action was constitutional, the university's quota system was not.
Citizens United v. Federal Elections Commission (2010)	The court ruled that restricting corporate donations to political campaigns was tantamount to restricting free speech; this ruling allowed the formation of influential super PACs, which can provide unlimited funding to candidates running for office.
Obergefell v. Hodges (2015)	The court ruled that same-sex marriage was legal throughout the United States.

SAMPLE QUESTIONS

31) Where did the Supreme Court's power of judicial review come from?
    A. the Judiciary Act of 1789
    B. an order by the president
    C. an amendment to the Constitution
    D. the court's own interpretation of the Constitution

    Answer:
    D. **Correct.** The court endowed itself with the power of judicial review in the case of *Marbury v. Madison*, when upon interpreting the Constitution, it found part of the Judiciary Act of 1789 unconstitutional.

32) Why are justices appointed for life?
    A. to insulate them from political pressure
    B. to prevent them from running for political office
    C. to ensure continuity of decisions
    D. to make the judicial branch the strongest branch of government

    Answer:
    A. **Correct.** The framers were very concerned about judges making unfair decisions based on fears of job security or political allegiances.

33) The Warren Court in the 1960s was accused of judicial activism, or legislating through court decisions. Whose rights were expanded under the Warren court?
    A. blacks
    B. women
    C. defendants
    D. youth

    Answer:
    C. **Correct.** Several cases during the 1960s expanded the rights of defendants in court. Two of the most notable were *Miranda v. Arizona* and *Gideon v. Wainwright*.

34) Which of the following would be written by a special interest to lobby the court?
    A. writ of certiorari
    B. amicus brief
    C. bill of attainder
    D. writ of habeas corpus

Answer:
- **B. Correct.** Amicus briefs are written by organizations, agencies, or other groups who hope to influence to court to take a particular decision.

CIVIL LIBERTIES AND RIGHTS

Influenced by revolution and the ideas of the Enlightenment, the framers of the Constitution valued **civil liberties**. Civil liberties are rights that protect individuals from arbitrary acts of the government. The framers protected some liberties explicitly in the Constitution via the prohibited powers, and expanded on them in the Bill of Rights, the first ten amendments of the Constitution. Each amendment *restricts* the actions of the federal government rather than actually granting a freedom to the people.

THE FIRST AMENDMENT

The liberties most central to the American identity are articulated in the First Amendment: freedom of speech, press, petition, assembly, and religion. No liberty is truly unlimited, however, and the court has imposed restrictions on speech over time. It has upheld laws banning libel, slander, obscenity, and symbolic speech that intends to incite illegal actions.

Freedom of religion comes from two clauses in the First Amendment: the **establishment clause** and the **free exercise clause**. The first prohibits the government from establishing a state religion or favoring one religion over another. The second prohibits the government from restricting religious belief or practice. However, the court has found that religious practice can be banned if it requires engagement in otherwise illegal activity. There are also debates on allowing prayer in schools and granting vouchers to students to attend parochial schools.

RIGHTS OF THE ACCUSED

Most of the civil liberties written into the body of the Constitution addressed the rights of the accused, including prohibitions on bills of attainder, ex post facto laws, and denials of writs of habeas corpus. Three of the amendments in the Bill of Rights address this as well.

The **Fourth Amendment** restricts unlawful searches and seizures. In *Mapp v. Ohio* (1961), the Supreme Court ruled that evidence obtained illegally—so in violation of the Fourth Amendment—could not be used in court. This **exclusionary rule** is very controversial, and the courts have struggled since to determine when and how to apply it.

The **Fifth Amendment** protects the accused from self-incrimination. Drawing on this amendment, the Supreme Court ruled in *Miranda v. Arizona* (1966) that arrestees must be informed of their due process rights before interrogation in order to protect them from self-incrimination. These rights, along with those in the Sixth Amendment, are now colloquially known as **Miranda rights**.

The **Sixth Amendment** guarantees the accused the right to a fair, speedy, and public trial, as well as the right to counsel in criminal cases. While originally this only applied at the federal level, in *Gideon v. Wainwright* (1963) the Supreme Court ruled that states must provide counsel to those who cannot afford it.

THE FOURTEENTH AMENDMENT

The Court's ruling in *Gideon v. Wainwright* was based on the Fourteenth Amendment's **equal protection clause**. Ratified in 1868, the amendment's original purpose was to ensure the equal treatment of African Americans under the law after the abolition of slavery. The equal protection clause has been used to protect the **civil rights**—protections against discriminatory treatment by the government—of individuals of a variety of groups.

The courts have regularly protected political and legal equality, as well as equality of opportunity. However, the courts do not recognize a right to economic equality. The Supreme Court also recognizes the need for reasonable classifications of people, and allows discrimination along those lines. For example, age restrictions on alcohol consumption, driving, and voting are all considered constitutional.

The Supreme Court has also used the Fourteenth Amendment over time to extend federal civil liberties to the state level. Today, all states are held to the same standard as the federal government in terms of civil liberties.

The second part of the Fourteenth Amendment extends the Fifth Amendment's due process guarantees to the state level. While this typically refers to the accused, it has also come to represent certain unnamed, or implied, rights. At the heart of most of these **implied rights** is the right to privacy, which is not specifically protected in the Constitution. However, the court has ruled that it is implied by the Fourth, Fifth, and Fourteenth Amendments. This was the basis for its decision to legalize abortion in *Roe v. Wade* (1973).

SAMPLE QUESTIONS

35) Which of the following is NOT considered protected speech?

    A. burning the American flag
    B. writing an article criticizing the government
    C. publishing a false list of supposed KKK members
    D. protesting outside of an abortion clinic

   Answer:

   C. Correct. Incorrectly alleging that someone is a member of a white supremacist group is considered libel (if written) or slander (if spoken). This is not protected by the Constitution.

36) Which of the following does NOT address a due process issue?
   A. a law prohibiting marriage between cousins
   B. a law establishing grounds for termination of parental rights
   C. a law prohibiting airplane travel by convicted felons
   D. a law prohibiting indecent exposure

   Answer:
   D. **Correct.** There is no fundamental right to public nudity. Nudity generally falls under the right to privacy; however, when it becomes a public act, the individual's rights only extend as far as those of others in society.

37) Which of the following is an absolute right?
   A. freedom to hold any religious belief
   B. freedom of speech
   C. freedom from search and seizure
   D. freedom to bear arms

   Answer:
   A. **Correct.** The government has no authority to restrict people's beliefs. They may, however, restrict religious activity if it violates other laws.

38) If the police search a home without a warrant, any evidence found could not be used based on:
   A. the equal protection clause
   B. the exclusionary rule
   C. the establishment clause
   D. Miranda rights

   Answer:
   B. **Correct.** The exclusionary rule prohibits any evidence obtained illegally from being used at trial.

AMERICAN POLITICAL SYSTEMS

A whole network of political systems has developed to support the US government since the Constitution was written. These systems operate within the framework of the government, impacting how it functions. As the federal government has expanded and grown in power, so have these institutions.

One of the biggest influences on the American political system is **public opinion**, the public's attitude toward institutions, leaders, political issues, and events. Analysts use the extent to which individuals believe they can effect change in the political system, called **political efficacy**, as a measure of the health of a political system.

Political Parties

Although the framers envisioned a political system without political parties, by the election of 1800, two official parties existed. A **political party** is a group of citizens who work together in order to: 1) win elections, 2) hold public office, 3) operate the government, and 4) determine public policy. Some countries have one-party systems; others have multiple parties. Although party names and platforms have shifted over the years, the United States has maintained a two-party system. Since 1854, our two major parties have been the **Democratic Party** and the **Republican Party**. Democrats generally follow a liberal political ideology, while Republicans espouse a conservative ideology. The parties operate at every level of government in every state. Although many members of a party serve in elected office, political parties have their own internal organization. Parties are hierarchical: they are comprised of national leaders, followed by state chairpersons, county chairpersons, and local activists.

The parties carry out important political functions to aid government operations. These include:

- recruiting and nominating candidates for office
- running political campaigns
- articulating positions on various issues
- connecting individuals and the government

In Congress, parties have become integral to the organization of both houses. The leadership of each house is based on the leadership of whichever party has the majority. The majority party also holds all of the committee chairs, assigns bills to committees, holds a majority in each committee, controls the important Rules Committee, and sets the legislative agenda.

While still very important, the power of political parties has declined dramatically since the beginning of the twentieth century. In response to the dominance and corruption of political machines, many states implemented **direct primaries** to circumvent the parties. Individual politicians can now build power without the party machinery.

Although the United States has a two-party system, third parties still emerge. These parties are relatively small and come in three types:

1. **Charismatic Leadership**: These parties that are dominated by an engaging and forceful leader. Examples include the Bull Moose Party (Theodore Roosevelt, 1912), the American Independent Party (George Wallace, 1972), and the Reform Party (Ross Perot, 1992 and 1996).

2. **Single-Issue**: These parties are concerned with one issue. Examples include the Free Soil Party and the Know Nothing Party in the 1840s, and the Right to Life Party in the 1970s and 1980s.

3. **Ideological**: These parties are organized around a particular non-mainstream ideology. Examples include the Socialist Party and the Libertarian Party.

Although they rarely succeed in gaining major political office, third parties play an important role in American politics. The two main parties tend to moderate their positions in an attempt to garner the majority of votes. Third parties, on the other hand, target select populations and are thus able to express strong views on controversial issues. Because their views are usually shared by the most extreme elements of one of the major parties, their stances can push the major parties into more radical positions. They also can affect the outcome of an election, even without winning it. By siphoning off a segment of the vote from one of the dominant parties, they can "spoil" the election for that party. For example, in the 2000 presidential election, Ralph Nader, the Green Party candidate, did not win any electoral votes. However, he drew away votes that most likely otherwise would have gone to Al Gore, contributing to George W. Bush's election.

SAMPLE QUESTIONS

39) All of the following result from the two-party system EXCEPT
    A. how the Speaker of the House is selected.
    B. the lack of effective third parties.
    C. the lifetime appointment of Supreme Court justices.
    D. how members are assigned to committees.

    Answer:
    C. **Correct.** While the appointment of Supreme Court justices can certainly be very political, their lifetime terms are constitutionally mandated and unrelated to political parties.

40) Third parties primarily impact presidential elections by
    A. increasing voter turnout.
    B. preventing either party from winning a majority in the Electoral College.
    C. encouraging more voters to officially join a political party.
    D. bringing forward issues to be adopted by the major parties later.

    Answer:
    D. **Correct.** Third parties address more controversial issues and espouse more radical positions. This often pushes the major parties to discuss the issues as well and take a stand.

INTEREST GROUPS

An **interest group** is a private organization of individuals who share policy views on one or more issues. The group then tries to influence public opinion to its own benefit. Interest groups play an important role in American politics. Much like political parties, they connect citizens to the government, bringing their members' concerns and perspective to government officials and educating their members about government policy. They wield more influence than the average citizen: they speak for many and raise funds for policymakers, thereby influencing policy. Interest groups play an increasingly dominant role in American political life. The number of groups increased from 6,000 in 1959 to 22,000 in 2010. Examples of major interest groups include the National Rifle Association (NRA), the American Association of Retired Persons (AARP), and the American Federation of Labor (AFL-CIO).

Interest groups **lobby**, or persuade, lawmakers to effect desired changes. There are about 30,000 lobbyists in Washington, DC, making $2 billion a year. It is their full-time job to advance the agenda of their interest groups. They do this by testifying before congressional committees, meeting with aides, connecting influential constituents to lawmakers, drafting legislation, and providing relevant technical information to members of Congress. Interest groups will even turn to the courts to achieve their goals, writing amicus briefs in Supreme Court cases or initiating court cases to challenge existing laws. They also can play a significant role in determining judicial nominees.

Interest groups also use **political action committees** (**PAC**) to influence policymakers. PACs raise money for political candidates who can work on behalf of interest groups. PACs are limited to contributions of $5,000 per candidate per election (primary elections count as separate elections). However, since the 2010 Supreme Court ruling in *Citizens United*, political committees known as *super PACs* have no limits on spending to advocate for or against certain candidates, though they may not contribute directly to campaigns or coordinate with them.

The role of lobbying, especially of PACs and super PACs, is hotly debated. Some political analysts are concerned that politics and money have become too closely tied. Others argue that the sheer number of special interest groups is a benefit because they each balance each other out. In order to accomplish anything, politicians must bargain and compromise, creating solutions that ultimately benefit more people. Others still argue that the number of competing interests leaves politicians scared to take any action at all out of fear of alienating one or more interest groups.

Mass Media

Any means of communication—newspapers, magazines, radio, television, or blogs—that reaches a broad and far-reaching audience is considered part of the **mass media**. Although certainly not a formal part of the political process, the mass media has a significant impact on American politics.

The media connects people to the government by providing them with information through reports, interviews, and exposés. The media also can help set the political agenda by drawing attention to issues through its coverage. For example, the medical treatment of veterans became a significant political issue after two lengthy exposés in the *Washington Post* on the conditions at Walter Reed Medical Center in 2007.

Mass media has also reshaped American campaigns. Especially since the advent of visual media, campaigns have focused more on candidates than issues. Candidates must consider their image on television and other video sources. They also have to be media savvy, making appearances on popular nightly shows and radio programs. The need for a strong media presence is largely responsible for increases in campaign spending, as candidates maintain an online presence and spend millions on television advertising.

Candidates' lives and pasts are also more visible to the public. In the 1960 presidential campaign, John F. Kennedy and Richard Nixon engaged in the first televised presidential debate in American history. Those who listened to it on the radio declared Nixon—who was confident in speech, but sweaty and uncomfortable on camera—the winner, while those who watched it on television saw the suave and image-savvy Kennedy as the victor. Many credit this debate for Kennedy's eventual win, demonstrating the new importance of crafting a public image for politicians.

SAMPLE QUESTIONS

41) Which of the following is an example of an issues-driven organization?

   A. Americans for Tax Reform
   B. the American Medical Association (AMA)
   C. the AFL-CIO
   D. the National Association for the Advancement of Colored People (NAACP)

   Answer:

   A. **Correct.** This organization was formed around the issue of tax reform. People who are interested in this issue then join this group.

42) Throughout the twentieth and twenty-first centuries, changes in politics have coincided with the emergence of new media or a change in the organization of media. This shows that:

   A. New media develops in response to political changes.
   B. Media has a greater impact on the functioning of government than other political systems.
   C. There is no connection between the functioning of media and politics.
   D. Politics is responsive to changes in how people communicate.

   Answer:

   D. **Correct.** Politicians are always trying to find the best way to connect to their constituencies; therefore they must be adaptable to new media as it emerges. Also, new media changes the way in which politics is reported, which then changes the way it functions.

43) The most effective task for a lobbyist is
   A. organizing protests.
   B. giving expert information to legislators.
   C. mobilizing letter-writing campaigns.
   D. leading politicians' campaigns for election.

   Answer:
   B. **Correct.** As a resource for legislators and their aides, a lobbyist can influence their thinking on a particular topic.

Comparative Politics and International Relations

All nations have governments; however, those governments come in very different forms. A government's structure is influenced by factors like geography, population size, economic strength, industrial development, and cultural diversity.

Types of Governments

Categories of governments can be divided up in three different ways.

TYPE OF RULE

Governments are either ruled by man or ruled by law. In an **autocracy** (*rule by one person*), decisions are arbitrary and absolute. There are two types of autocracies. In a **dictatorship**, the ruler derives power from political control, military power, or a cult of personality. In a **monarchy**, authority is derived from a **divine right** to rule given by God.

Some governments ruled by man are **oligarchies**, ruled by a powerful group, or **aristocracies**, ruled by an elite class. In both cases, the right to rule is based on wealth, social status, military position, or some level of achievement. In a **theocracy**, authority is also held by a small group—the religious leadership—and is derived from divine right.

Governments ruled by law are governed according to a code of law. Early legal codes include the Code of Hammurabi from ancient Babylon, the Twelve Tables of the Roman Empire, and the Byzantine Justinian Code. These became the basis of many modern legal systems, including that of the United States. Today, at least in theory, most nations are ruled by law.

GEOGRAPHIC DISTRIBUTION OF AUTHORITY

A second way to organize different types of governments is by how their authority is distributed across national territory. A **unitary government** vests all of its power in the central government and is most common. For example, Great Britain, France, and China all have unitary governments. On the other end of the spectrum are

confederate governments, such as is the first government of the United States under the Articles of Confederation. A confederate government is decentralized with power distributed among regional governments. Finally, power can be distributed through a **federal** system. In a federal government power is shared between the central government and the regional governments as in the United States.

SEPARATION OF POWERS

In an **authoritarian government**, there is no division of power. All aspects of government are controlled by the single ruler or a council, as in North Korea, for example. In a **parliamentarian government**, the legislative and executive functions of government are combined, with the judicial acting as a separate body. In this system, the head executive—the **prime minister**—and his or her cabinet are chosen from the legislature. The prime minister maintains power as long as his or her party maintains a majority in the legislature. The United Kingdom has a parliamentary government. The final type is the US-style, three-branch system discussed previously.

SAMPLE QUESTIONS

44) The British historian Lord Acton said, "Power corrupts; absolute power corrupts absolutely." Based on this, which of the following systems do you think he would have most likely supported?

   A. a monarchy
   B. a democratic republic
   C. a unitary government
   D. an aristocracy

   Answer:
   B. **Correct.** In a democratic republic, power is distributed across multiple branches of government.

45) In the Soviet Union, Joseph Stalin used secret police, purges, and censorship to rule. This type of government is called

   A. monarchy.
   B. democratic republic.
   C. dictatorship.
   D. oligarchy.

   Answer:
   C. **Correct.** An autocratic government in which power is maintained by force is a dictatorship.

Political Party Systems

Almost all modern governments are run by political parties. However, party systems come in three different types: one-party, two-party, and multi-party.

The simplest party system is the **one-party system**. In a one-party system, only one party controls the entire government without opposition or challenge. Elections are still held, but their purpose is to allow citizens to show their support for the existing government. China and Cuba have one-party systems.

In a **two-party system**, two major parties, usually liberal and conservative, compete for control. In these systems, fewer differences divide the parties, and each party trends toward the middle to amass as much public support as possible. The United States, Great Britain, and Australia all have two-party systems.

In **multi-party systems**, several different parties compete for government power. Unlike those in two-party systems, the parties in a multi-party system represent very different and often more radical ideologies. Because it is difficult for one party to win a true majority, parties seek **pluralities** (the largest percentage of votes) rather than **majorities** (half or more of the votes). Consequently, the government is run by a coalition of different parties that form alliances. Therefore, some parties must find consensus on issues for government to function. France, Italy, and Israel all have multi-party systems.

In both two-party and multi-party systems, citizens use their votes in elections to support certain policies or agendas. Several factors make a nation more receptive to a two-party or a multi-party system.

A key structural factor affecting the development of a party system is the apportionment of power within the legislature. In the United States, power is distributed among **single-member districts**. States are divided into districts, and each district elects one representative in a winner-take-all model. This discourages the growth of smaller parties, as they are unlikely to win a majority—the only way they can gain any power.

Italy, on the other hand, uses **proportional representation**. In this system, the number of seats any one party gets is based on the percentage of the vote it wins overall. This encourages smaller parties, for they can still win some seats with only a small percentage of votes.

Party-based proportional representation should not be confused with the proportional representation of the House of Representatives. In the House, *proportion* refers to how representatives are distributed among the states. Even though a state like Texas may have a greater proportion of the representatives than Delaware, in both cases the actual representatives are still chosen in a single-member district, winner-take-all style.

In the United States, these natural tendencies have been strengthened by legislation passed by the two major parties which makes it more difficult for third parties to gain a foothold. For example, only Democratic and Republican candidates automatically appear on the ballot; all other parties must petition to gain access. Finally, in spite of its diversity, the United States generally has a high level of consensus on core issues. This is likely because the nation was founded on a common ideology.

SAMPLE QUESTIONS

46) Autocratic governments typically have which kind of party system?

   A. a single-party system
   B. a two-party system
   C. a multi-party system
   D. no party system

   Answer:

   A. **Correct.** Because autocratic governments are controlled by one person or a small group of people, challenges to their authority are unwelcome. However, party affiliation usually indicates members of the ruling group and gives a semblance of democracy.

47) Which of the following is NOT true of multi-party systems?

   A. They lead to coalition governments.
   B. They have parties with more radical views.
   C. They result from single-member districts.
   D. Parties seek to win a plurality of votes instead of a majority.

   Answer:

   C. **Correct.** Two-party systems result from single-member districts where there is a winner-takes-all race for each individual seat. In a multi-party system, seats are apportioned based on the percentage of the vote received by each party.

Foreign Policy

Foreign policy describes how and why one nation interacts with the other nations of the world. As new technologies emerge and the world becomes more interdependent, foreign policy has become an increasingly important part of any nation's governance.

The goals for international engagement vary among countries and over time; these goals influence how policy is defined and communicated. Foreign policy goals include:

- protecting and increasing a nation's independence
- improving national security
- furthering economic advancement
- spreading political values to other nations
- gaining respect and prestige from other nations
- promoting stability and international peace

Nations use a variety of tools—military, economic, and political—to further their foreign policy goals. They may build up military resources, position troops in strategic locations, or even deploy troops to engage hostile nations or support allies. They also use economic tools. For example, a country may impose economic sanctions on another country to pressure it into changing a policy, or it may offer economic support in exchange for a favorable outcome. Countries may also use political pressure to influence the decisions of others by forming alliances or granting or withholding official recognition of another state.

Non-state ethnic minorities, world organizations, and multinational corporations are also important actors in foreign policy. While often indirect, they use many of the same tools to influence political leaders to form policy friendly to their own objectives.

American foreign policy has grown increasingly complex as the United States since the eighteenth century. In George Washington's Farewell Address, he warned against forming any "permanent alliances" with other nations. This call for **isolationism** set the tone for American foreign policy until the end of the nineteenth century.

But as American economic interests and power increased, so did American engagement with the rest of the world. The first half of the twentieth century saw divisions between groups favoring **internationalism** (more engagement in global affairs) and others favoring a return to isolation. After World War II, the United States became a global superpower, taking responsibility for affairs around the world. With the end of the Cold War and the fall of the Soviet Union, the political landscape shifted again. As the world has become more globalized, the United States has responded with a shift in its foreign policy to one of **interdependence**, mutual reliance with and on other countries.

The president, as commander in chief and head diplomat, is the primary foreign policy leader. He or she is supported from within the executive branch by the Secretary of State, the National Security Agency advisor, and the Secretary of Defense. Congress also plays a significant role as it controls the appropriation of money and declarations of war. The Senate also has the power to ratify treaties negotiated by the president and to control representation of the United States abroad by confirming diplomatic appointments.

SAMPLE QUESTIONS

48) The United States and the Cuban leader Fidel Castro were at odds following the Cuban Revolution. Which of the following is NOT an example of an attempt by the United States to influence Cuba during the twentieth century?

   A. encouraging emigration from Cuba to the United States
   B. placing severe economic sanctions on Cuba
   C. building a military base at Guantanamo Bay
   D. supporting the failed Bay of Pigs invasion

   Answer:

   C. **Correct.** The US military base at Guantanamo Bay was established before the Cuban Revolution.

49) US involvement in Europe after World War II is an example of

   A. internationalism.
   B. isolationism.
   C. interdependence.
   D. none of the above

   Answer:

   A. **Correct.** Learning from worldwide depression and the rise of totalitarianism after World War I, the US took on the responsibility of aiding the quick rebuilding of Western Europe. This is a clear example of internationalist foreign policy.

THEORIES OF INTERNATIONAL RELATIONS

International relations theorists posit that states always act in their own national interest, promoting their own foreign policy goals in their interactions with each other. However, theorists disagree on which of those goals is of utmost importance. There are two main schools of thought:

Realism: First articulated by Hans J. Morgenthau, realism argues that a state's primary interest is self-preservation, which can only be achieved by maximizing power. As a result, nations are always working to acquire more power than other states. This theory is a direct continuation of Machiavelli's political theory: morality has no place in policy.

Realists believe war is inevitable. They also do not believe any kind of global policing (in the form of a supranational law enforcement body) is truly possible, nor would they allow it insofar as it would threaten their own state's autonomy. If all states are acting in their own self-interest, there is no room for global interest. Realism guided Cold War politics from both the US and Soviet perspectives.

Liberalism: Liberal theorists argue that realism is outdated. Thanks to globalization (including international trade) nations are too interconnected for any one country to have a national interest separate from another's. Thus the consequences of military force usually outweigh the benefits, as it is impossible to strike another nation without serious repercussions in one's own. Instead, economic and social power is more effective. States will differ in their primary interests, but international cooperation is actually in the best interest of every state. Liberals argue that international organizations and rules—policing and otherwise—foster that cooperation, build trust, and lead to prosperity.

A sub-group of liberals, **idealists**, argues that states must follow moral goals and act ethically to serve their best interest. Woodrow Wilson was an idealist. His Fourteen Points envisioned a world beyond war and conflict—peace and prosperity through moral foreign policy.

SAMPLE QUESTIONS

50) Which of the following actions follows a realist approach?

　　A.　creating the United Nations

　　B.　building the Berlin Wall

　　C.　imposing economic sanctions on Russia following conflict with Ukraine

　　D.　sending economic aid to Afghanistan

Answer:

　　B.　Correct. East Germany built the Berlin Wall in order to prevent defections to the West. This is an example of self-preservation.

51) In 1994, over half a million people were killed in Rwanda during a genocide that lasted only a few weeks. An idealist response by the United States to this tragedy would have been to:

　　A.　take no action

　　B.　declare war on Rwanda

　　C.　insist that the UN or other international organizations take action

　　D.　impose economic sanctions on Rwanda

Answer:

　　C.　Correct. Idealists would insist on intervention as the only moral option. They would also believe in the enforcement power of an international organization like the UN to maintain peace.

CURRENT GLOBAL RELATIONS

Today, **international organizations** are as important as individual nations to global politics. There are two types of international organizations:

Nongovernmental Organizations (NGOs): Funded primarily by individuals or foundations, NGOs provide services or advocate for certain policy positions locally, nationally, or internationally. NGOs vary widely in their missions and practices; however they all work outside of national governments. Some are highly religious or political in nature, while others intentionally avoid all such associations. They address issues such as healthcare, the environment, human rights, and development. Doctors without Borders and the Red Cross are both examples of NGOs.

Intergovernmental Organizations (IGOs): IGOs are organizations comprised of individual sovereign nations (they can also be made up of other IGOs). Whereas NGOs are entirely private, IGOs are official governing bodies that must adhere to international legal guidelines. All members must sign (and ratify) a treaty establishing the organization's existence and outlining its mission. Not all treaties create IGOs. The North American Free Trade Agreement (NAFTA), for example, does not create an official organization, although the signatories may need to meet periodically. Three examples of IGOs are:

- **North Atlantic Treaty Organization (NATO):** Created after World War II, the NATO treaty was originally signed by ten Western European nations, the United States, and Canada. The treaty created an organization of countries that pledged to come to each other's defense in case of external aggression; this was mainly in response to the threat posed by the Soviet Union. Today, NATO has twenty-eight members.

- **United Nations (UN):** Also created after World War II, the United Nations was the second attempt at an international organization dedicated to promoting world peace. The UN addresses economic, health, social, cultural, and humanitarian issues throughout the world. The United Nations currently has 193 member states. While it is a significant player in world politics, its limited military power is subject to the consent of its members.

- **World Bank:** Another organization created after World War II, the World Bank provides loans to developing nations for capital projects. Its primary purpose is to eliminate poverty in the world; however—a product of its time—it is also designed to support and encourage the growth of capitalism. While an independent organization, the World Bank works closely with the United Nations.

SAMPLE QUESTIONS

52) **Which of the following is NOT an example of an NGO?**

   A. Amnesty International

   B. Wikimedia Foundation

   C. Oxfam

   D. The World Trade Organization

Answer:

D. Correct. The World Trade Organization is an IGO that governs the rules of trade between nations.

53) **Which of the following issues would be addressed by the United Nations?**
   A. the voting age in France
   B. the election of the president of the United States
   C. the national highway system in Canada
   D. disarmament after civil war in Sierra Leone

Answer:

D. Correct. From 1999 to 2005, the UN stationed peacekeeping troops in Sierra Leone to disarm combatants after the country's civil war. Creating a stable and peaceful Sierra Leone was directly in line with the UN's mission to promote global peace.

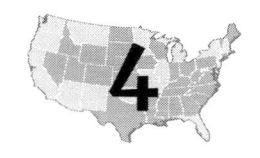

Geography

WHAT IS GEOGRAPHY?

In its most basic form, geography is the study of space. For geographers, the *where* of any interaction, event, or development is a crucial element to understanding it.

There are many sub-disciplines of geography: 1) regional studies, which examine the characteristics of a particular place, 2) topical studies, which look at a single physical or human feature that impacts the whole world, 3) physical studies, which focus on the physical features of Earth, and 4) human studies, which examine the relationship between human activity and the environment.

THE FIVE THEMES OF GEOGRAPHY

Geographers have developed five themes of geography: Location, Place, Region, Human-Environment Interaction, and Movement. Each of these addresses the basic geographic questions:

Location addresses physical site or placement. An example of location would be the address of someone's house or a description of where it is in the neighborhood.

Place studies the qualities and characteristics of location. **Region** asks, *what do different areas have in common and why?* While the address of a specific house is an example of location, a description of the neighborhood would be an example of *place*. Comparing that neighborhood to others in the area would be an example of *region*.

Human-Environment Interaction addresses how humans shape and are shaped by their environments. The development of cities illustrates human-environment interaction. For example, San Francisco is known for its steep streets, a result of the physical landscape on which it is built. In Chicago, engineers successfully reversed the flow of the river so that it pulled water from Lake Michigan rather than feeding into it, showing how humans shape their environment.

Movement investigates how places are connected and interact with each other. Blues music spreading from the South into the rest of the United States and beyond is an example of movement.

All of geography can be organized around these five themes.

SAMPLE QUESTIONS

1) Which of following is NOT an example of geographic study?
   A. patterns of volcanic eruptions
   B. climate change and global warming
   C. settlement patterns in Southern Europe
   D. the rise and fall of the American dollar

   Answer:
   D. **Correct.** A study of the rise and fall of the American dollar is solely an economic issue, not a geographic one.

2) Migration patterns are an example of which geographic theme?
   A. location
   B. place
   C. movement
   D. region

   Answer:
   C. **Correct.** Migration patterns show how people—or animals—move in and out of different areas. This is a clear example of the theme of *movement*. It describes how places are interconnected.

LOCATION

Location, the most concrete of the themes, describes where something can be found on Earth. When location is **relative**, the object in question is positioned in relation to something else. For example, if someone says that their house is located two blocks north of the school, they are providing a relative location for the house.

In formal geographic settings, **absolute location** is generally used. A location is absolute when it is described by its position on Earth without reference to other landmarks. For example, the tallest building in the world—the Burj Khalifa—is located at 25.2°N and 55.3°E.

Something's location can also be described by either its site or situation. When a place is described by its **site**, it is described by its internal physical and cultural characteristics. For example, the site of a football stadium could be described by the number of seats, the field, the concession stands, and even the fans.

When a place is described by its **situation**, its characteristics are described relative to those around it. So the football stadium might be described by its size as compared to the other buildings in the city, its accessibility, or the amount of foot traffic it receives. The more connected a place is to powerful places, the better its situation. For instance, the front row of seats in a stadium is better situated than the top row.

MAPS

Geographers use illustrations to articulate and visualize the absolute location of a place or thing. These illustrations are called globes and maps.

Globes are spherical representations of the earth. They show the correct size, shape, and location of land masses, and the accurate distance between places on Earth. However, because globes are models for the entire earth, it is impossible for them to provide much detail.

Maps, on the other hand, are flat representations of the earth or parts of it. The more specific the area a map covers, the more detailed it can be. Maps do, however, have drawbacks.

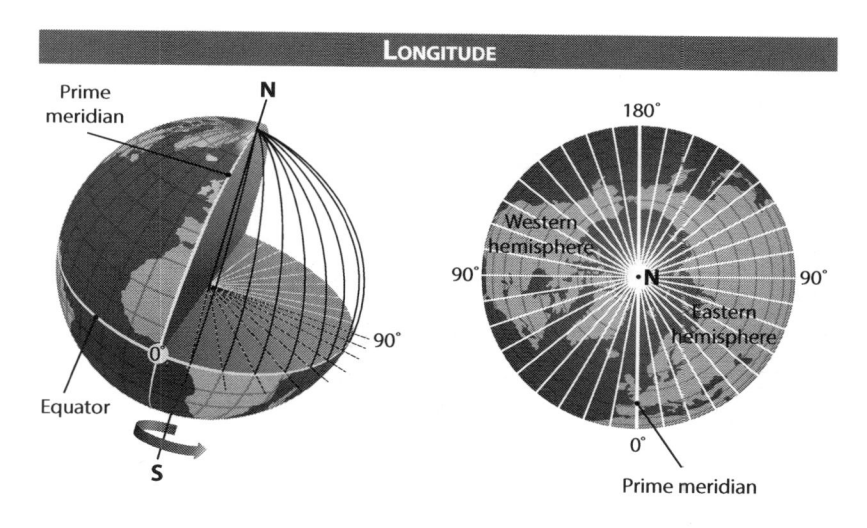

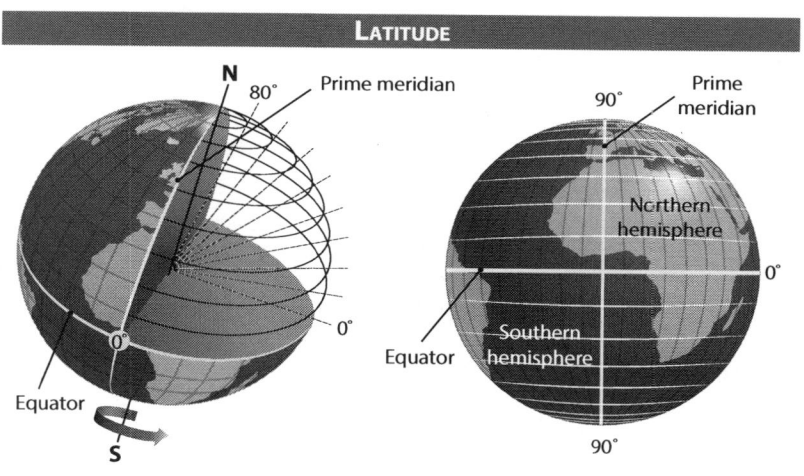

Figure 4.1. Longitude and Latitude

Whether map or globe, both types of illustrations use the same system for identifying location. The **grid system** divides the earth into imaginary, equidistant lines running vertically and horizontally to create a grid. Each line is measured as a **degree** (°), which can be subdivided into **minutes** (') and **seconds** (").

HELPFUL HINT
Which is longitude and which is latitude? Here is an easy way to remember: Lines of longitude are "long" so they stretch from pole to pole. Lines of latitude lie "flat" ("flat-itude latitude"), and so run horizontally.

The lines that run horizontally around the earth, parallel to the equator, are called lines of **latitude**. Degrees of latitude are numbered 0° to 90° running north and south from the equator (the equator is 0°). There are approximately 69 miles between each degree of latitude. This number shifts slightly because the earth is slightly egg shaped, not a true sphere.

The lines that run north and south from pole to pole are lines of **longitude**, or **meridians**. Because there is no natural "center" of the earth when measuring this way (like the equator), a 0° line was established by international agreement. Called the **prime meridian**, this line runs through the Royal Observatory in Greenwich, England. Meridians are then numbered up to 180° running east and west of this line.

Time zones around the world have been organized based loosely on the meridians, with each time zone representing approximately 15 degrees. Time is measured as an offset of Universal Coordinated Time (a system that measures time based on the rotation of the earth). However, there are exceptions to the rule. For example, China uses one time zone for the entire country.

At approximately 180° opposite of the prime meridian is the International Date Line. This is where the date changes in order to allow the global time zone system to work.

While the flat nature of maps provides greater flexibility in terms of focus and scale, representing something spherical—the earth—as flat inevitably leads to distortion. Every map is a **projection**, a representation of the earth's features on a flat surface.

Every projection has four main properties: the size of areas, the shape of areas, consistency of scales, and straight line directions. No map is able to accurately depict all four of these properties at once: every projection must sacrifice accuracy in at least one. In general, mapmakers choose to maintain the accuracy of one property and distort the others as needed. Which property is maintained is determined by the perspective of the mapmaker and the purpose of the map.

In an **equal area map**, the accuracy of the size of areas is maintained. Each land mass is kept to scale in its size. The best example of this type of map is the **Gall-Peters** projection. In order to preserve land mass size, the shape of land masses is distorted.

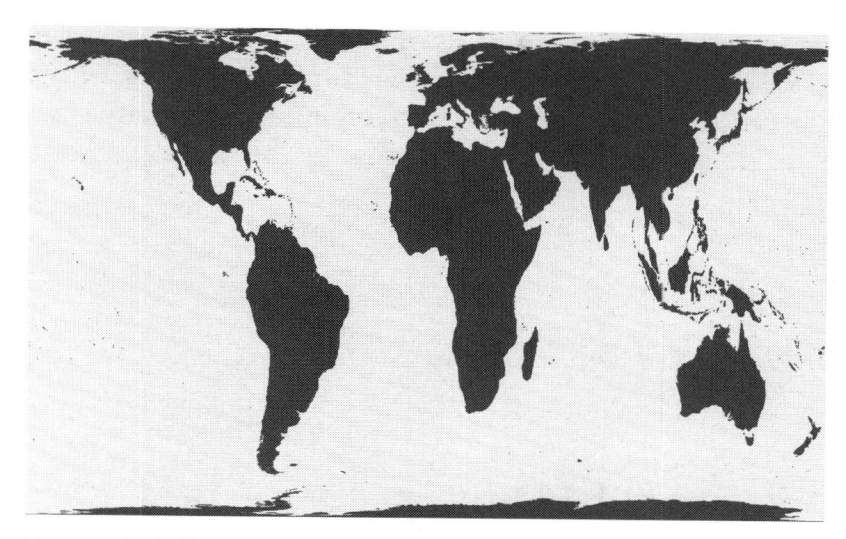

Figure 4.2. Gall-Peters Projection

Conformal maps, conversely, maintain the shape of areas at the expense of accuracy in size. The most used conformal map is the **Mercator** projection. It uses straight lines for latitude and longitude, rather than curving them to indicate the curve of the earth. It is made by wrapping the paper into a cylinder around a globe, called a **cylindrical projection**. On a Mercator projection map, the scale is accurate only at the equator or at two parallels equidistant from the equator. The farther from the equator, the more enlarged land masses appear. It is used primarily for marine navigation.

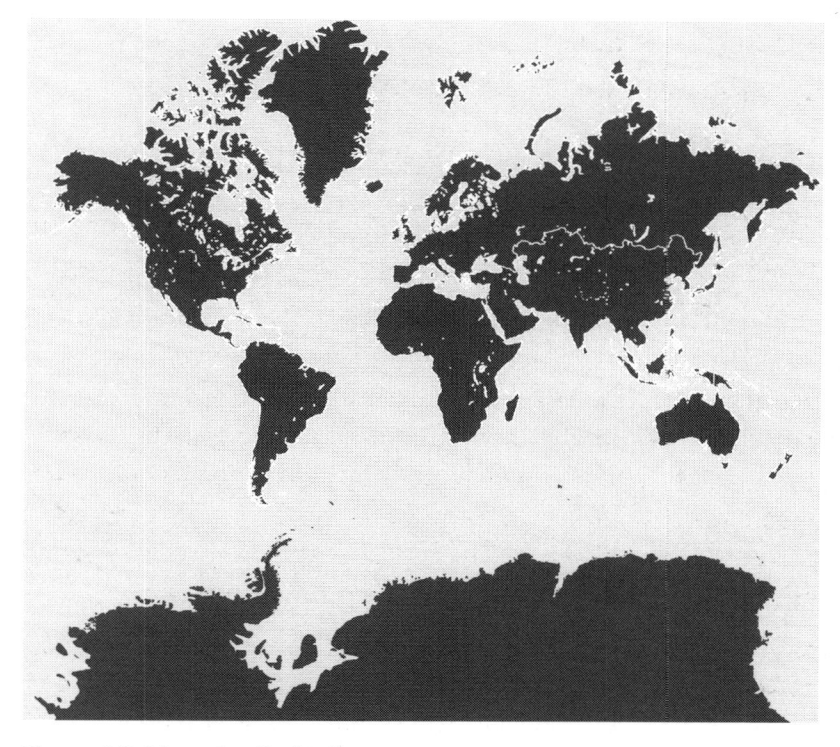

Figure 4.3. Mercator Projection

An **azimuthal equidistant projection** maintains accuracy in scale for distances from one single point on the map to all other points on the map. This kind of projection is most often used in showing airplane routes from one city to multiple other cities, for example.

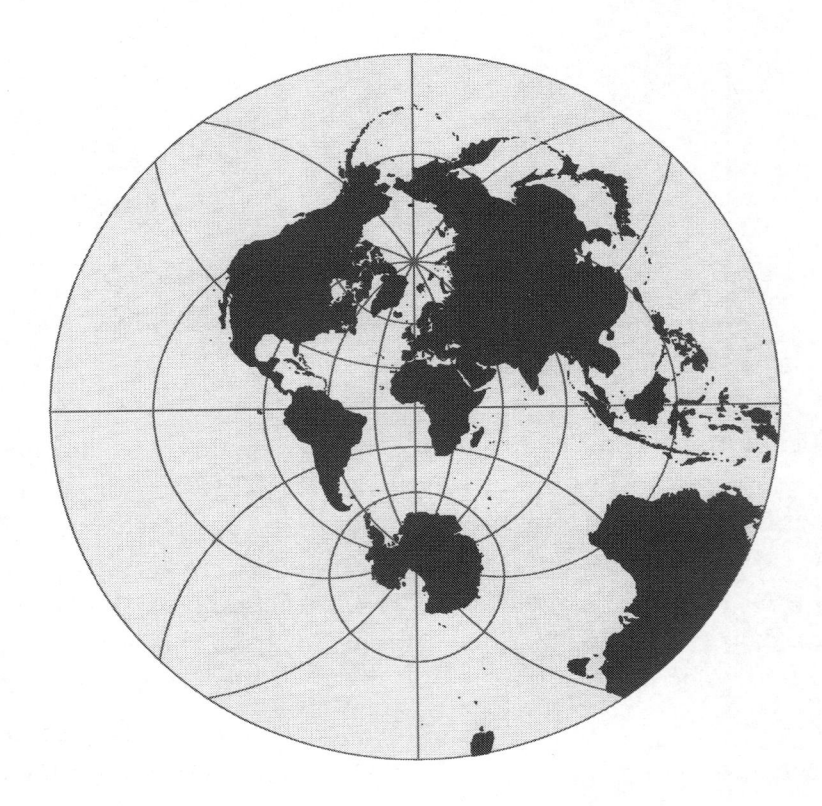

Figure 4.4. Azimuthal Equidistant Projection

A **gnomonic projection** preserves accuracy of distance. Every straight line on a gnomonic projection is the arc of a **great circle**, which represents the shortest distance between any two points on Earth. A great circle is any circle that bisects a sphere. In most projections, great circles are curved due to distortion resulting in the maintenance of one or more other properties. The gnomonic projection is the exception. This projection is particularly useful in navigation by sea or air where direction—for its own sake—is important. It is also often used to map the poles which are usually highly distorted in other map projections.

The most commonly used maps, however, are some sort of **compromise map**, which somewhat distort all four properties to minimize overall distortion. The most popular compromise maps are the Robinson projection and the Winkel tripel projection. Both projections balance size and shape, with minor distortions.

Most maps have five main tools:

The **title** of the map explains the purpose of the map and its area of focus.

The **scale** of the map describes the relationship between the unit of measurement used on the map and real distances on the earth.

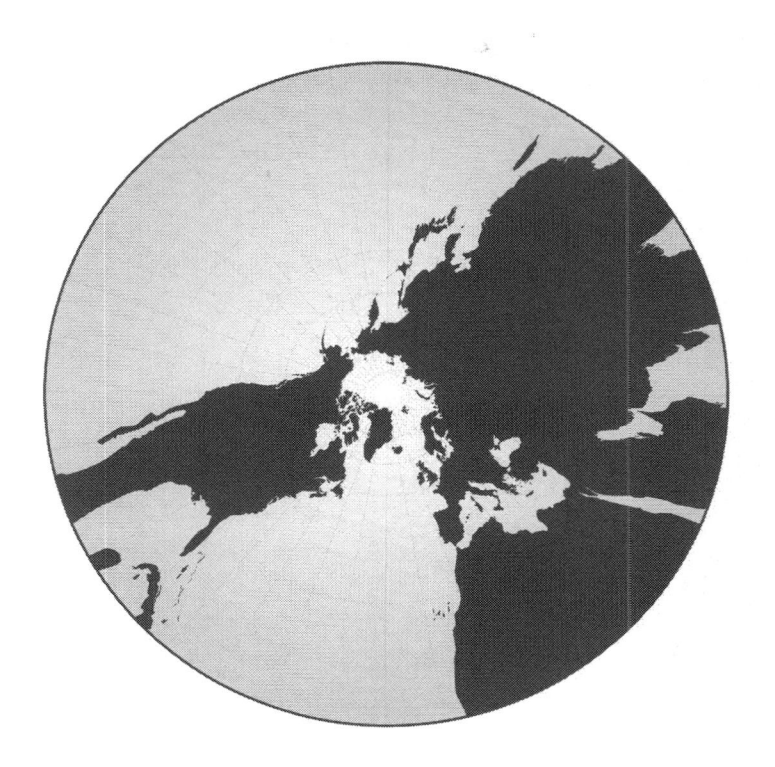

Figure 4.5. Gnomonic Projection

The **grid** consists of lines placed on the map to aid in finding locations. The grid is usually based on lines of longitude and latitude, but this may vary depending on the scope of the map.

The **legend** explains the meaning of any symbols used to convey information like population, natural resources, and more. For example, a dot map showing population would have a legend explaining how many people are represented by each dot.

Finally, a **compass rose** indicates the four cardinal directions: north, south, east and west, allowing the user to properly orient the map.

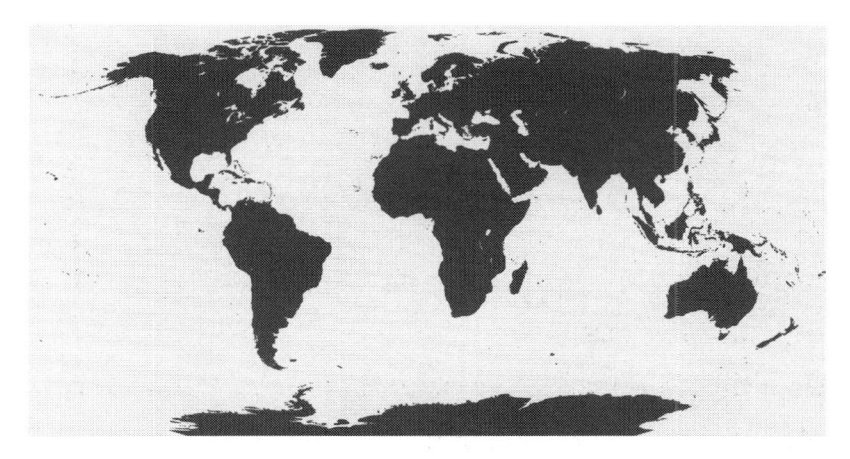

Figure 4.6. Robinson Projection and Winkel Projection

Some maps convey information other than location, direction, land mass, and shape. **Contour maps** illustrate levels of elevation in an area. Instead of showing latitude and longitude, the lines on these maps connect points of equal elevation, and the provided scale indicates the distance between the lines. **Relief maps** also depict elevation but do so through shading to create a three-dimensional effect.

> **QUICK REVIEW**
>
> Use a map to determine which city is at 41.9°N, 12.5°E.

An **isothermal map** is used to illustrate ranges of temperature. As in contour maps, the lines are used to show areas of equal or constant temperature.

SAMPLE QUESTIONS

3) In a conformal map, areas are represented accurately in terms of which of the following?

   A. shape
   B. size
   C. direction
   D. all of the above

   Answer:
   A. **Correct.** Conformal maps are designed to ensure the shape of all land masses are correct. In order to do this, they distort the other properties of the map: specifically, size.

4) Which of the following is an advantage of globes over maps?

   A. Globes provide more detailed information.
   B. Globes can be used to show a variety of sizes of areas.
   C. Globes are accurate models of the Earth without distortion.
   D. Globes show elevation levels in addition to size, shape, and location of areas.

   Answer:
   C. **Correct.** A globe is a model replica of the earth. It is precisely scaled to reflect the dimensions of the planet, accurately preserving size, shape, direction, and distance.

5) To determine the distance between Tokyo and Shanghai on a map of Asia, which of the following parts of the map would be used?

   A. compass rose
   B. scale
   C. legend
   D. grid

Answer:

B. Correct. The scale shows the ratio between distance on the map and true distance.

6) A scientist exploring Antarctica would most likely use which type of map?
   A. equal area projection
   B. azimuthal equidistant projection
   C. conformal projection
   D. gnomonic projection

Answer:

D. Correct. The gnomonic projection map allows for great circles and accurate straight-line directions. It is often used for mapping the poles; it would be an excellent choice for an explorer of Antarctica.

PLACE

The second theme of geography, **place**, is directly related to location. Studying place addresses all of the characteristics—human and physical—of a location. Physical attributes include climate, terrain, and natural resources, whereas human attributes include language, religion, art, political organization, and customs. Understanding place is at the core of any geographic study.

There are five physical characteristics of place: **land, water, climate, vegetation,** and **animal life.**

Land forms categorize areas by elevation, like **mountains, hills, foothills,** and **plateaus** on one hand and **plains** and **valleys** on the other. They also include areas created by water: **deltas**—the flat plains created by deposits from diverging branches of a river; **basins**—the bowl-like land that catches water and directs it toward a river; **marshes**—wetlands that are frequently inundated with water; and **swamps**—any wetland primarily covered in woody plants. Geographers also look at **soil**: how fertile it is, the kind of life it can support, and how it easily it is shaped by wind and water.

Bodies of water can be subdivided into several categories as well. The biggest bodies of water are the earth's five oceans:

- The **Atlantic Ocean** separates North and South America from Europe and Africa.
- The **Pacific Ocean**—covering almost one-third of the earth—separates North and South America from Asia and Australia.
- The **Indian Ocean** touches Africa, Asia, and Australia.
- The **Arctic Ocean** extends from the northern edges of North America and Europe to the North Pole and is composed primarily of ice for much of the year.

▸ The **Southern**, or **Antarctic, Ocean** extends from the southern tips of South America, Australia, and Africa to Antarctica.

There are other saltwater bodies called **seas**, which are smaller than oceans and surrounded by land. The largest is the **Mediterranean Sea**. The largest fully enclosed sea (or salted lake) is the **Caspian Sea**. Land-bound freshwater bodies are called **lakes**.

Finally, and most important for the development of civilization, are **rivers**, bodies of water that flow towards the ocean. The world's major river systems: the **Nile**, the **Tigris** and **Euphrates**, the **Indus**, the **Ganges**, the **Huang He (Yellow River)** and the **Yangtze**, the **Amazon**, and the **Mississippi** all gave birth to early and complex civilizations.

Another major defining physical characteristic of a place is its **climate**, the average weather for a specific location or region. Climate is based on monthly and yearly temperatures, as well as the length of the **growing season**. Climate is shaped by the latitude of a location, the amount of moisture it receives, and the temperatures of both land and water. Varying climates create different **ecosystems**, the communities of living organisms and nonliving elements of an area. These are discussed further below.

> **DID YOU KNOW?**
>
> While the majority of lakes are freshwater, there are some lakes that are salt-water lakes. The biggest example of these is the Great Salt Lake in Utah.

SAMPLE QUESTIONS

7) Which of the following is NOT a physical characteristic of Switzerland?

    A. mountain chains on both the northern and southern sides of the country
    B. three river valleys
    C. It shares borders with Germany, France, Italy, Austria, and Liechtenstein.
    D. over 1400 lakes

    Answer:

    C. **Correct.** Political borders are artificial, so they are considered human characteristics of a place.

8) Which of the following statements best illustrates the geographic theme of place?

    A. Northern Mali is primarily composed of desert.
    B. St. Louis is approximately 300 miles from Chicago.
    C. Beijing is located at approximately 40°N and 116°E.
    D. English is the dominant language in North America as well as Australia.

    Answer:

    A. **Correct.** "Place" addresses the defining features of an area.

Region

A **region** is a group of places that share common characteristics, whether human or physical. Regions can be large—incorporating multiple continents—or quite small.

There are three types of regions. In a **formal region** the shared characteristics define the region. For example, the Middle East is a formal region, as the area has common physical and cultural traits. A **functional region** is an area defined by common movement or function. Functional regions have a focal point, called a node, around which they are organized, related to their function. For example, a school district is a functional region organized around a school (or set of schools). The third type of regions are **perceptual regions**. These are areas grouped not by actual commonalities, but by perceived ones. For example, Africa is often addressed as a single region, even though the continent has a large number of differing cultural systems and physical characteristics.

To analyze global phenomena, geographers divide the world into **realms**, the largest logical regions possible. Realms are based on clusters of human population, economic, political, cultural, and physical traits.

There are twelve widely accepted realms: Sub Saharan Africa, North Africa and Southwest Asia, Europe, Russia, South Asia, East Asia, Southeast Asia, North America, Middle America, South America, the Austral Realm, and the Pacific Realms.

Regions are not static, and their borders are generally not sharply defined. The areas between regions, then, are called **transition zones**. Transition zones are marked by a greater diversity of cultural traits. Furthermore, they more often experience conflict.

Human geographers study regions the way they study place, applying the same concepts on a larger scale. While regions are defined primarily by their commonalities, geographers often study them in order to create comparisons. For example they might look at economic development, the growth of religions, or gender roles in different regions. The various theories and models apply as well. Geographers can use the Demographic Transition Model to understand demographic growth in a region as a whole, not just a specific place.

In physical geography, defining features of a region are its climate and ecosystems. The earth's ecosystems can be divided by latitude, with different latitudes having different climates.

The **low latitudes**, from the equator to latitudes 23.5° north and south, have three distinct climates. **Tropical rainforests** can be found in the equatorial lowlands. They experience intense sun and rain every day. Although temperatures in the rainforest rarely go above 90° Fahrenheit, the combination of sun and rain creates high humidity levels, leading to extreme heat.

North and south of the rainforest is the **savannah**. The savannah is dry in the winter and wet in the summer, experiencing an average of ten to thirty inches of rain. Temperatures generally stay below 90° Fahrenheit with lower temperatures (under 80° Fahrenheit) in the winter.

The **desert** lies beyond the savannah to the north and south. Deserts are the hottest and driest parts of the Earth. Deserts receive fewer than ten inches of rainfall a year. Temperatures swing widely from extreme heat during the day to extreme cold at night. The best known deserts in the world are the Sahara Desert, the Australian Outback, and the Arabian Desert.

The **middle latitudes**, from latitudes 23.5° to 66.5° north and south, have a greater variety of climates, determined more by proximity to water than by the exact latitude. While none of these climates are as wet as those in the low latitudes, three climates in the middle latitudes receive the most rain and therefore are the most fertile. The first is the **Mediterranean climate**. This climate can be found in lands between latitudes 30° and 40° north and south that lie along the western coast. These territories include land bordering the Mediterranean Sea, a small part of Southwestern Africa, southern and Southwestern Australia, a small part of the Ukraine near the Black Sea, central Chile, and southern California.

The Mediterranean climate features hot summers and mild winters. Unlike the savannah, the winters receive the most rain, and the summers are generally dry. This climate allows a year-round growing season.

The **humid subtropical climate** is located on coastal areas north and south of the tropics. This climate receives warm ocean currents and warm winds year round, leading to a climate that is warm and moist. The summers are long and wet, and the winters are short and mild. This creates a long growing season. This is also the climate that supports the greatest percentage of the world's population. Japan, southeastern China, northeastern India, southeastern South Africa, the southeastern United States, and parts of South America all have subtropical climates.

Areas that are near or surrounded by water experience the **marine climate**. This climate has very temperate weather, with winters that rarely go below freezing and summers that stay below 70° Fahrenheit. Marine climates are warm and rainy, resulting in part from the warm ocean winds. This climate can be found in Western Europe, the British Isles, the Pacific Northwest, southern Chile, southern New Zealand, southeastern Australia, and on the western coast of Canada.

The climate best for farming is the **humid continental climate**, the true four-season climate. Average temperatures vary based on an area's distance from the ocean, but regions with this climate all feature fertile land. Summers are warm to hot and usually humid. Winters range from cold to extremely cold, and precipitation is distributed evenly throughout the year. This climate can be found in the northern and central United States, south-central and south-eastern Canada, northern China, and the western and southeastern parts of the former Soviet bloc.

Those areas of continents far from the ocean are called **steppes**, or prairie. These are dry flatlands with minimal rainfall (ten to twenty inches annually). Steppes can even become deserts if rainfall consistently dips below ten inches per year. Summers are hot and winters are often very cold. Steppes can be found in the interiors of North America and Asia, as these continents are so large that their interiors are not subject to the ocean winds.

The **high latitudes**, from latitudes 66.5° north and south to the poles, are home to two climates: **tundra** and **taiga**. The tundra features extremely cold and long winters. While the ground is frozen for most of the year, during the short summer it becomes mushy. The tundra has low precipitation. With no arable land, it is home to few people, but features abundant plant and animal life.

> **HELPFUL HINT**
>
> In the low and high latitudes, the farther north, the drier the climate. In the middle latitudes, distance from the ocean determines how wet or dry the climate is.

The **taiga** is south of the tundra in Northern Russia, Sweden, Norway, Finland, Canada, and Alaska. This area is home to the world's largest forestlands. It also contains many swamps and marshes. The taiga has more extreme temperatures than the tundra because it is farther from the ocean. The growing season is so short that meaningful agriculture is impossible; thus, the taiga is sparsely populated. However, this region features distinctive and extreme mineral wealth.

SAMPLE QUESTIONS

9) **Which ecosystem experiences extreme temperatures—both hot and cold—in a single day?**

   A. tundra
   B. rainforest
   C. desert
   D. savannah

   Answer:

   C. **Correct.** The desert has extreme heat during the day and extreme cold at night.

10) **A congressional district is an example of which kind of region?**

    A. a functional region
    B. a formal region
    C. a perceptual region
    D. a node region

    Answer:

    A. **Correct.** A congressional district is a region with a common purpose—representation in Congress.

11) **According to the map below, if Biome 1 is tundra, which type of ecosystem is represented by Biome 2?**

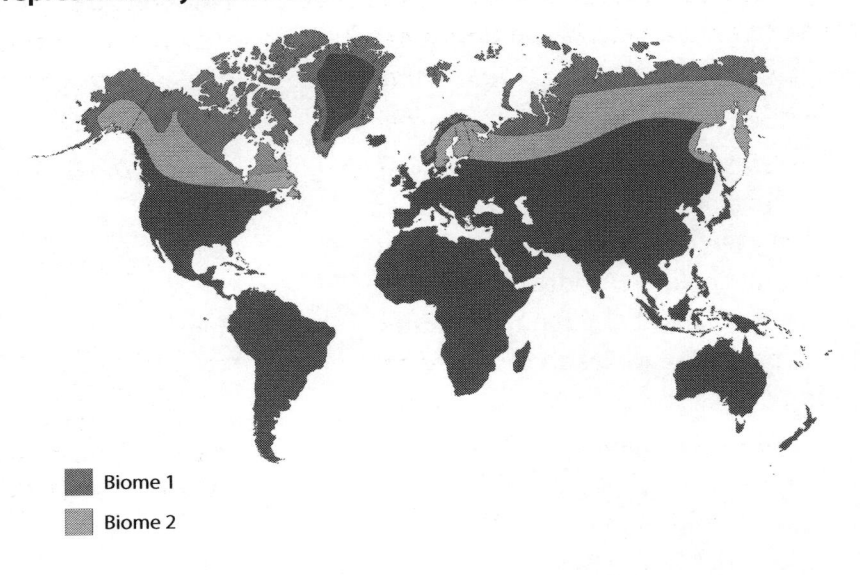

Biome 1
Biome 2

A. marine
B. taiga
C. desert
D. steppe

Answer:

B. **Correct.** Taiga is found just south of the tundra primarily in Sweden, Norway, Finland, northern Russia, Canada, and Alaska.

Human Characteristics of Place

The human characteristics of a place make up its **culture**. These include the shared values, language, and religion of the people living in a location or region. Cultures can be very specific or regional, like **folk cultures**, or they can be diffuse and widespread, like **popular culture**.

The Study of Culture

Human geographers or **cultural geographers** study how these characteristics are shaped by the physicality of a place. One key area of study for cultural geographers is the **material components** of a culture—the physical artifacts that can be left behind, like a bowl or a religious icon. They also look at the **non-material components** of a culture—the thoughts,

> **HELPFUL HINT**
>
> A folk culture is the sum of cultural traits of a localized, traditional group. Folk culture is often threatened by the spread of popular culture.

ideas, and beliefs of a people, like their code of law or their religion. Finally, they study a place's **cultural landscape**. Also called a *built landscape*, this is the impact a culture has on its environment: what kind of buildings or infrastructure did it create? For example, the development of railroads is an important part of the cultural landscape of the American West.

Human geographers use a variety of tools to interpret and analyze geographic information. A **histogram** is a graph that illustrates the distribution of data and shows how frequently various phenomena occur. **Scatter plots** show the relationship between two sets of data to allow for broader comparison. From tables and graphs, geographers can develop **descriptive statistics**, like the mean, mode, range, and average, which allow for more detailed understanding of the data.

> **TEST TIP**
>
> Interpreting graphs and tables is an important part of the Praxis Social Studies exam. Knowing and understanding various types of geographic tables, charts, and graphs will give you a leg up!

In order to recognize and understand spatial patterns, geographers use **geographic models**. For example, a **concentric zone plot** shows urban social structures, and the **Demographic Transition Model** explains the population patterns (this will be discussed later in this section).

Cars Through Tollbooth by Time of Day

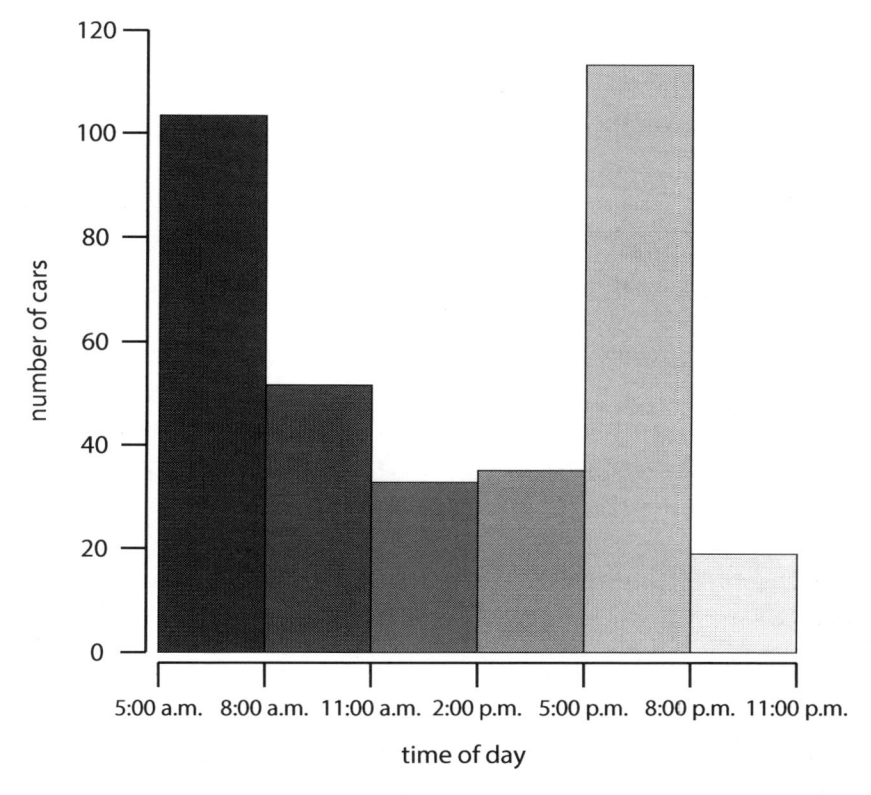

Figure 4.7. Sample Histogram

But where does the data come from to use in these various graphs, tables, and models? Geographers use both **primary geographic data** and **secondary geographic data** to build models and interpret information. They also use **geographic information systems (GIS)**, which are computer systems that store, manage, manipulate, or analyze spatial data.

SAMPLE QUESTIONS

12) **Which of the following is an example of a non-material component of a culture?**

    A. a statue of Buddha
    B. the teachings of Aristotle
    C. a newspaper from October 29, 1929
    D. a medieval sword

    Answer:

    B. **Correct.** While Aristotle's physical writings would be material components, his actual teachings—what he believed and said—are non-material.

13) **A geographer visits a village along the Amazon River and collects information about the role the river plays in the culture of the village. This is an example of**

    A. a descriptive statistic.
    B. a geographic information system.
    C. primary geographic data.
    D. secondary geographic data.

    Answer:

    C. **Correct.** Because the geographer is collecting the data on the river him- or herself, this is primary geographic data.

STRUCTURES OF CULTURES

Each culture is made up of countless, specific **culture traits**, single aspects of a culture, like shaking hands in greeting, or eating with a fork. A culture trait is not necessarily unique to one culture. For example, Eastern Orthodox nuns and conservative Jewish women cover their hair, but these are clearly two distinct cultures. This is because while the two cultures might have this one distinct trait in common, the combination of all of their culture traits—their **culture complexes**—are quite different.

In fact, no two cultures have the exact same complex. Therefore, wherever a difference in trait can be identified, two separate culture complexes exist. If, though, two culture complexes have many overlapping traits, they form a **culture**

system. For example, after the fall of the Berlin Wall there were distinct differences between East and West Germany, based on physical characteristics and differing histories. East Germans had a greater collective sense due to the socialist political and economic system they had experienced, while West Germans were more individualistic, having lived in a more capitalist society. The West had more access to technology; therefore television, movies, popular music, and video games were all a bigger part of West German culture. Even in terms of language there were differences: as a second language, the majority of West Germans spoke English, while the majority of East Germans spoke Russian. The East and the West made up distinct culture complexes.

However, they also had enough traits in common—a common language, a common government after reunification, and a shared history—to be a single culture system. And that culture system had linguistic and historical connections with the Netherlands, Norway, Denmark, and Sweden; these countries all, in turn, share history and have similar music and arts with France, Italy, Spain, and other neighboring countries. As such, they all make up a common **culture region** (Western Europe). That cultural region also has a shared history with Eastern Europe, as well as similarities in art and music. Together, they comprise a **culture realm**.

Development of Cultures

There are eight locations where formal culture—the development of agriculture, government, and urbanization—began. These locations are known as **culture hearths**.

In the Americas, culture began in Andean America and Mesoamerica. In Africa, the culture hearths were in West Africa and the Nile River Valley. In the Middle East, culture began in Mesopotamia, and in Asia, hearths existed in the Indus River Valley, the Ganges River delta, and along the Wei and Huang Rivers in China. In each of these hearths, similar innovations developed completely independently.

These innovations spread across the earth in a process called **cultural diffusion**, moving outward from the hearths in a variety of ways. Sometimes this occurred through inheritance, when one culture left an imprint on a place that was then used by the next culture to inhabit the same place. This is called **sequent occupancy**. New Orleans was founded by the French; it then switched between French and Spanish control several times, all the while attracting immigrants from Europe and importing slaves from West Africa and the Caribbean. The influence of each of these various cultures can be seen in New Orleans' hybrid culture today.

Other times, cultures change by coming into contact with each other, called **transculturation**. This can be symbiotic as in **cultural convergence**, when two cultures adopt each other's traits and become similar. For example, with the advent of national television programming, broadcasters and actors developed neutral accents and dialects which could be understood throughout the United States. These then diffused into the public, reducing regional language differences. Or it can be less balanced: for example, a culture may take on the qualities of another dominant culture. Called **acculturation**, examples of this throughout history abound, particularly anywhere that was subjected to colonization. In extreme cases, one culture fully **assimilates**, losing some or all of its unique aspects.

Cultures can also **diverge**, or change from being one culture complex into two. For example, as American mainstream culture modernized, the Amish diverged into a separate culture maintaining traditional ways.

SETTLEMENT PATTERNS

For cultures to grow, an area must first be settled. **Settlements** were the cradles of culture, permitting resource management, political development, and information transfer to future generations. Settlements all began near life-sustaining natural resources: water and a reliable food source. The success and growth of a settlement depends on its proximity to these natural resources and its ability to collect and move raw materials. As settlements became more sophisticated, local populations began to concentrate near the point of resource allocation and production.

A settlement's spatial layout was determined by its environment and primary function. For example, European villages clustered on hillsides to more easily protect against invaders, preserving flat areas for farming. Settlements fostered by trade, like those on the outskirts of the Saharan desert, concentrated around access to the trade routes and were generally more dispersed.

Later, successful settlements needed labor to generate products, and the ability to deliver these finished products elsewhere. Efficient transportation made people mobile, accelerating cultural diffusion and, eventually, the development of industrial centers. These industrial centers became cities. A **city** is a major human settlement with a high population density and a concentration of resource creation or allocation. Today, almost half of the world's population lives in cities. In more developed regions the percentages are even higher. With the development of cities, three types of areas emerged: **urban** (in the city itself), **suburban** (near the city), and **rural** (away from the city). Sometimes urban and suburban areas or multiple urban areas merge into a **megalopolis**, or super-city.

SAMPLE QUESTIONS

14) Which of the following statements is an example of cultural diffusion?
    A. Russia has the most lumber in the world.
    B. There is a Starbucks at the Mall of the Emirates in Dubai.
    C. Chopsticks are a key utensil in China.
    D. Spanish is the official language of Spain.

GEOGRAPHY

Answer:

    B.   **Correct.** Starbucks began in the United States, and is distinctly American. Its existence—and popularity—in Dubai is an example of cultural diffusion.

15) **The adoption of French as an official language throughout most of West Africa is an example of**

    A.   sequent occupancy.

    B.   cultural convergence.

    C.   cultural divergence.

    D.   acculturation.

Answer:

    D.   **Correct.** The adoption of French in West Africa as an official language is a classic example of a local culture overcome by a powerful force and taking on the traits of what would thus become the dominant culture. This occurred wherever colonization took place.

16) **The majority of people in the world today live in**

    A.   urban areas.

    B.   suburban areas.

    C.   rural areas.

    D.   megalopolises.

Answer:

    A.   **Correct.** More than half of the world's population lives in cities.

17) **Settlements developed near rivers would most likely**

    A.   be designed in a circular fashion a few miles away from the river.

    B.   be built into nearby hills.

    C.   be long and narrow to follow the shape of the river.

    D.   have clear access to land trade routes.

Answer:

    C.   **Correct.** In order to maximize the residents' access to the water, the settlement would grow along the bank of the river.

DEMOGRAPHIC PATTERNS

Demography is the study of human population. The **distribution** of people (how people are spread across the earth), and the **density** (the number of people in a particular area) are closely tied to other geographic factors.

Demographers use **population equations** to analyze changes in population. **Global equations** look at the total population of the earth, including the number of births and deaths that occur. **Sub-global equations** look at total population in a given area and also include immigration and emigration as factors.

Over the last 300 years, the population of Earth has exploded; population has been growing at an exponential rate, meaning the more people are added to the population, the faster it grows. In 1765, the global population was 300 million people. Today it is six billion. This increase has raised concerns for many demographers, particularly in the areas with a higher population concentration. To determine if an area is at risk, demographers determine its **carrying capacity**, the number of people the area can support.

The carrying capacity of various areas can differ greatly depending on technology, wealth, climate, available habitable space, access, and **infrastructure**, or institutions that support the needs of the people. When a country exceeds its carrying capacity, it suffers from **overpopulation**. Countries in danger of overpopulation may attempt to restrict their growth, like China did through its one-child policy. Conversely, they may attempt to increase their carrying capacity by increasing their resources using technology such as irrigation or desalination, or increasing their access to trade. For example, Japan greatly increased its carrying capacity by importing significant quantities of food. As a result, it is able to maintain a much larger population than it would otherwise be able to.

In spite of the population boom, some countries actually suffer from **underpopulation**. They have a much greater carrying capacity—due to their high levels of production, amount of land, or abundance of natural resources—than their population uses.

As discussed earlier, more than half of the world's population today lives in cities. While this is a relatively recent change, the population has always been unevenly distributed based on resources. Seventy-five percent of all people live on only 5 percent of the earth's land. Much of the world's wealth is concentrated in North America and Western Europe, but 80 percent of people live in poor, developing countries in South America, Asia, and Africa. The most populated area in the world is East Asia, which is home to 25 percent of the world's population. East Asia is followed by Southeast Asia, and then Europe.

> **QUICK REVIEW**
>
> Name one way a country can increase its carrying capacity.

DEMOGRAPHIC TRANSITION MODEL

In order to understand how populations will change, demographers use the **Demographic Transition Model**. This is a geographic tool which predicts changes in population using the **crude birth rate (CBR)**, **crude death rate (CDR)**, and the **rate of natural increase (RNI)**, or how much the population is increasing based on the first two factors. The model ties the changes in population to economic development by making two major assumptions: 1) all population growth is based on economic status, and 2) all countries pass through the same economic stages. While both of these assumptions have been challenged, the Demographic Transition Model is still the best indicator of population change.

The Demographic Transition Model outlines four states of economic and population growth (and one theoretical one):

- **Stage One**: This is a low growth stage. Both the CBR and CDR are high, making the RNI low or stationary. Some fluctuation will occur at this stage based on disease, war, and famine, all of which are somewhat common in Stage One economic development. Most of the population consists of subsistence farmers. Today, there are no countries that are still considered Stage One because of advances in medical technology which have eventually permeated down to every country. The prevention of disease—and death from it—decreases CDR, allowing RNI to increase.

- **Stage Two**: Because CDR has declined, but CBR remains high, this is a high growth stage. Medical advances can have an immediate impact on CDR, but CBR tends to be a deeply-rooted cultural tradition and is much more difficult to change. In Stage Two countries, the majority of the population still engages in subsistence farming. Many developing countries today are Stage Two countries.

- **Stage Three**: As countries move from only subsistence farming into industrialization, CBR begins to slow. Women have more choices in work and this, in conjunction with urbanization—and the reduced living space that goes along with it—leads to a decline in the birth rate. Most Latin American and Asian countries today are Stage Three countries.

- **Stage Four**: Industrialization leads to modernization. Once countries become fully industrialized and begin to develop more complex service economies, as well as advanced healthcare and education systems, CBR and CDR are once again equal but at a much lower rate, leading to a low RNI. This is a low growth stage. Stage Four is considered to be the ideal stage for population growth as the country is stable and prosperous, and population growth is slow and steady. The United States, Argentina, and Singapore are all Stage Four countries.

- **Stage Five**: The last stage of the Demographic Transition Model is mostly a theoretical one, although several countries are moving towards it. In Stage Five, medical advances not only succeed in limiting early deaths, but also in extending the life of the elderly. The decline in CBR continues, leading eventually to a negative RNI. Many countries in Western Europe and Japan are facing such graying populations.

United States Population (2015)

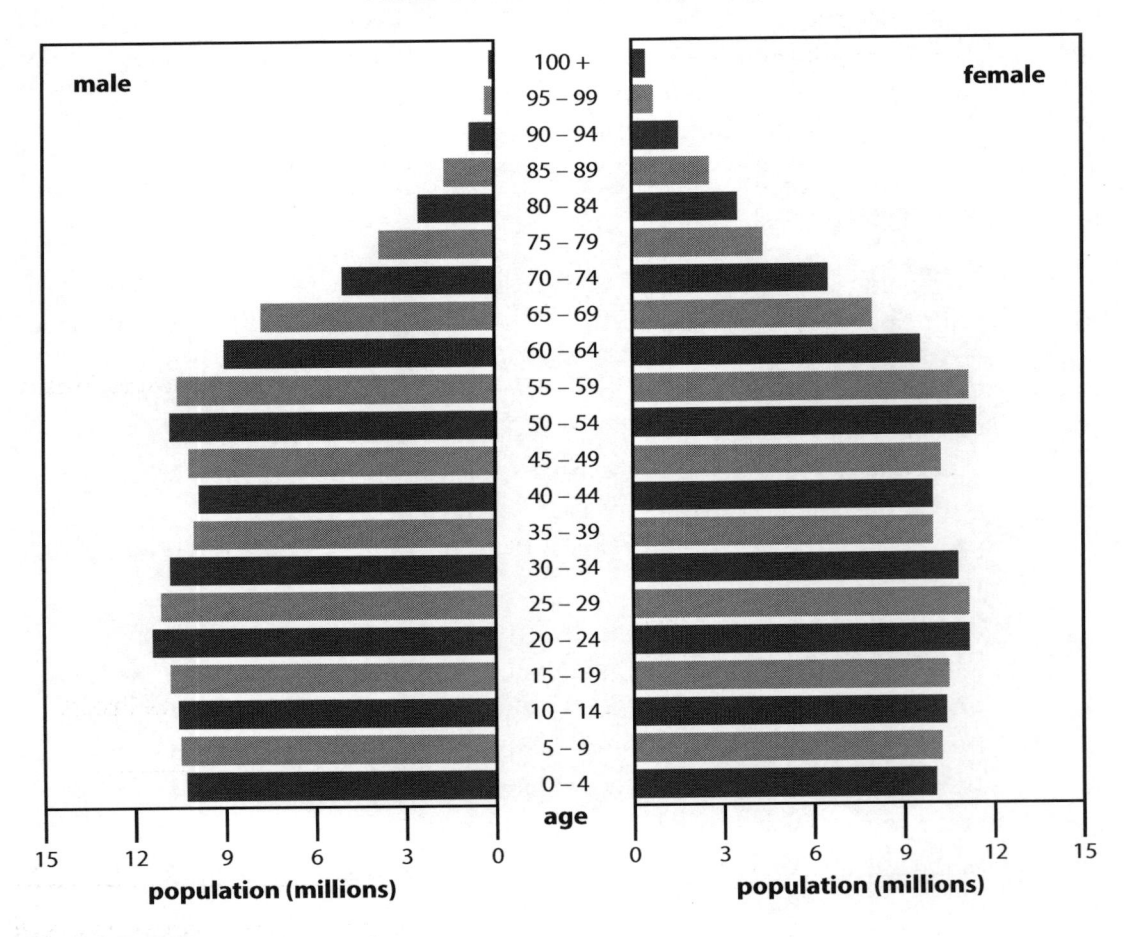

Figure 4.8. Population Pyramid

SAMPLE QUESTIONS

18) Overpopulation is most likely to occur in which stage of the Demographic Transition Model?

   A.   Stage One
   B.   Stage Two
   C.   Stage Three
   D.   Stage Four

   Answer:

   B.   **Correct.** In Stage Two, the crude death rate declines (as a result of medical advancements), but the crude birth rate remains high. This leads to high population growth, putting the country at risk of overpopulation.

19) Which of the following areas has the highest population density?
    A. India
    B. United States
    C. Germany
    D. Belgium

    Answer:
    A. **Correct.** The second biggest population center in the world is Southeast Asia (the first is East Asia).

20) Canada produces more resources than its population can consume. This is an example of
    A. overpopulation
    B. carrying capacity
    C. under-population
    D. graying population

    Answer:
    C. **Correct.** When a country does not have enough people to utilize its resources, it is underpopulated.

Economic Patterns

A country or area's **economy** is the system by which it produces, consumes, and distributes resources and goods. The economy is classified into five sectors:

- The **primary sector** focuses on the extraction of raw materials. This includes mining, farming, and fishing. In an industrialized economy, this is the smallest part of the economy.
- The **secondary sector** processes the raw materials extracted by the first sector. This sector is made up primarily of factories. Things like steel, canned tuna, and rubber are all secondary sector products.
- The **tertiary sector** moves, sells, and trades the products created by the secondary sector; it is also known as the *service economy*. Transportation companies, merchants, and stores are all parts of the tertiary sector.
- The **quaternary sector** creates and transfers information. University researchers, journalists, and information technology specialists are members of the quaternary sector.
- The **quinary sector** applies to the highest levels of decision-making and focuses on managing the overall functioning of the economy. Usually the quinary sector includes government agencies and officials.

Most economies also have an informal sector which encompasses all business transactions that are not reported to the government. The range of this sector includes everything from unregistered street vendors to neighborhood babysitters to illegal sales of drugs.

INDUSTRIALIZATION

With development and economic growth, manufacturing becomes increasingly important to the functioning of the economy. This is called **industrialization**. Because industrialization requires a shift in the labor force, it pairs with a decline in subsistence farming.

> **HELPFUL HINT**
>
> Throughout the 1990s, technology firms *agglomerated* in San Francisco, creating a *technopole*. However, in 1999 many companies lost their value. This resulted in *deglomeration*: many companies moved out of San Francisco because of the high rent and operational costs.

Industrialization is a relatively recent phenomenon. The **Industrial Revolution** began in Great Britain in the 1760s, then diffused to Western Europe and North America by 1825. The discovery of new energy sources like coal (later, petroleum) and technological advancements which allowed machine labor to replace human labor led to the emergence of manufacturing centers and a shift in the functioning of the economy.

Industrialization had significant spatial implications. The extraction of resources and building of factories changed the physical landscape of places. As transportation infrastructure improved and labor was commodified, migration from rural to urban areas increased. Also, population settlements grew up around energy sources. Called **agglomeration**, related industries often are developed near each other to share resource costs.

In some cases, an area can become over-agglomerated and pollution, traffic, restricted labor pools, and overtaxed resources can lead to the spreading out of industries, called **deglomeration**. Increasingly, industries also are moving their operations to places with lower labor costs.

> **SAMPLE QUESTIONS**
>
> 21) An owner of a grocery store is part of which sector of the economy?
>
>   A. primary
>
>   B. secondary
>
>   C. tertiary
>
>   D. quaternary

Answer:

C. Correct. The tertiary sector sells and trades processed goods. Any store is part of the tertiary sector.

22) **Which of the following is NOT a consequence of industrialization noted by geographers?**

    A. significant changes to the physical characteristics of the area in which industrialization takes place

    B. decrease in subsistence farming

    C. migration to suburban areas

    D. increasing importance of energy sources like coal and oil

Answer:

C. Correct. With industrialization, geographers note a rise in the migration of people from rural to urban areas, not suburban.

ECONOMIC DEVELOPMENT

The growth of economies is strongly connected to **development**, the use of technology and knowledge to improve the living conditions of people in a country. While economic in its foundation, development focuses on a range of quality of life issues like access to basic goods and services, education, and healthcare. Wealthier countries are called **more developed countries (MDCs)**, while others are called **less developed countries (LDCs)**. MDCs are concentrated primarily in the Northern Hemisphere. Their primary economic concern is maintaining growth. LDCs, found mostly in the Southern Hemisphere, face the challenge of improving their economic conditions by stimulating significant and sustainable economic growth.

Several different measures indicate development. A country's **gross domestic product (GDP)** is the value of the total output of goods and services produced in a country in a given period of time, typically a year. The GDP is usually calculated per capita. In MDCs the per capita GDP is more than $20,000. In LDCs it is less than $1,000. GDP should not be confused with another measure of development, the **gross national product**, which is the value of goods and services owned and produced by citizens of a country, regardless of where those goods and services are produced.

Neither of these, however, take into account the distribution of wealth in a country or non-monetary factors in quality of life. They also exclude the informal sector. Therefore, they are considered ineffective measures of development. Instead, two other measures provide a better understanding.

Purchasing power parity (PPP) is an exchange rate that determines how much currency it would take to buy the equal amounts of goods in two different countries. For example, a Big Mac in South Africa costs 19.45 rand, 9.50 real in Brazil, and $4.07 in the United States (as of 2011). So which is actually the most expensive? By looking only at the numbers, it seems that it is significantly harder to buy a Big

Mac in South Africa; therefore, it would seem that quality of life is lower in general for South Africans. However, once the purchasing power parity is determined (by dividing the numeric cost of each Big Mac), and then adjusted using the currency exchange rate, a Big Mac in South Africa actually costs US $2.87 and a Big Mac in Brazil costs US $6.17. Therefore, Big Macs are actually significantly less expensive in South Africa and significantly more expensive in Brazil. So, the perceived disparity between South African development and American development is less than it originally seemed (when measured by a Big Mac!).

The second measure is the **United Nations Human Development Index (HDI)**. The HDI assumes that development is actually best measured by the choices available to the population of a country. It focuses on quality of life measures like education, healthcare, and general welfare. It does use GDP, but only as one measure among others including life expectancy, level of education attainment, and literacy rates. It then creates a ranking system of the world's countries with the highest score being 1.000 and the lowest 0.000.

ROSTOW MODERNIZATION MODEL

In the 1950s, sociologist Walt Rostow created a model to explain the economic development of countries. He argued that each country goes through five stages.

- Stage One is the *Traditional Society*. An economy consists mostly of subsistence farming with little trade or industry.
- Stage Two he called *Preconditions for Takeoff*. In this stage, small groups of individuals initiate "takeoff" economic activities. They begin to develop small industries in pockets of a country.
- In Stage Three, called *Takeoff*, those small industries begin to grow very quickly and become a significant part of the economy. The shift from subsistence farming to industry begins.
- Stage Four is the *Drive to Maturity*. Advanced technology and development spread beyond the takeoff areas to the rest of the country. A skilled, educated workforce emerges and becomes sustainable. Other industries begin to grow rapidly.
- Finally, Stage Five is *High Mass Consumption*. In this stage the majority of the population is employed in service, rather than factory, jobs. Education is high. Economic development reaches new levels, leading to increased consumption.

LDCs are all in Rostow's Stages One, Two, and Three, while MDCs are in Stages Four and Five. Rostow's model has many critics who argue that is too Anglo-centric. They also point out that it unrealistically assumes countries develop independently of one another, and so it does not take into account the impact of colonization (discussed in the next section).

Critics also take issue with Rostow's fifth stage, arguing that increased consumption is not a necessary consequence of economic growth. Instead, they argue that the surplus wealth could lead to increased social welfare programs or sustainable activities. Northern Europe more closely models this version of a fifth developmental stage.

> **TEST TIP**
>
> The Demographic Transition Model (DTM) is based off of Rostow's Modernization Model. The five stages of each model align. This can help you with questions that ask you to analyze the relationship between population and development.

DEVELOPMENT GAP

By any measure, the gap between MDCs and LDCs is widening. In the last ten years, the GDP of MDCs has tripled while the GDP of LDCs has only doubled. RNI in MDCs has dropped by 85 percent in the same time period, while it has only decreased by 5 percent in LDCs. Several theories attempt to explain this trend.

Dependency theory argues that colonization is at root of the problem. According to dependency theory, the decisions and actions of one country directly impact those of others.

The majority of MDCs today were colonizers, while the majority of LDCs were colonized. The goal of the colonizing countries was to increase their wealth by using the colonies as both a source of natural resources and as a market for the sale of their finished goods. So industrialization was suppressed in the colonies. Even after colonization, MDCs needed LDCs in order to maintain economic growth and dominance. LDCs have relied on MDCs for aid and support. Therefore, LDCs are kept in a cycle of underdevelopment by the structure of the global economic system.

The **Core-Periphery Model** presents a similar perspective. It divides the countries of the world into three groups: the core, semi-periphery, and periphery. The *core* consists of industrialized countries, those with the highest per capita income and standard of living (the United States, Canada, Australia, New Zealand, Japan, and Western Europe). The *semi-periphery* is composed of newly industrialized countries like India, Brazil, South Africa, and China. These countries are distinguished by significant economic inequality. The *periphery* consists of countries with very low levels of industrialization, infrastructure, and per capita income and standards of living. Essentially, these are LDCs, and include most of Africa (not South Africa as noted above), parts of Asia, and parts of South America.

> **HELPFUL HINT**
>
> Most semi-periphery countries are spatially located between core and peripheral countries, and between two competing core areas. They also, typically, have larger land masses (like India, China, and Brazil); however there are exceptions to this (Poland, Greece, and Israel).

To explain this structure, sociologist Immanuel Wallerstein posited his **World Systems Analysis Theory** which states that the global system is a capitalist system interlocked by competition, both political and economic. This competition made the exploitation of some countries by others inevitable. Those that did the exploiting became the core, and those that were exploited became those on the periphery and semi-periphery (based on location and, to a degree, size).

IMPROVING ECONOMIC DEVELOPMENT

There are three main approaches for improving the economic development of LDCs. The first is the **self-sufficiency approach**. This is based on the idea that a country can only develop if the country provides for its people itself, rather than relying on outside aid and support. Countries must promote development across all sectors and regions rather than concentrate on just one industry (which is typical for LDCs based on the colonization model). Self-sufficiency requires a closed economic state with minimum imports and high tariffs to limit international trade. However, critics of this model argue that it stifles competition, which will ultimately inhibit growth.

The opposite approach is the **International Trade Approach**. In this export-oriented approach, a country focuses on products that it can provide to the rest of the world. By doing this, a country develops a **comparative advantage** in that industry, meaning it becomes better than the rest of the world in that industry.

For example, Japan chose to focus on developing a comparative advantage in high-tech products rather than food production. Instead, it imports much of its food. Critics of this approach argue it only works if a country is able to actually develop a comparative advantage. If a country invests in developing a comparative advantage in one industry, but is unable to become the "best," it has wasted its resources and crippled the rest of its economy. Also, even if it does develop a comparative advantage, this can still leave the country open to exploitation, particularly if its chosen market is an export-based product. This can best be seen in many African countries that export raw materials like gold, diamonds, rubber, and cocoa. While exportation levels might be high, development remains low, as the push to produce more leads to severe mistreatment of labor with limited opportunities for small business growth, market competition, or upward mobility.

Finally, intergovernmental organizations attempt to improve the development of LDCs through **structural adjustments**. Organizations like the **World Bank** or the **International Monetary Fund** offer loans in exchange for changes to a country's economic structure. These usually involve increasing privatization, which negatively impacts families reliant on resources previously provided by the government. However, advocates argue this is only a short-term negative impact that is necessary for longer-term gain.

GEOGRAPHY

SAMPLE QUESTIONS

23) The countries of West Africa remain LDCs because of their dependence on Western MDCs developed during French colonization of the area. This statement most reflects which of the following?

   A. Rostow's Modernization Model
   B. World Systems Analysis Theory
   C. International Trade Approach
   D. Dependency Theory

   Answer:
   D. **Correct.** Dependency Theory argues that colonization created a dependent relationship between LDCs and MDCs that cannot be broken due the global economic structure.

24) Which of the following is true of MDCs?

   A. They have GDP per capita in excess of $20,000.
   B. They are concentrated in Western Europe and North America.
   C. both A and B
   D. neither A nor B

   Answer:
   C. **Correct.** Both statements about MDCs are accurate descriptors.

25) Purchasing power parity is a better measure of economic development than gross domestic product because

   A. PPP allows for direct comparisons of what money can acquire in different countries.
   B. It is based on more accurate numbers than GDP.
   C. GDP is only calculated every ten years, whereas PPP is annual.
   D. PPP takes into account class differences in quality of life.

   Answer:
   A. **Correct.** By looking at the ratio of the cost of certain items (or groups of items) in different countries, PPP gives a more accurate comparative measure of development.

26) How does the UN Human Development Index differ from other measures of economic development?

   A. It focuses on the gap between the wealthy and the poor in a country.
   B. It considers non-monetary factors like healthcare, literacy rates, and education.
   C. It only examines the top fifty and bottom fifty nations in the world.
   D. It is the only measure focused on comparative economic growth.

Answer:

B. **Correct.** The HDI defines development as the expansion of choices for the people. As a result, it looks at many factors, many of which are non-monetary.

Globalization

Globalization is the trend of interdependence and interaction throughout the world. At its core, globalization is an economic trend; however it has significant cultural and political impacts as well. For example, the exportation of American fast food restaurants reflects the capitalist drive to find new markets. Furthermore, the introduction of this type of food has a significant impact on one of the major distinguishing cultural traits of other countries—cuisine.

The primary driving force of globalization is **multinational corporations (MNCs)** or **transnational corporations (TNCs)**. Often made up of several smaller companies that all contribute to the same production process, these are companies whose headquarters are located in one country (usually an MDC) and whose production is located in one or more different countries (usually an LDC). The process of moving production to a different country is called **outsourcing**, and it allows for several financial advantages for the MNC including reduced labor costs, lower tax rates, and cheaper land prices. The new country also often has more lax safety and labor standards. Although outsourcing increases transportation costs, this increase is offset by a lower cost in labor. This is called the **Substitution Principle**.

Some countries create **special economic zones (SEZs)** to encourage outsourcing. In these zones, companies are held to lower environmental and labor standards and can receive special tax breaks and other incentives. SEZs also encourage companies to invest directly in the economy of the hosting country to help maintain the government that is supporting their business.

Similar to SEZs are **export processing zones**, also known as free trade zones, in which duties and tariffs are waived, and restrictions on labor practices are significantly loosened. Again, the goal is to attract the factories of MNCs.

The globalization of the manufacturing process has created a **New International Division of Labor** in which different parts of a product are manufactured in different places of the world, then sent to yet another location to be assembled. Essentially, this is a globalization of the Fordist assembly line. The problem with this model is that LDCs become very dependent on MNCs. Furthermore, MNCs may engage in **direct investment** in the country as part of their activities there, investing directly into its economy. In the long run, local involvement allows

> **HELPFUL HINT**
>
> NICs are countries that are not yet developed, but are developing faster than other less developed countries. They have strong manufacturing export economies, a great deal of foreign investment, strong political leadership, and increasing rights for citizens.

MNCs to gain disproportionate influence over governmental affairs as they advocate for governmental policies favorable to their own financial goals, especially **free trade**, or no regulations, on outsourcing.

Advocates argue that outsourcing allows economic growth in otherwise struggling economies. They point to the Four Asian Tigers (Singapore, Hong Kong, South Korea, and Taiwan) as examples of countries that began as sources of production for MNCs, and then became **Newly Industrialized Countries (NICs)**, experiencing unprecedented economic growth. As a result, today many consider these countries to be MDCs.

Critics, however, argue that free trade only benefits MNCs because it does not protect local workers, local environments, or ensure an appropriate quality of life in the countries that provide the labor. They argue that the Asian Tigers succeeded not because of outsourcing, but because they shifted their focus from production for MNCs to developing a comparative advantage in service industries, namely high-end technology and financial management. These critics argue for **fair trade** in which governments oversee and regulate outsourcing to ensure all workers receive a living wage.

SAMPLE QUESTIONS

27) Special Economic Zones attract multinational corporations by doing all of the following EXCEPT

   A. offering them tax breaks.
   B. providing them space for their headquarters.
   C. lessening environmental standards.
   D. loosening labor laws.

   Answer:

   B. **Correct.** Most MNCs headquarter their companies in MDCs, and only use the LDC's SEZ for production purposes.

28) The Substitution Principle states that:

   A. Corporations headquarter their company in one country and produce their goods in another.
   B. Companies can invest money directly into a country's economy.
   C. Companies will accept increased transportation costs in exchange for decreased labor costs.
   D. New industrialized countries switch from hosting production to focusing on new cutting edge industries.

   Answer:

   C. **Correct.** Although outsourcing leads to higher transportation costs as companies have to pay to get finished goods back to their markets,

the reduced cost of labor is enough to offset it. This is called the Substitution Principle.

Political Geography

The study of political organization—another human characteristic of place—is called **political geography**. Political structures emerged over time in response to ongoing competition for control over territory, resources, trade routes, and people. In order to strengthen their positions, groups often cooperate with each other through alliances and agreements. For example, today the world is mostly divided into various state sovereignties as different groups came together in order to access different resources, solidify their power, or control strategic positions. In fact, the only unorganized area left in the world is Antarctica. Cooperation exists on the **supranational scale** as well in the form of multi-national organizations like the United Nations.

However, more often competition between groups leads to conflict. Those same agreements and alliances that allow for cooperation may also determine the sides of a conflict. These sides are often based on culture traits: religion, political ideology, national origin, language, or race. They can be local, regional, national, or global. For example, within a state different regions might compete for a greater share of government funds, or two towns might fight over access to roads or rivers. In the nineteenth-century United States, the North and South engaged in an ideologically and economically based armed conflict during the Civil War. In the twentieth century, the nations of the world divided into two sides—the fascist Axis and the western, democratic capitalist Allies (in an uneasy alliance with the Soviet Union)—during World War II.

Humans desire to establish ownership of their own specific, personal space. This **human territoriality** has manifested differently over time from tribes, clans, and villages to kingdoms and empires. In Europe, for example, city-states then emerged in Greece and Rome, followed by the rise of feudal society after the fall of these empires. Feudal society led into monarchy, which eventually transformed into nation-states (which has become the global organizing political principle since World War II). At the center of each of these political forms, though, was the concept of **sovereignty**, the public recognition of an individual or group's control over a place, its people, and its institutions.

States

In political geography, there is a distinction between the physical area and the people of a place. A **state** refers to the physical place: it is any area with defined borders, a permanent population, and a relatively effective government and economy.

The borders, or **political boundaries**, of a state can be drawn in three different ways. **Physical boundaries** are based on natural features like rivers or mountains, whereas **cultural political boundaries** are based on religion or language. The third type of boundary, **geometric political boundaries**, are drawn as straight lines without regard to natural or cultural features. The border between North and South Korea is such a boundary.

Most modern boundaries are the result of negotiation between states, or human settlement or interaction. These are called **subsequent boundaries**. **Antecedent boundaries** pre-dated human cultures. **Superimposed boundaries**, such as those in the modern Middle East, were imposed by an outside force. **Relict boundaries**, like the Great Wall of China, are boundaries that are no longer functioning but serve as a reminder that the boundary used to exist.

In order to create a legal political boundary, four steps must be followed.

- **Definition**: The boundary must be legally described. This is where most of the negotiation between states takes place.
- **Delimitation**: The boundary must be drawn onto a map.
- **Demarcation**: The boundary must be marked, in some way, on the physical landscape.
- **Administration**: The boundary must be policed and enforced.

In this process, there are many opportunities for disagreement and conflict. Disputes over borders can arise over the border's actual location, how that location is defined, how the border is administered, and how resources are distributed near and across the border. Disputes also arise in **frontiers**, areas where boundaries are either not well established or not maintained well.

On land, boundary negotiations can be tricky, but they become significantly more complicated in the oceans. States have agreed that each state has an **exclusive economic zone** up to 200 miles from its shore. If there is less than 200 miles between two countries, the ocean area is divided equally in half. This is called the **median line principle**.

Boundaries determine the outer edges of a state. From the inside, states are organized around a **core**, the location of the concentration of power. The core is essential in determining the functionality of a state. If the core is well integrated into the rest of the state, development is more likely to spread evenly. In this case, **centripetal forces** pull the state and the people together to create a unified identity. If however, the state has several cores—a **multicore state**—development can occur unevenly and in pockets. In South Africa, the executive capital is Pretoria, the legislative capital is Cape Town, and the judicial capital is in Bloemfontein. **Centrifugal forces** then can divide the state

> **QUICK REVIEW**
>
> Name one centripetal force and one centrifugal force at work in the United States.

and its people. Infrastructure is often underdeveloped and inefficient, and internal conflict is likely. This can lead to **balkanization**, the disintegration of a state into smaller pieces.

In some countries, there may be a single core, but it is not well integrated and development is not evenly distributed. Instead, the core is located in a **primate city**. This is a city in which all of the resources are concentrated, with smaller cities serving as support for the primate city. As a result, it serves as the political center for the country and holds greater economic power than any other city in the state.

Primate cities are common in less developed countries. For example Lagos, with a population of 13.4 million, is a primate city in Nigeria. The second biggest city in the country, Kano, has a population of only 3.6 million. They also can be found in very old nation-states, like Hungary (Budapest) and the United Kingdom (London). In these cases, the primate city not only has a concentration of political and economic power, but is the cultural center of the country as well.

Some states, in an attempt to disperse the concentration of power and resources, attempt to remove political power from the primate city by creating a **forward capital** which better serves national goals. So, while Lagos is Nigeria's primate city, Abuja is its capital.

Territorial Morphology

Territorial morphology—the relationship between a state's size, shape, and location and its political situation—is critical to political geography. The ideal state structure is a **compact state**, a state which is relatively small and nearly square or circular in shape. In these states, the center of power is always close, no matter where a group or individual is within the state. Switzerland is a compact state.

However, most states are not compact. **Fragmented states**—like Indonesia, which is comprised of 16,000 islands—exist in several pieces. **Elongated states**, like Vietnam and Chile, are long and thin, and **prorupted states**, like Thailand, have a piece that protrudes. In each of these cases, political administration is more challenging because it is difficult to maintain control over the areas that are far from the center of power.

Landlocked states face economic challenges because they have no direct access to the ocean for trade. They also have a greater potential for boundary disputes since they have more borders to administer. These states must rely more on their neighbors which can lead to political problems. Many small, landlocked states end up serving as **buffer states**, independent states that are sandwiched between two (usually larger) conflicting countries. Jordan is a buffer state between Israel and Iraq.

While most landlocked countries are simply surrounded by multiple other countries, others are actually **perforated states** and make a hole in the middle of another country. Lesotho perforates South Africa.

While sovereignty is a defining character of a state, not all states enjoy the same level of sovereignty. **Satellite states** are states that are technically independent, but are heavily controlled by another, more powerful state. Belarus is a satellite state of the Russian Federation.

Sometimes, states are divided. A **political enclave** is a state—or part of a state—that is surrounded by another. In contrast a **political exclave**, is part of a state that is separated from the rest of the state. During the Cold War, West Berlin was a political exclave of West Germany and a political enclave within East Germany.

SAMPLE QUESTIONS

29) The country of Panama is an example of which of the following kinds of states?

   A. landlocked state
   B. compact state
   C. fragmented state
   D. elongated state

   Answer:

   D. Correct. Panama is an elongated state because it is long and thin.

30) The mountains surrounding Switzerland create which kind of boundaries?

   A. physical boundaries
   B. relict boundaries
   C. geometric political boundaries
   D. superimposed boundaries

   Answer:

   A. Correct. Mountains are an example of physical boundaries because they are part of the landscape.

31) What is a disadvantage that results from a primate city?

   A. The primate city has limited access to political power.
   B. A primate city creates a multi-core state.
   C. A primate city has a disproportionate share of a state's resources.
   D. A primate city is particularly vulnerable to invasion and conflict.

   Answer:

   C. Correct. Because of its concentration of power, primate cities also have a much greater share of a country's resources.

32) Poland is considered a buffer state because of its location
- A. sharing a border with seven other states.
- B. between Germany and the Soviet Union during World War II.
- C. on the Baltic Sea.
- D. in Eastern Europe.

Answer:
- **B. Correct.** A buffer state is a state that lies between two states in conflict. A great deal of fighting took place in Poland during World War II as a result of the conflict between Germany and the Soviet Union.

NATIONS

A people who identify as a group and share a culture compose a **nation**. In most cases, a state is composed of one nation (and called a nation-state). However, in some cases, like the former Soviet Union, states can be multinational. There are also **stateless nations**, like the Romani people throughout Europe, who exist as a nation but do not have their own territory.

Conflict can often arise between stateless nations and the states in which they reside. For example, the stateless nation may be a minority within a state and at odds with that state in terms of cultural traits or political beliefs. In these cases, members of a stateless nation become **ethnonationalistic**, maintaining allegiance for their nation over the state. If a nation is dispersed across multiple states—as is often the case—that nation may strive to reunite its various parts: **irredentism**.

GEOPOLITICS

The study of the interaction between states—politically and territorially—is called **geopolitics**. Geopolitical theory has been very important in shaping the major global conflicts in history.

For example, Adolf Hitler used Friedrich Ratzel's **organic theory** to justify his aggressive actions toward neighboring countries. In the late nineteenth century, Ratzel posited that states are essentially living organisms that feed on land. So, in order to grow (as all living things must), they must obtain more land. Ratzel argued this process was the root of all state decision-making and conflict.

The Soviet Union's foreign policy was based on Halford John Mackinder's **Heartland Theory**. In 1904, Mackinder stated that the world was made up of the World-Island (Europe, Asia, and Africa), outlying islands (Great Britain and Japan) and offshore islands (North America, South America, and Australia). Therefore, global power was dependent on control of Eurasia (the World-Island). In order to do that, a country needed to control Eastern Europe—the heartland of Eurasia. This theory not only motivated Soviet aggression in Eastern Europe, but US attempts to curb it as well. Heartland Theory was the basis for the American concept of **Domino Theory**, the idea that if one country fell to communism, the whole region would fall.

Taking Mackinder's theories further, Nicholas Spykman developed the **Rimland Theory**, which argued for a balance of power in the periphery of Eurasia in order to prevent the emergence of a global power there (namely, a Soviet or Chinese global power). As a result, the United States developed **containment**, a policy to keep communism *contained* to the areas where it already existed. This policy, rooted in Domino Theory, drove both the Korean and Vietnam Wars.

SAMPLE QUESTIONS

33) **The Basque people in Spain are an example of**

    A. a nation-state.
    B. a stateless nation.
    C. a multinational state.
    D. a divided nation.

    Answer:

    B. Correct. Having a distinct culture complex from the rest of Spain, the Basque people make up a separate nation. However, as they do not have their own state, they are considered a stateless nation.

34) **The United States became involved in the Korean War primarily because of which geopolitical theory?**

    A. Organic Theory
    B. Heartland Theory
    C. Domino Theory
    D. Irredentism

    Answer:

    C. Correct. The domino theory states that if one country falls to communism, the rest around it will as well. Once communist forces began to gain power in the north, US officials became concerned that all of the peninsula—and then the rest of Asia—would become communist.

HUMAN–ENVIRONMENT INTERACTION

The relationship between humans and their environment is of utmost importance to geographers. Humans have always modified the environment to suit their needs. The environment has also shaped human activity.

Theories of Human–Environment Interaction

Theorists continually debate the cause and effect nature of the relationship between humans and their environment. There are four main schools of thought. **Environmental determinism** argues that human behavior is controlled by the physical environment.

Possibilism posits an opposing theory: while the environment does replace restrictions on the options available to a group of people, it is still ultimately the people who make the choice. Possibilists would point to Europeans and Americans who settled in Hawaii and built large and productive plantations, rather than becoming "lazy."

Beyond possibilism is **cultural determinism**, which reflected the changing ideology of the nineteenth and early twentieth century. Cultural determinists argue that the environment, in fact, places no restrictions on the development of culture, and that the only restrictions come from human limitations.

Finally, **political ecology** argues that the government of a region affects the environment which, in turn, affects the choices available to the people. For example, mountains blocked the building of a transcontinental railroad in the nineteenth century United States. However, the government allowed railroad companies to use dynamite to create tunnels in the mountains, leading to the construction of a transcontinental railroad.

The First Agricultural Revolution

The primary way humans have affected the earth is through the development of agriculture. With the domestication of plants and animals, humans transitioned from a nomadic existence to a sedentary one. Early domestication consisted of cutting a stem off of a plant and planting that stem or dividing a plant by the roots. This process diffused from multiple hearths: Southeast Asia, northwestern South America, and West Africa.

Approximately 12,000 years ago, humans began to collect and plant seeds and to raise animals for their own use. This was the start of the **First Agricultural Revolution**. Humans became stationary and self-supporting. Large communities became an asset for farmers. As communities grew, civilization emerged.

Not only did the advent of seed agriculture and animal domestication change the way people lived, but it also increased the carrying capacity of the earth. Attempts to increase yield led to the development of more advanced tools. With specialized tools came specialized skills. People began to use their skills to benefit the larger community rather than just themselves.

Increased agricultural efficiency eventually led to surplus that could be traded for other goods. As a result, markets and trade systems developed; so did the notion of **wealth** as the accumulation of goods.

The revolution did not bring about only positive change, however. Farmers were vulnerable to the weather and dependent on a harvest calendar. Also, those who had acquired goods were vulnerable to theft. Consequently, humans developed secure storage methods and began to construct fortifications to protect their communities.

Success in seed agriculture led to **subsistence farming** in which the farmer grows only enough food to feed his own family. This type of farming is still very common today, especially in less developed countries. Subsistence farming takes three main forms:

Extensive subsistence farming uses a large amount of land and is practiced mainly in areas with low populations. Farmers practice **shifting cultivation**, rotating crops in order to maintain healthy soil. Once the soil becomes worn out, fields are left fallow to rebuild nutrients.

Extensive subsistence farming has serious environmental ramifications. As populations grow and arable land decreases, farmers must replant fields too soon, leading to permanent soil damage. Land shortages lead to the destruction of other areas—like rainforests—to create new farmland.

Farmers will often use **slash-and-burn** techniques to clear the land for agriculture (called making it **swidden**). Most farmers who use this technique also practice **intertillage**, planting different crops in the same area to reduce the risk of crop failure and promote a healthier diet.

Intensive subsistence farming, found mainly in Asia, uses a small amount of land as efficiently as possible. This type of farming can be found in areas with high populations and very fertile soil. Intensive subsistence farming is marked by innovative farming techniques like terrace-farming pyramids, which make use of vertical *and* horizontal space for farming. Another technique is **double-cropping**, when farmers plant two subsequent crops in the same field in a single year.

Pastoralism emerged with the domestication of animals. Rather than raising crops, pastoralists breed and herd animals (primarily goats, camels, sheep, and cattle) for food, clothing, and shelter. Pastoralism is dominant in areas with very limited growing capabilities such as grasslands, deserts, and steppes like North Africa, central and southern Africa, the Middle East, and Central Asia. Pastoralists can be sedentary or nomadic, moving their herds in search of new food sources or improved climate depending on the season. However, the land used by pastoralists is shrinking as governments take control of it to use for other economic purposes like drilling and mining.

SAMPLE QUESTIONS

35) **All of the following are accurate descriptors of the First Agricultural Revolution EXCEPT:**

    A. Humans began to settle in stationary communities.

    B. Humans began to use technology to increase production of food.

    C. It led to the development of a more stable food supply.

    D. It allowed for significant population growth.

    Answer:

    B. **Correct.** The First Agricultural Revolution resulted from humans learning how to gather and replant seeds to grow crops. Technology did not play a significant role.

36) **Which of the following farming techniques would most likely be used in a Vietnamese rice field?**

    A. intertillage

    B. slash-and-burn

    C. double-cropping

    D. shifting cultivation

    Answer:

    C. **Correct.** Double-cropping is the intensive subsistence farming practice of planting subsequent crops within the same year. Vietnam's climate is ideal for this type of farming.

THE SECOND AGRICULTURAL REVOLUTION

The **Second Agricultural Revolution** began around 500 CE, was centered in Europe, and was marked by an increase in agricultural technology. This revolution occurred in two major bursts.

After the fall of Rome, the feudal village structure emerged. Agricultural production was organized by the **open-lot system** in which there was one plot of land for the community, and all members worked in it to provide for themselves and their families. Refinement of tools like the plow and the introduction of other, more complex tools like water mills increased production.

The second burst came about 1,200 years later. The growth of capitalism shifted the way people farmed, and individuals began fencing off their land in what was called the **enclosure movement**. This coincided with the Industrial Revolution and the decline of the feudal system. As people began to migrate to the cities, demand for food in urban areas skyrocketed. New innovations in farming like the steel plow and the mechanical reaper led to higher outputs and eventually triggered a population boom that continued the cycle.

Subsistence farming was replaced in industrialized countries by **commercial farming**, growing food to be sold on the market rather than to feed one's own family. There are several forms of commercial farming. However they all have one thing in common—they are designed to maximize profit.

Mixed crop and livestock farming is commercial farming that involves both crops and animals. It differs from subsistence farming in two notable exceptions: 1) these farms are generally much bigger than the average subsistence farm, and 2) most crops are raised to feed the animals, not for human consumption. The income from the farm comes from the sale of animal products: wool, eggs, and meat. Thus these types of farms are not as dependent on the seasons as crop-only farms.

Other types of commercial agriculture focus on one animal product. For example, **ranching**, the commercial grazing of animals, also became a profitable form of farming. The textile mills of Europe's Industrial Revolution demanded high quantities of wool, greatly increasing the value of sheep worldwide. In the United States, urban demand for meat led to a ranching boom in the second half of the nineteenth century. Ranching was, and remains, popular in areas where the climate is too dry to support crops but where land is abundant. Ranching has had a significant negative impact on the environment, destroying grasslands through overgrazing.

Another type of specialized commercial farming is **dairying**, farming which focuses solely on bringing milk-based products to market. Originally, farms within the **milkshed**, the area surrounding the market in which fresh milk could be safely transported, usually focused their efforts on milk and other fluid products because these are more perishable. Those outside of the milkshed focused mostly on more sustainable products like butter and cheese. Over time, the milkshed has grown as a result of technological advances in transportation and refrigeration.

The most common type of commercial farm is the **large-scale grain production farm**. These are farms that focus solely on the production of one to two key grain crops for both people and animals. In fact, more large-scale grain production is dedicated to animal feed than to food for humans to eat. These are found primarily (but not solely) in humid continental climates. Wheat is the most common crop, most of which is grown in the United States and Canada. Large-scale grain production is capital intensive.

Plantation farms also focus on producing only one or two crops. These farms are also large-scale; however, they are labor intensive rather than capital intensive. Plantation farms rely on large numbers of seasonal workers and are most used for crops that cannot be easily mechanized: bananas, cotton, and tea, for example. They also must be located near ports (and so are generally coastal) to allow for easy export of crops. The location of plantation farms reflects the global power structure: they are located primarily in less developed countries—mostly low-latitude Africa,

> **QUICK REVIEW**
>
> How does climate affect the type of farming that develops in a location?

Asia, and Latin America, but are owned by and produce crops primarily for export to more developed countries. They monopolize the high-quality land in these areas, leaving little for local farmers and impeding development within the host country.

Both the development of new technology and the growth of factories led to a globalization and industrialization of agriculture. It became increasingly cost effective to grow food in one place and process it in another. For example, the United Kingdom and the northeastern United States originally dominated the textile industry. However, the cotton they used was grown primarily in the American South, India, and Egypt.

The methods used to improve the efficiency and profit of industry were applied to agriculture as well. Developing seeds, fertilizing fields, farming, processing, packaging, distributing, and advertising all became part of a larger **agribusiness**. As a result, the number of people involved in agribusiness has increased, while the number of actual farmers has declined.

In the 1820s, Johann Heinrich von Thünen developed the first spatial economic theory, called **Agricultural Location Theory**. He created a theoretical model to determine how distance impacted human location decisions, treating all other factors as constants in order to isolate distance. Based on this model, he predicted that the city would be surrounded by rings of agricultural activity moving from the most intensive to the most extensive. Agricultural Location Theory was the first economic model to use a geographic lens.

SAMPLE QUESTIONS

37) **The Industrial Revolution impacted agriculture in all of the following ways EXCEPT:**

    A. The emergence of the feudal system created more labor-intensive farming.

    B. Increased technological innovations led to more efficient farming and greater production.

    C. The rise of capitalism led to the individualization of farmland.

    D. The demand for food made growing crops for the market more profitable.

Answer:

A. **Correct.** The feudal system was ending as the Industrial Revolution got underway, and farming actually became less labor-intensive with the introduction of new machinery.

38) According to Agricultural Location Theory, what is the relative location to the city of a dairy farm and a mixed crop-livestock farm that specializes in cheese and butter?

- A. The dairy farm will be closer to the city.
- B. The mixed crop-livestock farm will be closer to the city.
- C. They will be equidistant from the city.
- D. Their distance from the city cannot be determined with the information given.

Answer:

- A. **Correct.** Because the dairy farm is a more intensive farming practice that requires less land, it will be located closer to the city. It also carries a greater risk of spoilage (milk vs. butter and cheese), so it requires a shorter distance to market.

THE THIRD AGRICULTURAL REVOLUTION

The **Third Agricultural Revolution**, also known as the **Green Revolution**, centered on a dramatic increase in crop yields based on **biotechnology**, scientific modifications to seeds and fertilizers. In response to the burgeoning global population, scientists found ways to improve grain production capabilities. **Norman Borlaug**, seen as the father of the Green Revolution, won a Nobel Prize for his work in 1970. The world can grow enough food to feed the global population.

Unfortunately, however, hunger still exists. The world's food supply is unevenly distributed, and hunger persists as a global problem due to social and transportation problems. Yield was increased for many crops, but not all, and most Green Revolution crops like rice are not arable in Africa. Africa's main crops—sorghum and millet—have received very little attention. As a result, less than 5 percent of African farmers use Green Revolution seeds for farming.

Moreover, other problems emerged as a result of the Green Revolution. Farming jobs decreased as less labor was required to produce food. In addition, the higher yield crops are more susceptible to disease and pests, making crop failure more common. Using technology requires more fuel, thereby increasing pollution and consumption. These crops also require more water, straining water supplies. Pesticides cause pollution, soil contamination, and health problems. Finally, global genetic diversity in plant life has been reduced as local strains of various crops are phased out to make room for high-yield crops. While this has led to a growth of the food supply, it has also greatly increased its vulnerability.

RENEWABLE AND NONRENEWABLE RESOURCES

One of the most significant ways humans impact their environment is through the use of natural resources. Some resources are **renewable resources**, meaning they are virtually unlimited or can be grown and regrown. Wind, sun, and plants are all examples of renewable resources. Other resources are **nonrenewable resources** because they cannot be replaced once they are consumed. Iron ore, coal, and petroleum are three of the most important nonrenewable resources. Trees may be renewable or nonrenewable. If managed properly, they can be replanted and grown again. However, the rapid consumption of old growth forests uses up a resource that essentially cannot be replaced. Also, the land trees are on is often repurposed for farm land, urbanization, or mining once the trees are removed, resulting in a permanent loss of the resource.

Consuming nonrenewable resources—and consuming renewable resources too quickly—is a growing concern as industrialization has greatly increased overall consumption. Many countries are searching for ways to promote **sustainable development**, the use of natural resources and the growth of new ones at a rate that can be maintained from one generation to the next. The **United Nations Commission on Sustainable Development** defines several criteria for global sustainable development: caring for the soil, avoiding overfishing, preserving the forest, protecting species from extinction, and reducing air pollution.

Other sustainability efforts focus on indirect factors impacting Earth's natural resources. For example, efforts to reduce fuel consumption are both motivated by the finite quantity of oil in the world, and also by the **greenhouse effect** caused by industrialization. Industrial production unleashes carbon dioxide, methane, and other gases. These create a vapor that transforms radiation into heat, which leads to **global warming**, an overall rise in Earth's temperature. As a result, the ice caps are melting prematurely, leading to rising sea levels and changes in oceanic patterns.

SAMPLE QUESTION

39) Which of the following statements is true about sustainable development?

   A. Sustainable development requires the proper management of renewable resources.

   B. Sustainable development only applies to energy resources like wind, sun, oil, and coal.

   C. Sustainable development requires a prohibition on the use of nonrenewable resources.

   D. Sustainable development contributes to the greenhouse effect and increases global warming.

Answer:

   A. **Correct.** Sustainable development seeks to ensure resources are available to the next generation. Therefore, renewable resources must be properly managed, ensuring consumption does not outpace the rate of replacement.

Movement

Geographers study **spatial interaction**, the ways in which different places interact with one another through the flow of people, goods, or ideas. Transport of agricultural goods to market, movement of labor from rural to urban areas, and diffusion of culture are all examples of spatial interaction.

Distance is an important factor in the study of movement. Geographers examine the **friction of distance** in movement, or the extent to which distance interferes with the spatial interaction. The level of energy and resources required to overcome distance increases with the distance itself. So there is less friction of distance—and greater spatial interaction—between Boston and New York than between Boston and Shanghai.

Distance also impacts the intensity of phenomena that travel between places. This **distance decay** can be seen in the impact of an earthquake. Those closest to the earthquake will see the biggest changes to the physical characteristics of their place, as well as the most cultural, political, and economic ramifications. Those hundreds or thousands of miles away may feel little to no impact at all. However, the impact of distance decay has been decreasing over time. **Space-time compression**—the feeling that the world is getting smaller—resulting from globalization means that the 2011 earthquake and tsunami in Japan, for instance, had significant consequences as far away as Chicago. Markets were affected, trips were cancelled to and from Japan, and sadly, people around the world lost family and friends in the disaster.

Diffusion

The type of movement most commonly studied in geography is **spatial diffusion**, the spread, or movement, of people, things, and ideas across space. Cultural diffusion (discussed earlier in this chapter) is a subset of spatial diffusion. There are two main types of spatial diffusion.

The first, **expansion diffusion**, describes the process of a phenomenon remaining strong at its hearth while expanding outward to new places. As it spreads to a new place, the new adopters may modify the idea. This is called **stimulus expansion diffusion**. For example, the sport of tennis began in the royal courts of France and England, and was played on grass. As the game diffused to new areas and new groups of people, different playing surfaces were adopted.

In other cases, when the phenomenon spreads to a new area, it starts with a person or place in a position of power or influence and then spreads to others in a leveled pattern. This is called **hierarchical diffusion**. For example, sushi arrived in the United States from Japan as a result of stimulus expansion diffusion. It began in New York City, a city of significant cultural power, and then followed a hierarchical diffusion pattern by spreading to other large cities, then mid-size and smaller cities, and finally suburbs and towns.

CONTAGIOUS DIFFUSION

HIERARCHIAL DIFFUSION

early diffusion ⟶ later diffusion

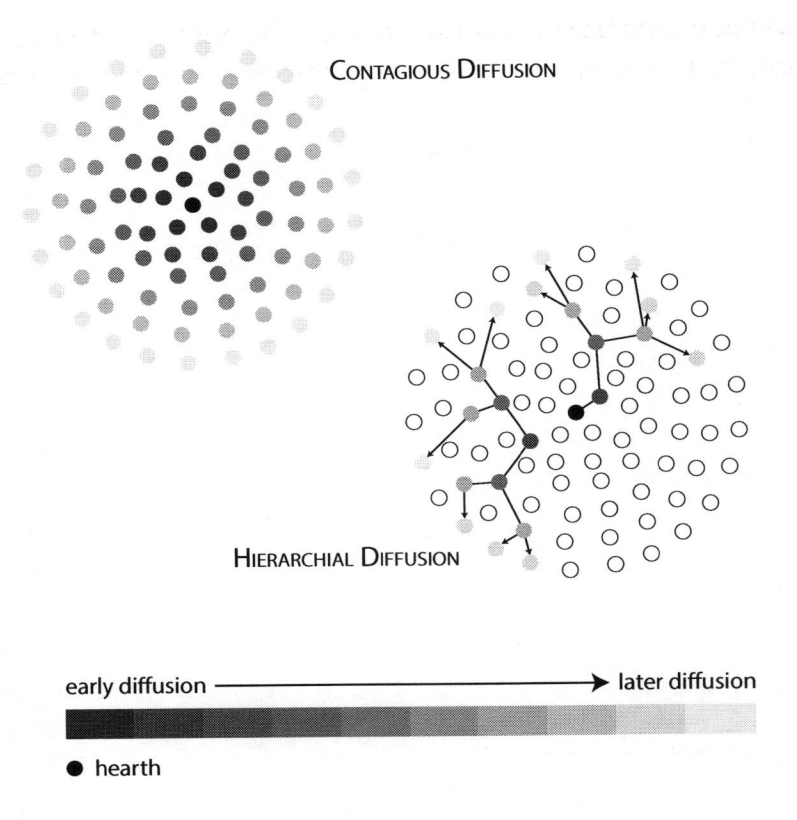

● hearth

Figure 4.9. Contagious and Hierarchical Diffusion

The final method of expansion diffusion is **contagious diffusion**. In this case, multiple places near the hearth become adopters, rather than the phenomenon spreading in a sequential manner. As the name implies, the classic example of contagious diffusion is a disease. This is the most widespread type of diffusion.

Diffusion does not always occur in an expansive manner. Sometimes, the original adopters move from the hearth to a new place, taking their ideas with them. This is called **relocation diffusion**. For example, in the 1850s, Mormons moved west from New York State to Illinois and then to what would become Utah. As they moved, the hearth of Mormonism moved with them as well.

> **QUICK REVIEW**
>
> Which type of diffusion is most closely associated with the spread of disease?

A variant on this is **migration diffusion**, when the original adopters move but the idea or trait lasts only a short while in the new place. This phenomenon occurs most often among immigrants, who move to a new place originally carrying the traits of their home culture. However, in a relatively short time they shed their original cultural traits and adopt the traits of the new culture.

In reality most diffusions follow more than one of these patterns. However, all diffusions follow an S-curve pattern when the number of users over time is plotted on a graph. For example, when a new technology is first introduced, only a small group of early adopters uses it. As time passes, the adoption rate increases and continues until most people use the new technology. Then, adoption tapers off.

Diffusion S Curve

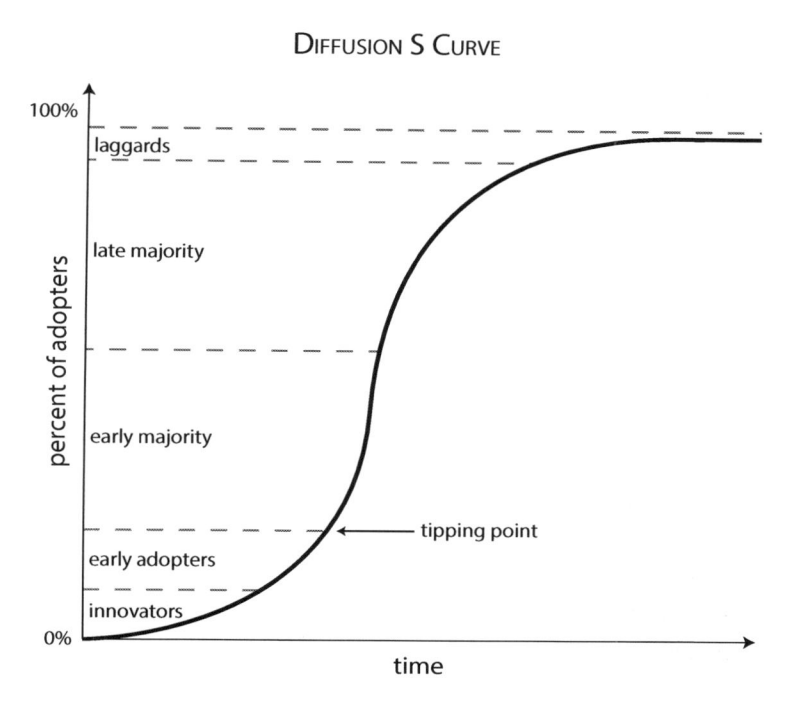

Figure 4.10. Diffusion S-Curve

SAMPLE QUESTIONS

40) **The diffusion of smartphones within the United States is an example of which kind of diffusion?**

    A. stimulus diffusion
    B. relocation diffusion
    C. hierarchical diffusion
    D. contagious diffusion

    Answer:

    C. Correct. Smartphones were first adopted by those who could afford them and who were in a position of power. They then diffused through economic levels as the prices changed and companies provided opportunities to make them more affordable.

41) **According to the S-curve graph, the LEAST number of new users emerges at which point(s) in the diffusion process?**

    A. the very beginning only
    B. the middle only
    C. the end only
    D. both the beginning and end

Answer:

D. Correct. Early adopters and laggards are the two smallest groups of adopters.

MIGRATION PATTERNS

Migration is the permanent relocation of an individual or group from one home region to another region. As globalization and space-time compression have increased, global mobility has increased as well. Some migration is internal, like urbanization. Other migration is regional or global.

Geographers study migration to understand *how* people move through space as well as *why* they move through space. To answer the question of *how*—the manner and numbers of people moving—geographers examine **migration streams**, the specific spatial movement from the starting location to the destination. These are mapped using arrows of differing thickness to indicate the number of migrants. Migration streams are usually paired with **migration counter-streams** of people returning home.

To answer the question *why?* geographers look at both **push factors**—negative aspects of the home region that make someone want to leave it—and **pull factors**—positive aspects of the new region that make someone want to move there. Push factors include high taxes, high crime rates, resource depletion, and corrupt governments. Migrants who cross international borders fleeing persecution, governmental abuse, war, or natural disaster are called **refugees**. People who migrate within a country are called **internally displaced persons**.

Figure 4.11. Migration Streams

Examples of pull factors include new, better-paying jobs, schools, abundant resources, and greater protection of individual rights. A common pull factor for new immigrants are previous immigrants to a place. This is called **chain migration**. For example, in the late 1990s Eritreans began to immigrate to the United States as the result of the Eritrean-Ethiopian War (a push factor). They settled primarily in Washington DC and Los Angeles, prompting other Eritreans to move to these two cities as well (a pull factor).

If a location attracts more **immigrants** (people moving into a place) than it has **emigrants** (people moving out of a place), it has **net in-migration**, and is considered to have **high place desirability**. Western Europe, the United States, and Canada all have net in-migration. On the other hand, if a place has more emigrants than immigrants, it has **net out-migration**. Today that includes most of Asia, Africa, and Latin America.

Geographers determine how likely someone is to migrate using **migration selectivity**. While personal, social, and economic factors all play a role, age is actually the most important factor in migration. Younger people tend to be more mobile. Research has also shown that greater education leads to greater mobility.

Not all migration is voluntary. History has many examples of **forced migration**, when a group of people is forcibly removed from their home and brought to a new region. The African slave trade and the removal of Native American tribes from the Southeastern United States are both examples of forced migration.

Migration patterns tend to be predictable and can be determined using three key theories:

Ravenstein's Laws of Migration: In the 1880s, geographer Ernst Georg Ravenstein developed his laws of migration which remain the basis for migration theory today:

1. Most migrants travel only short distances. Even when they do travel longer distances, they often use **step migration**, traveling in short steps to ultimately achieve a longer distance.
2. People living in rural areas are more likely to migrate, especially in areas that are industrializing.
3. Migrants who travel farther tend to choose big cities as their destination.
4. Large towns grow by migration instead of by natural growth.
5. Mostly adults migrate.
6. Young adults are more likely to cross borders than families, who tend to migrate internally.
7. Every migration stream has a counter-stream.

Gravitational Model: The gravitational model of migration estimates the size and direction of migration between two places. It is based on the assumption that the migrational "gravity" of a place is determined by its size and its distance. So places that are larger and/or closer attract more migrants. The limitation of this model is that it only considers location and does not include migration selectivity factors.

Zelinsky's Model of Migration Transition: Geographer Wilbur Zelinsky developed a model of migration based on the development stage of a country, using the Demographic Transition Model. Countries in Stage One of the DTM migrate locally to search for food and shelter materials. In Stage Two, the high RNI overstresses resources, resulting in out-migration. There is also a high rate of rural-to-urban migration. In Stage Three, rural-to-urban migration is surpassed by urban-to-urban migration, and immigration exceeds emigration. In Stage Four, urban-to-suburban migration (and vice versa) emerges as the dominant form of migration, stabilizing in Stage Five.

> **HELPFUL HINT**
>
> The DTM, Rostow's Modernization Model, and Zelinsky's Model of Migration Transition are all closely related. If you master one—probably Rostow's—you can use it as a tool to help you recall the others.

SAMPLE QUESTIONS

42) Which of the following events would be considered a pull factor for migration?

    A. the opening of a new factory in a different town
    B. a drought in the home region
    C. an increase in terrorist activity in the home region
    D. the construction of a high-speed train between the hometown and the nearest city

    Answer:
    A. **Correct.** A new factory would provide jobs and encourage migration into the area.

43) During the late 1990s, Ireland had such strong economy, attracting migration and investment. Recent Irish immigrants to the United States and even some Irish Americans began returning to their homeland with their families. This phenomenon is best explained by which of the following?

    A. the US' stage of development (Stage Four) based on Zelinsky's Model of Migration Transition
    B. the size of Ireland, based on the gravitational model of migration
    C. Ravenstein's law that young adults are more likely to cross borders than families
    D. Ravenstein's law that for every migration stream, there is a counter-stream

Answer:

D. Correct. Historically, the Irish fled poverty and oppression in Ireland, many settling in North America. The migration of Irish to Ireland from the United States constitutes a counter-stream to the migration stream of the Irish diaspora.

Economics

FUNDAMENTAL ECONOMIC CONCEPTS

SCARCITY

There are some basic concepts that are part of all branches of economics. Scarcity, choice, and opportunity costs all figure in day-to-day living for everyone. In economics, there is an assumption that all people have unlimited wants; however, there are limited resources to satisfy those wants. This concept is called **scarcity**. Scarcity forces individuals to make a **choice**, to select one want over another. In making choices, people seek to maximize their **utility**, the point of greatest happiness.

For example, a student wants to go to the movies with her friends, but also wants to do well on her exams the next day. Her resource—in this case, time—is limited, so she must choose between the options. She will weigh the cost, or value lost, of not studying for her exam, against the benefit, or value attained, of seeing the movie, and vice versa. The value of the option not selected is called the **opportunity cost.** So, the opportunity cost of staying home to study is the lost fun of seeing the movie and strengthening of bonds with friends.

Resources, also called **factors of production**, fall into four basic categories: labor, land or natural resources, physical capacity, and entrepreneurial ability, or know-how.

Each of the four factors of production is necessary to the process of producing anything in the marketplace and they are considered some of the most basic parts of the business equation.

LAW OF DIMINISHING MARGINAL UTILITY

Total utility is the sum of an individual's happiness or the extent to which an individual's needs are met. **Marginal utility** is the increase in happiness one gains from a product. For example, a child desires a treat. She receives an ice cream cone, thereby increasing her utility. Then, she receives a cupcake which further increases her utility. That increase is her marginal utility.

While needs are unlimited, an individual's need for a specific product can be met. In fact, the **law of diminishing marginal utility** states that the more units of a product one has, the less one needs. Think of a very hungry person. His need for food seems unlimited. However, with each bite he takes, his need—and the amount of additional utility a bite brings—is shrinking or diminishing, until he is finally sated.

Marginal Analysis

People tend to make decisions **at the margin,** meaning as an addition to the status quo. Looking back at our student, she has already studied for an hour (and she has already spent time with her friends and seen movies on previous days), so her choice is a marginal one; she is considering the **marginal benefit** (the additional benefit) and **marginal cost** (the additional cost) of studying for another hour or the marginal benefit and cost of going to the movies.

Marginal analysis is used in many economic decisions, including production, consumption, and hiring. For example, when a company looks at the extra costs of producing a good or service in regard to the benefit of producing that good, it uses marginal analysis. Marginal analysis is most helpful in company decision-making in regards to production. Changes in marginal costs and benefits can also affect decision-making in both the short and long term. If consumers are happy with an item and they buy it in quantity, then businesses flourish. A company would use marginal analysis to determine if the benefit of offering more of the item outweighed the cost of increasing production. Similarly, a new company would use marginal analysis to decide if the benefit of selling a popular item outweighed the cost of heavy competition from many similar companies on the market, or if the cost of a lower price was overshadowed by the benefit of potentially selling more units than the competitor.

SAMPLE QUESTIONS

1) Which of the following is NOT an example of the principle of scarcity?
    A. overfishing in key coastal waters
    B. a pharmaceutical company lowers the price of a commonly used generic drug
    C. drought reduces the amount of pumpkins sold in fall farmers' markets
    D. flu season ramps up and flu vaccines are hard to find

    Answer:
    B. **Correct.** The lowered price in and of itself does not create scarcity, as the supply of the drug is not impacted.

2) A company is looking to hire a new website designer to refresh its website. The first candidate is fresh out of college and this would be his first job. The second candidate has worked as a website designer for ten years; however, the company would have to pay him twice as much as the first candidate. Which of the following illustrates how the company uses marginal analysis to decide which candidate to hire?

   A. weigh the cost of hiring a web designer against the benefit of having customers
   B. weigh the cost of increased pay for the second against the benefit of more experience
   C. weigh the cost of the first candidate's lack of experience against the cost of the second candidate's high price
   D. weigh the benefit of the first candidate's price against the benefit of the second candidate's experience

   Answer:
   B. Correct. Here, the additional cost of the second candidate's higher salary is weighed against the extra ten years of experience he brings.

3) At an amusement park, a child takes her first rollercoaster ride. She loves it so much, she wants to go again. According to the law of diminishing marginal utility, which of the following is most likely to happen after the child's tenth ride?

   A. The child will have a greater desire to ride the rollercoaster than on her first ride.
   B. The child will never want to ride any rollercoaster again.
   C. The child will experience the same level of excitement as after her first ride.
   D. The child will be less interested—or uninterested entirely—in riding the rollercoaster again that day.

   Answer:
   D. Correct. The law of diminishing marginal utility states that the additional utility gained for acquiring new units of a product (rollercoaster rides) decreases with each new acquisition. In this case, each subsequent rollercoaster ride offered less marginal utility, until it no longer exists.

PRODUCTION POSSIBILITIES CURVE

A **production possibilities curve** determines if an individual, company, or nation is producing at its most efficient level and what product will likely make the highest profit. The curve assumes that there are two choices for production. A production possibilities curve demonstrates opportunity costs, economic efficiency, economic growth, and scarcity.

For example, a company that produces soccer balls is looking to diversify and produce basketballs as well. However, for each basketball the company produces, there is an opportunity cost in soccer balls. Perhaps it takes a worker twice as long and costs twice as much money to make a basketball as a soccer ball. The opportunity cost of making a basketball is two soccer balls. The production possibility curve plots the relationship between the number of soccer and basketballs produced to help the company find the most efficient combination of production. This curve is also called the **production possibility frontier** because it represents the maximum level of production. It is not possible for a company to produce soccer balls and basketballs beyond the curve. The scarcity of resources (materials for soccer balls and labor) creates this upper bound. At the points under the curve, the company is not using its resources to their maximum potential.

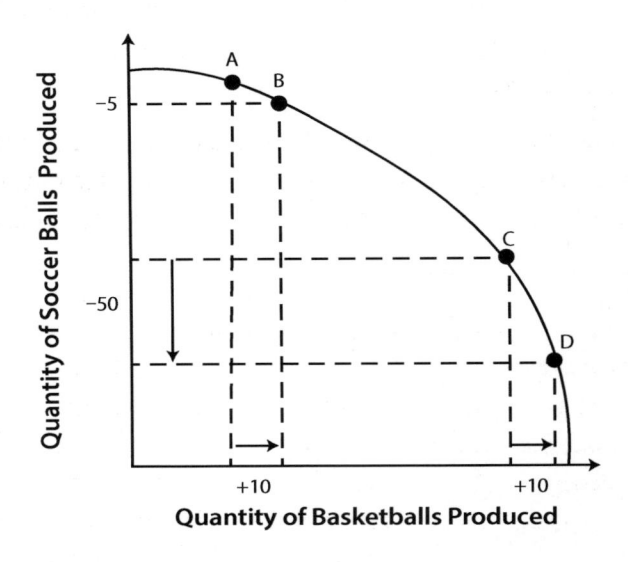

Figure 5.1. Production Possibilities Curve

Economists believe that the frontier expands over time, a process called **economic growth.** This results from one or more of the following: an increase in the quantity of resources, an increase in the quality of existing resources, or technological advancements in production. The reflection in the production possibility curve, however, is not proportional, as an increase in resources or new technology does not impact all sectors of the economy in the same way. A classic historical example is the invention of the cotton gin. The cotton gin was a technological advancement allowing cotton seeds to be separated from harvested cotton by machine rather than by hand. This dramatically expanded the production possibility of cotton, shifting the curve. However, it had no impact on the actual production of cotton plants.

Opportunity cost can be determined by calculating the slope of the curve: the slope represents the opportunity cost on the *x*-axis; the inverse of the slope represents the opportunity cost on the *y*-axis. The production possibility frontier is curved because opportunity costs increase as the quantity produced increases. This is called the **law of increasing costs.**

Economic efficiency is as necessary for consumers as it is for business entities. For consumers, setting a budget for monthly expenses is part of running a household. At the same time, businesses must continually analyze production possibilities curves to determine more efficient production processes, cost-cutting measures, and ways to boost profits.

MARKET EFFICIENCY

As discussed, an economy is working inefficiently if it is producing below the production possibility curve. This is called **productive inefficiency.** An economy's efficiency is not only measured by its use of resources, but by the benefit it provides to society, called its **allocative efficiency.** For example, a country could direct all of its resources to the production of hats. This economy might have high productive efficiency, maximizing its output, but it is providing little benefit to its citizens, and so has low allocative efficiency.

To offer a real world example, Equatorial Guinea is rich in petroleum; however, only the elite have profited from it, and the standard of living for most of the country remains extremely low. Equatorial Guinea therefore exhibits low allocative efficiency.

ABSOLUTE AND COMPARATIVE ADVANTAGE

When deciding between producing two different products, a company must also consider its production capabilities for each item relative to the rest of the market. If a company (or nation) can produce a good more efficiently than all competitors, it has an **absolute advantage** in that market. Consider, again, the soccer ball company. If that company can produce soccer balls more efficiently than all other soccer ball companies, it has an absolute advantage in soccer ball production. A company can have an absolute advantage in more than one product (if the company also produced basketballs most efficiently, for example).

It may then seem that the company should produce both products. However, that is not necessarily the case. For example, the ball company may be able to produce both soccer balls and basketballs more efficiently than its competitor. But, if the company has workers specifically trained in stitching high quality soccer balls very quickly, the opportunity cost of producing basketballs instead will be high. Their competitor, on the other hand, may have workers who may stitch quality soccer balls at a much slower rate, leading to a lower opportunity cost for producing basketballs (but the first company's opportunity cost for producing soccer balls will be lower). In this case, the competitor actually has a **comparative advantage** in producing basketballs, and the original company has one in producing soccer balls. Comparative advantage compares the opportunity cost of producing an item between companies. It would then be in the best interest of the original company to specialize in soccer balls and the competitor to specialize in basketballs, even though the original company can produce both more efficiently.

Specialization and Interdependence

Specialization occurs when an individual, company, or nation focuses on producing one thing, typically because it has a comparative advantage. For example, a doctor may also be the fastest wood chopper in a town. However, the doctor does not both chop the town's wood and tend to its patients; the opportunity cost of chopping wood is too high. So, he specializes in being a doctor, leaving the wood chopping to someone else (even though they are not as fast as he is). Specialization leads to increased profits and lower prices for consumers.

Interdependence is part of a larger global or regional economy. When countries or businesses are interdependent, goods from one are necessary to the economy of another and both must function together for both to work. Colonization is a classic example of interdependence. The mother country relied on the colony both for raw materials and as a market for its finished goods. On the other hand, the colony relied on the mother country as a market for its raw materials, and as a source for finished goods.

Both globalization and specialization lead to increased interdependence. Countries depend on treaties and business partnerships to provide goods necessary for production. One country provides lithium to another for cell phone battery production while the lithium-providing country is permitted to buy stockpiles of seed corn for its agricultural concerns. That means that both sides gain from this trading equation.

SAMPLE QUESTIONS

4) Company A can produce 900 pencils at the cost of producing 300 pens. For the same cost, Company B can produce either 200 pens or 1000 pencils. Which company has the comparative advantage and which company has the absolute advantage in producing pencils?

   A. Company A has the comparative advantage; Company B has the absolute advantage.
   B. Company A has both the comparative and absolute advantages.
   C. Company A has the absolute advantage; Company B has the comparative advantage.
   D. Company B has both the comparative and absolute advantages.

   Answer:

   D. **Correct.** Company B can produce 100 more pencils than Company A at the same cost, giving it an absolute advantage. Its opportunity cost for producing pencils is .2 (200/1000), whereas Company A's is .33 (300/900), giving Company B a comparative advantage as well.

5) **At point A on the production possibility graph below, which of the following is true about the economy?**

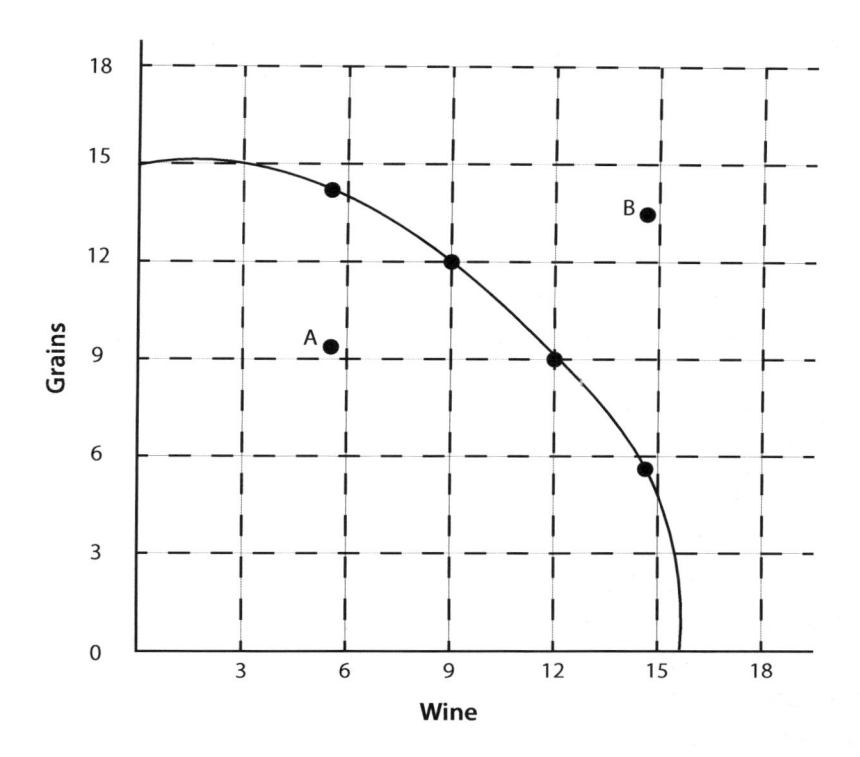

[Graph: Production possibility frontier with Grains on y-axis (0 to 18) and Wine on x-axis (0 to 18). Point A is located at approximately (6, 9), below the curve. Point B is located at approximately (13, 13), above the curve. Points on the curve include approximately (6, 14), (9, 12), (12, 9), and (15, 5).]

A. The economy should increase wine production and decrease grain production.
B. New resources are required before production can increase.
C. Some resources are being underutilized or wasted.
D. The economy is producing at its greatest efficiency.

Answer:

C. Correct. Point A is below the production possibility frontier, indicating that the use of resources is not being maximized.

6) **Which of the following is NOT a consequence of specialization?**

A. lower wages
B. higher quality goods
C. higher profits
D. lower prices

Answer:

A. Correct. Specialization does not cause low wages. Sometimes, specialization in the workforce, or the division of labor, can lead to lower wages because the skills required of a worker are reduced. However, specialization can also lead to higher wages because it may require a higher level of skill from a worker.

Types of Economic Systems

There are four kinds of economic systems.

A **traditional economy** is a pre-industrialized economy, guided by tradition, and often using bartering rather than currency.

A **pure command economy** is usually found in communist societies. In a pure command economy, the government—rather than the market—determines all aspects of production. Today, they are very rare; North Korea is an example.

A **pure market economy,** also known as capitalism, is governed by the laws of supply and demand with no outside interference.

A **mixed economy** is governed by both the market and the government. The people may decide what is produced by what they are willing to buy, but the government regulates different aspects of the economy with regards to the safety of the population. Most modern economies are mixed economies.

Functions of the Market

There are several defining principles of a market economy.

A pure market economy is a self-running entity; its internal forces govern its functioning, and it does not require outside intervention. Therefore, government has no place in a pure market economy. This leads to two key principles:

Private Property: The market favors private ownership of most economic resources. Private ownership leads to innovation and investment, which in turn lead to growth. It also allows for trade (of services and goods). Economists often point to the inefficiency of the United States Postal Service (USPS) as compared to private carriers like FedEx or UPS to illustrate this point. The owners of FedEx and UPS have an incentive to provide better service, in order to stay in business and grow. USPS, as a publicly owned entity, is guaranteed survival by the government.

Freedom of Choice: In a market economy, all individuals are free to acquire, use, and sell resources without restriction or regulation. This allows market forces to function properly. Two important elements in the market are supply and demand (discussed more in depth later). If there was a restriction on buying large cars, for example, this would artificially alter demand, and throw off the functioning of the automobile market.

Private property and freedom of choice create the two primary driving forces of the market:

Self-interest: Market theory assumes that people are motivated by self-interest in their use of their own resources. The seller in the market wants to maximize resources (or profit). The buyer wants to maximize utility (or happiness). As a result, the seller offers goods that will maximize the happiness of buyers in order to attract sales. Self-interest, then, leads to innovation and quality, as it creates a market where the best products are available to buyers. For example, Apple has noted that technological integration brings buyers a great deal of happiness, so the company works to continually innovate new ways of integrating technology (like the Apple watch) in its quest for profit.

Competition: Because all individuals are motivated by self-interest, new sellers will enter the market when they determine that there is a possibility for profit. And, because all individuals have freedom of choice, buyers will buy from the sellers whose products maximize their happiness (either through prices or quality usually). Therefore, sellers compete with each other to attract buyers by appealing to their maximum happiness. Competition leads to lower prices and higher quality.

Consequently, the primary communication tool of the market is **price.** Because of competition, prices are set by the market rather than by individuals. As a result, price signals buyers and sellers who, in turn, use it to make decisions about how to use their resources. Prices communicate the relative value of products in the market and deliver to both sellers and buyers what they seek through their own self-interest: profit and happiness, respectively.

SAMPLE QUESTIONS

7) In the 1870s in the United States, Americans favored laissez-faire economics, minimizing government regulations and controls on business. This most closely resembles which type of economy?

   A. traditional
   B. command
   C. market
   D. mixed

   Answer:

   C. Correct. Laissez-faire economics essentially means to leave the market alone to function. The United States came close to having a pure market economy in the 1870s.

8) A buyer decides to switch to a new brand of detergent that promises to leave clothes cleaner. Which of the following market principles is NOT involved in this decision?

   A. self-interest
   B. freedom of choice
   C. competition
   D. price

Answer:

D. Correct. The buyer makes his decision based on the effectiveness of the product rather than its price. Price does not come into play.

Supply and Demand

If price is the communication tool of the economy—determining the allocation of resources by both buyers and sellers—then what determines price? Price is the result of the interplay between two important economic forces: demand and supply.

Law of Demand

The **law of demand** is simple. As the price for a good or service increases, the demand for it will decrease, if all other factors are held constant. In other words, if the price goes up, purchases usually go down. For example, a coffee shop sells coffee for $1 a cup and sales skyrocket. The coffee shop then quadruples the price to $4 a cup, and sales plummet. It is important to note that only **relative (real) price** affects demand. The relative price of a good is its value in relation to other items of similar value (what else could you buy for $4?). For example, perhaps the same shop sells donuts for $2. Yesterday, the buyer could have gotten two cups of coffee for the price of one donut. Now two donuts are equivalent to the price of one cup of coffee. This is called the **substitution effect.** Relative price is also determined by the percentage of one's income the price demands (if the buyer makes $16 an hour, the cup of coffee is 25% of her hourly income versus the 6.25% that the $1 price was). This is called the **income effect.** The actual number of $4—the **absolute** price—does not impact demand.

Demand Curve

A **demand curve** shows how demand changes as prices increase. The curve actually measures **quantity demanded** in relation to price. In economics, this is different from simple demand.

Once again, a demand curve assumes all other factors remain constant. This is an assumption often made in economics to allow for the creation of models. If multiple factors were taken into consideration (e.g., price and weather and income), it would be impossible to determine causation. These other factors are called **determinants of demand** and include:

▸ Consumer income (buyer's ability to pay)
▸ Price of a substitute good (in the example above, tea)
▸ Price of a complementary good (in the example above, donuts)
▸ Consumer preferences

- Consumer expectations about future pricing (Do consumers anticipate the price will go down in the future?)
- Number of buyers in the market

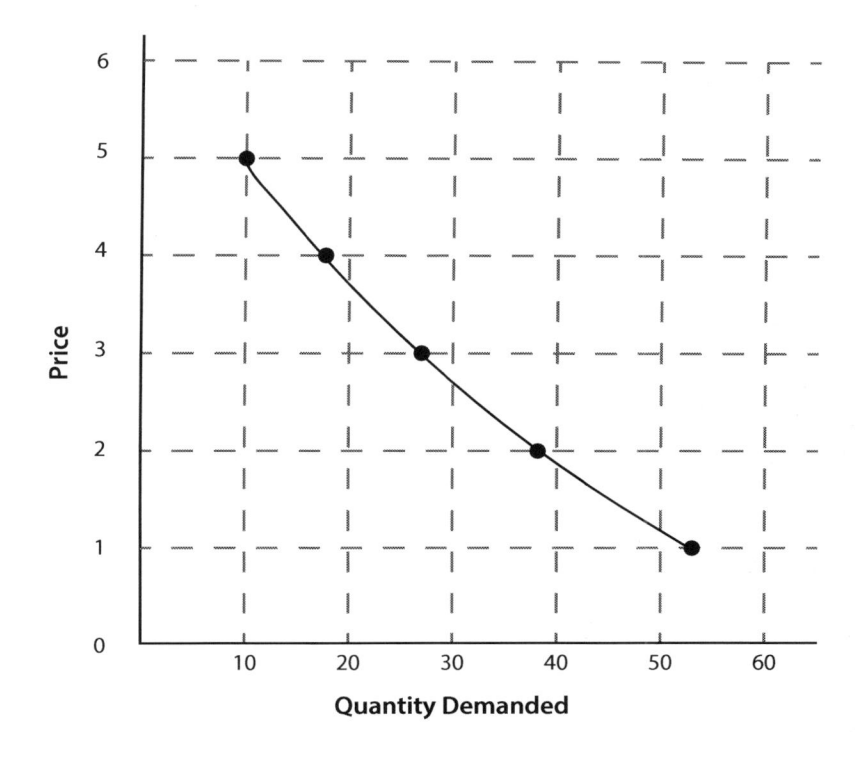

Figure 5.2. Demand Curve

While changes in price affect the quantity demanded, changes in determinants of demand lead to changes in demand overall—regardless of price—which are shown by a shift in the entire demand curve. For example, consider a fruit stand selling raspberries. As the end of the season approaches, buyers anticipate that prices will increase when less fruit is available. So, fruit buyers increase their demand for raspberries. This is translated into a rightward shift in the demand curve. This shift is unrelated to the current price, and—in fact—would be seen regardless of the price of raspberries. So, whether raspberries are $2 per pint or $4 per pint, there will be an increase in demand a week or two before the end of the season. A decrease in demand, conversely, is shown by a leftward shift in the curve.

LAW OF SUPPLY

Whereas demand addresses the behavior of buyers, supply deals with the behavior of sellers. The **law of supply** states that as the price of a good increases, suppliers will increase the quantity of the good they supply, if all other factors are held constant. This is because of **increasing marginal costs**: as suppliers increase the amount they are supplying, the marginal costs of production increase as well. Therefore, they will only increase supply if price is high enough to offset that cost. For example, at the holidays, a toy company decides to double its supply of its most popular toy. In order to do this, they must hire more workers, keep the factory open longer, run the machines longer, pay more in electricity, and pay more in packing materials and shipping costs to get the toys to the stores. If they decided to triple the supply, these costs would only increase. So, the price of the toy would need to be at a point that it could generate enough revenue to offset these additional costs.

Supply Curve

A **supply curve** shows the relationship between what something costs and how much a business is willing to supply for sale. In the graph below, the vertical line on the left indicates price while the horizontal line shows quantity produced for sale. The higher the price, the higher the supply (holding all other factors constant).

Just like with the demand curve, points on the supply curve represent the **quantity supplied** rather than the overall supply. Changes in the overall supply result from **determinants of supply** which shift the curve either rightward or leftward. These include:

- the cost of an input
- technology and productivity
- taxes or subsidies
- producer expectations about future prices
- the price of alternative goods that could be produced
- the number of similar companies in the industry

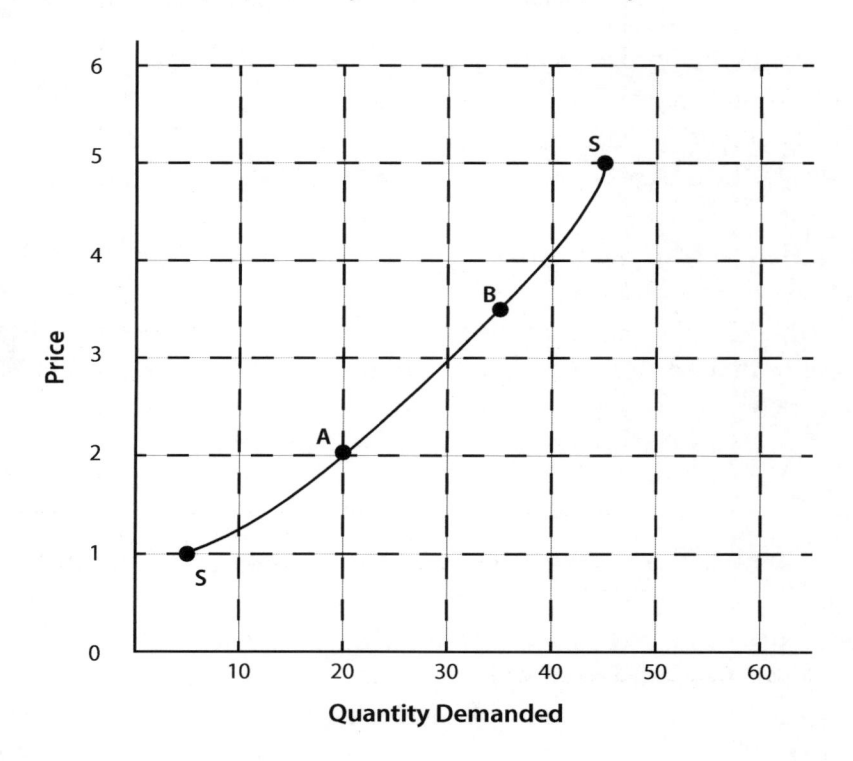

Figure 5.3. Supply Curve

For example, the price of flour drops. Because it now costs less to make baked goods, bakeries across the industry will increase their production of muffins and cakes. This is an overall increase in supply, shifting the curve rightward. In the same way, if flour suddenly became more expensive, bakeries would produce less (as cost of production increased), and the curve would shift leftward.

SUPPLY AND DEMAND

The interplay of supply, demand, and price is used to describe the state of the market. When the quantity demanded equals the quantity supplied at a given price, the market is in a state of **equilibrium**. Essentially, this means that both suppliers and buyers are satisfied with the price. In a graph, equilibrium is located where the supply and demand curves intersect. The other areas of the graph, where the supply and demand curves do not meet, are states of **disequilibrium**.

When the quantity demanded exceeds the quantity supplied, a **shortage**, or **excess demand,** exists. Shortages occur when prices are low because low prices lead to high demand but low supply. For example, if the market price of a television is $20, demand for these inexpensive TVs will be high, but the marginal cost of increasing supply at that price would quickly outweigh the revenue from sales, keeping the supply low.

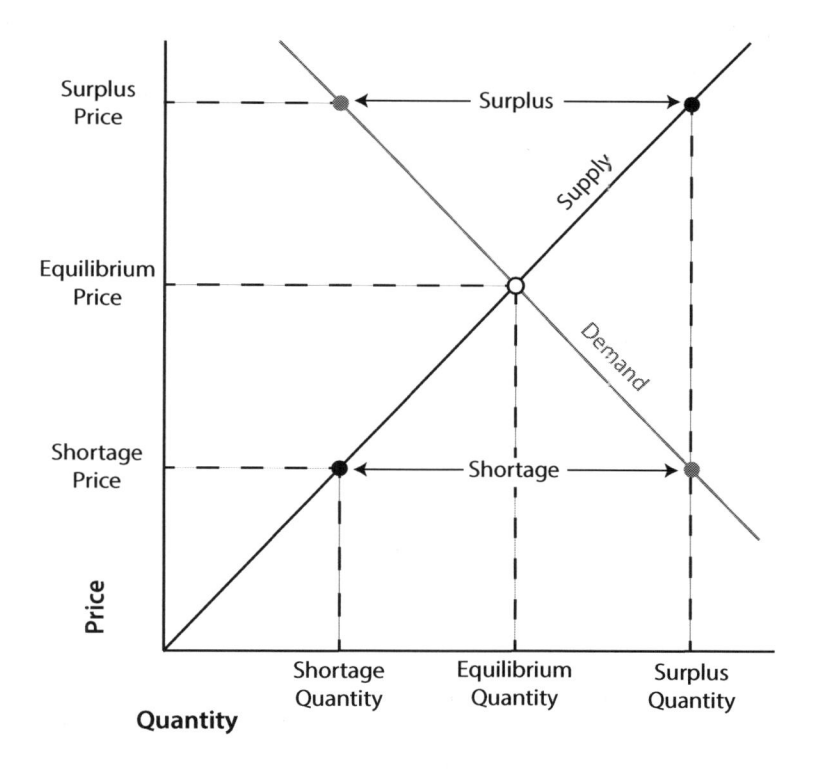

Figure 5.4. Equilibrium Price

When the quantity supplied exceeds the quantity demanded, a **surplus**, or **excess supply**, exists. Again, this is caused by the supply and demand's opposing relationships to price. If the TVs are now $2000 each, fewer buyers will be willing to purchase one. However, the high price allows the supplier to clearly outstrip her marginal costs.

The market always tends toward equilibrium. So, in the case of a shortage, buyers will offer to pay more—say $50—for the television, and suppliers will begin to increase supply. This trend will continue until they reach equilibrium. On the flip side, when a surplus exists, suppliers will lower prices in order to attract buyers, thereby increasing demand until equilibrium is reached.

Changes in overall supply and demand impact equilibrium as well. For example, the ability to stream television shows on a tablet or phone created an equivalent product. If the cost of a tablet dropped below the cost of a television, there would be a decreased overall demand, shifting the demand curve to the left. This would, in turn, shift the equilibrium price, also called **market clearing**.

If both supply and demand are changed (e.g., the price of tablets drop and a tornado destroys half of the television factories), the relative degree of each change must be gauged before a new equilibrium can be determined.

SAMPLE QUESTIONS

9) At the price of $15, a manufacturer of bowls expects to sell 10,000 bowls. If the bowls are instead offered at a price of $20 per bowl, how many can the manufacturer anticipate selling?

   A. fewer than 10,000 bowls
   B. exactly 10,000 bowls
   C. more than 10,000 bowls
   D. more information is needed to make the prediction

   Answer:
   A. Correct. The law of demand states that when price increases, demand drops. This means the manufacturer will make fewer sales.

10) Workers at pen factories earn minimum wage. When the state raises the minimum wage, what impact will that have on the market supply of pens?

    A. The supply curve will shift to the right.
    B. The supply curve will remain unchanged, but the quantity supplied will increase.
    C. The supply curve will shift to the left.
    D. The supply curve will remain unchanged, but the quantity supplied will decrease.

Answer:

C. Correct. An increase in the minimum wage increases the cost of producing pens, which in turn reduces supply (as pen manufacturers do not want to invest when their margins of profit are reduced).

11) **Which of the points below is the original equilibrium?**

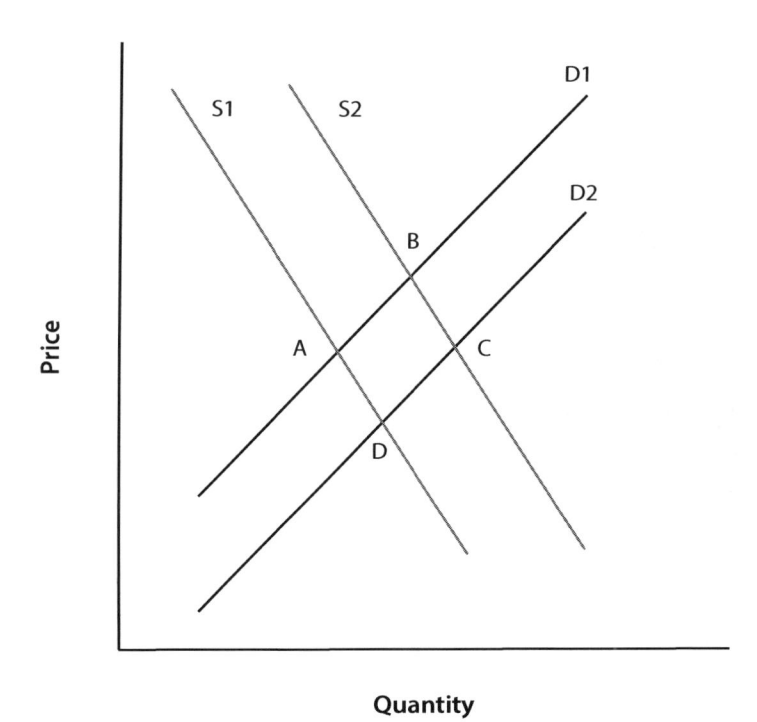

A. A
B. B
C. C
D. D

Answer:

A. Correct. The original equilibrium can be found at the intersection between the original demand curve (D1) and the original supply curve (S1).

ELASTICITY

PRICE ELASTICITY OF DEMAND

The law of demand states that demand increases when price decreases. It does not, however, provide a means for determining the magnitude of decrease. **Elasticity,** in general, is the measure of sensitivity to change. **Price elasticity of demand** measures the extent to which changes in price alter demand. For example, if the price of bread were to increase, price elasticity of demand would indicate the extent to which people would stop buying bread.

In a perfect world, the elasticity of the price will find equilibrium between price and demand (as in the diagram below). The upper line represents elasticity with demand at the same level. The mathematical equation for this is below:

$$E_d = \frac{\%\text{ of change in quantity demanded}}{\%\text{ of change in price}}$$

The greater this ratio is, the more responsive buyers are to the change in price. When the change in demand is greater than the change in price (so $E_d > 1$), demand is called **price elastic**. For example, the price of a car increases by 5% and there is a 20% decrease in quantity demanded ($E_d = {}^{20}/_5 = 4$). This shows that the change in price greatly affected quantity demanded.

When change in price is greater than the change in demand (so $E_d < 1$), demand is called **price inelastic**. Reverse the previous example. If the price of a car increased by 20% and there was a 5% increase in quantity demanded ($E_d = {}^5/_{20} = .25$), it is clear the change in price had only a small effect on consumer demand.

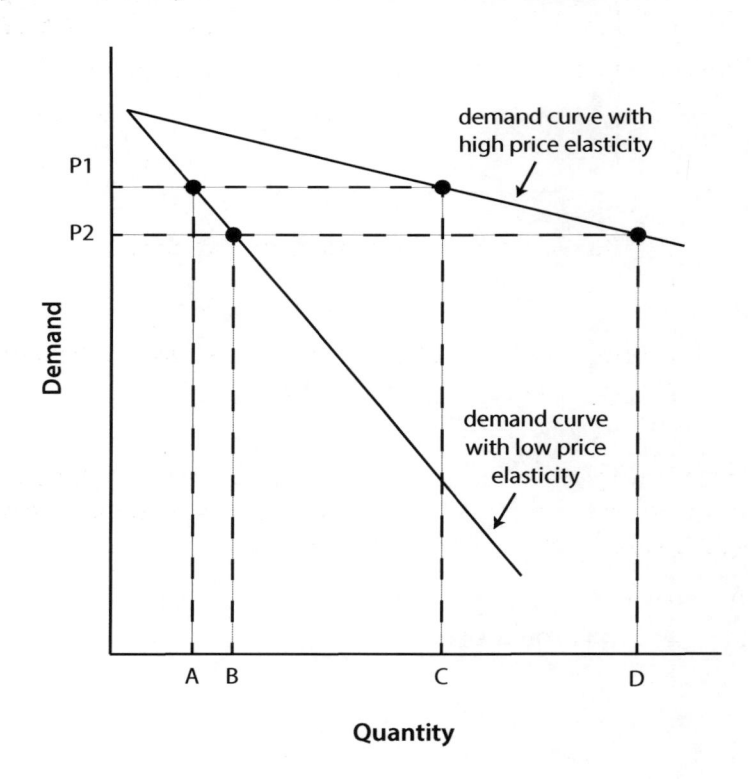

Figure 5.5. Price Elasticity of Demand

If any change in price will lead to unlimited demand, demand is **perfectly elastic**. This usually occurs in cases where there are many substitutes of the product. A coffee shop surrounded by other coffee shops might have perfectly elastic demand. If there is no change in quantity demanded based on a change in price, demand for that good is considered **perfectly inelastic**. For example, a life-saving drug for a rare disease might have perfectly inelastic demand: it does not change regardless of how expensive the drug becomes. A perfectly elastic demand curve is horizontal, whereas a perfectly inelastic curve is vertical. So, the steeper a demand curve, the less elasticity it has.

> **QUICK REVIEW**
>
> What are some perfectly elastic and perfectly inelastic goods?

Finally, if the change in price equals the change in demand ($E_d = 1$), demand is **unit elastic**. For example, the price for chewing gum decreased by 7% and the quantity of chewing gum demanded increased by 7%.

There are several factors that impact elasticity, including:

- proportion of income
- number of good substitutes
- time

SAMPLE QUESTIONS

12) The price elasticity of demand measures which of the following?

   A. The extent to which changes in demand impact price.
   B. The extent to which changes in price impact demand.
   C. Whether demand will decrease based on price.
   D. Whether demand will increase based on price.

   Answer:
   B. **Correct.** Price elasticity of demand measures how much demand will change based on changes in price.

13) If the supply curve for a product shifted to the right, creating a 5 percent decrease in price and a 4 percent increase in demand, the price elasticity of demand would be which of the following?

   A. 1.25
   B) 1
   C) 0.8
   D) The demand would be perfectly inelastic.

   Answer:
   C. **Correct.** When the change in demand (4) is divided by the change in price (5), the elasticity is 0.8.

Factors of Production

Labor

Just like production, labor is also subject to the market forces of supply and demand. A **supply curve of labor** shows the number of hours labor workers are willing to work at a given wage rate. Because engaging in labor is an individual economic decision, opportunity cost plays a role. As wages increase, workers are willing to forgo leisure activities in order to increase their labor and thereby increase their earnings. This is called the **substitution effect.** The demand for leisure, however, also increases as income increases. Therefore, when wages reach a certain amount, the number of hours workers are willing to work decreases as they increasingly choose leisure over labor. This is called the **income effect.** As a result, labor supply curves that extend to these high wages can take a backward-bending shape.

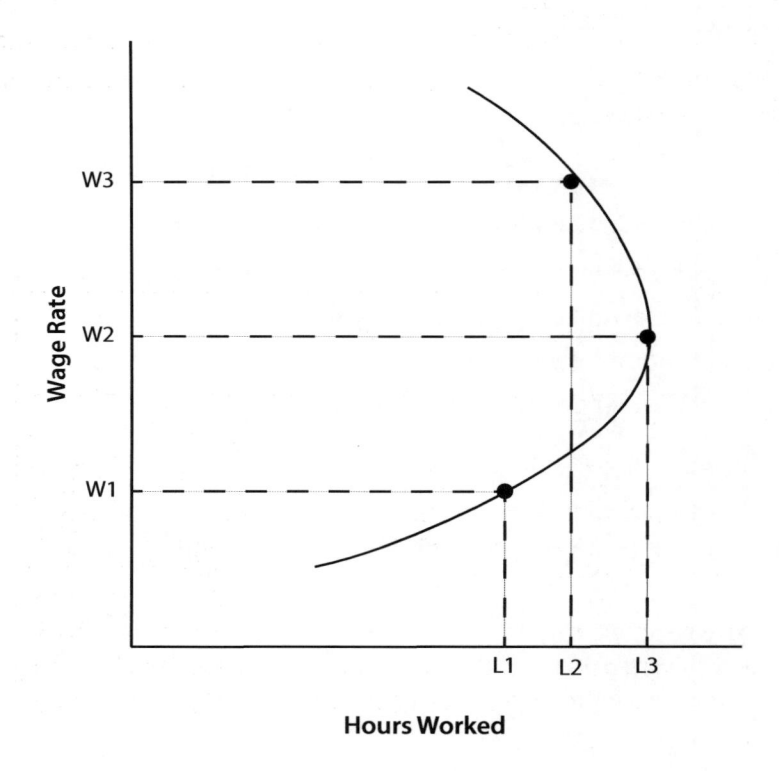

Figure 5.6. Supply Curve of Labor

The labor supply curve can shift overall based on the following factors:
- population growth or increased immigration
- changing worker attitudes
- changes in alternative opportunities

Labor demand is more complicated to calculate as it is a function of wage, desired quantity of production, and price of unit sold. Generally speaking, whereas labor supply curves are upward sloping overall, labor demand curves are downward sloping.

The **equilibrium wage rate** and quantity occurs where the quantity of demanded labor equals the quantity supply of labor.

THE BASIC CATEGORIES OF FINANCIAL ASSETS

Stocks and bonds are securities, monetary units that can be exchanged. Public and private interests and individuals may invest in stocks as stockholders, or in bonds as lenders. Stocks and bonds are traded on the stock market, a venue where private individuals, businesses, government agencies, and even foreign investors and foreign countries can invest.

Stocks are essentially shares of any given company or corporation that has "gone public" or offered its stock for sale to the highest bidder, whomever that may be. In the last century, the value of the stock market has come to reflect the state of the American economy as never before.

DOW JONES INDUSTRIAL AVERAGE

Stock Market Crash

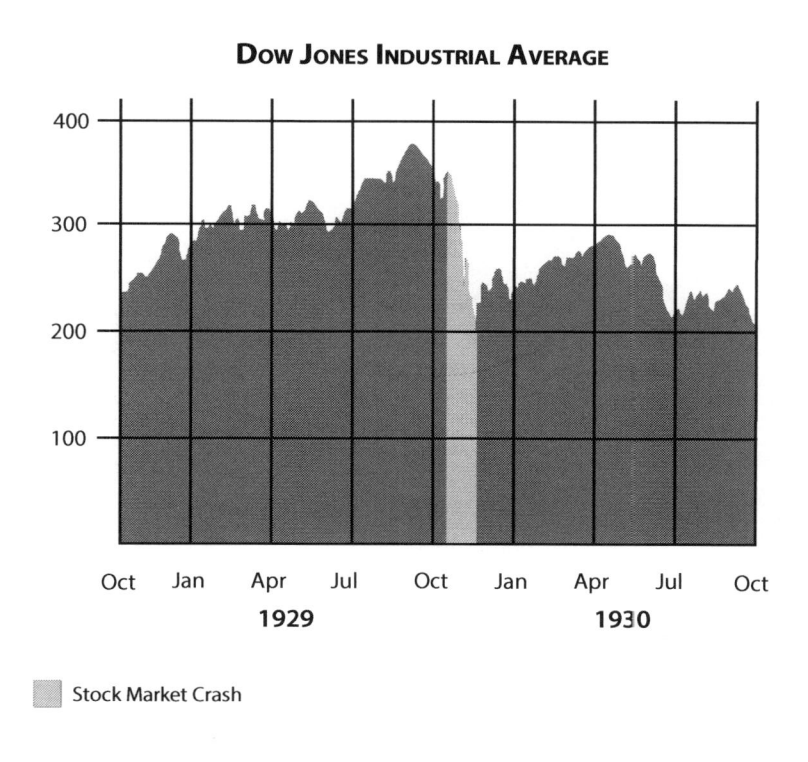

Figure 5.7. Stock Market Crash and Consequences

In 1929, the stock market was the precursor to an economic downturn that history has called the Great Depression. It was not just an American economic downturn. There were few nations unaffected by the stock market crash in 1929 and the decade of Depression that followed. The graph below shows the pitfalls of more than a decade of questionable buying practices by investors of all economic demographics.

The American economy is still more or less a mirror reflection of the American stock market. Its movement, both up and down, is the fodder of presidential campaigns and Congressional debate. For smaller investors, it's often boom or bust, bear or bull markets. There are fortunes to be made and lost for anyone who wants to take the risk. The graph below explores the three different stock measures over a period of several years.

STOCK MARKET TRENDS

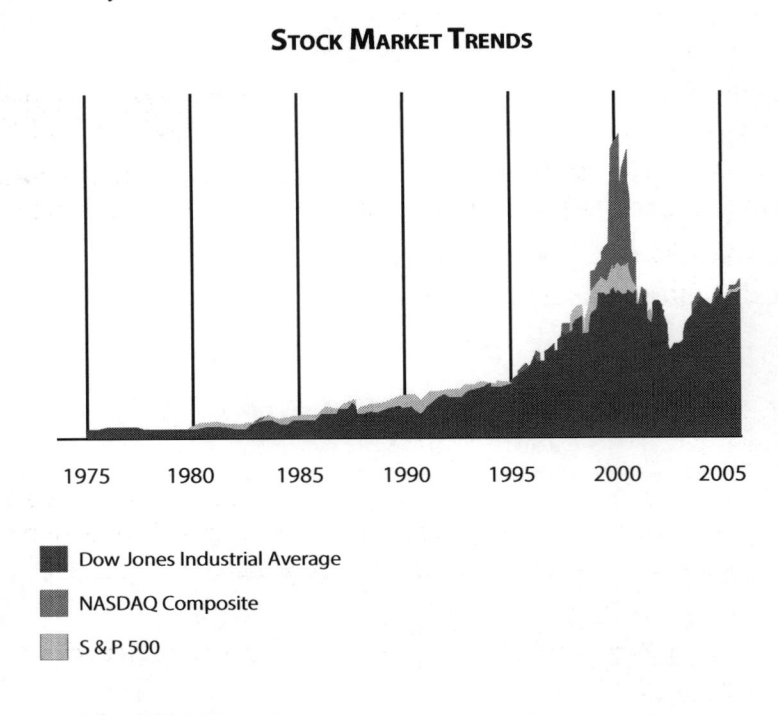

- Dow Jones Industrial Average
- NASDAQ Composite
- S & P 500

Figure 5.8. Stock Measures

Money market funds invest in short term investments like treasury bonds. These are considered safe and solid investments much like bank deposits, but encompass a broader scope for large scale investors.

THE ALLOCATION OF RESOURCES

Allocation of resources, or how resources are distributed across an economy, can fall to either the government or the market, depending on the type of economy. Within a specific firm, the allocation of resources is determined by profit maximization: how can the resources be used most efficiently?

One of the best ways to explain government control of the allocation of resources is to look at rationing during the Second World War in the United States. Rather than allow the public to hoard goods and create shortages, the federal government decided to control the flow of goods to civilians by allocating only a small amount of goods to the public on a weekly and monthly basis. Most resources are limited. In this case, economists determine the best way to allocate resources that does the least harm to all parties.

Public goods are products that an individual can consume without reducing their availability to other individuals. Public goods are also equally available to all. Basic television, plumbing infrastructure, and sewage systems are all examples of public goods. Some people now argue that internet access should be a public good. In a pure market economy, the market would provide for all public goods. However, in reality, often private markets fail to provide the allocatively efficient level of public goods and providing falls to the government.

SAMPLE QUESTIONS

14) When a new factory paying higher wages opens two towns over from Smallville, what will happen to Smallville's labor supply curve?

   A. It will begin to slope upwards.
   B. It will begin to bend backwards.
   C. It will shift to the right.
   D. It will shift to the left.

   Answer:
   D. **Correct.** Smallville's labor pool will shrink as workers leave Smallville to work higher-paying jobs at the new factory. A reduction of the labor pool results in a leftward shift of the graph.

15) Which of the following is NOT an example of a public good?

   A. air travel
   B. street lights
   C. public parks
   D. radio broadcasts

   Answer:
   A. **Correct.** Air travel is not available to everyone; it is restricted by price. Also, once one person "consumes" air travel by taking up a seat on a plane, the passenger prevents someone else from "consuming" that good.

BEHAVIOR OF FIRMS

In economics, any organization that uses factors of production to produce a good or service which it intends to sell for profit is called a **firm**. Firms can range from a child's lemonade stand to a multinational corporation like Walmart. While individuals make economic decisions to maximize their utility, firms make economic decisions to maximize their profit. **Economic profit** is different from simple accounting profit (subtracting costs from revenue). Economic profit also takes into consideration non-priced, or **implicit costs**. For example, a young entrepreneur starts a bicycle sandwich delivery business. She charges $4 per sandwich plus a $1 delivery fee. In her first month, she sells 200 sandwiches, which equals revenue of $1000. She spent $300 on bread, meat, and fixings, $50 on packaging and paid $50 for her bike and basket. These are her **explicit costs**. Her accounting profit for the month then was $600. However, economic profit takes into account other non-priced factors, including opportunity costs, like wages not earned from another job or interest not earned on money that has been liquidated. In this case, she passed up a job working at a coffee shop for $700 a month. Taking that into account, her economic loss would actually be $100.

Types of Firms

A **sole proprietorship** is a business belonging to a single individual. Either as the sole owner or the inventor, a sole proprietorship is dependent on the skills and income of a single individual.

A **partnership** is a joint venture between two individuals or two business entities. Some might say that a partnership is the next step in business ownership. A sole proprietor has too much business or too much inventory to manage alone, so he or she has the option to hire more help or bring in a partner to share both the risk and the profits.

A **corporation** is a group of individuals or businesses working together to share the business risk and the business profit. Of all the economic terms listed here, the corporation is the newest. It originated during the nineteenth century in the second phase of the Industrial Revolution, but it took off with the availability of credit at the end of the century and in the beginning of the twentieth century. Credit meant that the financial risk of the corporation was spread out among a larger pool of business leaders and therefore even more attractive than before.

Short Run Loss and Long Run Equilibrium

Firms make decisions in both the short and long term. The **short term,** in economics, is a period in which at least one production input is fixed and cannot be changed. For example, a store experiences a major increase in foot traffic and sales during the holiday season. It can respond by increasing staff and extending hours. It may even be able to order more merchandise. It cannot, however, increase the size of the store during that time. The **long term** refers to a period of time in which all production inputs are changeable. While that same store could not change its size for the few months of the holiday season, it could do so over the course of a year or two if high foot traffic continued.

Firms operating at a loss will continue to produce in the short run if money coming in—revenue—exceeds variable costs. Loss of profit in the short run is unimportant as long as there is a long term profit. If there is no long term profit, then the item will likely be discontinued and replaced with more cost-effective, profitable merchandise.

Of course, loss is not sustainable beyond the short run. If an industry is perfectly competitive, it will reach equilibrium (or **long run equilibrium**) when price is the same as the average total costs. This point is called **zero economic profit**; it is the amount of income that a business needs to break even in the marketplace.

FIXED AND VARIABLE INPUTS

Fixed inputs are any production inputs that cannot be changed in the short run. These are the costs that do not change and must be paid monthly or bimonthly, such as wages, rent, or materials costs.

Variable inputs are production inputs that can be changed in the short term, like the cost of labor (if the number of employees is increased or decreased). In the diagram below, fixed inputs or fixed costs appear as the stable bottom of the graph, while variable inputs or variable costs appear as an ever-changing line going up in terms of price.

Marginal costs are the costs of producing one more unit. Changes in any of the above costs can affect the final cost of production. Of all the costs in the productivity of a business, the ones most likely to change would be VC, or variable costs.

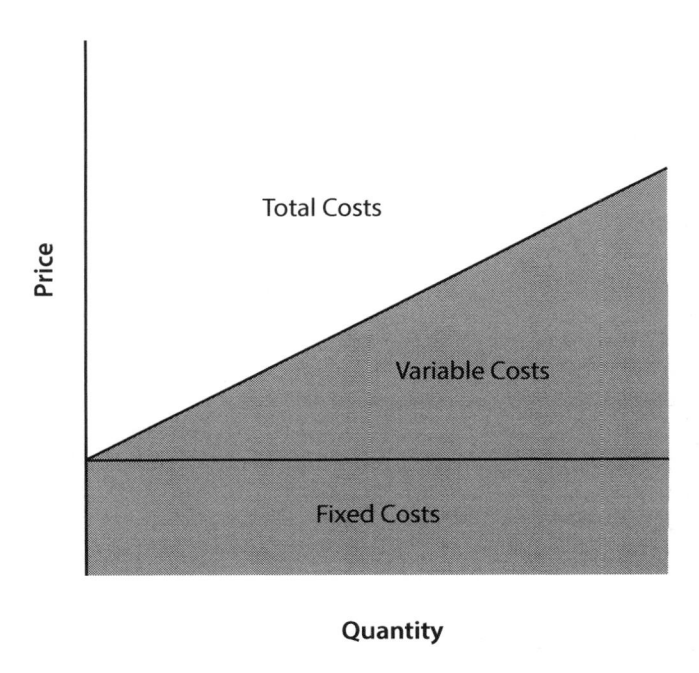

Figure 5.9. Fixed and Variable Inputs

Labor Analysis of Production

Economic analysis of production is based on production measures:

- **Total Product of Labor (TPL)** is best defined as the total amount of product at each quantity of labor.
- **Marginal Product of Labor (MPL)** is defined as the change in amount of product resulting from a change of labor.
- **Average Product of Labor (APL)** is the total product divided by the amount of labor which gives the average productivity of a market's labor.

For example, the sandwich entrepreneur's total product of labor is based on the variable inputs of the labor she put into her sandwich-making and her time on her bike. In her first month, she used 1 unit of labor, creating a TPL of 200 sandwiches. Her APL is calculated by dividing her TPL by her units of labor: 200/1 = 200.

Her business takes off and she decides to hire someone else to help her deliver sandwiches. The unit of labor increases to 2 and her TPL increases to 275. Her MPL is her change in TPL for the additional unit of labor. In this case, then, the MPL would be 75. Her new APL will then be 137.5.

Fixed and Variable Costs

Fixed costs are business costs that remain stable while **variable costs** change with the markets. As discussed earlier, fixed costs represent rent, wages, or insurance costs. Variable costs are the items needed for production or the cost of utilities that might change from month to month.

> **QUICK REVIEW**
>
> What are some variable costs a firm might have?

Total costs include all of the costs to reach a certain level of production. Total costs are the bottom line in a new business and will include both fixed costs and variable costs with a hope of profit at the end of the fiscal year.

Average costs include all of the costs to produce items divided by the number of items produced. This is the cost per item that a business must consider and hope to lower. Lower average costs of production means higher profits.

Marginal cost is the difference in price when production is increased by one unit. Marginal costs can either increase or decrease the overall price of the item produced. It depends on a whole variety of different factors and the market at the time.

Long Run Average Costs

How do firms determine how and when to expand? By examining long-run average cost (LRAC). A firm can calculate its LRAC by combining snapshots of its short-term average costs (SRAC) at various production points. For example, our entrepreneur could calculate her SRAC based on selling 0–100 sandwiches. She could then calculate her costs at 75–250, and so on. Her LRAC would combine these graphs to indicate when she should prepare to expand.

An LRAC graph would show a decrease in price with increasing quantity, followed by a leveling out, and then an increase in price with increasing quantity. The first section of the graph, in which price decreases, is called **economies of scale**. This shows the advantages (in decreased costs) of greater production and expansion. Labor and management are able to specialize. Our entrepreneur now focuses on assembling the prettiest sandwiches and hires others—who are faster and more efficient—to organize sandwich supplies, wrap the sandwiches, and make deliveries.

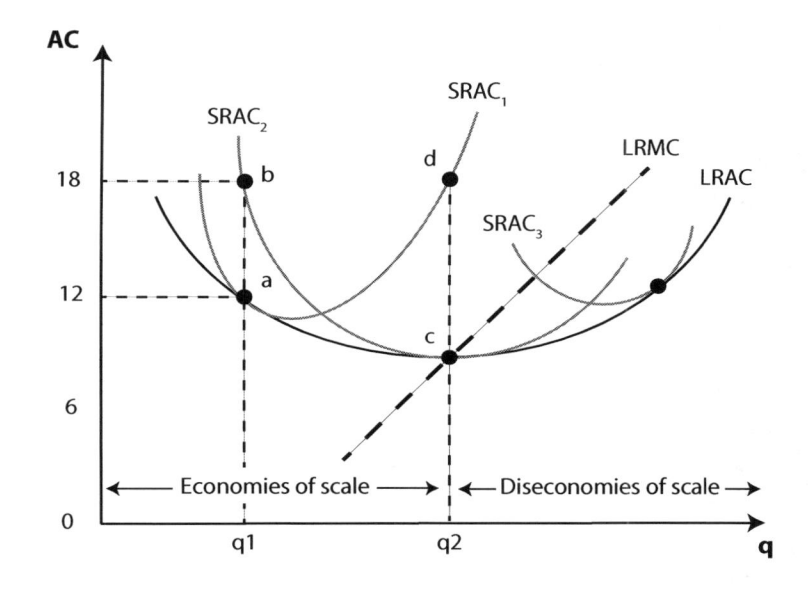

Figure 5.10. Long Run Average Costs (1)

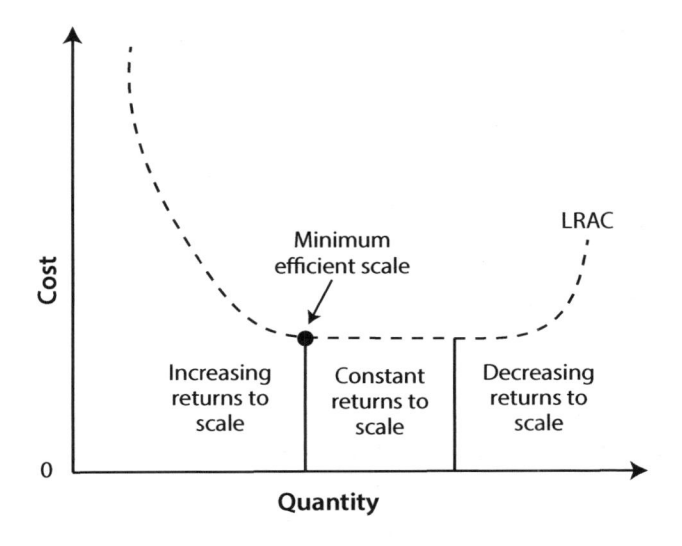

Figure 5.11. Long Run Average Costs (2)

However, she will eventually reach a point where adding more workers will bring fewer and fewer advantages. This is called the **law of diminishing returns.** For example, if she hires more riders than she needs at one time, she will not see the same benefit as she did when each new rider allowed deliveries to happen faster. This stage is called **constant returns to scale.**

Finally, a firm reaches a point where expansion hurts profit rather than helps. This is called **diseconomies of scale.** The increase in production becomes more costly. So our entrepreneur now has hired too many people to help in the sandwich preparation process, and they are bumping into each other and working inefficiently.

SAMPLE QUESTIONS

16) If a long run average cost curve is falling left to right, this indicates that a firm should do which of the following in that price range and quantity range?

    A. expand its operation
    B. maintain its operation at its current size
    C. decrease the size of its operation
    D. There is insufficient information to make a determination.

    Answer:

    A. **Correct.** A LRAC that falls left to right shows decreasing cost with increasing quantity, or economies of scale. In this situation, it is beneficial for a company to expand.

17) If a firm wanted to know the impact that hiring 100 new workers would have on production, it would examine which of the following?

    A. Total Product of Labor
    B. variable costs
    C. Marginal Product of Labor
    D. fixed costs

    Answer:

    C. **Correct.** In economics, the term marginal always means "additional." In this case, the Marginal Product of Labor is a measurement tool used to determine the additional output resulting from an increase in labor.

18) Which of the following is an example of a variable input?

    A. a contractor's work crew
    B. money obtained from a bank loan
    C. a caterer's kitchen
    D. a magazine's printing press

Answer:

A. Correct. A contractor can hire or cut employees in response to changes in the short term. That makes his crew a variable input.

19) **Which of the following is an example of an implicit cost?**
    A. the money an entrepreneur anticipates spending in the next six months to grow her business
    B. ad space purchased in a local newspaper to advertise an entrepreneur's new business
    C. money spent on certification courses to achieve a license in a field
    D. the time an entrepreneur spent researching information to launch a new business

Answer:

D. Correct. Time spent researching information is a non-priced cost. There are many other things the entrepreneur could have been doing but did not do. Therefore, this is an implicit cost.

Types of Markets

Perfect Competition

There are four main characteristics of **perfect competition**: there are many small and independent buyers and sellers; everybody produces the same product; there are no barriers to the entry of new or exit of old firms; and all firms must accept the price where it is and produce as much as they want at that price (because they cannot change it).

Put simply, perfect or pure competition occurs when there is no one business that controls the entire marketplace because no one business is big enough to do so. For example, three pizza restaurants compete against each other in a small college town. Price wars and showmanship may establish one of the restaurants as a leader for a time, but none of the three restaurants dominates the market because they all produce the same product for roughly the same price.

Monopoly

Not all markets are perfectly competitive markets. When one corporation or business controls one entire area or product of a given market, it is called a **monopoly**. In addition, monopolies are marked by a lack of close substitutes for the product, barriers to entry for new firms, and market power. Barriers can include legal barriers, like licensing restrictions or copyright laws. The advantages of producing large quantities (discussed later) also can edge newcomers out of the market. For example, big box stores like Walmart can purchase or produce products on a large scale. This allows them to decrease their costs and lower their prices. A small family-owned store in the same town—buying a small fraction of the same products—cannot compete. Finally, if a firm controls all of the resources needed in production, it can prevent others from entering the market. Andrew Carnegie used this technique at the end of the nineteenth century with his company, US Steel. He purchased every layer of production, allowing him to streamline costs and prevent competitors from accessing the resources.

Monopolies function best in a new market where competition is either too expensive or not possible because of legal roadblocks like patents.

Oligopoly

An **oligopoly** occurs when a few businesses control one market. As a result, they become interdependent; the action of one affects the others. For example, when one airline started to require payment for checked luggage, the others quickly followed suit. In an oligopoly, the product can be standardized as in a perfectly competitive market, or may be differentiated. For example, telephone service is essentially a standardized product, whereas the car industry is an oligopoly with differentiated products. Like monopolies, oligopolies have entry barriers.

SAMPLE QUESTIONS

20) If a market has perfect competition, which of the following is true?
    A. There are many buyers, but only a few sellers.
    B. There are many sellers, but only a few buyers.
    C. There are many sellers and buyers.
    D. There is an equal number of buyers and sellers.

    Answer:
    C. **Correct.** A perfectly competitive market has a large number of small buyers and sellers, which prevents any one (or two) entities from controlling price.

21) Which of the following types of markets have barriers to entry for new firms?
    A. monopolies and perfect competition markets
    B. oligopolies and perfect competition markets
    C. monopolies only
    D. monopolies and oligopolies

    Answer:
    D. **Correct.** Both monopolies and oligopolies are markets in which a very small number of firms—one or a few, respectively—control the market.

In order to maintain control, they must stifle competition from new firms. This is done by maximizing the benefits of large-scale operations or controlling relevant resources.

GOVERNMENT INTERVENTION

PRICE FLOORS AND PRICE CEILINGS

A **price floor** is the lowest price established by the government. Governments use price floors to aid producers in unfair markets with depressed prices. If the price floor instituted by the government is lower than the price the market will support, the price floor is ineffective as demonstrated by the figure below, line F being the price floor set by the government. When set above the market price, they can lead

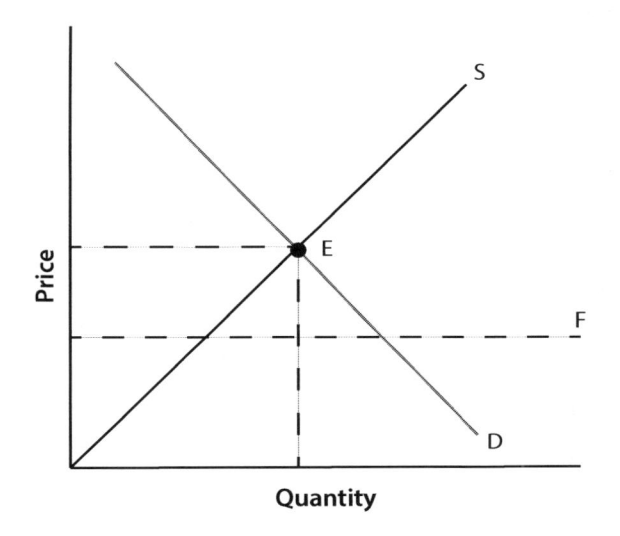

Figure 5.12. Ineffective Price Floor

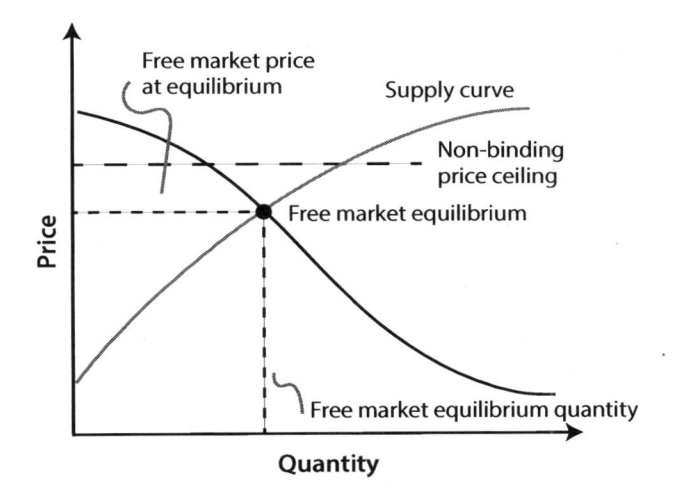

Figure 5.13. Price Ceiling

to a surplus. Price floors lead to overall inefficiency in the market as neither producers nor consumers are maximizing the available resources. They also can price people out of the market.

A **price ceiling** is the highest price allowed by government. Often the price ceiling dictated by the government is higher than the market actually allows as demonstrated by the diagram below where the government set price ceiling is indicated by line F. If the price ceiling is set below the market price, then demand will outstrip supply, leading to a shortage.

Antitrust Laws

Antitrust laws are used to promote a competitive market environment. Antitrust laws exist to protect consumers from illegal mergers and other unfair business practices. Antitrust laws emerged out of the Progressive movement of the nineteenth century in response to the monopolies and trusts dominated by banking and heavy industry in the Second Industrial Revolution.

The richest businessmen of the nineteenth century were called **robber barons** because they controlled vast amounts of money and property. For the robber barons, controlling all aspects of one given industry was simply good business practice. For example, a steel magnate might control the steel industry of a given region of the United States. That means he controls the mines where raw ingredients are mined from the earth as well as the miners, even providing company houses and a company store. Furthermore, the magnate controls the railroad that hauls raw ingredients to his steel foundries and the railroads that carry the finished product to its destination.

Competition is key to a market economy and a capitalist system. Establishing a **trust**—control over the entire industrial process—defeats that purpose. It was for that reason that the US government set out to break the trusts of the late nineteenth and early twentieth centuries.

Types of Taxes

Progressive taxes tax the income of the wealthy more than other groups in society, or so the theory goes. These taxes increase gradually as income rises for an individual, but, in a free market economy, taxes are adjusted to account for income losses in business, charitable contributions, and other circumstances. Therefore, in reality, tax rates may vary considerably across income levels.

Other forms of taxation include **proportional** and **regressive taxes.** Proportional taxes are similar to flat rate taxes in that all taxpayers are taxed at the same rate or at the same proportion of their incomes. Regressive taxes affect everyone at the same rate without a sliding proportional scale, making life more expensive for the lower classes.

SAMPLE QUESTION

22) Which of the following statements is true of antitrust laws?

    A. They are designed to modify perfect competition markets.

    B. They are designed to protect controlling firms in oligopolies.

    C. They are designed to shift perfect competition markets towards monopolies.

    D. They are designed to decrease the power of monopolists.

Answer:

    D. Correct. With the rise of the robber barons and the consolidation of market power in several industries (including steel, railroads, and oil), the government took action to reduce that power and restore balance in the market.

MACROECONOMICS

CIRCULAR FLOW MODELS

A **circular flow model** shows where money goes in any given economy. The circular flow model follows money as it enters the marketplace to be spent by consumers and to be invested by businesses. The model also reveals places in the economy where money is being wasted. In a **closed economy** model (Figure 5.14), households provide factors of production to firms, which the firms then transform into goods and services. The firms pay the households competitive compensation for those factors of production, providing income for the household. The household then uses that income to buy the goods and services created by the firms.

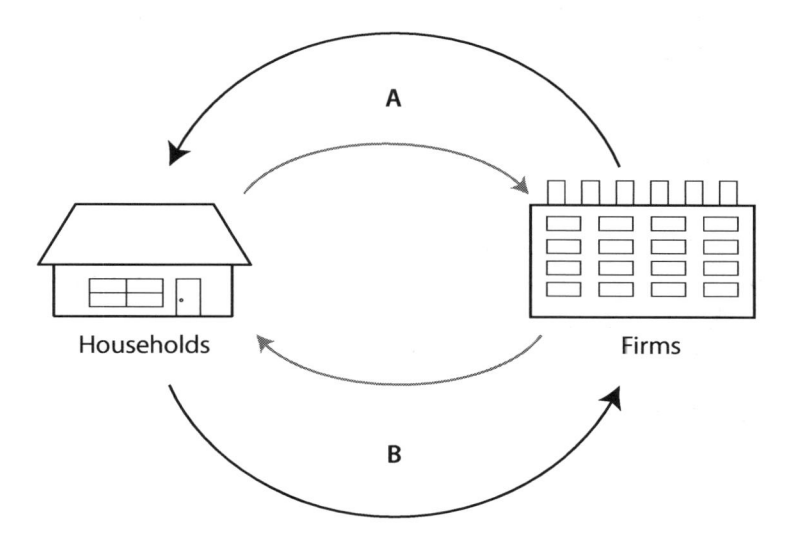

Figure 5.14. Circular Flow Model

Governments also play a role in the circular flow, acting as both recipients of factors of production (in the form of tax collection) and creators of goods and services.

The study of macroeconomics focuses on how to keep this flow moving at a strong and steady pace, primarily through the use of measurement tools.

Gross Domestic Product (GDP)

The **GDP**, the **gross domestic product**, is the total value of domestic production: the market value of all of the **final goods and services** produced within a nation in one year. Final goods are those that are ready for consumption. **Intermediate goods**, goods that still require more processing, are not counted. Tomatoes are intermediate goods; jarred tomato sauce is a final good. Also, to avoid **double counting**, the count takes place at the final sale.

GDP focuses on what was actually produced within a country, regardless of where it is headquartered. For example, if a shoe company has its headquarters in California, but all of its production takes place in Vietnam, the total production of shoes would contribute to Vietnam's GDP, not that of the United States.

The higher the GDP is for the nation, the better the economy for both business and individual citizens.

Secondhand sales, nonmarket transactions, and underground economies are all excluded from GDP. This means that a country (usually developing countries) in which these play a stronger role have relatively weak GDPs.

NOMINAL GDP IN BILLION U.S. DOLLARS IN 2014

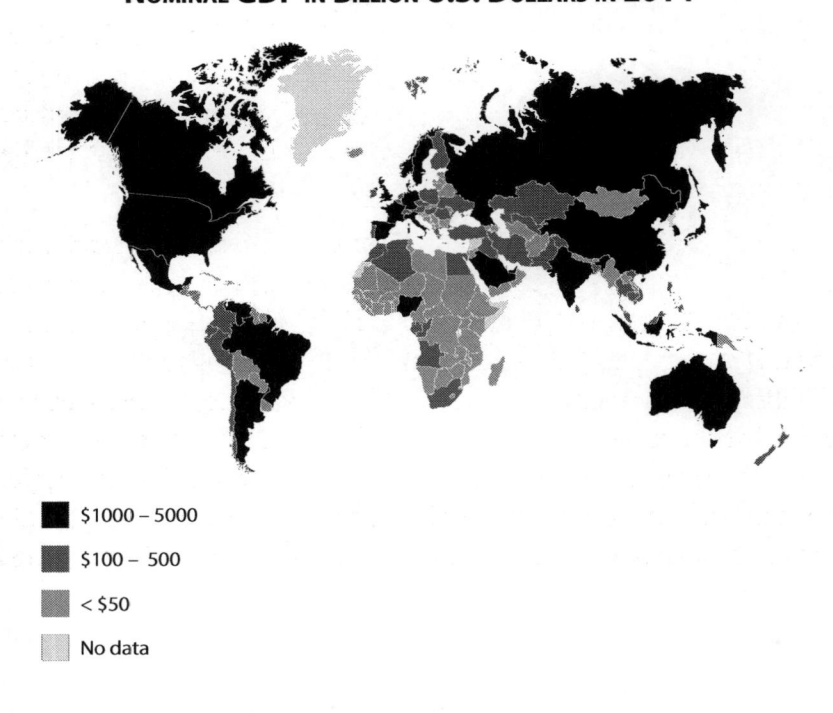

- $1000 – 5000
- $100 – 500
- < $50
- No data

Figure 5.15. 2014 World Economies Map

INFLATION AND THE CONSUMER PRICE INDEX

To measure the health of an economy based on consumer spending, economists use the **Consumer Price Index (CPI)**.

The **CPI** measures prices of goods and services as they change over time. It does this by selecting a base year and compiling a market "basket" of 400 consumer goods and services that year, ranging from gas to candy to refrigerators. A price index is created for subsequent years by measuring the change in prices. Here is an example:

Table 5.1. CPI Example

Items in the basket	Quantity Purchased (2010)	2010 Price	2010 Spending	2015 Price	2015 Spending (based on 2010 quantities)
Candy Bar	12	1.5	18	1.75	21
Books	10	12.0	120	14.00	140
Movie Tickets	6	10.0	60	12.00	72
Total Spending			= 198		= 233

$$\text{Current Year Price Index} = 100 \times \frac{\text{Spending Current Year}}{\text{Spending Base Year}}$$

$$\text{2015 Price Index} = 100 \times \frac{233}{198} = 117.68$$

This shows a 17.68 percent increase in price. To calculate the official CPI, the average price level of consumer goods is taken for the base year and the current year. The percent change from year to year is called **inflation**. Sudden or unexpected inflation—particularly inflation that does not keep up with wages—causes problems within an economy.

Figure 5.16 shows a sample of the CPI for the United States between 1913 and 2014, just over a century. The dark line shows the average CPI for each year with 1982–1984 as the "base year" (when CPI = 100). The graph shows that there has been an overall increase in CPI over time. The light line shows the percent change in average CPI from year to year. This is the measure that shows inflation within the economy. Inflation peaked in the 1970s, but there has been very little since. In the 1970s inflation reached an all-time high, and economists struggled to figure out how to bring it back down. Eventually, the Federal Reserve stopped issuing new money, leading to a sharp rise in unemployment but eventually curbing inflation.

U.S. Consumer Price Index

- Average Consumer Price Index
- Change in Average Consumer Price Index

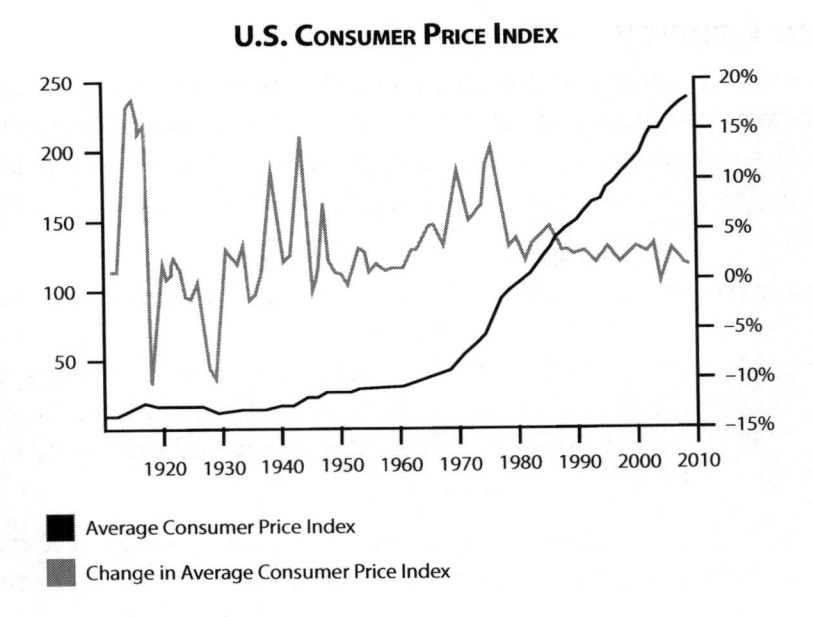

Figure 5.16. US Consumer Price Index

SAMPLE QUESTIONS

23) **Which of the following transactions would be used in a calculation of GDP?**

    A. compensation a teenager receives for raking a neighbor's leaves
    B. the resale of a coffee table on eBay
    C. the sale of strawberries to a jam manufacturer
    D. the sale of five pounds of carrots at a grocery store

    Answer:

    D. **Correct.** Because the carrots are going directly to a consumer, and not being used to create another item for sale, they are considered a final good.

24) **When is inflation an economic problem?**

    A. when it continues over a long period of time
    B. when it occurs unexpectedly
    C. when it is lower than wage increases
    D. It is always a problem.

    Answer:

    B. **Correct.** Unexpected and sudden inflation causes problems because people do not have time to prepare for it, and wages do not have time to catch up. This kind of inflation leads to the sudden loss of value of money, investments, and capital.

ECONOMIC GROWTH

In its simplest form, economic growth is the outward movement of the production possibility frontier over time, which in turn results from an increase in **productivity**. In economics, productivity is defined as the quantity of output that can be produced per worker in a prescribed amount of time. There are four main **determinants of productivity.**

Physical Capital: When the physical capital, or tools of production, are increased, productivity increases. For example, a bottle maker has a machine that can produce 100 bottles an hour. The company upgrades to a more efficient machine and can now produce 200 bottles an hour. On a macroeconomics level, governments should craft policies that encourage investment in capital.

Human Capital: Human capital refers to the knowledge and skills of the labor force. The more skilled its labor, the more productive the economy. This is reflected in the rapid economic growth of the four Asian Tigers: South Korea, Singapore, Hong Kong, and Taiwan. Each economy began to grow thanks to factory jobs requiring unskilled workers. However, economic growth really took off when their skilled labor forces allowed them to dominate international banking and manufacturing information technology. Increasing human capital does not simply mean encouraging education (although that is part of it). Health initiatives (like vaccination drives) that create a healthier workforce also increase human capital and productivity.

Natural Resources: Minerals, soil, timber, and waterways all constitute productivity resources that are provided by nature. Government policies that provide for sustainable consumption of renewable resources and protection of nonrenewable resources can foster economic growth.

Technology: Technology does not just mean computers and machines. Technology refers to a nation's knowledge and ability to efficiently produce goods. In this way, discovering how to make fire was a technological advancement on par with smartphones. Governments should create policies to encourage and incentivize innovation.

Social and cultural changes can impact economic growth as well. For example, significant economic reforms introduced market principles to the Chinese economy beginning in the early 1980s. Since then, China has experienced rapid economic growth fueled by government policies that capitalize on the country's huge labor pool.

Figure 5.17 looks at economic growth between the years of 1990 and 2006 in the United States and different countries. It gives a glimpse of the economic highs and lows of the last two decades and it also reveals the peaks and valleys that accompany not only the economic, but social, cultural, and historic events as well.

GDP Accumulated Growth

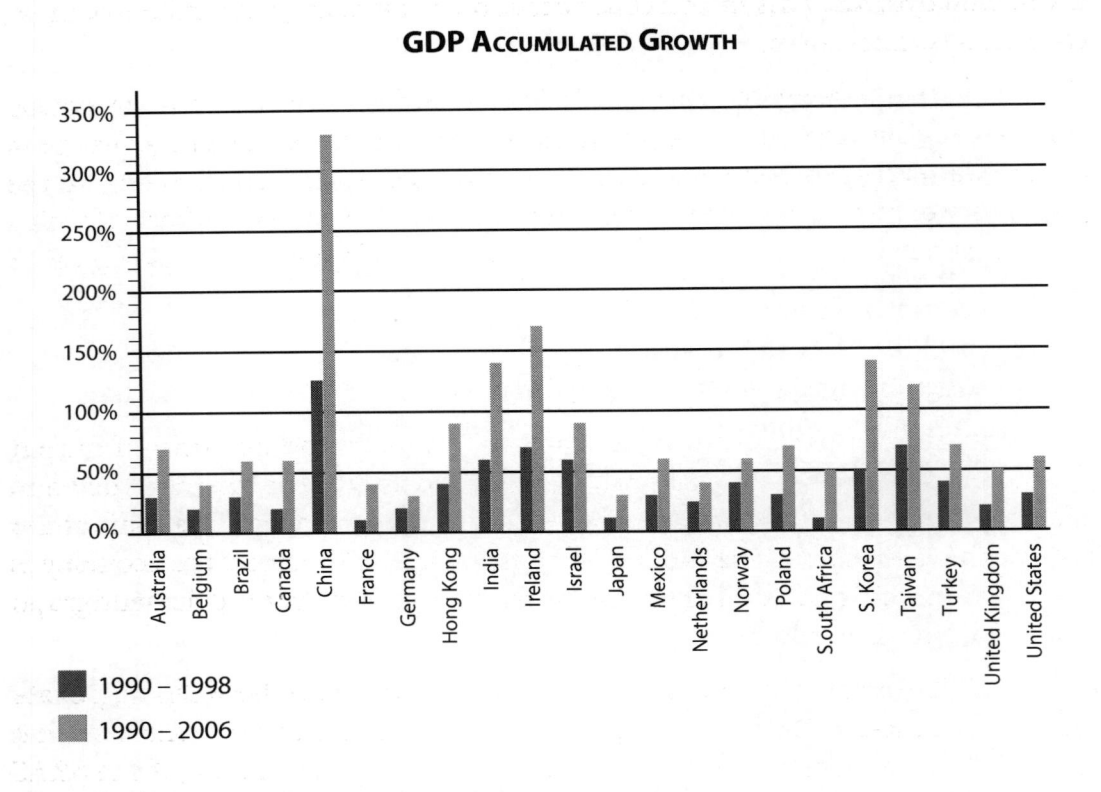

■ 1990 – 1998
■ 1990 – 2006

Figure 5.17. Global Economic Growth (1990–2006)

Aggregate Supply

Aggregate supply (AS) is the relationship between the total of all domestic output produced and the average price level. Essentially, it is the sum of all of the microeconomic supply curves in an economy. The **Long Run Aggregate Supply (LRAS)** assumes that input prices have had enough time to adjust to changes in the various product markets. All markets—product and input—are at equilibrium, and there

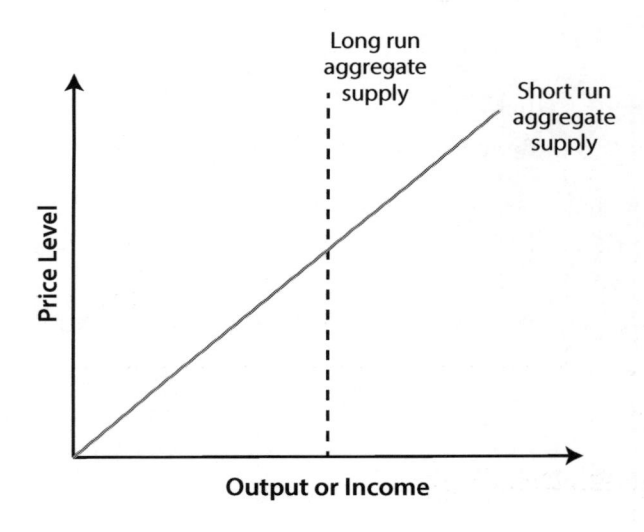

Figure 5.18. Aggregate Supply

is full employment. This means that output does not change, regardless of price, creating a vertical curve.

Short run aggregate supply (SRAS) curves fluctuate without impacting employment; however, if the long-run AS curve shifts, there must be a change in the output level at full employment. These changes result from a change in the availability of resources or changes in technology and productivity, both of which could alter a nation's output when working at full employment. In this way LRAS can be used as a measure of economic growth.

INFLATIONARY AND RECESSIONARY GAPS

An economy is in **macroeconomic equilibrium** when the quantity of output demanded in an economy (as shown by **aggregate demand**, the sum of all demand curves in an economy), is equal to the quantity of output supplied. This equilibrium does not always occur at full employment, though. If it does not, the economy is either experiencing inflation or recession—an aggregate supply and demand graph will reveal this information.

An **inflationary gap** occurs when the intersection point between **aggregate demand** and SRAS is at a higher output level than the LRAS curve. Remember that the LRAS curve represents the output level of full employment. So, if the SRAS curve and the aggregate demand curve intersect at an output level beyond the LRAS curve, the economy is producing at an output level that is higher than full employment. This usually happens when quantity demanded is suddenly increased through foreign or government spending, or even just very active consumers. When demand increases like this, factories stay open longer and pay their workers more overtime, thus exceeding full employment output.

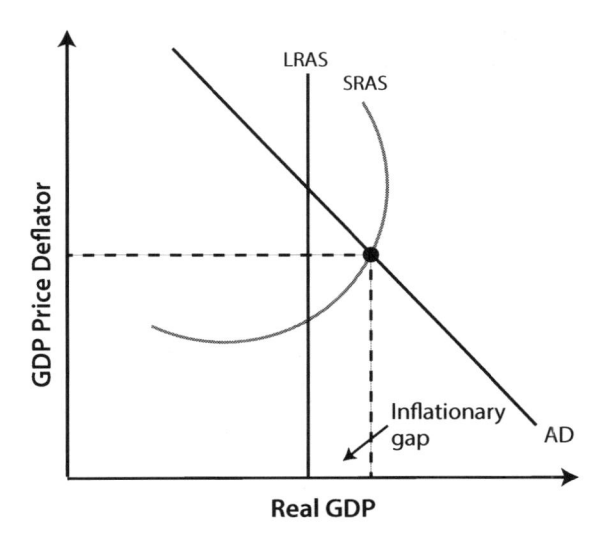

Figure 5.19. Inflationary Gap

On the other hand, if the equilibrium point is lower than LRAS, a **recessionary gap** exists. This indicates that the nation is experiencing high levels of unemployment.

SAMPLE QUESTIONS

25) In the New Deal, the government created new jobs for people in an attempt to counteract the recession (the Great Depression). Which of the following best describes the economic theory guiding that policy?

    A. Government-created jobs increase aggregate demand, which shifts the equilibrium point closer to the LRAS curve.

    B. Government-created jobs shift the LRAS curve to the left to bring it closer to the equilibrium point between short term aggregate supply and aggregate demand.

    C. Government-created jobs increase the nation's productivity, which eliminates recession.

    D. Government-created jobs increase aggregate supply, which shifts the intersection between SRAS and long-term aggregate supply.

    Answer:

    A. Correct. The jobs generated by the New Deal created new demand for labor, increasing aggregate demand and shifting the equilibrium point closer to LRAS (which is at full employment). The danger is in going too far the other way and creating an inflationary gap.

26) Which of the following policies would be least likely to increase a nation's productivity?

    A. a law providing free post-secondary education
    B. a national immunization campaign against malaria
    C. government funding for research into high-yield crops
    D. a government-mandated minimum wage

    Answer:

    D. Correct. Mandating a minimum wage does not affect productivity; it simply improve wages for labor and impacts the cost of production.

THE FEDERAL RESERVE

The Federal Reserve behaves as a central bank of the United States and ensures the safety of the American monetary system. In the century since its inception, the role of the Fed has expanded tremendously, but the Fed's primary role at the end of the day is to maximize employment and stabilize prices in the United States.

The Federal Reserve was created in 1913 to help thwart the rising numbers of so-called "panics" that seized the nation every few years. The Fed was created to stabilize the US money supply and to moderate interest rates. As mentioned earlier, the Fed's duties have also expanded to include for US banks. With its own seal and flag, the important components of the US federal government.

The Federal Reserve is the arbiter of interest rates for mortgages, the stock market, and any other monetary policy involving interest (such as money markets). **Equilibrium interest rates,** regulated by the Fed, occur only when interest rates and the money supply are roughly equivalent.

As of 2016, interest rates established by the Federal Reserve are at an all-time low. While the low interest rates can be a boon for borrowers, lenders also can take advantage of low interest rates to offer loans, sometimes questionable ones, to borrowers who historically were not eligible for loans in the past. This contributed heavily to a recent housing crisis that is still being felt throughout the housing industry.

Figure 5.20. The Federal Reserve

The interest rate set by the Federal Reserve is established by a number of factors, including the federal funds rate, the interest that the Federal Reserve charges banks. The chart below shows the fluctuating interest rates that banks have paid in recent decades and how they ultimately trickled down to consumers.

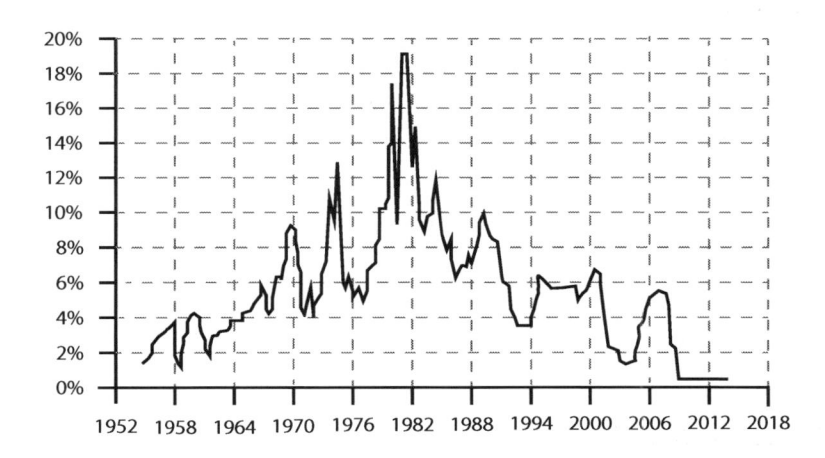

Figure 5.21. Federal Funds Rate

The Federal Reserve also monitors **monetary stabilization**: efforts to keep prices, unemployment, and the money supply, among other fiscal indicators, relatively stable. Monetary stabilization helps to prevent the economy from oscillating between inflation and recession.

Fiscal Policy

Fiscal policy is an approach to economic management in which the government is deeply involved in managing the economy. When an individual or firm spends or saves money, those choices impact that individual's or firm's own finances. When the government makes similar choices, the government's decisions impact the economy as a whole. These economic decisions are called **multipliers.**

In **expansionary fiscal policy**, the government either increases spending or decreases taxes in order to increase the aggregate demand curve to counteract a recession. When the economy experiences inflation, the government uses **contractionary fiscal policy**: reducing government spending or increasing taxes.

A **tariff** is a tax or duty paid on anything imported or exported into or from a given country. Low tariffs encourage foreign goods to enter the market. Countries may do this to stimulate trade or in exchange for other trade agreements. For example, the North American Free Trade Agreement (NAFTA) essentially eliminated tariffs among Canada, the United States, and Mexico.

High tariffs protect domestic industry by making foreign goods more expensive. However, they also risk slowing trade. For example, between World War I and World War II, the United States passed a very high protectionist tariff. In response, other countries instituted retaliatory tariffs to block American trade as Americans had blocked foreign trade. Consequently, world trade ground to a halt.

When governments make changes to spending and taxes, it affects the government's budget. When revenue (primarily money from taxes) exceeds spending, the government has a **surplus**. When spending exceeds revenues, the government has a **deficit**. A deficit is not the same thing as a debt. A deficit is simply the gap between what the government has spent and what it has earned. In order to cover that deficit, it must borrow money, generating government debt. National debt develops over years of deficits.

Changes in **currency** are caused by and impact the strength of a nation's economy. **Currency appreciation** occurs when a country's money gains value in national and international markets. This increases foreign investment, as other countries are able to gain more value for their money. However, a strong currency makes that nation's exports more expensive, which can affect trade.

Currency depreciation occurs when a country's money loses value in national and international markets. Currency depreciation may point to instabilities in the nation's economy (such as high rates of inflation). However, when carried out in an intentional and orderly manner, it can increase a nation's global competiveness by lowering the cost of its exports. For example, China has used intentional currency depreciation to build a strong export-based economy and foster economic growth.

SAMPLE QUESTIONS

27) Which of the following would NOT be an example of contradictory fiscal policy?

   A. freezing annual cost of living increases on the salaries of government employees
   B. reducing the operating hours of national parks
   C. increasing property taxes
   D. financing a new dam

   Answer:
   D. Correct. If the government builds a new dam, it injects new spending into the economy, thereby expanding the economy.

28) Which of the following is NOT a responsibility of the Federal Reserve?

   A. to set interest rates
   B. to determine government spending
   C. to maximize employment
   D. to stabilize prices

   Answer:
   B. Correct. Although the Federal Reserve plays an important role in fiscal policy, it has no control over government spending.

Psychology

Psychology is the study of the human mind and how it functions, with particular attention paid to human behavior. Although its roots can be traced back to the philosophical writings of ancient Greece, it only emerged as a science approximately 150 years ago. As a discipline, it has a home in both the social and biological sciences. Psychologists apply theoretical interpretations, explanations, and predictions to observations, measurements, and analysis based on objective and systematic procedures.

Lifespan Development

Developmental psychology studies the ways in which people change over time. Because the majority of change occurs during childhood, that is the emphasis of this field. There are several significant debates in developmental psychology:

Nature v. Nurture: Psychologists have determined that both biology and environment play a significant role in human development. Every person has certain biological traits that shape their personality traits. For example, research has found that some people have neurons that are sensitive to over-stimulation. These people tend to be introverts (in fact, as a general rule, introverts have these neurons). However, some of these people are raised in ways that help them overcome this sensitivity to an extent—perhaps their parents required them to engage in lengthy conversations with other adults frequently—leading them to become extroverts.

Stability v. Change: Do people maintain the same characteristics their whole lives or do they change over time? This has proven a very challenging question for psychologists, as it seems to vary greatly from person to person. It seems that some aspects of personality remain constant over the course of a person's entire life, while other aspects change.

Continuity v. Stages: Does development happen steadily from birth to death or does it happen in leaps (or stages)? Although many of the best-known developmental theories are stage theories, this is an ongoing debate among psychologists. They have been able to determine that some skills, like crawling and walking, are acquired in a continuous manner. Other skills, like language, come in a more segmented fashion.

There is consensus, however, that **critical periods** occur in development when certain skills must be acquired or they will never be able to be fully achieved. For example, human binocular vision must develop between three and eight months or it will not fully develop. Many psychologists believe a critical period also exists for language acquisition and possibly even memory development.

Motor Sensory Development

The greatest changes in sensory, motor, and perceptual development happen in the first two years of life. When babies are first born, most of their senses operate in a similar way to those of adults. For example, babies are able to hear before they are born; studies show that babies turn towards the sound of their mother's voice just minutes after being born, indicating they recognize the mother's voice from their time in the womb.

The exception is vision. A baby's vision changes significantly in its first year of life; initially it has a range of vision of only eight to twelve inches and no depth perception. As a result, infants rely primarily on hearing; vision does not become the dominant sense until around the age of twelve months. Babies also prefer faces to other objects. This preference, along with their limited vision range, means that their sight is initially focused on their caregiver.

While babies' senses might be similar to those of adults, their ability to interpret sensory inputs is very different. They must learn to **perceive**, or interpret the sensory information they receive. This occurs as they interact with their environment and their caregivers, and as they age. **Eleanor Gibson** conducted an experiment in which she created a "visual cliff" by extending a Plexiglass ledge off a wooden table. All babies looked to their mothers for guidance when they approached the cliff; older babies refused to cross it regardless of their mothers' expressions. Gibson posited that while all babies could see the cliff, the older babies had a more complex perception of it because of their more advanced development and their experiences with crawling (and falling).

In early psychology, babies were not believed to have any innate motor skills; the brain was considered to be **tabula rasa**, or a blank slate. However, later research revealed that all humans are actually born with certain reflexes which then later disappear. These include **rooting**, turning the head and opening the mouth in search of food when the cheek is touched; **sucking**, moving the mouth to draw milk from a nipple; **grasping**, the tight clenching of anything placed on a baby's palm; the **Moro reflex**, a startle reflex in which a baby throws its arms out and pulls them back in; and the **Babinski reflex**, when a baby extends its big toe when the bottom of the foot is touched.

These reflexes fade through the process of **maturation**, the biological process of aging. Maturation is also a key component of other motor development: a baby cannot perform certain skills until its body has properly matured. For example, no matter what a parent tries to do, a six-month-old baby cannot run or jump.

SAMPLE QUESTIONS

1) Which of the following is NOT a reflex a baby has at birth?

   A. Moro reflex
   B. rooting reflex
   C. smiling reflex
   D. Babinski reflex

   Answer:

   C. **Correct.** While babies do make many facial expressions from birth—including smile-like movements—these are not in response to any particular stimulus and so are not reflexes.

2) Which of the following statements is true?

   A. Humans are born as blank slates in terms of both senses and perception.
   B. Perception develops as the result of interaction with the environment.
   C. The majority of people remain stable in their personality for their entire lives.
   D. Biological factors have a much greater impact on development than environmental factors do.

   Answer:

   B. **Correct.** Babies learn how to interpret sensory information based on their experiences and their observations of those around them.

Cognitive Development

The study of cognitive development examines how people—mostly children—evaluate the world, and how that changes over time. The most significant figure in cognitive development is **Jean Piaget**. Piaget theorized that children view the world through **schemata**, cognitive rules for interpreting the world which are developed based on their experiences. When they encounter new information or have a new experience, they either incorporate it into their existing schemata, called **assimilation**, or—if the new information is contradictory or does not fit—they adjust their schemata based on the new information, called **accommodation**.

For example, all of the men in a girl's life may have short hair. She then believes that all men have short hair. If she encounters a young boy with short hair, she will assimilate the information into the existing schema: all males have short hair. If, however, she encounters a man with long hair, her first reaction might be surprise, confusion, or even amusement. She will then accommodate the information by adjusting her schema: most men have short hair, but some have long hair.

Piaget identified four stages of cognitive development:

- **Sensorimotor Stage** (Birth–Age 2): In this stage, a baby's behavior is governed by its senses, and its schemata are based on its reflexes. During this time babies develop **object permanence**, the understanding that, even if an object is outside of their perceptual range, it still exists. If a four-month-old baby is fussing for his father's keys, the father need only put the keys away, and the baby will forget they exist.
- **Preoperational Stage** (Ages 2–7): The most important development during this stage is **language**. Children learn to use symbols—through speech, drawing, letters, and numbers—to represent real-world objects. Their memories are developing, and they can use their imaginations. However, they still cannot understand more complex ideas like cause and effect, time and comparison. A three-year-old pours her milk over her dinner plate in an attempt to understand cause and effect. During this stage, children are also completely egocentric; they cannot think beyond their own worldview.
- **Concrete Operations** (Ages 8–12): During this stage, children begin to develop logical thinking. They understand the passage of time and comprehend that an action causes a certain reaction. Piaget identified **conservation** as the biggest developmental leap during this stage. Children in this stage can understand that the properties of an object stay the same even when its shape changes. For example, they understand that a rope is still a rope whether it is stretched out long or wrapped into an intricate knot.
- **Formal Operations** (Age 12–Adulthood): In this final stage, humans develop abstract reasoning and consider ideas and objects in their mind without physically seeing them. People are also able to engage in **metacognition**, thinking about *how* they think. While this is the final stage, Piaget argued that not everyone reaches this stage; some remain at the concrete operations stage.

In more recent years, critiques of Piaget's theory have emerged. Psychologists believe that many children go through Piaget's stages more quickly than he posited. Other psychologists question the validity of stages in general. These psychologists support the **information-processing model**, which follows the same development path as Piaget but in a continuous manner, rather than in stages.

An alternative theory, the **Cultural-Historical Theory** of cognitive development, was posited by **Lee Vygotsky**. Vygotsky believed that society and culture were critical in a child's cognitive development. Vygotsky's work is based on the assumption that children learn about their culture—and how it interprets and responds to the world—through their formal and informal interactions with adults. For example, a child is reading a book with her mother about animals that live in the forest. The mother points out the squirrels in the trees and the deer munching grass. In this way, the child learns how her culture classifies and talks about animals.

He also assumes that for cognitive growth to take place, children need both challenging tasks and room to play. Challenging tasks force children to stretch cognitively, making new connections and furthering their understanding. However, in order for this to be most effective, they need an adult—or anyone with more knowledge and experience—to **scaffold** their learning, by helping them through the process of acquiring the new skills. Vygotsky called this learning area—the area between what a child can do without help and what she can do with help—the **zone of proximal development (ZPD)**.

SAMPLE QUESTIONS

3) **A child that can consider multiple aspects of a problem has achieved which stage, according to Piaget?**

   A. Sensorimotor
   B. Preoperational
   C. Concrete Operations
   D. Formal Operations

   Answer:

   D. **Correct.** In this final stage, abstract and complex reasoning is developed. This would allow someone to determine the various parts of a problem.

4) **According to Vygotsky, which of the following is essential to cognitive development?**

   A. mental maturation
   B. social interactions
   C. genetic predisposition
   D. environmental interactions

   Answer:

   B. **Correct.** Vygotsky believed children learn about the world—how to understand it and interact with it—from the adults in their lives.

Language Development

Adults—and even children—cannot remember a time when language and thinking were separate. Once language is acquired, the two processes are completely intertwined. But how does language develop? Researchers have found that, regardless of the language a baby is learning, all babies go through the same stages of acquisition.

Around four months, babies begin to babble, practicing the sounds of the language (or languages) that they hear regularly. Around their first birthday, the babbling turns into single words, like "book." By eighteen months, babies begin to bring together their single words into two-word phrases with clear meaning but no syntax. So "book!" becomes "Mommy book!" Syntax begins to develop as the child advances into forming three- and four-word phrases. At first, young children often misapply or overuse grammatical rules, a process called **overgeneralization**. For example, knowing that one uses the suffix "-ed" to create the past tense, a child in the **telegraphic** phase might say, "Daddy throwed the ball," not understanding that it does not apply to every word. This is corrected through modeling: when adults or older children use correct grammar so that the younger child can model their mode of speaking.

> **QUICK REVIEW**
>
> Compare and contrast the perspectives of cognitive theory (nativist theory) and conditioning as regards language acquisition.

Some psychologists who study behavior have argued that language is acquired through a process called **conditioning** (discussed later in this chapter). Essentially, this means that when children properly use language, they receive praise and positive feedback (which may even be just receiving an item they request) from their parents or caregivers. This then encourages them to use the language in the same way again.

Cognitive psychologists argue, however, that people deprived of this kind of parental conditioning are still able to develop language. **Noam Chomsky** put forward the **nativist theory of language** which states that each person is born with a language acquisition device inside of them. This device allows for language acquisition unless it is interrupted or damaged during a critical period.

Current researchers have concluded that language is acquired both through behavior modification and through natural development in that critical period.

Attachment Theory

In 1953, psychologist John Bowlby posited his attachment theory to explain the nature of the relationship between caregiver and child. Bowlby argued that in infancy, babies form an **attachment**, an enduring emotional bond to a particular figure, usually the primary caregiver.

Whereas psychologists previously attributed attachment to the association between being fed and the caregiver, Bowlby noticed that babies often maintained a strong attachment to their mothers, even when they were not the ones doing the feeding. So he theorized that attachment is actually evolutionary in nature, developed for an infant's survival. Having someone who will provide that care allows babies to then use them as a base to explore their world, returning to them when they feel threatened. Attachment is not about food, but about care and responsiveness to needs. Thus, attachment is essential to development as a prototype for future relationships; disruption of attachment leads to difficulties in adulthood. He identified the ages of 0–5 as a critical period for the development of attachment.

Secure Attachment: In this case, the baby is very secure in its relationship to the attachment figure. The baby uses them as a base for exploration, and is soothed easily by them when upset. The baby is unhappy to see them go, but calms quickly when they return. Ainsworth found that secure attachment resulted from a caring and attuned caregiver.

Ambivalent Attachment: In this case, the baby exhibited extreme fussiness and clinginess. The baby was unhappy when left alone with the stranger, but was not easily soothed by the caregiver. This resulted from an inconsistent level of responsiveness from the caregiver.

Avoidant Attachment: In this case, the baby was completely detached from the caregiver. He or she explored the room without any orientation toward the attachment figure, and responded equally to the caregiver and the stranger.

Lifespan Developmental Theory

Piaget, Vygotsky, Bowlby, and Ainsworth focused primarily on infancy and early childhood in their theories, as this is where the majority of developmental change happens. Other psychologists, however, developed theories examining development across the entire lifespan of a human. The two most prominent are Erikson's psychosocial development theory and Kohlberg's theory of moral development.

The most well-known lifespan developmental theory is **Erik Erikson's psychosocial development theory**. Erikson was trained in the psychoanalytic school of psychology, so his theory is based in that rather than in evidence-based research. However, it has still heavily impacted psychology as a whole, particularly the treatment and schooling of children. Erikson theorized that development occurs in eight stages with each stage centered on a specific social conflict. The manner in which the conflict is resolved impacts who the person ultimately becomes.

Stage 1 (age 0–1): **Trust vs. Mistrust**: Babies determine if they can trust their caregivers. If they can, as adults, they will appreciate the value of relationships and interdependence. If they cannot, they will remain untrusting and disconnected.

Stage 2 (age 1–3): **Autonomy vs. Shame and Doubt**: Toddlers attempt to exert their will over their own bodies. This manifests itself through activities like potty-training and learning to dress themselves. If toddlers are able to develop a level of independence, as adults they will have a strong sense of autonomy. If not, they will be plagued by feelings of shame and self-doubt.

Stage 3 (age 3–5): **Initiative vs. Guilt**: This is also known as the "why?" stage. Children develop curiosity and a desire to exert control over their environment as well (because they feel they have some control over themselves and trust in the adults around them). If this initiative is encouraged, they will have a strong sense of curiosity and purpose going forward. If not, they feel guilt and avoid future curiosity.

Stage 4 (age 6–11): **Industry vs. Inferiority**: This is the beginning of a child's formal education. If they feel that they are as good academically and socially as their peers, they will develop confidence. If not, they will develop an **inferiority complex**, a generalized feeling of incompetence and performance anxiety.

Stage 5 (age 12–18): **Identity vs. Role Confusion**: During adolescence, the primary social task is to discover one's most comfortable social identity. All teenagers, then, try on different roles. If they find their identity, they will have a stable sense of self. If not, they will encounter an **identity crisis**, a period of profound identity confusion.

Stage 6 (age 19–40): **Intimacy vs. Isolation**: Young adults must develop loving relationships with others while balancing their work needs. Success leads to strong, lasting relationships; failure leads to isolation and loneliness.

Stage 7 (40–65): **Generativity vs. Stagnation**: Individuals in middle adulthood strive to create something that will outlast them—through raising children or engaging in meaningful work. Those who succeed feel fulfilled and accomplished. Those who do not become disengaged with the world or try to change the direction of their lives; they may change their identities or attempt to exert more control over those around them.

Stage 8 (65–death): **Integrity vs. Despair**: As individuals near the end of life, they will reflect to determine whether they are satisfied with their life choices. If they are, they will develop wisdom. If not, they will experience despair.

Lawrence Kohlberg took another perspective in examining human development, developing **Kohlberg's theory of moral development**. He became interested in the question *how does the ability to reason in ethical situations change?* To answer this question he posed several dilemmas to people of varying ages. The most well-known of these is the **Heinz dilemma**: A man must decide if he should steal a drug that he cannot afford in order to save his wife's life. Based on the responses he collected, Kohlberg articulated three levels of moral development, each composed of two stages.

Table 7.1. Kohlberg's Three Levels of Moral Development

LEVEL	STAGE	AGE RANGE	DESCRIPTION
PRE-CONVENTIONAL	1: Obedience/Punishment	Preschool	Focus on avoiding punishment: Heinz should not steal the drug because he might get caught and put in jail.
PRE-CONVENTIONAL	2: Self-Interest/Reward	Elementary School	Focus on rewards instead of punishment; goal is to maximize benefits to oneself: Heinz should steal the drug because having his wife live would make him happy.
CONVENTIONAL	3: Interpersonal Accord	Middle School	Focus on being perceived as a "good" person and being liked: Heinz should steal the drug because he will be seen as a hero.
CONVENTIONAL	4: Law and Order	High School	Reliance on perceived fixed rules of conduct (learned from parents, peers, etc.): Heinz should not steal the drug because stealing is wrong.
POST-CONVENTIONAL	5: Social Contract	High School/Young Adulthood	Understand that legally right and morally right are not always the same; laws are for majority benefit and may conflict with best interest of the individual: Heinz should steal the drug because, while theft is illegal, the protection of life is more important than the protection of property.
POST-CONVENTIONAL	6: Universal Principles (only achieved by some)	Adulthood	Self-defined and protected ethical principles: Heinz should steal the drug because life must be preserved at all costs.

There are many critiques of Kohlberg's research. The primary criticisms are that the situations were fictional and unfamiliar for many of the participants. The participants ranged in age from 10 to 16, and so had no frame of reference for making a decision about saving a dying wife.

Carol Gilligan critiqued Kohlberg for his bias. All of the participants in the original study were male, and when girls were tested later, they demonstrated slower moral development. However, Gilligan argued that there is a difference in moral development based on gender, and Kohlberg's stages only articulate the development of male morality. Gilligan posited that male morality is based on absolute abstract ideas, with justice being the fundamental moral principle. Female morality is based on specific, individual situations with caring for others being the fundamental moral principle. Later researchers have also questioned Gilligan's gender distinctions, and this debate continues.

SAMPLE QUESTIONS

5) A child is in the bathtub. When his mother begins to wash him, he insists on doing it himself. This child is in which of Erikson's developmental stages?

   A. Trust vs. Mistrust
   B. Autonomy vs. Shame
   C. Initiative vs. Guilt
   D. Industry vs. Inferiority

   Answer:

   B. **Correct.** In the Autonomy vs. Shame stage, the child attempts to assert control over his or her own body. By insisting on washing himself, the boy is asserting his independence.

6) A student is asked by a friend for answers on the math homework. The student refuses, saying that cheating is against the school rules. This student is most likely in which of Kohlberg's stages of moral development?

   A. Preconventional: Stage 1
   B. Preconventional: Stage 2
   C. Conventional: Stage 3
   D. Conventional: Stage 4

   Answer:

   D. **Correct.** A student at Stage 4 would base his or her decision on finite rules gleaned from outside sources, like the school rules.

INTELLIGENCE

While a key topic of research, intelligence is very difficult to define. In fact, psychologists have not settled on an agreed-upon definition. Loosely, intelligence can be described as the ability to gather and use information in productive ways. Intelligence comes in two forms: **fluid intelligence**, the ability to learn new skills and information and to solve abstract problems; and **crystallized intelligence**, the use of knowledge that has been accumulated over time. Whereas fluid intelligence decreases with age, crystallized intelligence remains steady or may even increase. For example, a teenager may be able to master a new smartphone more quickly than his grandfather, but his grandfather would most likely be able to use his more extensive vocabulary to beat him in a game of Scrabble.

In addition to its definition, psychologists also debate the nature of intelligence: is it composed of one single factor or multiple factors? The biggest proponent for the single-factor theory is **Charles Spearman**. He used statistical analysis to argue that at the base of all of the different abilities that make up intelligence is the same general intelligence factor, which he named the **g factor**. Therefore, people who perform well on one type of measurement of mental ability (e.g., mathematical skill or verbal fluency) generally do well on all measurements.

Howard Gardner is the most well-known psychologist on the other side of the debate. He argues that different people have different types of intelligence which are discrete from one another. His theory of multiple intelligences essentially defines intelligences that cover the breadth of human experience. His linguistic, logical-mathematical, and spatial intelligences are in line with abilities traditionally used to define intelligence. He has also, however, identified musical, bodily-kinesthetic, intrapersonal (ability to understand oneself), interpersonal (ability to communicate well with others), and naturalist. He continues to name others.

As hard as it is to define intelligence, it is equally challenging to measure it. Two main intelligence tests are used: the Stanford-Binet and the Weschler test.

Alfred Binet wanted to develop a test that would measure student intelligence in order to better meet the needs of individual students. He assumed that intelligence increases with age, and devised a "mental age" measurement. For example, if Bobby, a ten year old, has a mental age of ten, he is on par with his peers. If his mental age was eight, he would be behind, and if his mental age was twelve, he would be ahead.

Louis Terman, a professor at Stanford University, used Binet's mental age system to create an **intelligence quotient (IQ)** that linked intelligence to a number. In order to determine someone's IQ, their mental age is divided by their actual age, and then multiplied by one hundred. So, if Bobby's mental age was twelve, his IQ would be 120. In order to be able to apply this method to adults, Terman set an arbitrary age of twenty for calculating all adult IQs. The test Terman developed to determine IQ is called the **Stanford-Binet IQ Test,** and it asks test-takers a variety of questions, the answers of which determine a single score.

The other major intelligence test was created by David Weschler. It is also called an IQ test, although the resulting number is not actually a quotient. Instead, the test is standardized so that the mean (the average of the numbers) is 100, and the **standard deviation** (how spread out the numbers are) is 15 with a **normal distribution** (or bell-shaped curve). A test-taker's percentile (relative to the population of test-takers) is determined, and the score is based on the number of standard deviations the percentile is from the mean. For example, let's say that Sally is in the sixteenth percentile. That places her at 34 percent below the mean (fiftieth percentile), which is one standard deviation to the left of the mean. Her IQ score would therefore be 85.

The Weschler test comes in three different forms: the Weschler Adult Intelligence Scale **(WAIS)**, the Weschler Intelligence Scale for Children ages 6–16 **(WISC)**, and the Weschler Preschool and Primary Scale of Intelligence **(WPPSI)**. Each test is composed of different types of questions (e.g., verbal and performance on the WAIS) which yield subscores, which—taken together—in turn yield a total IQ score.

DISTRIBUTION OF IQ SCORES

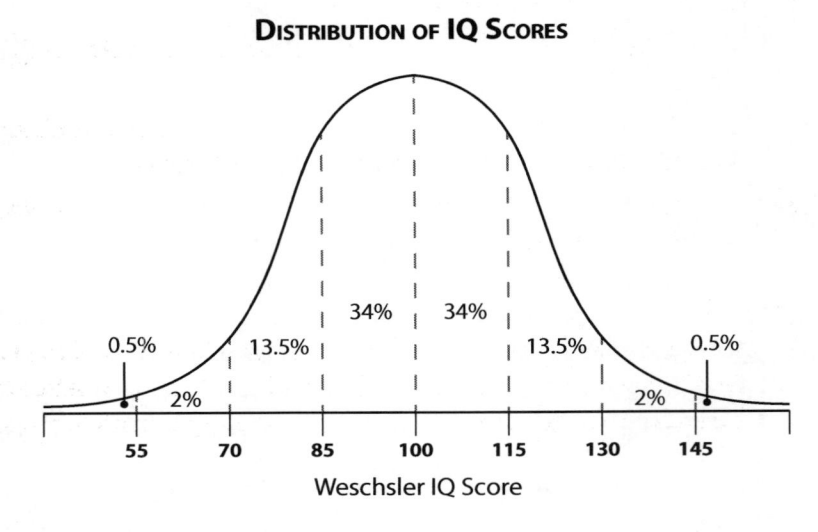

Figure 7.1. Weschler IQ Scores

There are several critiques of the efficacy of intelligence testing of any kind. First, the tests focus heavily on verbal skills. While the Weschler tests require more manipulation of objects, and other such performance skills, the verbal components can skew the scores of those whose verbal skills may not match their intelligence.

Additionally, intelligence tests are often accused of being biased. The questions are constructed on certain cultural norms and are not universal. If the question references information not regularly available to a certain individual, it can unfairly skew the results of the test. Defenders of the test argue that the test has the same validity—and predictive power on, for example, college grades—for all cultural groups. Others, however, respond by saying that the bias runs much deeper, setting certain groups up for success on both intelligence tests and college success, while unfairly impeding others.

SAMPLE QUESTIONS

7) Which of the following is NOT one of Gardner's intelligences?

   A. musical
   B. interpersonal
   C. linguistic
   D. auditory

   Answer:

   D. **Correct.** *Auditory* is a sensory descriptor, not a human behavior that can be measured as an intelligence.

8) Which of the following best describes the difference between Binet's original system and the Stanford-Binet test designed by Terman?

   A. Binet's original system was unreliable while the Stanford-Binet provides an accurate measure of intelligence.
   B. Binet's original system was culturally adaptable, while the Stanford-Binet is culturally biased.
   C. Binet's original system was designed as an education tool, while the Stanford-Binet is designed to measure intelligence.
   D. Binet's original system used standard deviations to determine scores, while the Stanford-Binet uses a quotient.

   Answer:

   C. **Correct.** Binet did not develop his system as a means of measuring intelligence, but to determine the needs of students relative to their peers. Terman adapted the system by creating the intelligence quotient.

LEARNING, MEMORY, AND COGNITION

The study of human development looks at how the mind grows and changes over time. Other subfields of psychology examine how the mind functions. These include learning, or how the mind acquires new information and skills; memory, or how the mind retains information and skills; and cognition, or how the mind makes sense of the world.

LEARNING

Learning is the process by which the mind acquires new knowledge, skills, and habits. In order to understand learning, psychologists look at long-term changes in behavior that result from an individual's experience, rather than innate or biological changes. There are two primary methods of learning: classic and operant conditioning.

Classical conditioning is the process by which an animal (including humans) learns to respond to a neutral stimulus in the same way that they respond to a reflexive stimulus by associating the two. This process was first observed by Ivan Pavlov in studying the digestion of dogs. He discovered that dogs salivated when they heard the sounds of the places where they were fed. Dog food, the **unconditioned stimulus** (US), elicits a reflexive reaction—in this case, salivating—which is called the **unconditioned response** (UR). Pavlov then took a neutral stimulus—in his study, the ringing of a bell—and paired it with the US. So every time the dogs were presented with food, the bell rang. In time, the dogs developed a **conditioned response** (CR) to the ringing of the bell: they began to salivate. As a result, the once-neutral stimulus (ringing of the bell) became a **conditioned stimulus** (CS). When they salivated to the bell alone (with no food present) they achieved **acquisition**, indicating that learning has occurred.

Order and timing determine the effectiveness of acquisition. The best method, called **delayed conditioning**, begins with presenting the CS, then introduces the US while the CS is still present. Studies have shown that a break between the presentation of stimuli or reversing the order greatly reduces acquisition. Frequency also is important to acquisition: more pairings of the CS and US increase the strength of the CR (although only up to a point).

Behaviors can be unlearned as well, a process called **extinction**. This is accomplished by repeatedly presenting the CS without the US.

Whereas classical conditioning facilitates learning involving reflexive behaviors, **operant conditioning** is a learning process in which consequences are associated with behavior. Psychologist B.F. Skinner coined the phrase based on his experiment in which he taught an animal to press a lever in order to receive food using **reinforcement**, a consequence that makes the behavior more likely. The animal received a **reinforcer** (food) as a consequence for the **targeted response** (pushing the lever). **Primary reinforcers** are consequences that are, in and of themselves, rewarding—like sleep, food, and water. **Secondary reinforcers**, things we have come to value (e.g., praise, money), can also be used. It is important to note that reinforcers do not affect all people in the same way.

> **QUICK REVIEW**
>
> Explain three key differences between classical and operant conditioning.

In this experiment, the animal was given **positive reinforcement** because its action resulted in a pleasant outcome (the receipt of food). **Negative reinforcement**, the removal of something unpleasant, can be used just as effectively. For example, the experimenter could play a high-pitched noise that stopped whenever the animal pushed the lever. In this case, the subject can be taught either **escape learning**, terminating the unpleasant condition (like the high-pitched noise) or **avoidance learning**, avoiding the unpleasant stimulus (e.g., the high-pitched noise is in one compartment, so the animal can avoid it by not entering that compartment).

Similar to classical conditioning, timing of reinforcement matters. When first being conditioned, a subject should receive **continuous reinforcement**, by getting a reward for the behavior each time. Once the behavior is learned, **partial reinforcement** makes the behavior more resistant to extinction.

Reinforcement schedules are determined by two factors: when reinforcement is delivered and the pattern of enforcement. Timing the delivery of reinforcement may depend either on the number of responses made (**ratio**) or the passage of time (**interval**); the pattern of reinforcement may be a constant (**fixed**) or changing (**variable**) pattern. There are four types of schedules:

Fixed-Ratio (FR): Reinforcement is given after a set number of responses. This is written as FR-#, where # represents the number of responses. So, if reinforcement is given after every three responses, it would be a FR-3 schedule.

Variable-Ratio (VR): Reinforcement is given after a number of responses but the number varies. In this case the # represents the average number of responses required for a reward. So if reinforcement was given after 3 responses, then 4, then 8, it would be a VR-5 schedule.

Fixed-Interval (FI): A set amount of time must pass before a successful response receives a reward. In this case the # represents the number of minutes. If the subject cannot receive a reward until 5 minutes have passed, it would be a FI-5 schedule.

Variable-Interval (VI): The amount of time that must pass before a successful response receives an award changes. The # represents the average number of minutes. So, if in the first trial the subject must wait 3 minutes, in the second 5, and the third 10, it would be a VI-6 schedule.

All schedules are not equally effective. Much like partial reinforcement, variable schedules are more resistant to extinction; the subject is more likely to continue the behavior if he or she is not sure when the reward is coming. Ratio schedules lead to higher response rates than interval schedules since reward is tied to the number of successful responses.

In more complex tasks, **shaping** is used to modify behavior. Desired responses are broken down into specific, related behaviors, each of which are then reinforced. For example, the animal could be shaped to move to the side of the box, approach the food station, and put some part of its body on the lever.

Punishment is the opposite of reinforcement: it decreases the likelihood of a behavior by providing unpleasant consequences for a response. **Positive punishment** gives the subject an unpleasant consequence, and **negative punishment** (also called **omission training**) removes something pleasant. While punishment can change behavior,

> **HELPFUL HINT**
>
> Don't confuse negative reinforcement and punishment! When you think of "positive" and "negative" think of a plus and minus sign. Positive reinforcement or punishment adds something, and negative reinforcement or punishment takes something away.

it must be immediate and it must be harsh. In these cases, it often has unintended consequences like fear or anger which could lead to new undesirable behaviors. Psychologists generally consider reinforcement a better tool.

SAMPLE QUESTIONS

9) The phone rings at Mary's house many times a day, but it is never for her. Finally, she stops answering the phone when it rings. This is an example of which of the following?

    A. positive punishment
    B. negative reinforcement
    C. shaping
    D. extinction

    Answer:

    D. **Correct.** Extinction is the ending of a behavior—in this case, answering the phone—because of the removal of the reward (having someone on the phone wanting to talk to her).

10) Which of the following would be the first step in a shaping procedure designed to teach a dolphin to push a ball with its nose?

    A. Reward the dolphin for facing the ball.
    B. Place the ball on the dolphin's nose and give it a reward.
    C. Reward the dolphin as soon as it enters the tank.
    D. Wait until the dolphin accidentally bumped into the ball and then reward it.

    Answer:

    A. **Correct.** Shaping requires reinforcing "step" behaviors leading up to the desired response. In this case, facing the ball would be the dolphin's first step in approaching it and pushing it with its nose.

MEMORY

In addition to how new information and behaviors are acquired, psychologists are interested in how that information and those experiences are stored. There are two main models of memory: **the three-box model** and the **levels of processing model**.

In the three-box model, the memory is conceived as having three storage areas: sensory memory, short-term memory, and long-term memory. **Sensory memory**, which processes all external events, is a split-second holding area for sensory information. George Sperling conducted an experiment where he flashed a grid of nine numbers at people for one-twentieth of a second and then asked them to recall one row. Participants were able to recall that one row perfectly, proving that all people have **iconic memory**, a split-second perfect photograph of what they have seen.

Later studies discovered **echoic memory**, the human ability to perfectly remember sounds for three to four seconds.

However, most of that sensory information is not encoded; instead people encode using **selective attention**, holding only to what we consciously try to or to what is important to us. The information that is encoded becomes part of the **short-term** or **working memory**. Short-term memory consists of the memories of which people are aware in their consciousness at any given moment. On average, people can hold up to seven separate things in short-term memory, and they fade if not used in ten to thirty seconds. This can be extended through **rehearsal**, the repeating of information over and over, but this still only keeps it in short-term memory.

Information that is used can then be encoded and moved to **long-term memory**, which is essentially permanent storage. There is no limit on the amount of information that can be stored in long-term memory; however, memories that are not used do eventually decay or fade. A few people in the world have **eidetic**, or **photographic**, memory. They are able to repeat lists of seventy letters or digits up to fifteen years later. Memories stored in long-term memory can either be **explicit** or **declarative memories**, conscious memories of facts or events intentionally remembered, or **implicit** or **nondeclarative memories**, memories that are stored unconsciously. For example, the smell of freshly cut grass could suddenly recall a memory of a picnic from when someone was young. Long-term memories are encoded in three formats:

Episodic Memory: These are memories of specific events that are stored sequentially. For example, a memory of one's tenth birthday would be an episodic memory.

Semantic Memory: These are memories of general knowledge which are stored as discrete facts, meanings, or categories without any sequential order. For example, knowing that Paris is the capital of France is a semantic memory.

Procedural Memory: These are memories of how to perform specific skills. These are stored sequentially, but are not easily articulated in words. Kicking a soccer ball is a procedural memory.

The second model of memory is the **levels of processing model**, which examines how deeply a memory was processed or considered. Rather than short-term and long-term memory, this model considers **deeply or elaborately processed memories** and **shallowly or maintenance processed memories**. The more cognitive time someone spends on information or a skill, the more deeply they process it, and the more it is remembered. For example, stories are more memorable than a random list of facts because the context requires greater cognitive work. The use of rehearsal to remember information—say for a test—is shallow processing. However, if someone familiarized themselves with the context of the test content, the information would become deeply processed.

Retrieval is the process by which information is pulled from memory (this applies to both storage models). There are two types of retrieval: **recognition**, matching new facts or events to those already in memory; and **recall**, retrieving a stored memory. When trying to recall a series of information, research shows that order matters.

The **primacy effect** states that people are more likely to recall items that are at the beginning of a list. The **recency effect** states that people are also more likely to recall items at the end of a list. It is the middle of a list that is least remembered.

Context is also an important factor in retrieval. The brain forms new memories by linking them to existing ones creating a **semantic network**, or web of interconnected memories. The more connected a memory is, the less likely it is to fade or decay. Memories can also be connected to mood and state. If someone is happy, they are more likely to remember happy memories.

If someone is repeatedly asked leading questions about an event, this can create a false memory, called a **constructive memory**.

Like creating memories, **forgetting** is an active process of the mind. Some forgetting occurs as the result of **decay**, the fading of memories from a lack of use. In this case, memories do not actually disappear and the information can be **relearned** quickly. For example, a parent helping his or her child with homework will be able to learn (really relearn) high school algebra faster than the child, who is learning it for the first time.

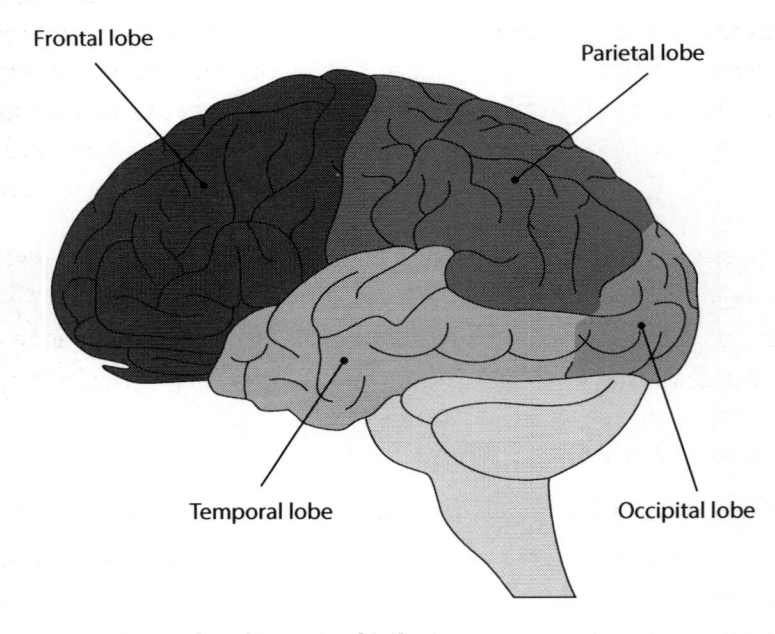

Figure 7.2. Frontal and Temporal Lobes

Other forgetting is a result of **interference**, competition between the information being recalled and other memories. **Retroactive interference** occurs when new information interferes with the recall of old information. For example, after listening to an updated version of a song on the radio, it might be difficult to recall the original song. **Proactive interference** occurs when older information interferes with the recall of more recently learned information, such as attempting to shift gears when learning to drive an automatic car.

It is still mostly unclear how memories are physically stored in the brain; however, research has determined that the hippocampus (located in the temporal lobe) plays an important role in encoding new memories. If the hippocampus is damaged, an individual can become unable to encode new memories, an illness called **anterograde amnesia**. However, these individuals can learn new skills (although they will not remember learning them), demonstrating that procedural memory must be stored elsewhere.

> **HELPFUL HINT**
>
> To remember the difference between retroactive and proactive interference, remember that the prefix refers to the information that is trying to be recalled—or the information you want "active" (rather than the interfering memory).

Two parts of the **cerebral cortex**, a sheet of neural tissue that covers the brain, are known to be involved in memory. The **frontal lobe** processes short-term memories and organizes information, helping to retain long-term memories. The **temporal lobe** houses the hippocampus and helps to form long-term memories.

Finally, neurons are most likely connected to long-term memory through a process called **long-term potentiation**. The more often two neurons fire simultaneously, the more sensitized they become to each other, and the more likely they are to fire together in the future. Since memories are spread throughout the brain, these neuron connections create a neural map that allows for more efficient access of memories, or **memory consolidation**. As the brain creates new connections, it discards old ones. So as memories are recalled, the brain discards little-recalled memories in order to strengthen the connections of the recalled ones. Researchers theorize that much of consolidation takes place during sleep. Therefore, better sleep can lead to a stronger memory.

> **QUICK REVIEW**
>
> Describe one way in which memories can be disrupted or lost.

There are several methods one can use to improve memory, including:

- **Chunking**: Grouping information into similar groups or concepts can increase retention both in short- and long-term memory (creating stronger connections between ideas).
- **Mnemonic Devices**: By associating an idea with a common item, a rhyme, a song, a joke, or an acronym, context is created for that idea, leading to deeper processing.
- **Visualization**: Visual images are better retained than abstract ideas. Creating a mental image increases retention. One approach is the method of **loci**, imagining a familiar place and then associating memories with physical objects in that space.
- **Elaborative Rehearsal**: Basic rehearsal can hold information longer in short-term memory, but does not aid in the transition to long-term

memory. Elaborative rehearsal involves not only repeating the information, but learning more about it, relating it to previously acquired information, or teaching it to someone else. This creates the context needed for deep processing.

SAMPLE QUESTIONS

11) A memory that is held in conscious awareness is called

   A. a declarative memory.
   B. an implied memory.
   C. an iconic memory.
   D. an echoic memory.

   Answer:
   A. **Correct.** A declarative memory, also known as an explicit memory, is one of which the individual is aware.

12) If Paul reads the chapter on World War II right before bed when he is very sleepy, he will best remember the information when

   A. he wakes up in the morning.
   B. he actively recalls the information during his exam.
   C. he is dreaming.
   D. he is very sleepy again.

   Answer:
   D. **Correct.** Mental state has a significant impact on recall. People are more likely to recall information when they are in the same mental state as when they learned it.

COGNITION

Cognition is the sum of the mental processes involved in acquiring and understanding knowledge, specifically problem solving, memory, and thinking. Memory was discussed in the previous section; this section will address the other two aspects.

There are three types of thoughts: **concepts** (organizational rules), **prototypes** (typical examples), and **images** (sensory mental "pictures"—does not have to be visual). Motherhood is an example of a concept: one's own mother might be a prototype, and a visual of a mother hugging a child might be an image. The process of acquiring and understanding information uses rules called **schemata** that help to organize categories of information and the relationships among them. While a schema increases efficiency, it can also create problems. People are more likely to notice things that fit into their schema, and are unlikely to alter their schema to fit new information. When someone is confronted with evidence that conflicts with their schema, called **cognitive dissonance**, it causes discomfort, so they typically distort the information to fit the schema.

When solving problems people either use **algorithms**, rules that use formulas or other foolproof methods; or **heuristics**, rules that are generally, but not always, true. For example, when trying to figure out a two-letter password for a computer, one could apply an algorithm and try all possible combinations until finding the right one. The advantage of an algorithm is that it guarantees the right solution; however, it can be inefficient. For example, instead of a two-word password, imagine trying to figure out a ten-word password. The number of possible combinations makes the algorithm unrealistic. Instead, a heuristic permits trying different ten-letter words (since most people use words for passwords).

Heuristics are helpful shortcuts, but people often mistakenly treat them as infallible rules. Misuse of heuristics can lead someone to make illogical conclusions in order to confirm their preexisting beliefs, called **belief bias** or **perseverance**. For example, the person trying to crack the password may conclude something is wrong with the computer if they cannot find a ten-letter word that works (rather than considering that the password is not an actual word). They are also susceptible to **confirmation bias**, looking for evidence that confirms their beliefs while ignoring evidence that contradicts them. Both of these are particularly dangerous in evidence-based research (like psychology).

When solving a problem, people also must avoid **mental set**, using old strategies to solve new problems, and improper **framing**, presenting a problem in a way that is detrimental to the research.

SAMPLE QUESTIONS

13) Gender is an example of which kind of thought?

   A. concept
   B. image
   C. prototype
   D. schema

   Answer:
   A. **Correct.** A concept is an organizational idea or rule. Gender is a category that helps a person categorize other people.

14) While conducting a study on aggression in boys and girls, a researcher (who believed boys were more aggressive than girls) did not record several instances of female aggression while recording every instance of male aggression. This is an example of which of the following:

   A. belief bias
   B. framing
   C. mental set
   D. confirmation bias

Answer:
- **D. Correct.** The researcher omitted information that did not support her preexisting views on the subject.

Personality

The study of personality is essentially the study of what makes a person who they are. This is a complicated question, but one that is fundamental to psychology. There are four general approaches to answering this question: psychoanalytic, trait, social-cognitive, and humanistic.

Psychoanalytic Theories

The most well-known **psychoanalytic** psychologist is **Sigmund Freud**. He believed that personality was set in early childhood. If a child progressed through the stages of development without a problem, she would be well-adjusted. If, instead, she experienced an unresolved conflict at a certain stage, she would become stuck at that stage; this conflict would affect her adult personality. For example, if an individual experienced a conflict in the first stage—the oral stage—he may develop an oral fixation and need to constantly have something in his mouth.

Freud also theorized that the personality was composed of three parts:

- **Id**: The unconscious or unknown mind that operates on instinct. Emotions reside here as these are instinctive and not actively created by the individual.
- **Ego**: Existing partly in the unconscious mind and partly in the conscious mind, the ego follows the **reality principle**, and it negotiates between the id and the limitations of the environment.
- **Superego**: The superego is a person's conscience, determining right from wrong. It can influence the ego to account for moral considerations.

While extremely popular, Freud's theories face significant criticism. They are not based upon empirical evidence, and the nature of many of his structures (e.g., the id) make them unprovable. His theories also have no predictive power. While they can be used to explain why someone acted the way that they did, they cannot predict how someone will act in the future. Freud is also criticized for overemphasizing early childhood and sex and for being offensive to women (e.g., he claimed all women have penis envy).

> **EXAMPLE**
>
> Janet sees a huge cookie on top of the bakery counter. Her id tells her to take it and eat it. Her superego tells her that stealing is wrong, and she should leave the cookie where it is. Her ego recognizes the potential problems with taking the cookie and determines that the best course of action is to pay for the cookie.

On the opposite side of Freud is Alfred Adler's **individual psychology.** Diverging from Freud's pessimistic view of humanity, Adler had an inherently optimistic view, arguing that people are all ultimately striving for success or superiority. If a person enjoys success—meaning that he contributes to the community benefit while maintaining his personal identity—his personality is unified. If not, or if the person strives for superiority (personal gain without real regard for others), he will be ultimately unfulfilled.

Trait Theories

Trait theories describe personalities by identifying main traits or characteristics. Characteristics of an individual's personality are considered stable and motivate their behavior. **Nomothetic theorists** argue that the same set of traits can be used to describe all personalities. For example, Hans Eyesenck posited that a transection of an introversion-extraversion scale (essentially how shy or outgoing one is) originally created by **Carl Jung** and a neuroticism scale (how anxious or fearful one is) could classify all personalities.

Idiographic theorists, on the other hand, argue that one set of traits cannot be used to describe everybody. Instead, people should be defined by the few traits that best define them, which can vary from person to person.

The primary criticism of trait theory is that it assumes that personalities are stable, when in fact people might behave very differently depending on the situation. For example, someone might be extremely talkative and social among their family, but shy and reserved in public.

Social–Cognitive Theories

According to social-cognitive theories, personality is the result of a combination of environment and patterns of thought. **Albert Bandura's** theory of **reciprocal determinism** posits that personality results from the interaction between the person (their traits), the environment, and the person's behavior. For example, a person might be naturally optimistic, but become less so after a series of disappointments and failures. **Julian Rotter's locus of control theory** posits that personality is determined by whether one feels in control of what happens to them. Those who have an internal locus of control—those who feel in control of their lives—tend to be healthier and more engaged, while those with an external locus of control—those who feel luck or destiny controls their lives—tend to be less successful.

Humanistic Theories

Humanistic theorists challenge the **determinism**—the idea that personality is determined by past events—innate in other personality theories. Instead, they argue that people are able to exercise free will to determine their own destinies. According to humanistic theory, an individual's personality is determined by their overall feeling about themselves (called **self-concept**) and the level of confidence they have in their own abilities (called **self-esteem**). **Abraham Maslow** argued that people strive to reach **self-actualization**, the maximizing of their own potential (Maslow's theory will be discussed in more depth later in the chapter). **Carl Rogers** posited that people need blanket acceptance, which he called **unconditional positive regard**, from other people in order to self-actualize.

Humanistic theory is criticized for being overly optimistic and vague. For example, it is difficult to measure if someone has reached their full potential.

Assessment of Personality

Different schools of thought use different tools to assess personality. Psychoanalysts primarily use **projective tests**, assessments in which the subject must interpret some type of ambiguous stimuli. The most well-known of these is the **Rorschach inkblot test**, in which subjects are asked to describe what they see in an inkblot. The **Thematic Apperception Test (TAT)** is another projective test in which the subject describes what is happening on different cards featuring people in ambiguous situations. Overall, projective tests are seen as unreliable because they rely heavily on the interpretations of the therapist.

Psychologists in the trait, social-cognitive, and humanistic schools use **self-report inventories**, questionnaires in which people provide information about themselves in response to various prompts. The most commonly used is the **Minnesota Multiphasic Personality Inventory (MMPI-2)**. These assessments are considered objective because the scores assigned to each response are predetermined (rather than based on individual interpretation). However, people are often dishonest about their answers, which diminishes the assessments' reliability.

SAMPLE QUESTIONS

15) When a parent tells a child they love him no matter what he does, this is an example of which of the following?

   A. self-actualization
   B. self-esteem
   C. unconditional positive regard
   D. locus of control

   Answer:

   C. **Correct.** Unconditional positive regard is blanket acceptance by those around a person. Parental love without restrictions is a prime example of this.

16) The zodiac system is an example of which approach to determining personality?

    A. idiographic
    B. nomothetic
    C. psychoanalytical
    D. humanistic

    Answer:

    B. Correct. Nomothetic trait theory argues that there are established, limited groups of traits that can define all people. The zodiac limits all personality to twelve types.

17) According to Freud, emotions reside in which of the following parts of the mind?

    A. the id
    B. the ego
    C. the superego
    D. none of the above

    Answer:

    A. Correct. The id resides entirely in the unconscious mind which is also where emotion can be found.

Social Psychology

Social psychology is the study of how people relate to each other. It examines how individuals perceive, label, and categorize others; it also studies how they interact with each other based on those labels and categorizations. Much of social psychology is based on **social cognition**, the application of cognition concepts to individuals' conceptions of themselves and others. Just as people collect data from their environments to develop schemata for understanding the world, they also collect data to develop systems for understanding other people.

Attitude

An **attitude** is an evaluative set of beliefs and feelings. Attitudes are applied to everything: people, places, objects, and ideas. Research shows that positive attitudes are primarily formed by the **exposure effect**: the more someone is exposed to something, the more they will like it. Advertisers exploit this; companies like McDonald's, for example, advertise on billboards, radio, television, online, and at bus stops to reach the consumer and ultimately increase sales. Messages are also more persuasive (more effective at shaping attitude) if they utilize expertise, attractiveness, or celebrity; persuasive information is better processed through the content of the message or via the secondary characteristics of the communicator—the person imparting the message—like fame or beauty.

Finally, research shows that education—general education level as well as knowledge of the specific subject of the attitude—decreases the ability to persuade. For example, someone who is informed on immigration issues is less likely to be persuaded by a specifically anti- or pro-immigration argument.

The following are two common persuasion techniques. *Foot in the door*: The communicator asks for something small, and then follows it up with a bigger request. For example, a charity asks for a small donation of $10, then later sends a request asking for a monthly donation of $20. *Door in the face*: The communicator asks for something large and unreasonable knowing it will be rejected, and then follows it up with a more reasonable request. For example, a child asks her parent for permission to stay out all night after the prom. When rejected, she asks for a 2:00 a.m. curfew, which is then more likely to be accepted.

ATTRIBUTIONS

Attribution theory addresses the way in which people determine the cause of what they observe. For example, a woman gets a new, very competitive job. Her friends might determine it is because she is highly skilled in what she does. This is called **dispositional** or **person attribution**. Alternatively, her friends might determine she only got the job because the company needed to hire more women. This is called **situation attribution**. Whether a dispositional or situation attribution is made is based largely on how others responded in the same situation (called **consensus**). For example, if many other women applied, were they also offered jobs or was she the only one?

Attributions can also be **stable** (e.g., this woman has always excelled) or **unstable** (e.g., this woman performed really well in this particular interview). This determination is made based on how similarly the individual acts in similar situations over time (called **consistency**). For example, is this woman usually offered jobs she applies for or was this one of the only times?

Attributional biases, mistakes in determining cause, are common and frequently repeated. Providing undue credit to the person rather than the situation is called **fundamental attribution error**. For example, if someone greets a colleague at work and the colleague does not respond, they are likely to determine the colleague is unfriendly (rather than having a bad day or distracted by something else). People are more likely to make dispositional attributions about others, but situational attributions about themselves. However, if the outcome of a person's behavior is positive, they are more likely to make a dispositional attribution about themselves. This is called **self-serving bias**. For example, if a student does

> **QUICK REVIEW**
>
> Explain the difference between an *attitude* and an *attribution*.

well on a test, he will most likely conclude that he was well-prepared. If he performs poorly, he is more likely to argue that the test was too hard or poorly designed.

On the other hand, people also exhibit a **just-world bias**, a belief that bad things happen to bad people. For example, if a child throws a tantrum in a store, other people most likely will assume the mother or father is a bad parent. Victim-blaming in cases of crime or abuse is a result of just-world bias.

STEREOTYPES

A **stereotype** is a pre-formed idea—positive or negative—about the characteristics of a group of people. Stereotypes impact how a person treats individual members of that group. For example, if a teacher stereotypically assumes that all Asian students are good at math, she may check an Asian student's understanding less often. Stereotypes are even harder to change than schemata; their uncritical application often results in **prejudice**, a negative attitude towards a group of people based on no real information. Taking action based on that prejudice is called **discrimination**.

IMPACT OF GROUPS

Research has shown that individual behavior is strongly influenced by the presence or actions of other people in a number of ways. For example, people tend to perform better in front of an audience. This phenomenon, **social facilitation**, holds true unless the person is trying to perform a particularly difficult task. In these cases the audience actually impedes his or her performance in a phenomenon called **social impairment**.

In addition, when in a group people tend to **conform**, or to follow the views and actions of the rest of the group. **Stanley Milgram** conducted obedience experiments in which subjects were told to administer electric shocks to someone in a different room. (The subjects were unaware that they were not actually harming the person.) In spite of hearing what sounded like cries of pain, over sixty percent of people continued to obey the experimenter, delivering all possible shocks. Interestingly, when other people in the room with the subject objected to the shocks, the likelihood of the subject objecting increased significantly.

Subsequent experiments showed that people were less likely to obey when they could see the person they were supposedly shocking (versus just hearing the cries of pain), and even less so when they had to physically place the person's hand on the shock plate—although thirty percent of people still continued to obey. Milgram's experiments have been criticized as being unethical, as subjects were made to believe they were seriously harming another person.

All people belong to multiple groups—families, social, racial, and cultural—and all groups have **norms**, rules determining how members of the group should act. Each member of the group also has a **role**, an identity within the group. The **group dynamic**, the way people function within a group, impacts the behavior of individual members. Often when acting as part of a group, individuals put forth less effort than when they act alone. This **social loafing** occurs because people feel less pressure to impress, since their individual work stands out less.

People also typically show less self-restraint when acting as a member of a group. In the **Zimbardo Stanford prison experiment**, students were divided into two groups: prisoners and guards. The experiment eventually was ended prematurely because the guards were treating the prisoners so poorly.

Furthermore, groups think differently than individuals do. Groups tend to make more extreme decisions than individuals would, a phenomenon called **group polarization**. Responsibility for actions is diffused over the whole group (**responsibility diffusion**), so each individual feels less responsibility. For example, an individual may have reservations about a proposed tuition increase on a university campus. When grouped with others who feel the same way, they are much more likely to take action by protesting. Responsibility diffusion also leads to the **bystander effect**, the tendency of people to ignore wrong acts or allow them to continue when part of a crowd of witnesses.

> **EXAMPLE**
>
> The best example of the bystander effect is the case of Kitty Genovese. Kitty was followed home by a man and attacked in full view of thirty-seven people in the nearby apartment building. The people watched the assailant attack Kitty, leave, and return, eventually killing her. Not one person called the police or took action to help her.

Groups also often make very bad decisions, a phenomenon Irving Janis identified as **groupthink**. In a group discussion of an idea, individuals tend to suppress reservations they may have because of their tendency to conform to the group. The result can be a poor decision that may have been avoided if an individual was making it alone.

SAMPLE QUESTIONS

18) In deciding on a prom theme, the senior class of a high school ends up choosing a zombie theme that no one particularly likes. This is an example of which of the following?

   A. bystander effect
   B. group polarization
   C. groupthink
   D. fundamental attribution error

   Answer:

   C. Correct. The senior class ended up making a poor choice (one that students would not have made individually) as a result of working as a group. This is an example of groupthink.

19) Simon ate very little at dinner. His wife decided he must be sick. This is an example of which of the following types of attribution?

- A. person-stable attribution
- B. person-unstable attribution
- C. situational-stable attribution
- D. situational-unstable attribution

Answer:

- **B. Correct.** Simon's wife assumes the cause of Simon's lack of appetite is himself, not the food or the environment. She also attributes it to a temporary condition: his illness.

Motivation and Stress

The reason for an individual's behavior is called **motivation**. Motivations can be either conscious and obvious, or unconscious and subtle. Much of motivation theory is based on research in learning and personality.

Maslow's Hierarchy of Needs

Abraham Maslow theorized that motivation was based on need, but all needs are not equal. He identifies five levels of need from basic biological needs for safety and survival to the need to fulfill life goals and self-actualization. According to Maslow, each level of need must be fulfilled before the next can be addressed. However, there are examples that contradict this model. For example, Buddhist monks who practice self-immolation (lighting themselves on fire) during the Vietnam War prioritized the need of self-actualization over the need for survival.

Sources of Motivation

Motivation comes from a variety of sources: internal, external, and environmental. The individual attitudes and goals of those people in an individual's life, as well as broader societal attitudes and goals, may serve as motivation for an individual. An example of this **social motivation** would be a student who works hard in school to gain admission to college because of the value society places on a college education. If, however, that same student sought admission to college in order to master high level skills and to better understand the world, he or she would be propelled by **achievement motivation**. People who are motivated by achievement continually seek greater challenges.

All motivators can be classified as either **extrinsic motivators**—coming from outside of one's self—or **intrinsic motivators**—coming from within. For example, the person motivated to gain admission to college in order to get a good job or to be held in high esteem by others is extrinsically motivated. The student who seeks admission to college in order feel a sense of accomplishment or achieve mastery in a particular discipline is intrinsically motivated. Both types of motivation are effective in encouraging desired behaviors; however, once extrinsic motivators end, so does the behavior. Once the student looking for peer approval gains admission to college, he is more likely than his intrinsically motivated counterpart to perform poorly. Therefore, extrinsic motivators are suitable for short-term behavior goals, while intrinsic motivators are better at encouraging long-term positive behaviors.

Self-Actualization Needs
creativity, spontaneity, morality, problem solving, lack of prejudice, acceptance of facts

Esteem Needs
self-esteem, confidence, respect by/for others

Love and Belonging Needs
family, friends, sexual relationships

Safety Needs
security in health, employment, morality, property, family

Physiological Needs
food, water, air, sex, sleep

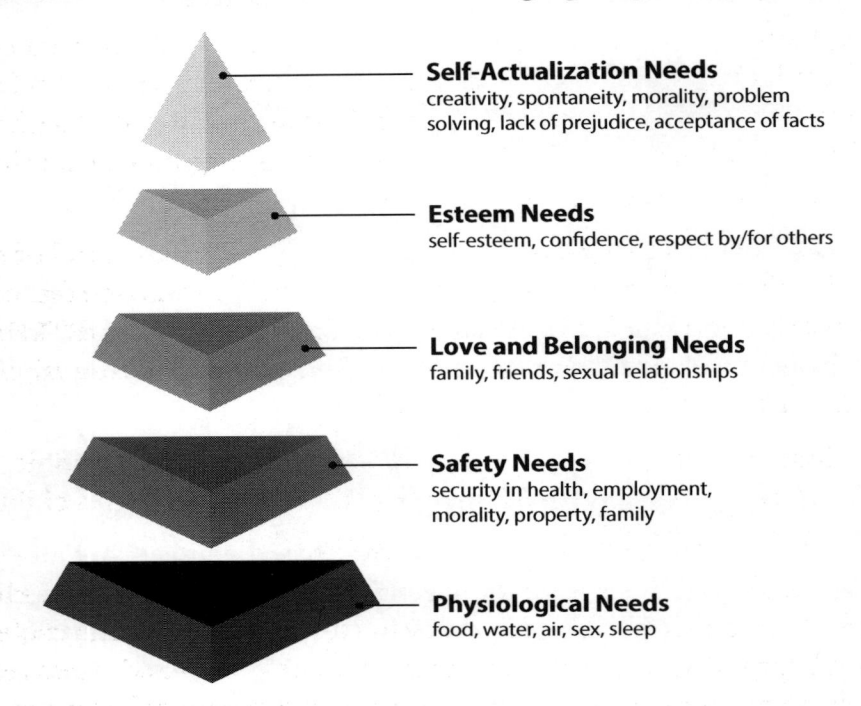

Figure 7.3. Maslow's Hierarchy of Needs

Stress

Any situation that taxes one's coping abilities by threatening—or seeming to threaten—a person's wellbeing is considered **stress**. Common stressors include life changes, external and internal pressure, environmental factors, frustration, and conflict. **Acute stressors** are relatively short in duration and have a clear endpoint, whereas chronic stressors are relatively long in duration and have no apparent time limit. Acute stressors have little negative impact and can even be beneficial at times. For example, short-term frustration, the thwarting of the pursuit of a goal, can act as a motivator for further achievement. **Chronic stressors**, on the other hand, have significant physiological and psychological consequences.

Hans Selye detailed the body's stress response in his **General Adaptation Syndrome (GAS)** as it applies to all animals:

- **Alarm reaction**: The heart rate increases; blood is diverted away from other body functions to prepare the animal for action. This is also known as the **fight-or-flight response**, as the animal is prepared to either attack or flee.
- **Resistance**: Hormones are released to maintain the state of readiness. In chronic stress, this state is maintained for too long of a period of time, leading to a depletion of the body's resources.
- **Exhaustion**: The body returns to a normal state. If the resistance state lasted too long, the body will be more vulnerable to disease and sustain long-term damage. This is why chronic stress is associated with major health problems like arthritis, ulcers, asthma, migraine headaches, heart disease, and depression.

The maintenance of a resistance state resulting from some kind of stressful event—either acute or long-term (e.g., war, rape, watching someone die, or almost dying themselves) can also lead to **post-traumatic stress disorder (PTSD)**. People suffering from PTSD experience disturbed behavior—including nightmares, jumpiness, and temper flares.

Chronic stress also disrupts attention and inhibits memory. Chronic, or **toxic stress**, related to poverty can even change the chemical makeup of a child's brain, disrupting and weakening its circuits.

The best way to deal with stress is to use **constructive coping mechanisms** like confronting a problem directly, breaking it down into manageable pieces, maintaining flexibility, and remaining aware of one's coping and stress resources. Studies have also shown that maintaining **perceived control**, or the feeling that one is in control of a stressor, reduces the overall stress level. For example, the patient who is given control of his own pain control medication reports a lower overall pain level than the patient who is prescribed doses, even when the amount of medicine received is the same.

SAMPLE QUESTIONS

20) Offering discounts on auto insurance for a safe driving record is an example of which of the following?

   A. achievement motivation
   B. social motivation
   C. an intrinsic motivator
   D. an extrinsic motivator

   Answer:

   D. **Correct.** Giving a discount in exchange for safe driving offers an external reward for the desired behavior.

21) According to Maslow's hierarchy of needs, the need of friendship, can only be fulfilled once

   A.   self-actualization has occurred.

   B.   self-esteem and confidence are assured.

   C.   safety and survival are secure.

   D.   It can be obtained at any time.

   Answer:

   C.   **Correct.** Safety and survival are the first two levels in the hierarchy; friendship is the third.

22) Which of the following is NOT a result of chronic stress?

   A.   cardiovascular problems

   B.   ulcers

   C.   toxic stress

   D.   perceived control

   Answer:

   D.   **Correct.** Perceived control is the sense that one can control one's stressors. This is a coping mechanism, not a consequence of chronic stress.

Sociology

Sociology is the scientific study of a society's social behaviors and its origins, development, networks, and institutions. As a science, it requires critical thinking, critical analysis, and empirical investigations to develop a body of knowledge about social order, social disorder, and the changes that affect them.

The primary goal of most sociologists is to conduct research applicable to **social policy** and **the common welfare**; others focus on refining and clarifying theoretical understanding and social progress. The range of subject matter can be as specific as individual agencies and direct communal interaction to the broader concepts of social structure systems.

While the main focuses of sociology include **social class and social mobility**, sociologists have increasingly explored **religion, secularization, law, gender, sexuality,** and **ethnicity** in their studies. Increasingly, nearly every sphere of human activity is viewed through the sociological lens. With more global interconnectivity due to improved telecommunications and media, all institutions are subject to sociological study. **Health, military, penal, educational,** and even **individual family institutions** can play a role in understanding social activity on a scientific level.

As sociology became a more mainstream science in the late twentieth and early twenty-first centuries, scientific methods used to analyze social activity increased in number and diversified to meet the needs of those individual activities and the individuals who took part in them. Researchers have made use of both philosophical and theoretical processes as well as mathematical and computational programs.

Social research is used by a broad selection of actors in the modern world, including politicians and policy makers; urban and rural planners and developers; market researchers; and for-profit and non-profit organizations. This total data plays a crucial role in developing and reforming the institutions that define our modern world.

> **SAMPLE QUESTION**
>
> 1) Since its inception, sociological study has become increasingly
>   A. widespread.
>   B. informal.
>   C. scientific.
>   D. A and C only
>
> **Answer:**
>
> D. **Correct.** Sociology is more widely used as a lens to better understand the world and is more formal and scientific than at its inception as a field of study.

Social Perspective and Methods of Inquiry

There are three major categories of **social perspective** in the field of sociology, which cover both the **micro** and **macro** levels of analysis. They are **symbolic interactionism, functionalism,** and **conflict theory**. These three perspectives are the basic paradigms through which sociologists seek to understand and explain the world around us. These perspectives individually interpret society, its influences, and human behavior, yet they are imperfect; multiple perspectives may seem applicable to the same sociological topic.

As its name implies, **symbolic interactionism** seeks to understand society through the symbols and details of our everyday lives. It argues that both the surface level meanings and the subconscious meanings of those symbols actively affect the ways in which we interact with one another. German sociologist and philosopher Karl "Max" Weber was instrumental in bringing symbolic interactionism to the modern sociological field; philosopher George H. Mead introduced symbolic interactionism to the United States in the 1920s.

According to symbolic interactionism, at a micro level people attach meanings to symbols. Human action is then affected or driven by those meanings. These symbolic interpretations are not limited to objects; the very words we use in verbal conversations can also serve as symbols. Words can have specific meanings for both the speaker and the receiver in a conversation. Conversation is more than an exchange of ideas; it is replete with symbols expressed and interpreted by individuals in an effort to better understand their environment.

Words carry an intention, or can at least can be received with an ascribed intention by the receiver that can affect the conversation and, thus, the world surrounding that conversation. For example, if a boss greets a subordinate with a terse, one word "hello" or even "yes?", the subordinate may receive or interpret the message as a sign of trouble, when the boss's intention may not be as negative as the subordinate thinks. But if the boss is a particularly verbose or involved individual, the simple one-word "hello" could be received as a sign that the boss is having a bad day or that the subordinate is about to have a bad day. On the other hand, a slightly longer exchange of pleasantries, or perhaps even a difference in how the word is delivered—nuance in inflection, eye contact, or the overall look on a boss's face—gives that word a very different meaning when in fact both at heart mean the same thing. The tone could be entirely unrelated to the subordinate.

Symbolic interactionists believe that anything can serve as a symbol, but they go a step further, arguing not just that anything can but often that anything does. Choice of adjectives affect meaning. "Severely" and "extremely" can technically mean the same thing when used as adjectives—both argue a greater number—but the former implies a more negative sensibility while the latter is more emotionally neutral.

Defining a symbol is simple: it is anything embodying a larger idea or element. Symbolic interactionists observe people's actions to understand what meanings they self-assign and what meanings they ascribe to the actions of others.

Because of that potential simplicity, many sociologists criticize symbolic interactionism as being too micro, distracting from the bigger picture understanding of social behavior and projecting one's own personal biases and opinions of symbolic meaning.

A common example cited for symbolic interactionism is the western (particularly American) marriage ceremony. The most notable symbols include wedding rings, a white bridal dress for the bride and a black tuxedo for the groom, the wedding cake, flowers, music, etc. Perhaps most importantly are the vows of lifetime commitment, which are not particularly subtle symbols of the ceremony's purpose. All of these symbols have had meanings thrust upon them by American society, and individuals layer their own understandings upon these symbols as well. The wedding band is perhaps the most notable example: a collective American society recognizes wedding rings as symbols of marriage. Some individuals might consider the circle to be a symbol of stability and constant motion that is a marriage. Other individuals might take the rings to be a symbol of financial power; specific materials and sizes can, for many people, imply social status on top of marriage. But collectively, these symbols direct behavior. Their importance is widely recognized, yet differences of interpretation create contrast in a society.

Symbolic interactionism's critics charge that this perspective neglects the macro perspective of sociology and instead focuses on the day-to-day, micro perspective. By ignoring the "big picture," critics charge that the perspective doesn't allow for wholesale change. For instance, by focusing on wedding rings, symbolic interactionists may better understand what people feel about what a ring means but will not address the state of marriage as a whole. The perspective also receives criticism for assigning responsibility solely to the influences of social forces and institutions; critics believe it ignores personal responsibility and individual opinions altogether.

Another category of social perspective, the **functionalist perspective** (also referred to as **functionalism**) argues that every aspect of modern society is connected, and that they rely on one another so that society can function. In exchange for taxes, state governments provide security and education to help families grow. Families rely on the safe environment and education a government provides to generate future taxpaying, law-abiding, productive members of society. The government can only provide these assets if families support it through taxes. If the process works, those families will grow, generating more productive taxpayers who in turn will generate even more; thus, they continue to sustain the system to which they belong.

If the process does not work, society either crumbles or adapts to a newer order that ensures productivity and stability. Functionalists would point to bank or real estate bailouts during times of major recession, or insurance for the unemployed as examples of a government functioning to right its course in order to maintain stability and thus productivity. They would also point to the sacrifices that come with a recession, such as tighter budgets on behalf of both the state and the individual or family, as a sign of functionalism at work. Both provide stability and productivity and both work in concert. A new social order, stability, and productivity are born out of those circumstances, and while they may lead to aesthetic changes, the basic construct of society remains intact.

Functionalists argue that social consensus holds society together; a society in which members agree and work together on what benefits the society as a whole will be strongest. French sociologist **Emile Durkheim** believed that consensus manifested as **mechanical solidarity** or as **organic solidarity**.

In **mechanical solidarity**, social cohesion is exhibited when a society maintains near identical beliefs and values; furthermore, people actively work together to maintain that society. Amish societies in the United States of America are good examples of mechanical solidarity. With an economy that is primarily farm based, families work together to produce goods and maintain a tight-knit social community that makes use of religion to provide a central, unifying moral code.

In **organic solidarity**, social cohesion appears in a society in which people are interdependent on a broad level (they may share security, education, transportation) but independent on a specific level (in terms of personal belief systems, moral values, etc.). Industrialized societies, such as most major American cities, are more likely to exhibit organic solidarity. Individuals must coexist in an urban environment and consequently must cooperate to provide stability; however, productivity is motivated by the individual or family, not the overarching society.

Functionalism achieved its greatest popularity in America during the post-World War II era due to renewed interest in nationalism and infrastructural development. While European functionalists concentrated on studying social mechanisms, American functionalists began to branch out into studying the behavior of individuals and humans.

The American functionalist Robert Merton theorized two types of human functions: **manifest functions** and **latent functions**. Manifest refers to obvious functions; for example, the manifest function of voting in a national election is to choose government leaders. Latent functions refer to unintentional or not obvious functions—the deeper reasons for a behavior. The latent function in voting in a national election is to define the long-term values of a society and to give the individual a sense of connection.

Critics of functionalism argue that this perspective neglects negative functions and encourages complacency. They believe that a functionalist society discourages dissent, leading oppressed groups to accept their current states. Other criticisms of functionalism point out that even beneficial change is foregone in a functionalist society, because it would lead to a destabilization of society or a new status quo that would differ minimally from the old. Critics consider this perspective at best defeatist and at worst a tool of the powerful to keep the lower classes under control.

Finally, the **conflict perspective** presents a drastically different (and far more negative) take on society than either the symbolic interactionist or functionalist perspectives. Based on the theories of class struggle postulated by the German political scientist **Karl Marx**, conflict theory argues that entrenched political leadership and aristocracy actively repress the poor and working classes.

Unlike functionalism, conflict theory promotes social change. Conflict theorists, for example, may interpret a scholarship program for underprivileged students as a moral justification of the position of the elite. They may even view the program as a tool of the elite that elevates only the best and brightest of the lower classes at the expense of the remaining poor, separating gifted students from their home communities in order to exploit their skills and further weaken the lower class.

Conflict theory came to prominence in America during the 1960s as a reaction to the functionalist perspective of the 1950s and also a natural evolution in that decade's well-documented tumultuousness. Perhaps because of that decade's debates on matters of race, gender, politics, and religion, conflict theorists added those categories and many more to the scope of conflict theory analysis. No longer were economic divisions the sole indicator of inequality and potential conflict. Conflict theorists argue, in essence, that there is no true status quo as different (and often unequal) groups have different values and competing agendas, and that the constant societal competition among those agendas requires a constant shift in the status quo.

Critics of the conflict perspective believe this perspective is perhaps gratuitous in its negative view of society, and that it discourages positive behaviors such as altruism by arguing that they are motivated by controlling the masses rather than preserving and benefitting a society.

Culture, Socialization, and Social Organization

Culture
Culture is the collective behaviors and beliefs characteristic of a particular group, be they ethnic, social, or religious in nature. English anthropologist and founder of

the cultural anthropology movement Sir Edward Burnett Tylor referred to culture as "that complex whole which includes knowledge, belief, art, morals, law, custom, and any other capabilities and habits acquired by man as a member of society." It is, in effect, the texture of societal structure: if society is the lines, culture is the color that goes within them. Shared traits include norms of behavior (greetings and interactions on a day-to-day level), values (the moral beliefs and codes that guide that culture's textual and sub-textual behavior), and language (cultural communication, generally through proper language but also including slang and colloquialisms).

Culture affects human behavior both directly and indirectly. Specific groups of people behave in different ways. For example, some East Asian cultures promote a more formal style of public social interaction. In South Korea, for example, shaking hands is customarily reserved solely for men, while women customarily bow. However, western (or western-influenced) visitors of any gender should be comfortable shaking hands with a Korean man but are expected to bow when greeting a woman. While deviating from the cultural norm may cause an interaction to become awkward, many Korean people are aware that their cultural traditions are not necessarily shared with the rest of the world, particularly western nations. So it would generally be socially and culturally acceptable for a western woman to shake hands with Korean men (though not Korean women). This example illustrates cultural compromise: individuals of different cultures can change their direct behavior, cooperating to meet each other's differing values halfway.

This is unfortunately not common. Some cultures view the rest of the world through the lens of **ethnocentrism**, or the belief that one's culture is superior to others, judging those other cultures by the former's values and assumptions. The western news media, for example, is often criticized as being too ethnocentric in its coverage of the developing world, particularly the more religious Middle East. Some argue that western media unfairly judges some Middle Eastern societies by the standards of the more secularly inclined West. This is a challenge created due to the emergence of **global culture**, improved quality and global distribution of communications and media.

The world is increasingly interconnected when it comes to the arts, entertainment, and news available on television and the internet. This shared information may have brought multiple cultures closer in terms of knowledge, but may not have brought them closer in terms of how they interpret and value that knowledge. Critics of global culture argue that it has robbed individual cultures of their own identities, while others argue that there is no one identity; rather, that only one identity (usually a more Western identity) is given top priority and influence in global culture. Put simply, on the plus side, global culture has exposed most of the world to more diverse ways of life. On the minus side, it risks privileging one or a few ways of life at the expense of others.

Subcultures and **countercultures** are parts of culture. Subcultures are subsets within a greater culture, often with beliefs or interests at variance with their greater culture. Modern America is a feast of subcultures that focus on issues ranging from religious to socioeconomic to personal interest. They include serious and intellectual subcultures, such as the academic elites; religious subcultures like those of the Southern "Bible Belt"; and even subcultures organized around hobbies or other shared interests. Video game and "nerd" subculture—fans of science fiction and fantasy books, comic books, and film—is currently experiencing a renaissance in American culture, as social media has brought fans together from across the country and has provided a serious infrastructure for a fan-based community to come to cultural prominence.

Counterculture is similar to subculture, but differs in that while a subculture may run against societal norms, countercultures are explicitly designed to oppose society's norms. These groups specifically exist to challenge the status quo and promote a new, different way of life. In previous generations of American history, groups like the hippies, yippies, and beatniks compromised the 1960s counterculture, designed to oppose what they considered to be the shallow, superficial era of the 1950s. Today's countercultures similarly are drawn along political lines; both the Tea Party and Occupy Wall Street movements were born out of the 2008 market crash as a response to the United States' bank bailouts. While they have differing ideologies (the former more conservative, the latter more progressive), both oppose a government they consider to be spending wild amounts of money on things that should not be national priorities.

All four of these forms of culture provide unique perspectives that ultimately comprise a strong social identity. Ethnocentrism provides a certain amount of stability—a specific vantage point with which to judge the world—while global culture serves a reminder that the world is a big place and individual points of view, while valid, are only part of the whole. Subcultures and countercultures add to that perspective; in effect, they are reminders that individual vantage points, while perhaps stable, are not necessarily perfect.

Gender

Gender remains perhaps the single most prominent example of the basic differences between humans. It is unavoidable: indeed, from the moment we are born, we are likely going to encounter someone of a different gender in the role of one of our two parents. Gender socialization is the process individuals undergo when learning and conditioning themselves to the expectations and attitudes of their own genders. Sociologists often explain the roles of men and women using gender socialization, arguing that an individual society's attitude towards different genders informs the behaviors of the individual.

The role of gender is ever-expanding and changing. It has been traditionally understood that generally, early men acted as hunters and early women acted as gatherers. It has been postulated that men made use of their theoretically more aggressive nature to hunt and catch food, while women's supposedly more organized, passive natures facilitated housekeeping and food preparation.

This has, of course, changed over the course of history. Today, it is not unheard of for men and women to have intentionally swapped roles; many women are the "breadwinners" in their households, while some men have taken steps towards being caretakers of the home. According to a study from the US Census Bureau and the Bureau of Labor Statistics, as a result of the global economic recession in the early 2000s, the number of men considered homemakers in the United States doubled between 2002 and 2012, increasing from 1.6 percent to 3.4 percent. That number has continued to grow, and while it is still low in comparison to the estimated thirty-five percent of women who are homemakers in the United States, it must also be taken into account that women now comprise forty-seven percent of the US workplace. The roles are changing.

But this change has taken a very long time and likely will continue to evolve. The role of gender in society is to define how individuals relate to each other and to delineate their social roles. However, gender roles are not consistent across the globe. In Saudi Arabia, for example, women were only granted voting rights in 2015, while German Chancellor Angela Merkel was, that same year, selected as *Time Magazine*'s Person of the Year. Indeed, the role of gender has varied from nation to nation. As of 2015, 0.3 percent of the United States population identified as transgender, someone who self-identifies as one gender but is born genetically as the opposite sex. As this constantly shifting playing field evolves, sociologists continue to reform and reevaluate the role of gender in society. Debates on that role seem to touch every major aspect of society, from religion to politics to sports and entertainment.

Recognizing the major cross-cultural differences in gender socialization is important to help understand current trends and perhaps predict the future of gender socialization. While biology of course plays a role, most scientists and experts disagree on whether the differences between men and women are biological in nature and generally believe they are a mix of nature and nurture, possibly more influenced by culture than by physicality.

Indeed, we learn gender best by observing those around us—our parents or parental figures. How women and men behave dictates their children's understanding of gender roles. Even the least gendered parenting styles must coexist with a world that enforces gender roles. For example, the toys and games a parent selects for their child unconsciously enforce gender roles. Dolls are aggressively marketed to girls, socializing them for their roles as mothers, while a boy will receive action figures designed to bring out, as the name implies, a sense of action or aggression. That said, recent changes in parenting styles have encouraged a less gender-focused style of parenting. Without ignoring a child's gender, many parents have made efforts to allow children to pursue their interests in non-gender-binary terms. It is not uncommon in many average US city parks to see a young girl playing baseball or a young boy playing with dolls. Parents have made progress, forcing society to catch up.

Similarly, education affects how children perceive themselves along gender roles. Much of the sociological research beginning in the 1950s focused on how young women were being neglected in the classroom. Because young men were believed to be more analytical, educators stressed the importance of math and science to their male students. Consequently, these students' ideal career paths included engineering, finance, and similar fields. In the 1990s, however, research began to indicate that the current educational climate was failing young men. As the grade point averages for young men fell, the dropout rate for young men rose; meanwhile, young women increasingly excelled in academics and went on to higher education. Some sociologists have theorized that this was biological in nature: young women mature faster than young men both physically and emotionally, while perhaps the allegedly more aggressive male nature makes it harder for young men to sit still in class. As educational methods developed into more structured, stationary processes, sociologists argued that those methods benefitted the abilities of young women over young men.

This snapshot of gender differences in American culture shows the importance of understanding not how gender roles differ, but that they differ at all. A clear vision of gender roles in one culture allows cross-cultural comparison of gender roles around the world. Indeed, these cross-cultural differences serve as a reminder that society still has much to learn about gender socialization, but comparison also allows for compromise and improved communication. Going back to handshakes in South Korea, on the one hand, the westerner, regardless of gender, would ideally show respect for Korean cultural norms by only offering a handshake to a male business partner and not offend a woman by offering a handshake, even though that gesture might seem sexist (an ethnocentric western viewpoint). On the other hand, ideally, a Korean man would offer his hand to a western woman, respecting her culture as well. Recognizing these differences is not a passive acceptance but rather an active, if subtle, method of provoking potential cross-cultural influence and change.

SAMPLE QUESTION

2) **Which best describes a gendered parenting style?**

   A. Parents provide their baby daughter with a pink nursery, dolls, and toys mimicking traditional household roles played by women.

   B. Parents encourage their daughter to participate in team sports played by both boys and girls.

   C. A family takes the children on a road trip to learn about historical monuments.

   D. Children are left unsupervised by their parents, and the eldest child must take on parenting responsibilities.

Answer:

   A. **Correct.** These parents are presenting expectations to their daughter that reflect traditional women's roles in western society.

SOCIALIZATION

The major theories of socialization were primarily postulated by American sociologists **George Herbert Mead** and **C.H. Cooley**.

Mead's theory, sometimes referred to as the **Development and Assumptions of the Self**, argues that social interaction generates personality, which itself is made up of self-awareness and self-image. This idea led to three major assumptions: that social interaction alone generates the self; that interchange of symbols comprises social interaction; and that empathy—the ability to see things from another's point of view—or being able to understand intention, allows the individual to understand symbols.

C.H. Cooley offered the **Looking Glass Self,** a theory that itself emerged from the theories of American psychologist William James. It argued that other people's views build, change, and maintain the self-image—that people develop their own images of themselves through the images others present to them. Individuals develop self-image based on their actual treatment by others in social interactions; they also develop self-image through their own assumptions about others' perspectives. These assumptions are actually based on the individual's own opinions or insecurities. The development of the looking-glass self is essentially a continuous process, growing with each new person an individual encounters.

There are four types of socialization: primary, secondary, anticipatory, and resocialization.

Primary socialization occurs when a child learns the values, actions, and attitudes that are appropriate for members of their particular culture. Primary socialization influences are generally those closest to the child, such as family and friends. For example, if the family unit makes it a point to have dinner together every night, that child will likely assume that the closest and most important people need to be regularly communicated with, perhaps on a daily basis.

Secondary socialization occurs when the individual learns the appropriate values, actions, attitudes, and behaviors as a member of a smaller group within a larger society. This generally occurs outside of the home in schools or places of employment. These organizations may require a very different set of behaviors from home.

Secondary socialization generally occurs in adolescence or young adulthood, and influences will be teachers, employers, and other figures of either definitive or assumed authority. For example, if one's employer encourages all employees to eat at their desks and work through lunch, the learned behavior would be to prioritize work over anything else.

Anticipatory socialization is the process of analyzing the behaviors from the previous two forms of socialization and rehearsing for future relationships, both professional and personal. The most frequently cited example of anticipatory socialization would be a young couple moving in together before marriage in order to anticipate what life together will be like. It is an active form of socialization which gives the individual more power to explore his or her behavior. Another example would be professional internships, where a student or young employee does limited work for limited money but gains experience working for a company and understands the basic responsibilities required for full-time employment.

Resocialization is the process of discarding previous behaviors, values, and attitudes and learning new ones as part of a transition to a new place in life. This occurs constantly in the human life cycle and is usually a very difficult process; challenging an individual to break with attitudes held for a very long time, potentially a lifetime.

The most extreme examples of resocialization involve penal and psychological institutions wherein inmates learn to let go of the negative or dangerous behaviors they have developed over the course of their lives, in order to coexist with the predominant society. However, in recent years as global culture has led to the awareness of different religious faiths or cultural lifestyles, sociologists have seen any number of resocializations. Resocialization can include experiences like religious conversion, gender reassignment, political transitions, and more; it has gone from a requirement for the extremely troubled to a process anyone may undergo.

SOCIAL ORGANIZATION

The way society is arranged is referred to as **social organization**. Although really nearly everything factors into the organization of our society, the three major building blocks of social organization are **institutions**, **networks**, and **individual roles** as they pertain to status.

Institutions are any formally structured groups that comprise our society. At the macro level they include government, private enterprise, religious institutions, and academic institutions. At the micro level, they include local communities and the family unit. They are comprised of a usually formal, often top-down structure with a small governing body in charge (either the executives in a government or private company, or the parents in the family unit).

Networks are slightly less formal; they are the relationships built between individuals or organizations based on common interests and purpose. These usually emerge from common professional interests. For example, the formal elected officials in a government institution will, day-to-day, function as a part of that institution; however, they likely also are a part of a political network of likeminded individuals who may not work in government but rather private, public, or religious institutions. Even so, their shared political or ideological goals will lead them to work together as a network, where those private, public, or religious concerns can provide something the elected official needs (financial support for a campaign, the votes in an election those groups can provide, or some technical or financial support for a government initiative), and that elected official in turn can provide for the needs of that network (serving as an advocate on matters of policy or causes that the network supports or believes in).

Individual roles and statuses exist at the very micro level: they describe how individuals contribute to society and treat each another. Individual roles in a society vary based on what part of that society they interact with. When dealing with a family unit, a mother will likely be the primary decision-making authority. Her status in that role is higher. But that mother may be employed in a mid- or lower-level-job where she provides a service to an employer; in that case, her status is slightly lower. At the same time, that mother may also be an active participant in her society's religious or governmental institutions, and then her status varies based on the needs of that institution. In short, roles are a combination of those assigned to the individual through employment or life choices, but also result from individual behavior and choices.

A mid- or lower-level position at a company may not carry with it a great deal of authority, but how an employee approaches the job can affect that employee's status anyway. For example, the mailroom manager who runs that station with lightning quick efficiency may have less authority in the company than an executive, but if the executive puts in less effort around the office—excessive delegation, consistent lateness, etc.—the mailroom manager may prove indispensable while the executive may prove expendable. Roles define us as much as we choose to define our roles.

Furthermore, how roles and status are explored in larger institutions and organizations depends on the makeup of those institutions. In government, the chief executive in a given government wields a great deal of power and, with it, the status of the person in charge. But the makeup of that government also dictates the limits of his or her power.

For example, the presidency of the United States carries with it an immense amount of power, but built into the system are two major factors that limit the amount of power that chief executive holds: term limits and the lack of ability to make laws. The presidency is not a lifetime position. A president must be elected and re-elected in order to execute a full agenda. But he or she cannot be elected more than twice, thus ensuring that presidents use their power wisely. They must also work with a legislative body in order to push through much of their agenda. Thus, while the presidency enjoys a high status and a strong role, it is not impervious to interaction. Presidents must employ cooperation and exchange in order to accomplish their goals.

Similarly, leaders in most successful organizations ensure a chain of accountability: the chief executive of a major company is still accountable to a board of directors, the leader of a religious institution is accountable to the members of that institution, etc. This accountability exists so that while the strong role and status of the person in charge may drive the expansion and evolution of society, it also empowers other members of society by giving them a voice in the process of that society's evolution, thus ensuring their own engagement and productivity within the structure.

Conversely, an institution where one person retains supreme executive authority generally exists at the expense of the members of that society. Recent examples in nations like North Korea demonstrate the lack of productivity that can come from supreme authority. The nation of North Korea is notorious for its extreme poverty, weak economy, food shortages, and a general lack of national productivity, all attributed to the supreme authoritarian leadership. Kim Jong-un, supreme leader of North Korea, has avoided making necessary compromises on the issues like nuclear weapons, humanitarian affairs, and more democratic government that would allow the country to have a productive relationship with most of the developed world. Without any way to check his power, no one is able to force him to work with other nations in such a way that would provide for his people. But his supreme authority (among other things) prevents that type of progress.

The importance of these building blocks—institutions, networks, and individual roles—cannot be overstated. In order for a society to operate at peak efficiency, sociologists argue all three must be employed. The structure of an institution provides boundaries, rules, and stability. The energy of a network provides texture to that society and ensures that everyone at every level feels a certain amount of engagement in that society's development. The clarity of roles allows daily functioning as well as giving individuals something to aspire towards, particularly in a society that not only allows but encourages advancement. They are three distinct, different concepts that combine to tell us who we are, where we are, and where we are going.

Social Interaction

While social organization describes the arrangement of society, that organization is itself determined through three primary forms of social interaction: **conflict**, **cooperation**, and **exchange**.

Conflict is the process of disagreement. It occurs when at least two groups or individuals with opposing views, needs, or interests come into contact over a shared desire. Typical modern conflicts are over property, usually land. Conflict is usually ended when one of the two parties receives either the entirety of their desired goal or at least a substantial enough component of their goal to be satisfactory.

Cooperation is the process of working together to achieve similar goals. It occurs when at least two groups or individuals with shared views, needs, or interests come into contact over a shared desire. Typical modern forms of cooperation are involved in either the establishment or expansion of a society. Cooperation between businesses usually leads to development in energy or transportation, for example. On a smaller scale, farm cooperatives allow groups of individuals to work together to produce their own food and vegetables. The end result of cooperation is usually that of a larger established society or group.

Exchange is the process of giving one thing and receiving another (usually with similar value) in return. It occurs when at least two groups or individuals with potentially different views and often likely different goals agree to work together in order to each achieve their own separate goals. The most common form of exchange in modern society is at the commercial level as consumers exchange currency for goods or services, but exchange can also happen between two societies on a non-commercial level. International trade is a form of exchange between nations that allows for the expansion of commerce and friendly relationships between nations. Exchange is also commonly used in conflict resolution.

Conflict interaction generally occurs between two different societies, but can occur within a society, even leading to a realignment of a society's goals and values. The American Civil War is a prime example of conflict within a society over the issue of slavery, ultimately ending with its abolition.

Examples of cooperation may exist within the prism of both the exchange and conflict perspectives. Cooperation may primarily occur within a society, but can also occur between two different and potentially competing societies. During the Second World War, the United States and Great Britain allied with the Soviet Union—fierce rivals before and after the war—but they worked together in order to achieve the common goal of thwarting the Axis powers. Exchange often happens both inside and outside of a society and can be applied to either conflict or cooperative interactions.

There are many theories of interaction in sociology, but perhaps the most prominent are **dramaturgical**, **ethnomethodological**, and **symbolic interactionism**.

Dramaturgical sociology argues that elements of human interactions are based on where and when those actions take place as well as who is watching it take place (in other words, an audience). Pioneered by Canadian sociologist Erving Goffman, the presentational concerns of this sociology are why it takes its name from the world of theater—it argues that individuals do not necessarily have to be present during interactions but rather play a part in a scene.

This approach argues there are three stages of behavior. On the front stage, people as "performers" adhere to all societal norms as expected by mass culture, performing appropriately for the "audience" in public. Backstage, these performers are present but the general audience is not—so while individuals need not perform for that audience, they must still perform for the fellow actors in their "cast," such as family, professional colleagues, friends, or anyone with whom they consider themselves equals and with whom they present an act. Offstage, individual members of the audience or society may be present, but the whole collective of society is not.

Perhaps the best example of dramaturgical sociology in action is how a soon-to-be married couple interacts at a wedding or during wedding activities. They are in the expected attire and sometimes literally reading lines from a script for a gathered audience, but the activity being performed is really that of an intimate transaction.

Ethnomethodology refers to an individual's interpretation of his or her actions in the everyday world. Developed by American sociologist Harold Garfinkel, this perspective argues that all people are rational actors who employ practical reasoning rather than formal logic in order to function in society. It is, at heart, the mechanics of daily routine.

When engaging in a conversation, people adhere to certain behaviors (head nod, eye contact, etc.) that are universally understood as the mechanics of a conversation. People unconsciously use these mechanics in a conversation not because they mean them but because these mechanics are expected behavior. Such actions visually communicate to conversation partners that we are, in fact, communicating. From a practical standpoint, this makes sense; we want it to be known that we are communicating with our partner. But from a logical standpoint, the extra effort doesn't really make sense. Another example would be how an employer speaks to his or her employees. It would be most logical to simply convey information, but a more practical tactic would be to try to relate to employees in a more casual and personal level—to form a relationship. This is what an individual or group expects. Unlike the dramaturgical method, this doesn't require as much performance but it does take appearance into account. It is often employed to improve communications in professional organizations.

Symbolic interactionism as explored in the previous chapter, argues that individuals understand society and communicate through symbols in daily life. Inspired by Max Weber and George H. Mead, symbolic interactionism focuses on the intentional decisions people make to use symbols to interact with fellow members of society. For example, a teenager may meet a new friend who skateboards and performs exciting but also dangerous tricks. The teenager may be well aware of the personal risks of performing stunts on a skateboard, but that reality is meaningless to the teenager; the skateboard is a symbol of excitement and popularity. The friend possesses this popularity and sense of adventure by possessing the symbol of the board. It can also become a symbol of friendship between the two teens. The emotional weight projected onto that skateboard will outweigh any real or logical factors.

SAMPLE QUESTION

3) Which of the following is an example of exchange?

   A. Two small companies merge to increase their share of a market.
   B. A group of students decides to form a cooking club in order to exchange ideas and knowledge about French cuisine.
   C. Two countries at war engage in peace talks; one agrees to give up land if the other agrees to return prisoners of war.
   D. Two children fight on a playground.

   Answer:

   C. **Correct.** Even though these countries have been in conflict, they are engaging in exchange: they are exchanging things they hold of equal value (land and prisoners) in order to achieve a common interest—peace—despite their enmity toward one another.

Social Hierarchy

Social Class

Social class refers to how we arrange our positions within society. Early sociologists based this generally on wealth and income, but in recent years education, occupation, lifestyle, and personal interests have begun to factor into how individuals and groups are assigned their "places" in the world.

At the macro level, class deals with economics. The term *upper class* is generally reserved for the wealthy or very successful. This would include executives in major private companies, or talented practitioners of in-demand services (medical, legal, sports, entertainment, etc.). Members of this class likely have advanced degrees. The *middle class* generally refers to the working class. This includes business professionals, laborers, teachers, and more. Its definition has shifted in the last two decades, but it usually applies to those who have achieved a certain amount of financial security and potentially home ownership, yet who must work full time in order to maintain that lifestyle. Members of this class may have advanced degrees of education or may not, but are at least likely to have high school diplomas or an equivalency. Lastly is the *lower class*, which includes both the poor and working poor. This usually includes those in the service industry and other similar professions. Financial struggles are real for these lower classes. It is not unusual for members of this group to work multiple jobs or rely on financial assistance. Members of this group often have lower academic accomplishments, often failing to complete high school.

In recent years, classes have begun to develop their own subsets: the educated class, for example (people possessing advanced degrees of education and potentially employed in academia) may be aware of and enveloped in upper class events or social circles, but perhaps financially belong to the middle class. Conversely, someone born into wealth may choose to limit his or her academic pursuits and exhibit lower academic accomplishments.

In the last decade, sociologists have begun to address the creative, or artistic, class. This class, a group of professional artists or creators, all share the same goal (to present their work to an audience) but have differing tastes; furthermore, not all will be as successful as others. For example, two professional comedians may have the same day-to-day lifestyle of writing and performing, but one may have achieved real financial success with a more in-demand act, while the other may still need a day job to provide income. Both are technically part of the same social class but live in different financial classes. In an increasingly global culture-centered world, class is evolving. Income will likely always dictate it to a certain degree—those with means will enjoy different experiences and possessions than those without—but the individual participants can and often will change as a culture evolves.

> **SAMPLE QUESTION**

> 4) A writer attends fundraising events with wealthy patrons and participates in exclusive literary readings. However, she maxes out her credit cards in order to wear the same designer clothes as her friends, and she has a small apartment in a poorer neighborhood. She would belong to the
>
>   A. upper class
>   B. lower class
>   C middle class
>   D. working poor
>
> **Answer:**
>
> **C. Correct.** The writer cannot afford many luxury goods, but she has a middle class creative job, a home, access to credit, and participates in some expensive events.

SOCIAL STRATIFICATION

Social stratification is the system by which a society ranks categories of people within the society's hierarchical order.

On a global scale, social stratification is defined by four underlying principles. **Principle A** is that social stratification is a property of society rather than of individuals in that society. **Principle B** argues that social stratification is generational, meaning it is both passed down from one generation to the next and interpreted by each individual generation. **Principle C** posits that social stratification is universal and variable all at once. This means that while each society has a concept of stratification, those concepts differ from one society to another on both a macro and micro level. For example, stratification in the Western nations of the United States and the European Union will be very different from stratification in India or China, but even within the United States there exist differing levels of social stratification based on ethnic and economic lines. Lastly, **Principle D** argues that social stratifications involve not just the quantitative but also the qualitative. Economic inequality leads to stratification, but belief systems do as well; as discussed earlier in this chapter, the educated class may exist in both the middle and upper classes.

As with previous aspects explored in sociology, stratification operates within the **functionalist perspective**, the **conflict theory** perspective and the **symbolic interactionism** perspective.

The functional perspective's take on stratification draws from the Davis-Moore thesis, the 1945 writing by sociologists Kingsley Davis and Wilbert Moore which put forth that the greater the functional importance of a social role, the greater the reward. Put simply, it argues that social stratification represents the differing value of work. For example, the scope of the work of a business executive (creating and providing jobs for a larger swath of society, thereby stimulating a society's economy and infrastructure) is larger and perhaps more important to society than, say, the grocery store owner (stimulating a local economy, providing for a smaller region or portion of a greater society) and thus serving a greater function and possessing a greater value of work.

Conflict theorists criticize social stratification, arguing that it benefits only the higher end of society. They would argue that the executive of a corporation is paid not based on the value of his or her work but rather based on his or her position: not for creating jobs and benefitting society but rather because executives hold a higher position within that society. The grocer, conflict theorists would argue, serves a more crucial and immediate role in society, fulfilling a true need (food) and having a greater impact on day-to-day life in a society as an active, visual member of that society. Conflict theorists argue that stratification creates barriers rather than lines of delineation.

Lastly, **symbolic interactionists** argue that social stratification is something people inflict upon themselves—that people delineate society themselves based on visual symbols. These may be as simple as fashion or home decor, to metaphorical symbols (such as educational accomplishments, etc.) to personal imagery like race, religion, or ethnicity. Symbolic interactionists argue that people group themselves together based on the symbols of the world around them.

Systems of Social Stratification

Different stratification systems have different lines of delineation. **Social class** is most commonly used in the western world and refers often to simple economics. As of 2015, the United States Bureau of Labor Statistics claims the lower class earns up to $47,000 annually. An annual income of $48,000–$140,000 reflects the middle class, while $141,000 and above normally defines the upper class.

Beyond economics, the **caste system** is used primarily in India. It has five tiers: the Brahmins, the Kshatriyas, the Vaishyas, the Shudras, and the Dalits. Caste is based on birth. People of the lowest tier are often referred to as the "untouchables" and are ostracized from greater society. While the caste system used to be a static phenomenon that kept individuals in their place, in recent years it has become apparent that there is some flexibility. While someone cannot move officially move out of their caste, there is no longer explicit economic repression for differing castes.

The **estate system** is another common system of social stratification in the modern world. Similar to feudalism, the estate system represents a broad division of labor. Three different estates exist within this system: clergy, nobility, and commoners. Clergy are allowed, by virtue of their position, to possess land. Nobility generally owns and is born into land, while commoners either own much smaller portions of land or rent from the nobility. One's ability to move up in this system depends on income and value of land. While this system is widely known as the basis of French society before the French Revolution, it is still in use today in some developing countries.

Power, Prestige, and Status

Power, prestige and **status** exist within nearly every level of social stratification.

Power, defined as the capacity to exert influence over others, often relates to the relationship between social classes—the upper classes tend to wield more power than the lower and middle classes, for example—but also relates to the relationships within those classes. Within the lower classes there are still people in positions of authority, from religious and community leaders to the head of a household.

Prestige refers to the widespread admiration of an individual or group based (usually) on the appearance of success or achievement. Again, the upper classes may appear more prestigious based on income levels, manner of dress, and physical possessions that demonstrate accomplishments (like home ownership). But again within those different classes, different concepts of prestige are apparent. One immediate image of the lower classes, popularized in Jacob Riis's *How the Other Half Lives*, is that of someone poorly dressed—with ratty clothing and an unkempt appearance. It is for that reason that the 1960s Civil Rights movement encouraged (and in some cases, forced) protesters and participants to be neatly attired in appearance. The image of these well-dressed, clean-cut citizens of multiple races being attacked in the streets caught the nation's sympathy and attention while also restoring dignity and humanity to the protesters. Taking a less dramatic example, when going in for a job interview, someone of any class is expected to wear business attire and look appropriate for work. Prestige is thrust upon the individual but can also be individually controlled to help them advance to a different position.

Status concerns how individuals are viewed in the world. It is demonstrated not just by income or education, but also by attitude and behavior. Individuals born into the upper-class may enjoy a higher social status, but their conduct—the business they choose to pursue, the people they associate themselves with—will impact that status. Likewise, the person born into a lower-class family is more likely to grow up living in a lower status but has, in theory, the ability to change that by pursuing a higher education and acting in accordance with the group they aspire to join.

Social Mobility

Social mobility is the idea that an individual or group can move out of their place and into a new place in society. Lower classes aspire to the middle class; the middle class aspires to the upper class, etc. There are two major forms of social mobility: horizontal and vertical.

Horizontal social mobility refers to the notion of moving within one's social level. This includes changing jobs, marriage, moving apartments or between social groups, all while staying at relatively the same status. These moves are generally superficial while still reflecting subtle changes. Moving to a larger house in the same neighborhood or to a better job that is still below management level would represent horizontal mobility.

Vertical mobility pertains to moving from one social level to another. This includes major promotions, marrying into a wealthier family, or moving from a lower economic class neighborhood to a more affluent neighborhood. These changes are far more drastic and usually involve a major change in economic status or a major educational accomplishment.

Two other forms of mobility involve **intergenerational** and **intragenerational** mobility. These almost always pertains to ethnic or family-based societies. Intergenerational mobility refers to changes of social status between different generations of the same family. This could mean the advancement of one family based off the work of each generation; a father and mother work middle income jobs to provide an education for their child, who uses that education to become an executive in business and in turn provides an education for his child who then becomes a doctor, advancing in social status with each generation. Intragenerational mobility refers to the changes of an individual's social mobility during the course of their lifetime. Everything, from one's race and ethnicity to level of educational accomplishment, personal talents, and even personality can affect upward mobility in social stratus. Outside factors, like the economy and stability of that individual's society, can affect this as well. In theory mobility is possible for anyone, but both internal and external factors can affect that mobility.

SAMPLE QUESTION

5) Which of the following represents horizontal mobility?

  A. A working-class individual marries a wealthy individual from the upper class.
  B. A laborer who works overnight shifts is given a daytime shift.
  C. A server at a restaurant is promoted to manager.
  D. A small business owner breaks even on an investment.

Answer:

  B. **Correct.** While the laborer has not received a promotion to a managerial or executive position, his or her life has been improved.

Prejudice, Discrimination, and Inequality

Prejudice, discrimination, and **inequality** are the major impediments to a society that allows members of a class to evolve and move up within that society. **Prejudice** refers to pre-judgments of an individual or group based off of stereotypes. The male employer may decide the female employee is less competent because of his own preconceived notions about women in the workplace. The store owner who has strict religious views on homosexuality may limit his direct interactions with the LGBT community based on his beliefs. The teacher who has limited interaction with the black community and experiences with one or two unruly black students may decide all black children share similar behaviors.

Discrimination occurs when one acts on their prejudices. The aforementioned male employer may give a female employee more menial tasks and pass her over for promotion in favor of a male counterpart. The store owner may refuse service to a gay couple that would like to frequent his store. Discrimination can also occur subconsciously: the teacher may call on more white children than black children in class, limiting the confidence those black children could develop when ignored by a teacher.

Inequality is the result of discrimination. Because more women are passed over in the workplace, the income level for their male counterparts begins to dwarf the income level for women. Because the store owner refuses service to the LGBT community, that community's consumer options become limited. Because the black child is passed over by the teacher for the white child, that child may become disillusioned with the notion of education and thus limit her academic pursuits, suffering grave repercussions throughout her life.

The causes of prejudice generally date back to a society that is either closed off or naturally combative and conflict oriented. The above examples could reflect communities where women actively take a secondary role in life, where religion is stressed as important over all other people and things, or where interracial interaction is limited or perhaps even nonexistent. It is possible that the male employer's only experience with women was an abusive father and a subservient mother. It is possible the store owner is an otherwise loving man who found religion to be the bedrock of his otherwise problematic life and will not deviate from it. It is possible the teacher simply never met a black person before.

The long-term consequences of prejudice are an increasingly polarized society: groups that choose to remain static. Prejudice may also lead to groups leaving that society altogether in order to find somewhere more beneficial (such as the Great Migration of African Americans from the South) and as a result upsetting the social order. Any number of negative factors can and often will occur in the face of discrimination. Change will inevitably occur, whether a society evolves or dissolves.

DEVIANCE AND CONFORMITY

Deviance, in terms of sociology, applies to any actions or behaviors that violate the established social norms. This can apply to explicit criminal violations of official rules and laws, as well as violations to the accepted informal behaviors and social norms; people who choose to live an unconventional lifestyle in comparison to the rest of society, for example.

Deviance is often considered a negative trait and deviants are often the victims of what sociologist Erving Goffman considered the theory of social **stigma**, in which an attribute of behavior or reputation is used to socially discredit a group or beliefs. But in an increasingly global culture where newer ideas and beliefs are shared and adapted by different groups, the notion of some deviance or deviation from the norm has become accepted by broader society. **Positive deviance**, for example, is an approach to social or behavioral changes and transformation based on the observation that in a given community, those with uncommon but successful behaviors or strategies may be able to make use of those differences to better themselves and potentially the world around them. Alternate forms of medicine, particularly the holistic kind, could be considered forms of positive deviancy. Deviants can also form their own subcultures within the greater subculture that can be added to the whole; the hippie and yippie subcultures in 1960s America were often considered deviant, but their outlook on a more inclusive society can be considered fundamental to the slightly more integrated society reflective of the United States today.

The most commonly qualifying terms involved in deviancy are **primary deviance** and **secondary deviance**. Primary deviance is the first stage in the formation of deviant identity, generally the initial act or behavior that is considered a violation. An example would be a child who steals a toy from a local toy store. The small child is behaving in what is considered childhood activity; as an initial infraction executed by someone unaware, this primary action may be considered an aberration. Secondary deviance is the act of integrating deviancy into one's behavior. That same child, for example, having never truly received consequences for his or her behavior, may learn stealing to be a personal benefit and thus becomes a criminal, violating laws in an act of deviance.

Deviance on the criminal level can generally be linked back to social problems. At the simplest level, economic inequality often can and will lead to crime, or an act or omission that constitutes an offense that may be prosecuted by the state and punishable by the law. Those in desperate need monetarily may be more likely to commit crimes related to those needs—stealing money, stealing items of value to attain money, or stealing that which the individual needs. But sociologists theorize that an unstable society or family unit can lead to crime due to a lack of positive influences. Absentee parents, particularly fathers, have been considered to be prime contributors to crime in young children, particularly boys. The lack of a positive influence leads to an aggressive need for attention and personal rebellion against the morals of a society. Sociologists argue that a stable environment with clearly defined rules, boundaries, and positive roles and functions for all members of the society will keep that society productive.

In theory, the criminal justice system exists to police and protect the members of a system. Ideally, law enforcement exists to protect and serve citizens while enforcing the laws of the society to which they belong. The justice system itself exists to determine the nature of punishment or rehabilitation needed in order to preserve the safety of a society and its individual members. The more stable the criminal justice system, the stronger the society, though stability doesn't necessarily mean total power is given to that system. Strength includes measured judgment.

Sociological perspectives on deviance vary as much as those perspectives themselves vary. The functional perspective considers deviance to have a role in the stability of society. Functionalists argue that deviants help determine where the lines between normal and abnormal behaviors are drawn. Conflict theorists are mixed on the issue. Karl Marx never explicitly wrote on the notion of deviance, but he argued that certain behaviors considered deviant were the result of alienation; that alienation itself created deviant behavior. Other theorists argue that deviance causes alienation. But where conflict theorists agree is that deviance is used as an excuse by those in power to enforce the differences between those in power and those out of power. Symbolic interactionism argues that there are no behaviors that are intrinsically deviant. Rather, deviance is essentially in the eye of the beholder. Whatever people are exposed to as normal behavior will become normal behavior; only upon interacting in a society with different behaviors will they discover any difference. The ascription of deviance will come from one group to the other based on the compatibility of the two societies.

SAMPLE QUESTION

6) Which of the following sociological theories argues that deviance and alienation are intrinsically connected?

   A. conflict theory
   B. symbolic interactionism
   C. functionalism
   D. Sociology does not connect deviance with alienation; it is a psychological problem.

   Answer:
   A. **Correct.** Marx argued that alienation caused deviance.

Social Change, Movement, and Demography

Factors of Social Change

Social change is based on **external causes, internal causes, technological advancements**, and **social movements**. External causes can include weather, climate, and other natural causes like erosion, earthquakes, etc. These natural events demand changes within a society and how it lives. Other external causes can include relationships with other societies, which includes both positive adaptations and, thus, evolution of a society, as well as negative interactions like war and other conflicts. Internal causes include a shifting economy, advancement of differing individuals or groups (ethnic, religious, education, etc.) from one social class to the next, or a political overhaul of leadership from one philosophy to another. Technological advances include everything from the advancement of computer hardware and software used by individuals to infrastructure development. Social movements are internal causes that lead to change, like elections, protest movements, and educational advancements; these usually spring from intellectual or philosophical debates.

The role of the major theories within social change is reflective of the theories themselves. Functionalism is often criticized for not taking social change into account, as this perspective tends to enforce the social order. However, functionalism allows for change if that change serves a purpose for that society. While functionalism states that everyone has a role in society, those roles do involve changing and developing our society. Therefore, social change is its own function. On the other hand, social change nearly defines conflict theory, a theory which relies on constant evolution and encourages a shakeup of the status quo. Conflict theorists would argue constant social change is necessary in order to grow and develop a society.

Symbolic interactionists would argue that social change is represented by imagery. For example, a society that is turning away from religion may focus on more secular imagery (trees, lights, etc.) and away from religious imagery (the Nativity scene, menorahs, etc.) during the holiday season. Those visual changes can stimulate social change faster than perhaps some in a society would like. They would argue the visual symbols that play a role in social change as well—the iconography of a protest movement or even the very visual symbols of crowds holding signs—push social change more than any idea ever will. For example, while a war for independence had already begun in the United States before 1776, it was the symbol of the Declaration of Independence that turned a few rebellious uprisings into a full-fledged revolution.

Collective behavior and social movements define social change. While ideas and theories abound, it takes the movement of a group to see it completed. Whether by protesters taking to the streets, activists raising awareness on social media, or bodies of government taking action, a collective human effort must coalesce around an idea for change to happen. In short, society in its entirety must want social change in order for it to become a reality.

SAMPLE QUESTION

7) Which of the following would symbolic interactionists view as indicative of social change?

A. signs indicating a sale at a major retail chain

B. the government making road signs for national parks brown, while keeping other road signs on the interstate green

C. a popular rock band unexpectedly changing its hairstyles and makeup

D. an unmarked red coffee cup distributed during the holidays by a popular US chain of coffee shops in lieu of a cup decorated specifically for Christmas

Answer:

D. **Correct.** This secular symbolism—declining to privilege one religious tradition during the holiday season—shows secular hegemony on the part of a widely popular consumer brand in the United States and therefore, according to symbolic interactionists, increased secularism throughout the country.

Practice Test

UNITED STATES HISTORY

Directions: Read the question carefully and choose the best answer.

1

All of the following contributed to the destruction of Native American populations in North America except

- A. intentional transfer of smallpox from Europeans to Native Americans.
- B. unintentional transfer of smallpox from Europeans to Native Americans.
- C. violent conflict over land and resources between Europeans and Native Americans.
- D. geographical displacement by colonists.

2

How did the colonies in New England differ from southern ones like Virginia, the Carolinas, and Georgia?

- A. Farms tended to be larger in the southern colonies and produce cash crops like tobacco, using slave labor; in the north, smaller family farms predominated and early urbanization was more widespread.
- B. Farms tended to be larger in the northern colonies and produce cash crops like tobacco, using slave labor; in the south, smaller family farms predominated and early urbanization was more widespread.
- C. The southern colonies were wealthier than the northern colonies, with a more educated population.
- D. There were no major differences between the northern and southern colonies before independence.

3

How did the views of the Federalists and the Anti-Federalists differ during the Constitutional Convention?

- A. The views of the Federalists and Anti-Federalists did not significantly differ at the Constitutional Convention.
- B. The Anti-Federalists did not believe in a Constitution at all, while the Federalists insisted on including the Bill of Rights.
- C. The Anti-Federalists favored a stronger Constitution and federal government, while Federalists were concerned that states would risk losing their autonomy.
- D. The Federalists favored a stronger Constitution and federal government, while Anti-Federalists were concerned that states would risk losing their autonomy.

4

Which of the following best describes the conditions faced by Latinos and Latinas who had remained in western territories won by the US in the Mexican-American War?

- A. They were treated with derision; many lost land and wealth they had held under Mexico, and did not enjoy the same rights under the law as citizens, even though they had been promised American citizenship in the Treaty of Guadalupe Hidalgo.
- B. While many had lost land and wealth they had held under Mexico, they were entitled to and received restitution from the government of the United States.
- C. They were treated equally in social and political situations under the United States.
- D. Most Latinos and Latinas left the western territories for Mexico following the Mexican-American War, due to discriminatory conditions they faced under the United States government.

5

The early Democratic Party (the Democratic-Republicans) was mainly concerned with which of the following?

- A. agrarian issues, small landowners, and maintaining a weaker federal government
- B. fiscal policy in support of urban areas and big businesses
- C. limitations on federal oversight of business and banks
- D. maintaining a strong federal government

6

What advantage did the colonists have in the American Revolution?

A. vast financial wealth

B. superior weaponry

C. strong leadership and knowledge of the terrain

D. a professional military and access to mercenaries

7

What did the Compromise of 1850 accomplish?

A. It admitted California and Maine as free states and strengthened the Fugitive Slave Act.

B. It admitted California as a free state, Utah and New Mexico with slavery to be decided by popular sovereignty, and strengthened the Fugitive Slave Act.

C. It admitted California, Utah, and New Mexico as free states, and strengthened the Fugitive Slave Act.

D. It admitted California, Utah, and New Mexico as states with slavery to be decided by popular sovereignty, and strengthened the Fugitive Slave Act.

8

What was a consequence of the Kansas-Nebraska Act?

A. the Fugitive Slave Act

B. the Compromise of 1850

C. violence between pro- and anti-slavery advocates in Kansas over the legalization of slavery ("Bleeding Kansas")

D. the Missouri Compromise

9

How did the Lincoln-Douglas Debates impact the nation before the 1860 presidential election?

A. They reflected the national mood: that the country was deeply divided over the question of slavery and whether states had the right to determine its legality.

B. They reflected the national mood: that the country was deeply divided over the question of slavery—Lincoln called for abolition, while Douglas favored the practice.

C. They reinvigorated the debate over slavery, which had been overshadowed by debate over states' rights.

D. They reinvigorated the debate over states' rights, which had been overshadowed by debate over slavery.

10

What did the Missouri Compromise accomplish?

A. It admitted Missouri as a free state.

B. It admitted California as a free state.

C. It allowed slavery in New Mexico and Utah to be decided by popular sovereignty.

D. It banned slavery north of the thirty-sixth parallel, so that new states formed in northern territories would be free.

11

Following the Civil War, the United States ratified the Thirteenth, Fourteenth, and Fifteenth Amendments to the Constitution. What did these amendments guarantee?

A. an end to slavery, equal rights for all Americans, and voting rights for all Americans, respectively

B. an end to slavery, equal rights for all Americans, and voting rights for all African Americans, respectively

C. an end to slavery, equal rights for all American men, and voting rights for all African American men, respectively

D. an end to slavery, equal rights for Americans, and voting rights for African American men, respectively

12

A major consequence of the Civil War was

A. the rise of the Federalist Party.

B. the destruction of the South's economy and the growth of the North's economy.

C. the emergence of the Republican Party.

D. the growth of the South's economy and the destruction of the North's economy.

13

During FDR's terms in office, which of the following was created?

A. Medicare

B. Social Security

C. the Federal Reserve

D. all of the above

14

Even after the end of slavery, African Americans in the rural South still suffered due to

A. sharecropping, which kept them in heavy debt, often to their former "masters."

B. the Colored Farmers' Alliance, which was organized to limit their efforts to become independent farmers.

C. the Reconstruction Acts, which specifically punished Southern blacks who did not join the Union army.

D. labor unions, which advocated for white workers' rights in factories in urban areas and ignored rural issues.

15

The New Deal was intended to

A. provide immediate economic relief to those suffering from the Great Depression.

B. stimulate longer-term economic and social recovery for US society through various targeted programs.

C. implement permanent reforms in banking and finance to prevent a reoccurrence of the failures that led to the Great Depression.

D. all of the above

16

The Spanish-American War

A. brought the United States territories in Asia, the Pacific Ocean, and the Caribbean.

B. was triggered in part by public support generated by sensationalist yellow journalism.

C. could be viewed as a precursor to Theodore Roosevelt's Roosevelt Corollary to the Monroe Doctrine.

D. all of the above

17

The Cuban Missile Crisis ultimately resulted in

A. the installation of the Castro regime.

B. the fall of the Castro regime.

C. a new opening of dialogue between the United States and the Soviet Union.

D. the end of a period of détente between the United States and the Soviet Union.

18

During periods of high tension between the United States and the Soviet Union in the 1950s, how was the US affected?

- A. Fear of communism was pervasive, and during the McCarthy era, accusations were made against public figures.
- B. Fearing Soviet communism, the United States supported Maoism in China as a counterweight to Leninism.
- C. During the McCarthy hearings, several members of Congress were found to be communist and so were removed from office.
- D. During the McCarthy hearings, several members of Congress were found to be Soviet spies and so were removed from office.

WORLD HISTORY

Directions: Read the question carefully and choose the best answer.

1

An important tenet of Judaism held that

A. There is only one God and Muhammad is God's Prophet.

B. A harmonious society is the ideal society.

C. The moral codes provided by God in the Ten Commandments apply to all, even slaves.

D. The son of God is both human and divine.

2

The Qur'an

A. contains the legal teachings of Islam.

B. contains the legal teachings of Judaism.

C. is believed to have been transmitted from Allah and is the holy book of Islam.

D. was written by Muhammad and is the holy book of Islam.

3

Which of the following best describes the Caste system in India?

A. It is a defined, unchangeable social and religious hierarchy, determined by birth.

B. It is a changeable social hierarchy.

C. It is a hierarchy determined by skills and education wherein one's position can be changed.

D. It is a defined, unchangeable social hierarchy, determined by birth.

4

During the Peloponnesian War,

A. the dominant Hellenic powers, Crete and Sparta, went to war with each other.

B. the dominant Hellenic powers, Athens and Sparta, went to war with the Ionian Greeks in Anatolia.

C. Greece was able to unite as the dominant powers, Athens and Sparta, fought against Persia and the Ionian Greeks.

D. the dominant Hellenic powers, Athens and Sparta, went to war with each other.

5

The Hittites were able to expand from Anatolia due to

A. superior seafaring technology, allowing expansion into the Mediterranean.

B. superior military technology, including chariots and weaponry.

C. advanced technology imported from Greece.

D. their development of bronze metallurgy.

6

How did the Neolithic Era mark a major development in human evolution?

A. the development of agriculture and beginning of settled societies

B. the early use of the wheel

C. the use of bronze to develop basic tools

D. early medical treatment

7

Despite the period of relative stability enjoyed by Europe during the High Middle Ages, the Black Death resulted in which of the following outcomes?

A. European powers were made vulnerable to attacks by the Magyars, who toppled the disorganized Holy Roman Empire.

B. Instability in Europe led to military conflict, division within the Catholic Church, and weakening of the Holy Roman Empire.

C. The Mongols were able to expand their empire into Eastern Europe.

D. Islamic powers were able to completely conquer the Iberian Peninsula as a result of instability there.

8

One reason the Muslim Arabs were able to take over Byzantine- and Persian-controlled areas was

A. Muslims were ambivalent towards Christian minorities who may have opposed the Greek Orthodox Byzantines or the Zoroastrian Persians; these groups therefore preferred Arab-Muslim rule to more oppressive power structures.

B. Arabic-speaking people in the region were more responsive toward Arabic-speaking rulers.

C. Muslims already living in the Byzantine and Persian empires welcomed Islamic rule.

D. A and B only

9

Many scholars argue that modern banking began in Venice in the fifteenth century. Which of the following strengthens this argument?

A. Venice was the first major colonial power, developing mercantilism.

B. Venice was a center of intellectual and cultural development.

C. Venice was a commercial center, ideally situated to profit from goods imported on the Silk Road and from Africa.

D. Venice was not badly affected by the plague.

10

Which of the following best describes the motivation for Protestant reformers?

A. Protestants, including Martin Luther, originally sought to develop a new form of Christianity separate from the Catholic Church.

B. Protestants like Martin Luther were unhappy with the teachings of the Church, including Papal indulgences and corruption in the Church, and originally sought reform.

C. Protestants were initially influenced by European political leaders, who used them to limit the power of the Church.

D. Protestants, including Martin Luther, originally sought to topple the Catholic Church, believing it to have become too corrupt.

11

The Hundred Years' War

A. is an example of European unity against an outside, non-European invading force.

B. showed the technological dominance of the powers aligned with the Catholic Church, whose resources were massive.

C. indicated a shift in European politics from allegiance to one's ethnicity or nation to allegiance to the empire.

D. described ongoing ethnic conflict in Europe.

12

Which of the following best describes the consequences of the Opium Wars?

A. British occupation of China

B. Chinese victory over Britain

C. unequal trade treaties favoring China

D. unequal trade treaties favoring Britain

13

How were European empires affected by nationalism in the eighteenth and nineteenth centuries?

A. European empires like the Austro-Hungarian Empire benefitted from nationalism, as Austrians and Hungarians were more loyal to the imperial government.

B. The Austro-Hungarian Empire lost its Balkan territories to the Ottoman Empire, which was perceived to be more tolerant of Muslim minorities.

C. Given the nature of empire—consolidated rule over an extended region home to diverse peoples—nationalism threatened empire as ethnic groups began to advocate for representation in imperial government.

D. Given the nature of empire—consolidated rule over an extended region home to diverse peoples—nationalism threatened empire as ethnic groups began to advocate for their own independent states.

14

How was Europe affected by the Civil War in the United States?

A. European powers were inspired to make slavery illegal following the American Civil War.

B. Industrializing European powers relied on Southern cotton, but were encouraged not to trade with the Confederacy so as not to support slavery, which had already been abolished in Europe and most European empires.

C. Industrializing European powers relied on Southern cotton, and traded with the Confederacy, supplying them with needed income during the Civil War.

D. none of the above

15

Following the collapse of the Ottoman Empire after the First World War, European countries took control of the Middle East, establishing protectorates according to arbitrary boundaries and installing rulers in accordance with European strategic interests. What effect has this had on the Middle East in the twentieth and twenty-first centuries?

A. The Middle East has not been greatly affected.

B. Illegitimate national borders and rulers have led to instability in the region.

C. Improved governance, thanks to the protectorates, improved stability following the decline of the Ottoman Empire in the region.

D. European investment in strategic resources supported long-term political stability in the Middle East.

16

Choose the best description for the Russian strategy of empire-building.

A. Russia focused on colonizing overseas, strengthening its navy to build a trans-oceanic empire.

B. Russia focused on overland expansion, moving eastward into northern Asia across Siberia and westward into Eastern Europe.

C. Russia remained isolated, avoiding expansion and focusing on industrialization instead.

D. Russia lacked the resources to build an empire and struggled to maintain its agrarian-based society.

17

The Treaty of Westphalia

A. marked the end of the Thirty Years' War.

B. was indicative of a shift in European politics, towards international relations based on non-interference and emerging concepts of independent states, rather than empires dominated by the Catholic Church and other forces.

C. is often viewed as the foundation of modern European relations.

D. all of the above

18

Which of the following best explains the economic impact on Germany following the First World War?

A. Overspeculation on German farmland caused the market to crash.

B. Wartime reparations mandated by the Treaty of Versailles and the worldwide Great Depression caused inflation to skyrocket, plunging the German economy into crisis.

C. Germans were forced to pay extra taxes to cover reparations, and due to high prices, many could not afford to do so.

D. The Reichsmark was removed from circulation and replaced with the dollar as a means of punishment, forcing many Germans into poverty.

GOVERNMENT

Directions: Read the question carefully and choose the best answer.

1

The framers instituted a system of checks and balances because they were concerned about

- A. one branch of government gaining too much power.
- B. mob rule.
- C. the military taking over the government.
- D. the states overpowering the national government.

2

What can Congress do if the Supreme Court declares a law unconstitutional?

- A. override the decision with a two-thirds vote
- B. pass the law again
- C. amend the Constitution
- D. request a veto from the president

3

If no presidential candidate wins a majority in the Electoral College, how is the president chosen?

- A. The Electoral College votes based only on the top two candidates.
- B. The House of Representatives selects the president.
- C. Whichever candidate had a plurality of the popular vote wins.
- D. The Supreme Court selects the president.

4

Which of the following is currently true about the Supreme Court's interpretation of the right to free speech?

- A. The expression of ideas or opinions even without words is protected.
- B. Citizens who believe certain laws are unjust are constitutionally allowed to disobey them.
- C. Newspapers are protected even if they knowingly print a false story about someone.
- D. It cannot be restricted.

5

Which of the following is an example of a legislative check on another branch?

A. a visit to Israel by a congressional delegation
B. Congress passing the Crime Bill after revisions in conference committee
C. the 2002 expulsion of Representative Jim Traficant after he was convicted of bribery
D. the 1999 Senate rejection of the Nuclear Test Ban Treaty

6

Which of the following is the best example of federalism?

A. The president sends troops to Iraq.
B. Congress rejects the Treaty of Versailles.
C. The Department of Agriculture is created.
D. State legislatures elect senators.

7

If a person believes they can effect positive change in their government, they have a high level of

A. political aptitude.
B. political allegiance.
C. political efficacy.
D. political insight.

8

Which of the following is true about political action committees (PACs)?

A. They are managed by political parties.
B. They are prohibited in state elections.
C. The amount of money they can contribute in each election is restricted.
D. They must work closely with the candidate that they support.

9

Which of the following differentiates district courts from appellate courts?

A. An appellate court has original jurisdiction.
B. A district court only hears criminal cases.
C. An appellate court reviews previous court decisions.
D. A district court is beholden to the state government.

10

According to the original Constitution, who is eligible to vote?

A. all citizens

B. Congress has the power to determine voter eligibility.

C. all white men

D. The states have the power to determine voter eligibility.

11

Which of the following describes the means by which a president can be removed from office?

A. The Senate votes by a majority to impeach the president; the House delivers a guilty verdict with a two-thirds vote.

B. The House votes by a majority to impeach the president; the Senate delivers a guilty verdict with a two-thirds vote.

C. The Senate votes to impeach the president with a two-thirds vote; the House delivers a guilty verdict through a simple majority.

D. The House votes to impeach the president with a two-thirds vote; the Senate delivers a guilty verdict through a simple majority.

12

If a developing nation needed help funding a new network of state-run hospitals, which of the following IGOs would it most likely ask for financial help?

A. The World Health Organization

B. NATO

C. The World Bank

D. The World Trade Organization

13

Which of the following is an accurate example of checks and balances?

A. The president signs treaties, and the Senate ratifies them.

B. A bill becomes a law when Congress votes on it and the Supreme Court declares it constitutional.

C. The Senate appoints justices to the Supreme Court, and the House of Representatives approves them.

D. Congress has the power to remove the president, and the Supreme Court has the power to remove members of Congress.

14

John Locke's theory of a social contract is best reflected in which section of the Constitution?

A. the Bill of Rights
B. Article V, which refers to amending the Constitution
C. the Preamble
D. Article VII, which refers to ratification

15

How do the two major parties officially select their nominees for the presidency?

A. through public opinion polls
B. through a discussion among the party's national leadership
C. at nominating conventions
D. through party votes in each state

16

To which of the following does the Supreme Court's power of judicial review NOT apply?

A. laws passed by Congress
B. laws passed by state legislatures
C. executive orders
D. lower-court decisions

17

Which clause of the Constitution best supports the idea of the rule of law?

A. the supremacy clause
B. the elastic clause
C. the advise and consent clause
D. the due process clause

18

Which of the following constitutional provisions was NOT a change from the Articles of Confederation?

A. a bicameral legislature
B. the possibility of amending the Constitution
C. a three-branch government
D. the creation of a standing army

Geography

Directions: Read the question carefully and choose the best answer.

1

The International Date Line is

A. the same as the Prime Meridian.
B. the same as the Equator.
C. 180° from the Prime Meridian.
D. 90° north of the Equator.

2

A farmer in Maine who grows fruits and vegetables only to feed his family is practicing

A. swidden farming
B. subsistence farming
C. intensive farming
D. traditional farming

3

Ireland has a "right to return" law granting Irish citizenship to anyone with at least one Irish grandparent. This type of law is an example of

A. irredentism
B. balkanization
C. ethnonationalism
D. centrifugal force

4

Which of the following factors most greatly contributes to a country's transition from Stage Two to Stage Three of the Demographic Transition Model (DTM)?

A. the changing roles of women
B. advances in agricultural technology
C. advances in medicine
D. increased industrialization

5

Which of the following statements is true about the political geography of Antarctica?

A. Antarctica is governed by the United Nations.

B. Antarctica is governed jointly by the United States, Great Britain, and Russia.

C. Antarctica is the only unorganized territory left in the world.

D. Antarctica is governed jointly by its four nearest neighbors: Argentina, Chile, South Africa, and Australia.

6

The Robinson map (which slightly distorts shape, size, and straight line direction) is an example of which kind of map?

A. gnomonic projection

B. azimuthal equidistant projection

C. equal area projection

D. compromise projection

7

Which of the following would be considered a push factor for migration?

A. the discovery of oil in a new region

B. the outbreak of civil war in a new region

C. a new law in the home country requiring the practice of Catholicism

D. the relocation of a major company to the home region

8

Silicon Valley is an example of which economic pattern?

A. deglomeration

B. agglomeration

C. industrialization

D. modernization

9

Boston, New York, Philadelphia, Baltimore, and Washington D.C., as geographically close urban areas, form a(n)

A. urban realm

B. world city

C. megalopolis

D. transition zone

10

Looking at the map below, what kind of boundary separates the United States and Canada?

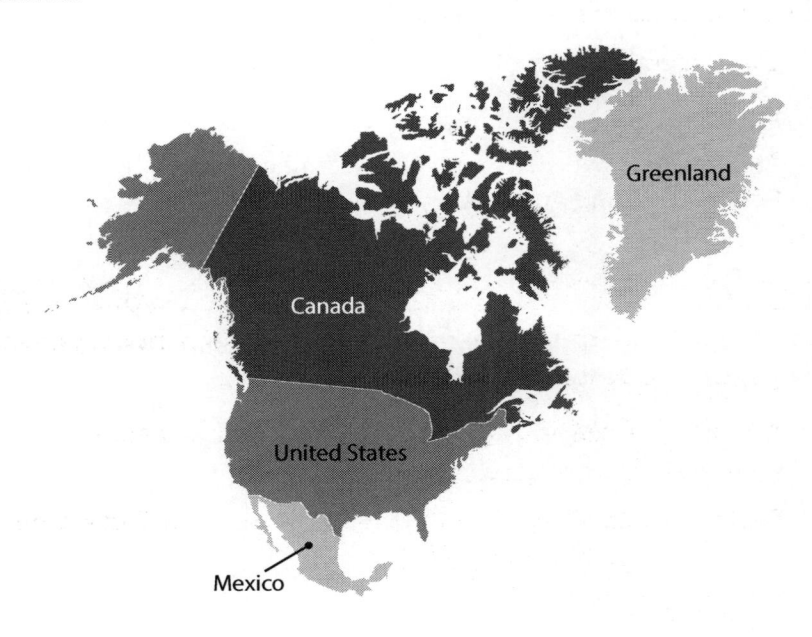

A. physical
B. cultural political
C. relict
D. geometric political

11

According to dependency theory, Senegal's low development is a result of which of the following?

A. its dependence on funding from the World Bank
B. its status as a Stage Two country based on the DTM
C. its status as a peripheral country
D. French colonization of West Africa

12

In the nineteenth century, Scotch-Irish families moved to Chicago, aided by glowing letters from family and friends who had migrated earlier. This is an example of which kind of migration?

A. chain migration
B. internal migration
C. step migration
D. net migration

13

Based on the core-periphery model, the majority of periphery countries are in

A. Africa, parts of Asia, and parts of South America.
B. Asia, parts of Eastern Europe, and parts of South America.
C. North America, Africa, and parts of Asia.
D. South America, parts of North America, and parts of Eastern Europe.

ECONOMICS

Directions: Read the question carefully and choose the best answer.

1

Paul decides that, having already completed two revisions of his resume, he should read through and revise it one more time. Which of the following is most likely true?

A. The marginal benefit of the third revision is less than the marginal cost of the third revision.

B. The marginal benefit of the third revision is at least as great as the marginal cost of the third revision.

C. Without knowing Paul's opportunity cost of revising his resume, there is no way to determine if the marginal benefits outweigh the marginal costs.

D. The second revision's marginal benefit was most likely less than its marginal cost.

2

In the production possibility curve below, economic growth would be indicated if the curve moved

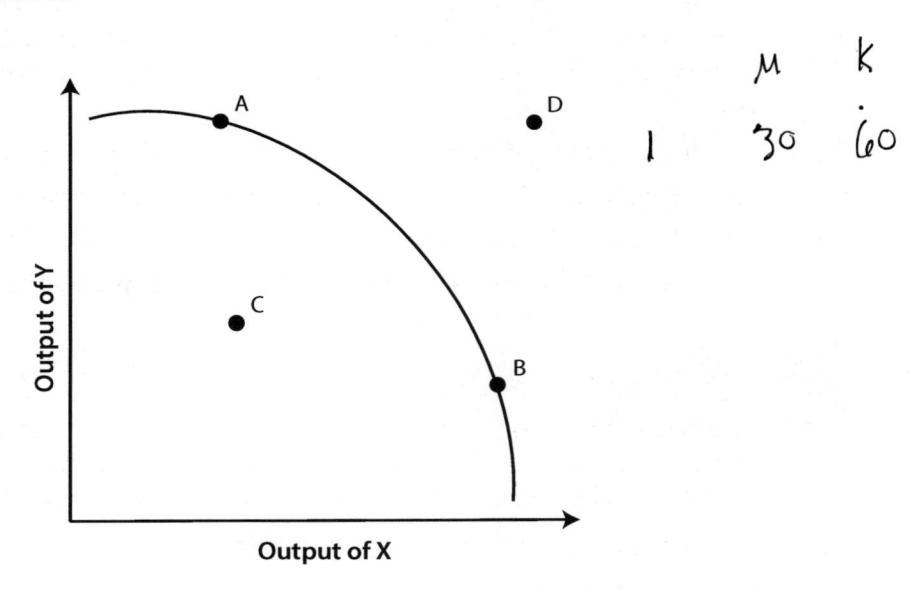

A. from point C to point A
B. from point A to point B
C. from point A to point D
D. from point D to point C

3

Max and Karen can both make desserts and peel carrots for the restaurant's evening service. For every dessert made, Max can peel thirty carrots and Karen can peel sixty carrots. Based on this information, which of the following is true?

A. Max peels carrots since he has absolute advantage in making desserts.
B. Karen peels carrots since she has absolute advantage in making desserts.
C. Karen makes desserts since she has comparative advantage in dessert making.
D. Max makes desserts since he has comparative advantage in dessert-making.

4

According to the law of demand, when the price of cucumbers increases, which of the following should happen?

A. The quantity of cucumbers demanded increases.
B. The quantity of cucumbers demanded falls.
C. The demand for cucumbers falls.
D. The demand for cucumbers increases.

5

The market for wool sweaters is in equilibrium. The price of hooded sweatshirts, a substitute good, rises. What impact will this have on the wool sweaters market?

A. Supply will rise, increasing price and decreasing the quantity.
B. Supply will fall, increasing the price and increasing the quantity.
C. Demand will fall, increasing the price and decreasing the quantity.
D. Demand will rise, increasing the price and increasing the quantity.

6

The price of the type of tomatoes used in ketchup drops dramatically. At the same time, the price of mustard, a substitute for ketchup, increases. What impact will these two events have on the supply and price of ketchup?

A. Price falls, but quantity is hard to determine.
B. Price rises, but quantity is hard to determine.
C. Price is hard to determine, but quantity rises.
D. Price is hard to determine, but quantity falls.

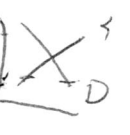

7

A startup software company determines that price elasticity for their software is 4.2. They wish to raise their total revenue. Which of the following will help them do that?

A. decrease price as demand is inelastic
B. increase price as demand is inelastic
C. decrease price as demand is elastic
D. increase price as demand is elastic

8

When is a price floor put into place?

A. The equilibrium price is perceived as being too high.
— B. The equilibrium price is perceived as being too low.
C. There is a surplus of a good.
D. There is a shortage of a good.

9

What is the price elasticity of the demand for salt (E_d). if the price of salt rises 4 percent and the quantity demanded for salt falls 2 percent?

A. $E_d = 0.5$
B. $E_d = 4$
C. $E_d = 2$
D. $E_d = 1$

10

Which of the following production inputs would least likely be able to be changed in the short run?

A. the number of cashiers at a grocery store
B. number of chocolate chips in a cookie
C. the size of a restaurant's dining room
D. the amount of electricity used at a high school

11

All of the following are basic factors of production except

A. labor
B. land
C. consumers
D. capital

12

Choosing among scarce items demonstrates the relationship between choice and

A. opportunity cost.
B. product cost.
C. marginal cost.
D. total cost.

13

Which of the following is NOT true of a production possibility curve?

A. It depicts maximum output possibilities.
B. It requires two goods.
C. It is based on a particular set of production inputs.
D. It maximizes utility.

BEHAVIORAL SCIENCES

Directions: Read the question carefully and choose the best answer.

1

Which of the following senses is most different at birth as compared to adulthood?

- A. sight
- B. smell
- C. hearing
- D. taste

2

If a person scored in the 97.5th percentile on the Weschler scale, what would his or her IQ be according to the graph below?

DISTRIBUTION OF IQ SCORES

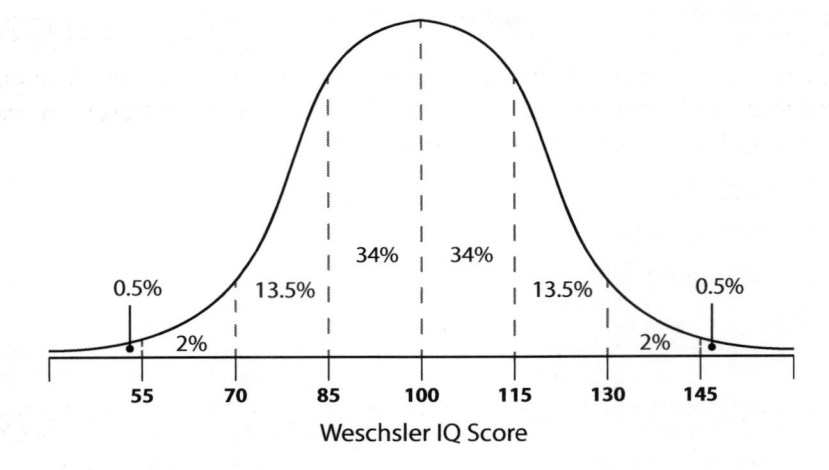

- A. 85
- B. 115
- C. 130
- D. 70

3

The process of accessing a memory is called

- A. retrieval
- B. encoding
- C. rehearsal
- D. repression

4

"In fourteen hundred and ninety-two, Columbus sailed the ocean blue…." is an example of which of the following memory techniques?

A. chunking
B. mnemonic device
C. visualization
D. elaborative rehearsal

5

Ben expected the French to be very rude, so when he was in Paris he noted every shopkeeper who spoke curtly to him (while paying little attention to those who were friendly). This is an example of which of the following?

A. confirmation bias
B. belief perseverance
C. mental set
D. misuse of an algorithm

6

Bandura's theory of reciprocal determinism—that personality is the result of the interaction between the individual, their behavior, and their environment—is part of which school of personality theory?

A. Humanistic
B. Psychoanalytical
C. Social-Cognitive
D. Trait

7

The primary goal of sociology is to conduct research applicable to

A. the common good and social stratification.
B. social policy and the common welfare.
C. the class system.
D. demographic determination.

8

Which of the following are the three major perspectives of sociology?

A. symbolic interactionism, ethnomethodology, and dramaturgical sociology
B. cooperation, exchange, and conflict
C. symbolic interactionism, conflict theory, and functionalism
D. primary, secondary, and anticipatory

9

The three major sociologists whose work best defined the applicable theories of sociology are

A. Max Weber, Emile Durkheim, and Karl Marx
B. Max Weber, Emile Durkheim, and Robert Merton
C. Karl Max, Emile Durkheim, and Robert Merton
D. Max Weber, Karl Marx, and Robert Merton

10

Which of the following best explains symbolic interactionism and three symbols related to that process?

A. a national election: the ballot box, candidates, and signs help achieve the common goal of electing a leader
B. the exchange of goods and services: the currency used, the customer, and the server all cooperate to carry out a mutually beneficial exchange
C. the establishment of currency: the texture, color, and logos reflect a national history and shared experiences
D. the ceremony of marriage: the ring, the outfits, and the venue model social values about relationships

Essay Questions

Read the information below, then complete the exercise that follows.

1 World History

The collapse of the Roman Empire led to a period of instability in Western Europe and a loss of the learning and infrastructure that had characterized Rome. However, imperial organization, brisk trade with partners in Asia, and philosophical and scientific learning continued in the Eastern Mediterranean and Middle East under the Byzantine Empire, and later under the Arab-Islamic and Ottoman Empires.

Using your knowledge of world history, explain how the knowledge and organization sustained in the Eastern Mediterranean eventually impacted the European Renaissance.

2 Social Sciences

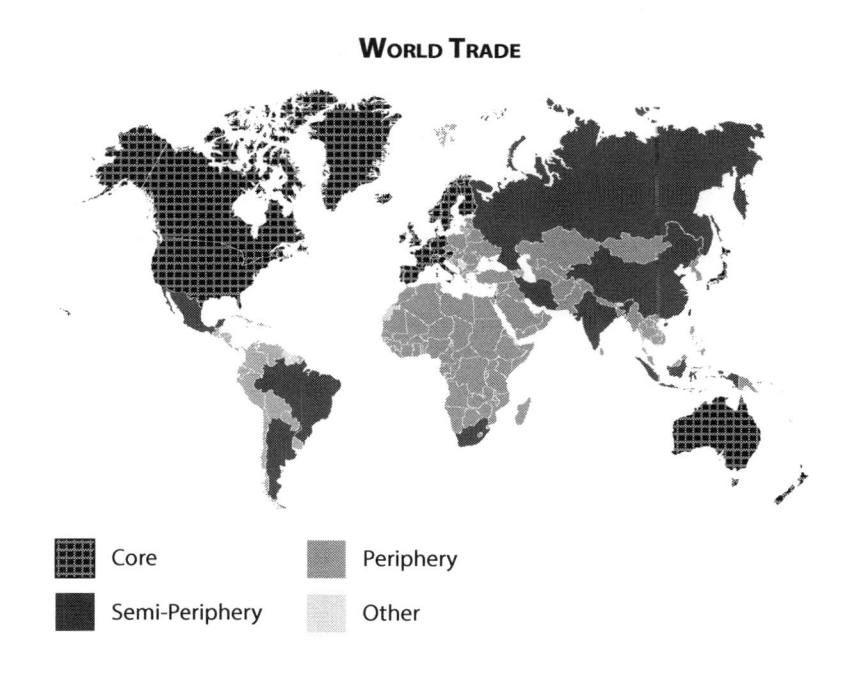

WORLD TRADE

- Core
- Semi-Periphery
- Periphery
- Other

According to World Systems Analysis and Core-Periphery Theory, Iran is in the "semi-periphery." How would a dependency theorist interpret this finding?

3 U.S. History

I shall see, this day, and its popular characteristics, from the slave's point of view. Standing, there, identified with the American bondman, making his wrongs mine, I do not hesitate to declare, with all my soul, that the character and conduct of this nation never looked blacker to me than on this Fourth of July! Whether we turn to the declarations of the past, or to the professions of the present, the conduct of the nation seems equally hideous and revolting. America is false to the past, false to the present, and solemnly binds herself to be false to the future. Standing with God and the crushed and bleeding slave on this occasion, I will, in the name of humanity which is outraged, in the name of liberty which is fettered, in the name of the constitution and the Bible, which are disregarded and trampled upon, dare to call in question and to denounce, with all the emphasis I can command, everything that serves to perpetuate slavery—the great sin and shame of America!

Frederick Douglass, "What to the Negro Is the Fourth of July?", July 5, 1852

Douglass condemned United States policy and society regarding slavery. Using your knowledge of US history, cite at least two examples of legislation that Douglass would likely have criticized, and explain how they reinforced slavery in the years preceding the Civil War.

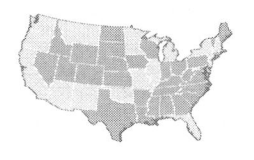

Answer Key

UNITED STATES HISTORY

1)

A. **Correct.** In early exploration of North America, European colonists were interested in spreading Christianity, extracting tribute and labor from Native Americans, and establishing trade agreements, not intentionally spreading disease.

B. Incorrect. Smallpox decimated Native American populations, which had never been exposed to the disease.

C. Incorrect. Ongoing violent conflict between European colonizers and Native Americans over hundreds of years caused thousands of deaths and led to social breakdown among some Native American societies.

D. Incorrect. Colonization and related conflict forced tribes to move from their traditional lands; for example, the Lenape were forced to move from Delaware west to the Great Lakes region. Later, many tribes were forced from their land during the Trail of Tears to Indian Territory (later, Oklahoma).

2)

A. **Correct.** Southern geography and climate lent itself to labor-intensive plantation agriculture, for which the colonists exploited slave labor. Natural harbors in the north fostered urban development, while the land was more appropriate for smaller farms.

B. Incorrect. The reverse was true.

C. Incorrect. All the colonies had wealthy, elite classes, in addition to working classes, indentured servants, and slaves.

D. Incorrect. Economic and cultural differences developed among the colonies.

3)

A. Incorrect. The views of the Federalists and Anti-Federalists differed a great deal.

B. Incorrect. The Bill of Rights was a compromise measure; it was not originally a Federalist contribution.

C. Incorrect. The reverse was true.

D. **Correct.** The Federalists were the driving force behind a stronger Constitution that would empower the United States federal government; the Anti-Federalists worked to protect state sovereignty and ensured the passage of the Bill of Rights to protect certain rights not explicitly guaranteed in the Constitution itself.

4)

A. **Correct.** Hispanic residents of the land the United States gained in the Treaty of Guadalupe Hidalgo did not obtain all they were promised; in fact, many lost their property and were not treated equally under the law or in society.

B. Incorrect. Those Hispanic residents of Mexico who were living on territory ceded to the United States did not receive restitution for losses suffered in violation of the Treaty of Guadalupe Hidalgo.

C. Incorrect. Latinos and Latinas living in United States territory often experienced unequal treatment under the law and in social situations.

D. Incorrect. Many people of Mexican descent stayed in what became the United States following the Mexican-American War.

5)

A. **Correct.** The Democratic-Republicans, descended from the Anti-Federalists, opposed a strong federal government and urban business interests, focusing on agrarian issues.

B. Incorrect. The Democratic-Republicans focused on rural constituents.

C. Incorrect. While the Democratic-Republicans surely did not favor a strong federal government, their priority was not supporting big business or banking.

D. Incorrect. The Democratic-Republicans were against federalism.

6)

A. Incorrect. While some colonists were quite wealthy, colonial wealth paled in the face of British wealth.

B. Incorrect. The colonists did not have superior weaponry.

C. **Correct.** The colonial military did have strong leaders, and an intimate knowledge of the terrain, many having been born there.

D. Incorrect. Britain had an experienced military with substantial experience fighting in Europe and elsewhere. In addition, King George III hired Hessian mercenaries from Germany to supplement British troops.

7)

A. Incorrect. Maine was admitted as a free state in the Missouri Compromise.

B. **Correct.** The Compromise of 1850 admitted California as a free state; however it strengthened the Fugitive Slave Act. The legalization of slavery in Utah and New Mexico would be decided by the voters.

C. Incorrect. Slavery in New Mexico and Utah would be decided by popular sovereignty.

D. Incorrect. Slavery would never be permitted in California.

8)

A. Incorrect. The Fugitive Slave Act was already in existence.

B. Incorrect. The Compromise of 1850 had already taken place.

C. **Correct.** Violence broke out over the question of legalizing slavery in Kansas, where it had previously been prohibited.

D. Incorrect. The Missouri Compromise had taken place decades before and was essentially undone by the Kansas-Nebraska Act.

9)

A. **Correct.** The Lincoln-Douglas Debates showed how divided the country was over slavery.

B. Incorrect. Douglas was not so much in favor of slavery as he was a proponent of states' rights.

C. Incorrect. Slavery and states' rights were intertwined.

D. Incorrect. The question of slavery was at the root of the debate over states' rights.

10)

A. Incorrect. The Missouri Compromise allowed slavery in Missouri.

B. Incorrect. California was not admitted as a state until 1850.

C. Incorrect. This was a feature of the Compromise of 1850.

D. **Correct.** The Missouri Compromise prohibited slavery north of the thirty-sixth parallel in new US territories, permitting slavery in Missouri.

11)

A. Incorrect. The Fifteenth Amendment only enabled African American men to vote. No American women could vote in national elections until the ratification of the Nineteenth Amendment in 1920.

B. Incorrect. African American women were still unable to vote, even though the Fifteenth Amendment allowed African American men to exercise that right. African American women would not be able to vote until 1920.

C. Incorrect. The Fourteenth Amendment ensures equal protection under the law to all Americans, regardless of race, gender, or other categories.

D. **Correct.** The Thirteenth Amendment abolished slavery; the Fourteenth Amendment promised equal protection under the law to all US citizens; the Fifteenth Amendment ensured that (male) African Americans and former slaves could vote.

12)

A. Incorrect. The Federalist Party had declined in the early nineteenth century and never returned to the political scene.

B. **Correct.** The Civil War devastated the South's economy due to infrastructural damage and international isolation.

C. Incorrect. The Republican Party appeared before the Civil War.

D. Incorrect. The Southern economy suffered from the Civil War.

13)

A. Incorrect. The Medicare Act was passed under the Johnson administration.

B. **Correct.** The Social Security Act was part of the New Deal.

C. Incorrect. The Federal Reserve Act was passed in 1913 following the Panic of 1907.

D. Incorrect. Only answer choice B is correct.

14)

A. **Correct.** Sharecropping perpetuated racial inequality in the South.

B. Incorrect. The Colored Farmers' Alliance assisted African American farmers.

C. Incorrect. The Reconstruction Acts did not include this provision.

D. Incorrect. While labor unions championed urban workers, most of whom were white, this was not in direct opposition to efforts to advance African Americans in the South; indeed, the Progressive Movement brought together activists for these and many diverse causes.

15)

A. Incorrect. While many New Deal programs targeted impoverished Americans, the New Deal had a wider scope than short-term poverty alleviation.

B. Incorrect. Several New Deal programs and projects sustained economic and social development in the United States, but this does not describe the breadth of the New Deal.

C. Incorrect. New Deal legislation did indeed address needed banking reform; however, the New Deal had other components as well.

D. **Correct.** The New Deal encompassed programs providing immediate relief for impoverished Americans, long-term development projects, and financial reforms to prevent a repeat of the Great Depression.

16)

A. Incorrect. While the United States gained control over former Spanish colonies in these regions, this answer choice does not completely answer the question.

B. Incorrect. One of the major driving forces behind the war was public pressure, which had indeed been boosted by yellow journalism; however, this answer choice is incomplete given the other options.

C. Incorrect. The Spanish-American War asserted United States military dominance in the Western Hemisphere, but this answer choice is inadequate in this context.

D. **Correct.** All of the answer choices are true.

17)

A. Incorrect. Castro was already in power at the time of the Cuban Missile Crisis.

B. Incorrect. Fidel Castro has remained in power, at least in name, through 2015; his brother Raul controls Cuba and despite many reforms, the same government is in place.

C. **Correct.** Following the extreme tensions between the two countries, the United States and the Soviet Union improved dialogue in the early 1960s, leading to a period of détente.

D. Incorrect. The Cuban Missile Crisis led to a period of détente; it did not end one.

18)

A. **Correct.** Public paranoia over communism was widespread, and many public figures were accused of being communist.

B. Incorrect. The United States never supported Maoism.

C. Incorrect. No members of Congress were removed from office due to the McCarthy hearings.

D. Incorrect. No members of Congress were revealed to be Soviet spies during the McCarthy hearings.

… ANSWER KEY 331

WORLD HISTORY

1)
- A. Incorrect. This is an important tenet of Islam.
- B. Incorrect. This is a core belief of Confucianism.
- **C. Correct.** This was a teaching of Judaism.
- D. Incorrect. This was a major teaching of Christianity.

2)
- A. Incorrect. While the Qur'an is a major source for Muslim legal scholars, Islamic law draws primarily from the Hadith.
- B. Incorrect. The Qur'an is not a holy book in Judaism; Jewish law relies on the Talmud.
- **C. Correct.** The Qur'an is the holy book of Islam and it is believed that the book was transmitted directly from God to Muhammad.
- D. Incorrect. While the Qur'an is the holy book of Islam, it is not believed that Muhammad himself wrote it.

3)
- **A. Correct.** The caste system is a social hierarchy rooted in religious tradition. It is not possible to change the caste into which one is born.
- B. Incorrect. While the caste system is a social hierarchy, and while there is more social and economic flexibility within it than before, it is not possible to move from one caste to another.
- C. Incorrect. One's position in the hierarchy is determined by birth; a person is born into his or her caste, and that position is permanent.
- D. Incorrect. While this definition is true, it leaves out the traditionally religious nature of the caste system.

4)
- A. Incorrect. The Peloponnesian War was between Sparta and Athens, not Sparta and Crete.
- B. Incorrect. The Peloponnesian War was fought between Greeks in Peloponnesus and Central Greece, not in Anatolia.
- C. Incorrect. The Peloponnesian War did not involve Persia.
- **D. Correct.** The Peloponnesian War was between the major Greek powers.

5)
- A. Incorrect. The Hittites expanded overland.
- **B. Correct.** The Hittites were skilled charioteers and were early pioneers of iron weaponry.
- C. Incorrect. The Hittites created their own weapons; furthermore, they preceded ancient Greek development.
- D. Incorrect. The Hittites worked with iron.

6)
- **A. Correct.** Developing agricultural practices in the Neolithic Era allowed humans to establish settled societies sustained by reliable food sources.
- B. Incorrect. While the wheel was an important development in the Neolithic Era, it was just one part of the major change in human behavior exhibited in that era: the development of settled societies.
- C. Incorrect. The use of bronze was a defining characteristic of the eponymous Bronze Age, which followed the Neolithic Era.
- D. Incorrect. While it is likely that early medical treatment developed in the Neolithic Era, again, this was not a

defining characteristic of this period; furthermore it was made possible by the development of settled societies.

7)

A. Incorrect. The Magyars did not topple the Holy Roman Empire; furthermore, their incursions into Europe had been several hundred years prior.

B. **Correct.** The continental—indeed, global—impact of the Black Death destabilized much of Europe.

C. Incorrect. The Black Death actually destabilized the Mongol Empire.

D. Incorrect. The Umayyads reached Iberia long before the Black Death.

8)

A. Incorrect. While this is true, it is not the complete answer given the other options presented.

B. Incorrect. Again, while this is true, it is not the complete answer.

C. Incorrect. Islam had not yet spread to these areas.

D. **Correct.** Even though the peoples living under Byzantine and Persian rule were not Muslim or Arab, the Islamic tradition of tolerance toward the "People of the Book" and, to an extent, Zoroastrians, made them more acceptable rulers than the oppressive and disorganized collapsing regimes; furthermore, many people in the region spoke Arabic, which made it easier to accept Arab rule.

9)

A. Incorrect. Venice was not a major global colonial power, nor did it develop mercantilism.

B. Incorrect. While Venice was a center of intellectual and cultural development, this was not a major reason for development of modern banking there.

C. **Correct.** As a commercial center and well-situated to handle goods arriving in Europe from the Silk Road and from Africa, Venice developed banking institutions that influenced modern banking.

D. Incorrect. As a center of international trade, Venice was strongly affected by the plague.

10)

A. Incorrect. Martin Luther was a Catholic monk; he originally sought reform within the Catholic Church.

B. **Correct.** Martin Luther and his followers opposed corruption in the Church and wanted changes.

C. Incorrect. The Reformation was not originally a political movement.

D. Incorrect. Again, Martin Luther wanted reform, not to overthrow the papacy or the Church.

11)

A. Incorrect. The Hundred Years' War was an intra-European war.

B. Incorrect. The Hundred Years' War occurred before the Reformation and was a conflict mainly between England and France; the Church was not a major figure.

C. Incorrect. This was not a factor of the Hundred Years' War.

D. **Correct.** The Hundred Years' War was really an ongoing conflict between different European ethnic groups (mainly, the French and the English).

12)

A. Incorrect. Britain did not occupy China, although it did control Hong Kong, which remained a colony until 1997.

B. Incorrect. China was not successful in the Opium Wars.

C. Incorrect. Trade treaties at the time did not favor China.

ANSWER KEY 333

D. Correct. Britain gained economic and commercial privileges in China it had previously not had, including gaining Hong Kong, freedom of movement in China, and access to ports.

13)

A. Incorrect. Nationalism did not benefit the Austro-Hungarian Empire: smaller ethnic groups living in territory controlled by the empire wanted their independence due to nationalism.

B. Incorrect. The Austro-Hungarian Empire began losing control over its Balkan territories due to nationalism and due to interference from Russia, which supported Slavic minorities in the Balkans.

C. Incorrect. Nationalism drove ethnic groups to seek self-rule and independence, not representation in government.

D. Correct. Nationalism triggered independence movements and advocacy.

14)

A. Incorrect. Some European powers had already made slavery illegal (legally, if not in practice).

B. Correct. Abolitionist European powers were unwilling to support the South economically, due to the Confederacy's stance on slavery.

C. Incorrect. While rapidly industrializing Europe needed cotton, many European countries ceased trade with the states that seceded from the Union and developed sources of cotton elsewhere (in Egypt and India, for example).

D. Incorrect. B is the correct answer choice.

15)

A. Incorrect. Many of the boundaries are the modern borders of Middle Eastern countries today, so the region has been greatly affected.

B. Correct. Borders did not take into account history or ethnic groups; installed rulers did not necessarily have legitimacy in the eyes of the people, leading to political instability and violence.

C. Incorrect. The protectorates did not improve governance or stabilize the region following the decline of the Ottoman Empire.

D. Incorrect. Outside investment in strategic resources (like oil) has contributed to instability in the region by providing support to illegitimate rulers and contributing to income inequality and conflict.

16)

A. Incorrect. Russia's strategy was land-based expansion; it did not have a strong navy until the twentieth century.

B. Correct. Russia expanded to the east, taking control of Siberia. Russia also extended westward to an extent, controlling part of Eastern Europe.

C. Incorrect. Russia expanded and employed developmental strategies under a number of czars, including Catherine the Great and Peter the Great. In terms of industrialization, some efforts were made under the Romanovs; however, industrialization accelerated under the Soviets.

D. Incorrect. Russia engaged in empire building throughout Eurasia well into the twentieth century; some argue that it has continued to do so in Crimea and Ukraine today.

17)

A. Incorrect. While the Treaty of Westphalia did end the Thirty Years'

War, this answer choice is incomplete given the other possibilities offered.

B. Incorrect. Again, while this is true, it is incorrect due to the other options presented.

C. Incorrect. The Treaty of Westphalia is considered the foundation of modern international relations as it is based on the idea of state sovereignty; however, the due to the other answer choices this one is incorrect.

D. **Correct.** All of these answer choices are correct.

18)

A. Incorrect. This explanation is insufficient.

B. **Correct.** The main factors in post-WWI German economic collapse are all addressed here.

C. Incorrect. This explanation does not account for global economic depression.

D. Incorrect. This is untrue.

Government

1)

- **A. Correct.** The purpose of checks and balances was to prevent tyranny in any branch of the government.
- B. Incorrect. While there was some concern among the founders about the dangers of a pure democracy, checks and balances do not address the relationship between the government and the people.
- C. Incorrect. Separation of powers kept the military in check. Also, with a civilian commander in chief, the military remains accountable to civilian authority.
- D. Incorrect. Checks and balances do not refer to the relationship between the state and national governments.

2)

- A. Incorrect. The two-thirds override only applies to presidential vetoes.
- B. Incorrect. Once declared unconstitutional, a law remains unconstitutional.
- **C. Correct.** Once a law has been declared unconstitutional, the only way to make it constitutional is to change the Constitution. This can only be done through a formal amendment.
- D. Incorrect. The president cannot veto Supreme Court decisions.

3)

- A. Incorrect. The Electoral College only votes once on the initial candidates.
- **B. Correct.** The House of Representatives selects the president from the candidates by a majority vote of its state delegations.
- C. Incorrect. The national popular vote has no bearing on presidential elections. However, today members of the Electoral College vote based on the popular vote within their state.
- D. Incorrect. The Supreme Court has no role in presidential elections.

4)

- **A. Correct.** Symbolic speech—the expression of ideas through actions—is protected speech.
- B. Incorrect. The rule of law is still paramount. There is no justifiable reason for breaking the law under the Constitution.
- C. Incorrect. This is called defamation and is not protected under the First Amendment.
- D. Incorrect. There are restrictions on freedom of speech; specifically, speech that defames someone, is considered obscene by the courts, or is designed to incite violence is prohibited.

5)

- A. Incorrect. The visit of a congressional delegation to another country is an unofficial diplomatic function of Congress. It does not limit the power of any other branch.
- B. Incorrect. Passing a bill after committee revisions only involves the legislative branch. The complex nature of the process is designed to limit chances for abuse of power, but only limits the legislative branch itself.
- C. Incorrect. The House of Representatives' power to expel one of its members is a check of abuse on itself, not on another branch of government.
- **D. Correct.** The rejection of the treaty shows the Senate checking the

power of the executive branch, as the president had negotiated the treaty.

6)

A. Incorrect. Presidential troop deployment is an example of an expressed executive power, not of the relationship between the central government and the states.

B. Incorrect. Congressional rejection of a treaty is part of the system of checks and balances.

C. Incorrect. Creating an executive department through an Act of Congress is an expressed legislative power.

D. **Correct.** State election of senators demonstrates how the Senate was originally beholden to the states.

7)

A. Incorrect. Aptitude refers to how well one can perform an action.

B. Incorrect. Allegiance refers to one's level of loyalty.

C. **Correct.** Political efficacy is a measure of an individual's belief in the importance of his or her role in the political system.

D. Incorrect. Insight is a strong understanding of the inner workings of a system.

8)

A. Incorrect. PACs are separate from the parties and are run by special interest groups, organizations, or corporations that are trying to advance a particular cause or candidate.

B. Incorrect. PACs operate at every level of government; there are no restrictions on whom PACs can support.

C. **Correct.** PACs may only contribute up to $5000 per election. Super PACs may provide unlimited funding.

D. Incorrect. PACs are not allowed to collaborate with the candidate that they support; they must remain independent.

9)

A. Incorrect. In most federal cases, district courts have original jurisdiction. In cases between two states, cases involving an ambassador, or cases in which a citizen is suing his or her state, the Supreme Court has original jurisdiction. The appellate courts never do.

B. Incorrect. There are both criminal and civil district courts. Appellate courts hear both kinds of cases.

C. **Correct.** The purpose of the appellate court is to review the decisions of the district courts in order to determine if an error of law has been made.

D. Incorrect. Both district and appellate courts are federal courts. The states have no authority over them.

10)

A. Incorrect. The Constitution does not provide for voter eligibility. The pool of eligible voters increased over time; now, the majority of the population may vote. However, there are still restrictions based on age and criminal record.

B. Incorrect. Determining voter eligibility is not an expressed power.

C. Incorrect. Again, the Constitution does not provide for voter eligibility. And, for the first fifty years, only propertied white men were eligible to vote.

D. **Correct.** Because it is not an expressed power, voter eligibility was left up to individual states. However, the Fifteenth, Nineteenth, and Twenty-Sixth Amendments all expanded the right to vote under the Constitution.

11)

A. Incorrect. The House is responsible for impeachment, the Senate for removal.

B. Correct. The House has the power to impeach, and it only requires a simple majority to do so. The Senate acts as a jury and delivers the verdict. Two-thirds of the Senate must vote guilty for the president to be removed.

C. Incorrect. While the Senate does require a two-thirds majority, that is to remove the president, not to impeach him or her.

D. Incorrect. The House is responsible for bringing formal charges against the president, but it is in the Senate that two-thirds of the members must vote for impeachment.

12)

A. Incorrect. The World Health Organization focuses on research and investment in the eradication of disease rather than developing healthcare infrastructure.

B. Incorrect. NATO—or the North Atlantic Treaty Organization—is a defense agreement among the United States, Canada, and several countries in Europe.

C. Correct. The World Bank promotes development and capitalism in developing countries around the world by providing loans for infrastructure and internal development.

D. Incorrect. The World Trade Organization determines the rules of trade between nations.

13)

A. Correct. The Constitution empowers the president to make treaties with the advice and consent of the Senate.

B. Incorrect. In order for a bill to become a law, Congress votes on it, and the president must sign it. The Supreme Court rules on it only if a relevant case comes before the court.

C. Incorrect. The president appoints justices to the Supreme Court and the Senate approves them.

D. Incorrect. Congress does have the power to impeach and remove the president, but members of Congress can only be removed by the House or the voters.

14)

A. Incorrect. The Bill of Rights is an example of Locke's theory of natural rights: it lists rights protected from government interference.

B. Incorrect. Article V is an example of the rule of law: it states that the only way to override the provisions of the Constitution is to legally change it.

C. Correct. The Preamble states, "We the People," supporting the idea that the government exists with the consent of the governed.

D. Incorrect. Article VII is an example of federalism: the federal government could not exist without the approval of the states.

15)

A. Incorrect. Opinion polls play no official role in the election process.

B. Incorrect. Candidates were chosen this way before the 1820s but no longer are today.

C. Correct. Each party holds a nominating convention the summer before the election. Delegates from each state cast votes for the candidate they support.

D. Incorrect. Each party does hold primaries and caucuses, which are elections at the state level. However, these determine how delegates at the convention should vote and technically do not determine the candidate.

16)

A. Incorrect. The Supreme Court may determine the constitutionality of laws passed by Congress. In fact, the case that created the power of judicial review, *Marbury v. Madison*, dealt with a law passed by Congress (the Judiciary Act of 1789).

B. **Correct.** The Supreme Court's power—as well as the rights and powers listed in the Constitution—only apply to the federal government. The states are beholden to their own constitutions, which are interpreted by their own supreme courts.

C. Incorrect. As acts of the federal government, executive orders are subject to judicial review.

D. Incorrect. Using a writ of certiorari, the Supreme Court has the power to demand any case within its jurisdiction be sent up for review.

17)

A. **Correct.** The supremacy clause declares the Constitution the highest law in the land. The only way to change the Constitution is through the amendment process; no individual has authority higher than the Constitution.

B. Incorrect. The elastic clause, also known as "necessary and proper," provides room for Congress to utilize powers not specifically listed in the Constitution. It does not assert the law's authority over individuals.

C. Incorrect. The advise and consent clause gives the Senate the power to approve presidential appointees. This is a prime example of a check on executive authority.

D. Incorrect. The due process clause is one of the clauses of the Fourteenth Amendment. It guarantees all citizens fair treatment under the law. While it does deal with the relationship between individuals and the law, it does not explicitly restrict any individual's authority from superseding the law.

18)

A. Incorrect. Under the Articles of Confederation, the legislature was unicameral. It became bicameral under the Constitution.

B. **Correct.** The Articles of Confederation could also be amended. However, amendment required a unanimous vote in the legislature, making it extremely difficult.

C. Incorrect. The Articles of Confederation provided for no judicial or executive branches, only a legislative one.

D. Incorrect. The Congress of the Confederation was not empowered to maintain an army. Under the Constitution, Congress is empowered to do so.

Geography

1)

A. Incorrect. The Prime Meridian is the internationally accepted 0° longitudinal line.

B. Incorrect. The International Date Line is a longitudinal line. The equator is at latitude 0°.

C. **Correct.** The International Date Line is where the date changes when following time zones around the world. This location was selected primarily because it was located almost entirely in open ocean and so would disrupt the fewest number of people.

D. Incorrect. Like with answer B, the International Date Line is a longitudinal line.

2)

A. Incorrect. "Swidden" is the term used for a field that has been prepared for planting by burning the remaining crops.

B. **Correct.** Subsistence farming is the process of growing crops primarily in order to feed one's own family. No extra crops are grown for sale.

C. Incorrect. Intensive farming is a type of subsistence farming. There is nothing in the question to indicate which type of subsistence farming the farmer uses.

D. Incorrect. Traditional farming would refer to the techniques used by the farmer, which are not discussed in the question.

3)

A. Incorrect. Irredentism is the process by which a state tries to reunite its various pieces that were previously divided. It applies to land, not people.

B. Incorrect. Balkanization is the process by which a state is broken into smaller pieces. The "right to return" law aims to bring people of Irish descent together.

C. **Correct.** Ethnonationalism is when an individual or group identifies with its ethnicity, in this case Irish, over its state affiliation. Ireland's right to return law places ethnic heritage before political affiliation or location in terms of determining membership to the nation.

D. Incorrect. Centrifugal forces are those that divide the people of the state. A right to return law, for the most part, has the opposite effect.

4)

A. **Correct.** The biggest difference between Stage Two and Stage Three is the slowing of the birth rate. This occurs as women are given more opportunities and societal views about their purpose shift.

B. Incorrect. Changes in agricultural practices do not have a direct impact on the birth rate of a country.

C. Incorrect. Advances in medicine transition countries from Stage One to Stage Two.

D. Incorrect. While industrialization does help open up new opportunities for women, it alone does not decrease the birth rate.

5)

A. Incorrect. The United Nations does not govern Antarctica.

B. Incorrect. While several different countries have research stations in Antarctica, no country or group of countries has authority over it.

C. **Correct.** In 1961, a treaty was signed banning any individual claims on

Antarctica and preserving it for scientific research. It is the only land in the world not claimed by a state.

D. Incorrect. While each of these countries has a research station in Antarctica, none of them has any claim on the territory.

6)

A. Incorrect. A gnomonic projection distorts size and area in order to maintain accurate straight-line directions.

B. Incorrect. An azimuthal equidistant projection distorts shape, size, and overall straight-line direction in order to maintain accuracy of direction from a single point to all other points.

C. Incorrect. Equal area projections preserve the size of land masses by distorting shape and direction.

D. **Correct.** The Robinson map distorts all map characteristics in order to minimize overall distortion.

7)

A. Incorrect. The discovery of oil would lead to new job opportunities and act as a pull factor in migration.

B. Incorrect. If the outbreak of civil war was in the home region, then it would be a push factor. However, because it is in a new region, it would not impact migration in the home region.

C. **Correct.** This new law would push out any individuals who did not wish to practice Catholicism.

D. Incorrect. The relocation would likely provide new job opportunities in the home region, discouraging migration out.

8)

A. Incorrect. Deglomeration is the process by which industries spread out due to the over-exploitation of a place's resources. This is the opposite of what has happened in Silicon Valley.

B. **Correct.** Agglomeration is the bunching together of like industries in order to reduce costs by sharing resources. Tech companies have come together in Silicon Valley for just this reason.

C. Incorrect. Industrialization is the process by which a country moves from an economy based on sustainable agriculture to one based on manufacturing. Silicon Valley is the product of a post-industrial society.

D. Incorrect. Modernization is the process by which a society's economy develops according to Rostow's model. This is unrelated to Silicon Valley.

9)

A. Incorrect. An "urban realm" is not a geographic term. A realm is the largest unit the world can be divided into, and includes multiple regions.

B. Incorrect. A world city is a locus of global economic, cultural, or political power. While New York City is a world city, these five cities do not make up one.

C. **Correct.** A megalopolis is a large urban area formed by the close proximity of multiple urban centers. These five cities are sometimes called the "BosWash megalopolis."

D. Incorrect. A transition zone is an area between culture regions where traits from both regions exist. It does not relate to urban zones.

10)

A. Incorrect. Physical boundaries are borders created by natural aspects of the landscape like hills, mountains, or rivers. The map shows that the

US-Canada border mostly does not follow a natural physical boundary.

B. Incorrect. Cultural political boundaries are based on religion, language, or other cultural traits. The culture on either immediate side of the US-Canadian border is very similar. The border is not based on any cultural difference.

C. Incorrect. A relict boundary is one that is no longer functional, which is clearly not the case with the US-Canadian border.

D. **Correct.** The border is drawn essentially as a straight line with little to no regard for physical features, making it a geometric political boundary.

11)

A. Incorrect. While Senegal does receive a great deal of funding from the World Bank, dependency theory argues that development is based upon a country's history.

B. Incorrect. Dependency theory does not address population growth.

C. Incorrect. The core-periphery model is a separate model of economic development linked to the World Systems Analysis Theory.

D. **Correct.** Dependency theory argues that past colonization crippled the colonized countries, preventing them from being able to develop economically.

12)

A. **Correct.** Chain migration describes the movement of people from their home region to another region, following earlier migrants.

B. Incorrect. Internal migration describes the process of moving from one place to another within the same country.

C. Incorrect. Step migration is the process of moving a long distance in short intervals.

D. Incorrect. Net migration is used to describe the total migration (in and out) for a particular region or place.

13)

A. **Correct.** Periphery countries are essentially LDCs, all of which can be found in Africa (with the exception of South Africa), parts of Asia, and parts of South America.

B. Incorrect. While some periphery countries are in Asia, not all of Asia is considered part of the periphery. Eastern Europe mostly belongs to the semi-periphery.

C. Incorrect. North America is not considered part of the periphery.

D. Incorrect. Some countries in South America like Brazil and Argentina are part of the semi-periphery. North America (specifically the United States and Canada) are part of the core.

Economics

1)

- A. Incorrect. Because we do not what Paul could be doing instead of the third revision or how much he improved his resume during the second revision, this cannot be said with any certainty.
- B. Incorrect. It may seem this way because Paul has decided to complete a third revision. However, there is no information to support or refute this statement.
- **C. Correct.** There is not enough information here to determine the opportunity cost of revising his resume. So, it is impossible to know the marginal cost or the marginal benefit of a third revision.
- D. Incorrect. Since Paul has decided to complete a third revision, it would seem likely that the marginal benefit of the second revision was greater than the marginal cost. However, there is not enough information to determine either way.

2)

- A. Incorrect. Point C represents under-utilization of resources. Movement from C to A simply demonstrates that resources are now being used at their full potential.
- B. Incorrect. Movement along the production possibility frontier indicates a shift in the ratio of output for the two products. This is not economic growth but simply a reallocation of resources.
- **C. Correct.** Economic growth is shown by an overall outward shift in the production possibility curve, as would happen if A moved to D.
- D. Incorrect. Movement from D to C would indicate an inefficient use of resources, not a shift in overall economic growth.

3)

- A. Incorrect. We do not know if Max has an absolute advantage in making desserts. In addition, the decision should be made based on comparative advantage, not absolute advantage.
- B. Incorrect. Much like above, we do not know whether Max or Karen has an absolute advantage in dessert-making. Instead, we need to look at who has the comparative advantage in each task.
- C. Incorrect. Karen's opportunity cost of making desserts is sixty carrots, compared to Max's opportunity cost of thirty carrots. This means that Karen should peel carrots, because she will "lose" more by making dessert.
- **D. Correct.** Because Max's opportunity cost of making dessert is less than Karen's, he should make dessert. He has the comparative advantage in dessert-making.

4)

- A. Incorrect. Price and quantity demanded have an inverse relationship. When prices rise, consumers are less willing to buy the product.
- **B. Correct.** The law of demand states that, holding all else constant, an increase in price causes a fall in demand.
- C. Incorrect. Demand—rather than quantity demanded—is affected by changes in determinants of demand, including consumer income and

prices of substitute or complimentary goods.

D. Incorrect. Demand only increases when consumer income increases or there is a change to another determinant of demand. Changes in price impact quantity demanded.

5)

A. Incorrect. A change in a substitute good is a determinant of demand, not supply. Supply will not change in this situation.

B. Incorrect. The increase in price of hooded sweatshirts will not affect the wool sweater market.

C. Incorrect. If demand were to fall, price would increase. However, an increase in a substitute good does not lead to a decrease in demand of a product.

D. **Correct.** When the price of a substitute good increases, the demand for a product also increases, as people are more interested in buying what is now a less expensive alternative. When demand rises, price rises as well and the entire production possibility curve shifts rightward, demonstrating an increase in quantity as well.

6)

A. Incorrect. With two opposing forces on the ketchup market, it is impossible to tell the impact on price without knowing which force is stronger. The hypothetical does not give us that information.

B. Incorrect. There are too many factors in this situation to determine the impact on price without more specific information.

C. **Correct.** Price cannot be determined from the information given; however, the lowered tomato price will increase the supply of ketchup, and the higher mustard price will increase the demand for ketchup. Together, these will increase the overall supply of ketchup.

D. Incorrect. If tomatoes became more expensive or mustard less expensive, the supply of ketchup would fall because both would act as deterrents to ketchup production. However, that is not the case in this situation.

7)

A. Incorrect. With $E_d > 1$ (4.2), the demand for the software is certainly elastic.

B. Incorrect. If the demand was inelastic (which it is not since $E_d > 1$), changing the price would not impact demand, and so would not increase revenue.

C. **Correct.** Because $E_d > 1$, demand is elastic and changes at a faster rate than price. Decreasing the price by even a small amount will increase demand, thereby increasing revenue.

D. Incorrect. Although demand is elastic in this case, increasing the price would decrease demand and negatively impact revenue because price and demand are inversely related.

8)

A. Incorrect. A price ceiling is set when the equilibrium price is perceived as being too high. The ceiling prevents the price from rising above a certain point.

B. **Correct.** Price floors set a minimum price below which the market is not allowed to fall. This is done when the equilibrium price is seen as too low to allow producers to profit.

C. Incorrect. Price floors create a surplus because the price is above the equilibrium price, which decreases quantity demanded and increases quantity supplied.

D. Incorrect. Shortages result from price ceilings. A price ceiling is below the equilibrium price, which increases quantity demanded and decreases the quantity supplied.

9)

A. Correct. Elasticity of demand is calculated by dividing the change in demand (2) by the change in price (4). This yields 0.5.

B. Incorrect. For $E_d = 4$, the change in demand would need to be much larger at 16 percent, or the change in price would need to be much smaller at 0.5 percent.

C. Incorrect. If the demand changed by 4 percent and price by 2 percent, then $E_d = 2$.

D. Incorrect. $E_d = 1$ when the change in price is the same as the change in demand (the demand is then unit elastic).

10)

A. Incorrect. A grocery store can quickly hire more people in order to increase production.

B. Incorrect. The number of chips in a cookie is a flexible production input.

C. Correct. It is very difficult to change the plant size of a firm. In this case, the restaurant would have to wait until its lease term was up or embark on an expensive remodeling campaign, both of which would be possible in the long run, but not the short run.

D. Incorrect. Electricity usage at the high school most likely already has some variability; the amount used could be easily reduced through basic conservation efforts.

11)

A. Incorrect. Labor is an essential factor of production, involved in all economic activity.

B. Incorrect. While some industries may no longer require physical land, most do. Land is stil considered a basic factor of production.

C. Correct. Consumers provide the demand for products. They do not play a role in production.

D. Incorrect. All businesses require capital to start and to maintain production. This is an essential factor of production.

12)

A. Correct. Opportunity cost is the idea that whenever an individual makes a choice, he or she is giving up something else.

B. Incorrect. Product cost is simply the cost of purchasing a product. This often factors into determining opportunity cost.

C. Incorrect. Marginal cost is the change in cost to produce an additional unit of the product. Marginal cost is considered in cost-benefit analysis, but relates to choosing something again, rather than simply choosing between scarce items.

D. Incorrect. Total cost is the total amount including explicit and implicit costs (including opportunity costs).

13)

A. Incorrect. The curve itself does show all possible maximum outputs. It is important to remember it only shows possibilities, not actual production levels.

B. Incorrect. A production possibility curve has one product on the x-axis and the other product on the y-axis. The curve shows the relationship between the production of each.

C. Incorrect. A production possibility curve holds all else the same, meaning it assumes no variability exists in production inputs.

D. **Correct.** A product's utility is the amount of happiness it brings to the consumer. A production possibility curve does not measure the impact of products on consumers, but rather an entity's production capacity.

Behavioral Sciences

1)

- **A. Correct.** At birth, babies can only see from eight to twelve inches in front of their faces. They do not gain full sight until they are one year old.
- **B.** Incorrect. Babies have a keen sense of smell and can identify their mothers by smell.
- **C.** Incorrect. Babies' dominant sense is hearing because of their limited sight. Babies can hear before they are even born.
- **D.** Incorrect. Babies are born with a fully developed sense of taste. Taste preferences are already set, and—like adults—babies show a preference for sugar.

2)

- **A.** Incorrect. A score of 85 is one standard deviation below the mean. This would be the IQ score of someone in the 16th percentile.
- **B.** Incorrect. A score of 115 is one standard deviation above the mean. This would be the IQ score of someone in the 84th percentile.
- **C. Correct.** A score of 130 is two standard deviations above the mean; a person with this score would fall in the 97.5th percentile.
- **D.** Incorrect. A score of 70 is two standard deviations below the mean; a person with this score would fall in the 2.5th percentile.

3)

- **A. Correct.** Regardless of the memory model being used, the process of recalling a memory is called retrieval.
- **B.** Incorrect. Encoding is the process of incorporating something into the memory.
- **C.** Incorrect. Rehearsal is the process of keeping something in the memory by repeating it over and over.
- **D.** Incorrect. Repression is the process by which the brain pushes out unused memories to make room for the storage of new ones.

4)

- **A.** Incorrect. Chunking is grouping items together in order to increase the number of things held in short-term memory. Chunking would be grouping the "Nina, the Pinta, and the Santa Maria" as the three ships of Columbus's fleet.
- **B. Correct.** A mnemonic device is a rhyme, song, joke, etc. that helps anchor information in a person's mind. This quote uses rhyme to help students remember the date Columbus sailed.
- **C.** Incorrect. Visualization is the process of creating a mental image of the information rather than using words.
- **D.** Incorrect. Elaborative rehearsal is the process of learning more about information and then repeating it in order to process the information more deeply. The phrase above does not increase understanding of Columbus or his journey, and so does not lead to deeper processing.

5)

- **A. Correct.** Because Ben had a pre-existing idea of how the French would act, he gave too much credence to the experiences that confirmed that idea, and not enough to those that contradicted it.
- **B.** Incorrect. Belief perseverance is the insistence on maintaining a belief, even when the evidence contradicts it. Ben would have exhibited this if

ANSWER KEY 347

he had only encountered friendly people and dismissed it as an anomaly.

C. Incorrect. Mental set is the use of old strategies to try to solve new problems. Ben is not trying to solve a problem.

D. Incorrect. An algorithm is a fool-proof rule that can be used to solve a problem. The attitude of the French is not a fool-proof rule.

6)

A. Incorrect. Humanistic theory is based on the concept of free will; it directly rejects determinism.

B. Incorrect. Psychoanalytical theory is based on the idea that childhood events greatly impact adult personality. It does not particularly take into account current behaviors.

C. **Correct.** Social-cognitive theory looks at the ways in which individual thought and overall environment impact personality. Bandura was a prominent social-cognitive theorist.

D. Incorrect. Trait theory argues that personality is determined by specific traits an individual may have. It does not see environment as a factor.

7)

A. Incorrect. While these are areas of sociological inquiry, their research is not the primary goal of sociology.

B. **Correct.** The primary goal of sociology is to conduct research applicable to social policy and the common welfare.

C. Incorrect. Some sociologists do study the class system, but it is not the main goal of the entire discipline.

D. Incorrect. Demographic determination is not the primary goal of sociological study.

8)

A. Incorrect. Symbolic interactionism, ethnomethodology, and dramaturgical sociology describe theories of interaction, not major sociological perspectives.

B. Incorrect. Cooperation, exchange, and conflict are the primary forms of social interaction that describe it.

C. **Correct.** Symbolic interactionism, conflict theory, and functionalism are the major categories of social perspective; the theorists Weber, Marx, and Durkheim, respectively, developed them.

D. Incorrect. These terms describe types of socialization.

9)

A. **Correct.** Weber, Durkheim, and Marx studied symbolic interactionism, functionalism, and conflict theory, respectively.

B. Incorrect. Weber was central to symbolic interactionism; Durkheim and Merton were major scholars of functionalism. However, this response does not address conflict theory.

C. Incorrect. Marx studied conflict theory, and Durkheim and Merton studied functionalism; however this response fails to address symbolic interactionism.

D. Incorrect. All three scholars studied all major schools of sociological inquiry; however, Durkheim was more central to functionalism than was Merton, so the best answer choice would include him.

10)

A. Incorrect. These are examples of political process; better examples of symbolic interactionism would include a social ceremony or process. The variables cited do not direct social behavior.

B. Incorrect. While the exchange of goods and services could be a social interaction, it is still an economic process, and could occur regardless of the cultural or social circumstances in the same manner. Again, the variables cited do not direct social behavior.

C. Incorrect. Like answer choice B, while some elements of a currency could reflect a society's values or shared history or culture, currency does not necessarily direct social behavior; most societies treat currency in the same manner.

D. **Correct.** While most societies celebrate marriage, the venue, outfits, and ring may have different meanings in different societies and symbolize different values (such as wealth or stability).

Answer Key

Essay Questions

World History

The Eastern Roman Empire transformed into the Byzantine Empire, thanks largely to Justinian II's strong organization, rule of law, and successful military conquest. The strength and organization of the Greek Orthodox Church fostered intellectual development; classical civilization was protected in Greece and the Eastern Mediterranean, where scholarship and art were safeguarded from chaos as Western Europe became unstable and unsafe. Byzantine missionaries spread Christianity in the region; Constantinople also became a trading hub, as international trade remained strong within the Mediterranean but also into Asia thanks to relative political stability.

Although Christian Byzantium itself fell into decline and became isolated to Anatolia as Damascus, the Levant, and eventually the whole of the Middle East and North Africa fell to Arab Muslims from the Arabian Peninsula, Islam valued art, science, and scholarship. Arab-Islamic civilization boasted achievements in navigation, astronomy, medicine, and mathematics. European Crusaders returned to Western Europe with this knowledge, helping spark the Scientific Revolution.

Christians in Constantinople who had cooperated with the Catholic Church in Rome began leaving Greece and Anatolia as the Muslim Ottomans gained power in Anatolia; when the Ottomans took Constantinople in 1453, the Byzantine Empire fully collapsed and Christians fled westward, bringing ancient classical learning with them. Centuries after the collapse of the Roman Empire, the remnants of Classical civilization enjoyed a resurgence, or Renaissance, beginning in Italy, which inspired a generation of artists and thinkers to develop new forms of human expression and scholarship.

This essay would receive a score of three because it cites the specific examples of the Byzantine Empire under Justinian II, the Greek Orthodox Church and Byzantine missionaries and scholarship, the contributions and stability of the Arab-Islamic caliphates, and the impact of the Crusades. It also cites the post-Ottoman migration of Byzantine Christians to Western Europe.

Social Sciences

World Systems Analysis recognizes the "core" countries as those countries that exploit, or most benefit, from the "periphery." Given that the core countries are the most industrialized ones, they rely heavily on the periphery for both raw materials to create goods, and for markets where they can sell those goods. Dependency theory perceives these relationships through a historical lens; often those same countries had a colonial relationship wherein the core country was the colonial power, and the periphery country was the exploited colony.

Iran was never colonized. However, it did come under the influence of European imperial powers in the late nineteenth century. The Qajars entered into an agreement with Britain to explore petroleum resources; the Anglo-Persian Oil Company, also known as the Anglo-Iranian Oil Company (and today, British Petroleum or BP) was founded to explore and exploit Persian reserves. While Iran remained independent, the Qajars had driven the country deeply into debt; foreign powers controlled domestic interests beyond petroleum, including the postal service and even the printing of currency. Despite an attempt to nationalize the oil industry in 1951 (which ended in the CIA-engineered assassination of the nationalist prime minister Mossadegh and reinstatement of the western-backed Shah Pahlavi), Iran remained beholden to western interests until the revolution in 1979.

At the same time, Iran had been a world power in ancient times, again under the Safavids, and had an important stabilizing force in Asia during the British Raj and Ottoman eras. Unlike many "periphery" countries, Iran had stable infrastructure, developed urban areas, and a diversified economy that was not wholly engineered to support a colonial power. Even though it was dominated by outside powers for a period, the country had a strong enough homegrown infrastructure and domestic economy due to its own long history that it would be able to sustain a position in the semi-periphery.

This essay would receive a score of three because it cites specific examples (the debts generated by the Qajars, the Anglo-Persian Oil Company, the nationalization of oil by Mossadegh, the various Persian regimes, and their accomplishments) as well as historical interpretations that dependency theorists would make. It also clearly defines Core-Periphery Theory, Wallerstein's World Systems Analysis Theory, and Dependency Theory.

United States History

The writer, abolitionist, activist, and former slave Frederick Douglass vehemently condemned slavery in the years preceding the Civil War. Indeed, the nineteenth century reflects division over the ethnics and legality of slavery in the United States. From the 1820 Missouri Compromise, debate ensued over permitting the expansion of slavery with the expansion of US territory. As of 1820, slavery would not be permitted north of the thirty-sixth parallel. However, pro-slavery activists continued to press for expansion of the practice and protection of the powers of slave owners. As a result, the Compromise of 1850 was reached, in which California was admitted as a free state, but the Utah and New Mexico Territories were admitted with slavery to be decided by popular sovereignty, allowing the expansion of the practice. Four years later, the Kansas-Nebraska Act permitted slavery to be decided by popular sovereignty in that territory as well, effectively repealing the Missouri Compromise and permitting slavery to spread across the US-dominated continent.

The Compromise of 1850 also strengthened the Fugitive Slave Act. The Fugitive Slave Act affected not only slaves in slave states but escaped slaves in free states as well. According to this Act, slave owners could pursue escaped slaves to free states and force them back to a life of slavery. In *Scott v. Sandford*, the Supreme Court found that slaves had no rights as American citizens to sue for their freedom in court even once they had escaped to a free state (as the escaped slave Dred Scott himself had). Activists like Douglass who participated in the Underground Railroad, helping escaped slaves to safety in the North and even to escape to Canada, were at even more risk, too. Douglass would likely have considered this series of legislative compromises, federal acts, and judicial cases as part of the "hideous and revolting" conduct described in his speech above.

This essay would receive a score of three because it cites specific pieces of legislation (the Missouri Compromise, the Compromise of 1850, the Kansas-Nebraska Act, and the Fugitive Slave Act). It also explains the impact of each in historical context. Furthermore, it cites the Supreme Court case of *Scott v. Sandford* **in historical context. It even invokes the Underground Railroad to bring social context and a personal perspective that Douglass may have had on the tumultuous period.**

Follow the link below to take your second Praxis Social Studies (5086) practice test and to access other online study resources:

www.cirrustestprep.com/praxis-5086-online-resources

Made in the USA
Lexington, KY
30 March 2019